IDEAS

# IDEAS

## GENERAL INTRODUCTION TO

## PURE PHENOMENOLOGY

### *Edmund Husserl*

TRANSLATED BY W. R. BOYCE GIBSON

**COLLIER BOOKS**
*A Division of Macmillan Publishing Co., Inc.*
*New York*
**COLLIER MACMILLAN PUBLISHERS**
*London*

*First Collier Books Edition 1962*

*15   14   13   12   11   10   9   8*

*The German original,* Ideen au einer reinen Phänomenologie und phänomenologischen Philosophie, *was published in 1913.* Ideas *was published in a hardcover edition by Macmillan Publishing Co., Inc. Macmillan Publishing Co., Inc., 866 Third Avenue, New York, N.Y. 10022. Printed in the United States of America.*

# Author's Preface to the English Edition

MAY THE AUTHOR of this work, which first appeared in the year 1913, be permitted to contribute to the English Edition certain explanations that may prove of use to the reader, both before and as he reads?

Under the title "A Pure or Transcendental Phenomenology," the work here presented seeks to found a new science —though, indeed, the whole course of philosophical development since *Descartes* has been preparing the way for it—a science covering a new field of experience, exclusively its own, that of "Transcendental Subjectivity." Thus Transcendental Subjectivity does not signify the outcome of any speculative synthesis, but with its transcendental experiences, capacities, doings, is an absolutely independent realm of direct experience although for reasons of an essential kind it has so far remained inaccessible. Transcendental experience in its theoretical and, at first, descriptive bearing, becomes available only through a radical alteration of that same dispensation under which an experience of the natural world runs its course, a readjustment of viewpoint which, as the methods of approach to the sphere of transcendental phenomenology, is called "phenomenological reduction."

In the work before us transcendental phenomenology is not founded as the empirical science of the empirical facts of this field of experience. Whatever facts presents themselves serve only as examples similar in their most general aspect to the empirical illustrations used by mathematicians; much, in fact, as the actual intuitable dispositions of numbers on the abacus assist us, in their merely exemplary capacity, to grasp with insight, and in their pure generality the series 2, 3, 4 . . . as such, pure numbers as such, and the propositions of pure mathematics relative to these, the essential generalities of a mathematical kind. In this book, then, we treat of an *a priori* science ("eidetic," directed upon the universal in its original intuitability), which appropriates, through as pure possibility only, the empirical field of fact of transcendental subjectivity with its factual (*faktischen*) experiences, equating these with pure intuitable possibilities that can be modified at will, and sets out as its *a priori* the indissoluble essen-

5

tial structures of transcendental subjectivity, which persist in and through all imaginable modifications. Since the reduction to the transcendental and, with it, this further reduction to the Eidos is the method of approach to the field of work of the new science, it follows (and we stress the point in advance) that the proper starting-point for the systematic unravelling of this science lies in the chapters which treat of the reductions we have indicated. Only from this position can the reader, who follows with inner sympathy the indications proffered step by step, judge whether something characteristically new has really been worked out here—worked out, we say, and not constructed, drawn from real, general intuition of essential Being, and described accordingly.

Eidetic phenomenology is restricted in this book to the realm of pure eidetic "description," that is to the realm of essential structures of transcendental subjectivity immediately transparent to the mind. For this constitutes in itself already a systematically self-contained infinitude of essential characteristics. Thus no attempt is made to carry out systematically the transcendental knowledge that can be obtained through logical deduction. Here we have one difference (though not the only one) between the whole manner of this new *a priori* science and that of the mathematical disciplines. These are "deductive" sciences, and that means that in their scientifically theoretical mode of development mediate deductive knowledge plays an incomparably greater part than the immediate axiomatic knowledge upon which all the deductions are based. An infinitude of deductions rests on a very few axioms.

But in the transcendental sphere we have an infinitude of knowledge previous to all deduction, knowledge whose mediated connexions (those of intentional implication) have nothing to do with deduction, and being entirely intuitive prove refractory to every methodically devised scheme of constructive symbolism.

A note of warning may be uttered here against a misunderstanding that has frequently arisen. When, in an anticipatory vein, it is stated right from the start that, according to the author's views (to be established in those further portions of the whole work which are still to be published), all radically scientific philosophy rests on the basis of phenomenology, that in a further sense it is phenomenological philosophy right through, this does not mean to say that philosophy itself is an a *priori* science throughout. The task which this book was planned to carry out, that of establishing a science of the eidetic essence of a transcendental subjectivity, is as far as it can be from carrying the conviction with it that philosophy itself is entirely a science *a priori*. A glance at the mathematical sciences, these great logical instruments for corresponding sciences of fact, would already lead use to anticipate the contrary. The science of fact in the strict sense, the genuinely rational science of nature, has first become possible through the independent elaboration of a "pure" mathematics of nature. The science of pure possibilities must everywhere precede the science of real facts, and give it the guidance of its concrete logic. So is it also in the case of transcendental philosophy, even though the dignity of the service rendered here by a system of the transcendental *a priori* is far more exalted.

The understanding, or at any rate the sure grasp, of the distinction between *transcendental phenomenology* and "*descriptive*," or, as it is often called nowadays, "*phenomenological*" *psychology*, is a problem that as a rule brings great difficulties with it, which indeed are grounded in the very nature of the case. It has led to misunderstandings, to which even thinkers who subscribe to the phenomenological line of thought are subject. Some attempt to clarify the situation should prove useful.

The change of standpoint which in this work bears the name phenomenological reduction (transcendental-phenomenological we now say, to be more definite) is effected by me, as the actually philosophizing subject, from the natural standpoint as a basis, and I experience myself here in the first instance as "I" in the ordinary sense of the term, as this human person living among others in the world. As a psychologist, I take as my theme this I-type of being and life, in its general aspect, the human being as "psychical." Turning inwards in pure reflexion, following exclusively "inner experience and "empathy," to be more precise), and setting aside all the psychophysical questions which relate to man as a corporeal being, I obtain an original and pure descriptive knowledge of the psychical life as it is in itself, the most original information being obtained from myself, because here alone is perception the medium. If, as is often done, descriptions of all sorts, which attach themselves purely and truly to the data of intuition, are referred to as phenomenological, there here grows up, on the pure basis of inner intuition, of the intuition of the soul's own essence, a phenomenological psychology. A right form of method (on this point we shall have something further to say) gives us in point of fact not only scanty, superficially classificatory descriptions, but a great self-supporting science; the latter, however, properly speaking, only when, as is possible also here, one first sets before oneself as goal a science which deals not with the factual data of this inner sphere of intuition, but with the essence, inquiring, that is, after the invariant, essentially characteristic structures of a soul, of a psychical life in general.

If we now perform this transcendental-phenomenological reduction, this transformation of the natural and psychologically inward standpoint whereby it is transcendentalized, the psychological subjectivity loses just that which makes it something real in the world that lies before us; it loses the meaning of the soul as belonging to a body that exists in an objective, spatio-temporal Nature. This transformation of meaning concerns myself, above all, the "I" of the psychological and subsequently transcendental inquirer for the time being. Posited as real (*wirklich*), I am now no longer a human Ego *in* the universal, existentially posited world, but exclusively a subject *for* which this world has being, and purely, indeed, *as* that which appears to me, is presented to me, and of which I am conscious in some way or other, so that the real being of the world thereby remains unconsidered, unquestioned, and its validity left out of account. Now if transcendental description passes no judgment whatsoever upon the world, and upon my human Ego as belonging to the world, and if, in this description, the transcendental Ego exists (*ist*) absolutely in and for itself prior to all cosmic being (which first wins in and through it existential validity), it is still at the same time evident that, at every conversion of meaning which concerns the phenomenological-psychological content of the soul as a whole, this very content by simply putting on another existential meaning (*Seinssinn*) becomes transcendental-phenomenological, just as conversely the latter, on reverting to the natural psychological standpoint, becomes once again psychological. Naturally this correspondence must still hold good if, prior to all interest in the development of psychological science, and of a "descriptive" or "phenomenological psychology" in particular, a transcendental phenomenology is set up under the leading of a philosophical idea, to that through phenomenological reduction the transcendental Ego is directly set up at the focus of reflexion, and made the theme of a transcendental description. We have thus a remarkable thoroughgoing parallelism between a (properly elaborated) phenomenological psychology and a transcendental phenomenology. To each eidetic or empirical determination on the one side there must correspond a parallel feature on the other. And yet this whole content as psychology, considered from the natural standpoint as a positive science, therefore, and related to the world as spread before us, is entirely non-philosophical, whereas "the same" content from the transcendental standpoint, and therefore as transcendental phenomenology, is a philosophical science—indeed, on closer view, *the* basic philosophical science, preparing on descriptive lines the transcendental ground which remains henceforth the exclusive ground for all philosophical knowledge. Here in fact lie the chief difficulties in the way of an understanding, since it must be felt at first as a most unreasonable demand that such a "nuance" springing from a mere change of standpoint should possess such great, and indeed, for all genuine philosophy, such decisive significance. The wholly unique meaning of this "nuance" can be clearly appreciated only when he who philosophizes has reached a radical understanding with himself as to what he proposes to bring under the title "philosophy," and only in so far as he is constrained to look for something differing in principle from positive science: the theoretic control, that is, of something other than the world ostensibly given to us through experience. From such understanding with one's own self, carried out in a really radical and consistent way, there springs up of necessity a motivation which compels the philosophizing Ego to reflect back on that very subjectivity of his, which in all his experience and knowledge of the natural world, both real and possible, is in the last resort the Ego that experiences and knows, and is thus already presupposed in all the natural self-knowledge of the "human Ego who experiences, thinks, and acts naturally in the world." In other words: from this source springs the phenomenological transposition as an absolute requirement, if philosophy generally is to work out its distinctive purposes upon a basis of original experience, and so contrive to begin at all. It can make a beginning, and generally speaking develop all its further philosophical resources, only as a science working from the transcendental-philosophical standpoint. For this very reason the immediate *a priori* phenomenology (portrayed in this work in its actual functioning as that which directly prepares the transcendental basis) is the "first philosophy" in itself, the philosophy of the Beginning. Only when this motivation (which stands in need of a very minute and comprehensive analysis) has become a vital and compelling insight, does it become clear that the "change in the shading," which at first appears so strange, transforming as it does a pure psychology of the inner life into a self-styled trancendental phenomenology, determines the being and non-being of philosophy—of a philosophy which knows with thorough-going scientific assurance what its own distinctive meaning calls for as the basis and the method of its inquiry. In the light of such self-comprehension, we understand for the first time that deepest and truly radical meaning of "psychologism" (that is, of transcendental psychologism) as the error that perverts the pure meaning of philosophy, proposing as it does to found philosophy on psychology, on the positive science of the life of the soul. This perversion persists unmodified when, in sympathy with our own procedure, the pure psychology of the inner life is set up also as an *a priori* science; even then it remains a positive science, and can provide a basis for positive science only, never for philosophy.

In the course of many years of brooding over these matters, the author has followed up different lines of inquiry, all equally possible, in the attempt to exhibit in an absolutely transparent and compelling way the nature of such motivation as propels beyond the natural positive realism of life and science, and necessitates the transcendental transposition, the "phenomenological Reduction." They are the ways of reaching the starting-point of a serious philosophy, and as they must be thought out in conscious reflexion, they themselves belong properly to the Beginning, as is possible, indeed, only within the beginner as he reflects upon himself. For each of these ways the point of departure is, of course, the natural unsophisticated standpoint of positive reality (*Positivität*) which the world of experience has as the basis of its being, and is confessedly "taken for granted" (the nature of such Being never having been questioned). In the work here presented (§ 33 f.), the author selected that way of approach, which then appeared to him the most effective. It develops as a course of self-reflexion taking place in the region of the pure psychological intuition of the inner life, or, as we might also say, as a "phenomenological" reflexion in the ordinary psychological sense. It leads eventually to the point that I, who am here reflecting upon myself, become conscious that under a consistent and exclusive focusing of experience upon that which is purely inward, upon what is "phenomenologically" accessible to me, I possess in myself an essential individuality, self-contained, and holding well together in itself, to which all real and objectively possible experience and knowledge belongs, through whose agency the objective world is there for me with all its empirically confirmed facts, in and through which it has for me at any rate trustworthy (even if never scientifically authorized) essential validity. This also includes the more special apperceptions through which I take myself to be a man with body and soul, who lives in the world with other men, lives the life of the world, and so forth. Continuing this self-reflexion, I now also become aware that my own phenomenologically self-contained essence can be posited in an *absolute* sense, as I am the Ego who invests the being of the world which I so constantly speak about with existential validity, as an existence (*Sein*) which wins for me from my own life's pure essence meaning and substantiated validity. I myself as this individual essence, posited absolutely, as the open infinite field of pure phenomenological data and their inseparable unity, am the "transcendental Ego"; the absolute positing means that the world is no longer "given" to me in advance, its validity that of a simple existent, but that henceforth it is exclusively my Ego that is given (given from my new standpoint), given purely as that which has being in itself, in itself experiences a world, confirms the same, and so forth.

Within this view of things there grows up, provided the consequences are fearlessly followed up (and this is not everybody's business), *a transcendental-phenomenological Idealism* in opposition to every form of psychologistic Idealism. The account given in the chapter indicated suffers, as the author confesses, from lack of completeness. Although it is in all real essentials unassailable, it lacks what is certainly important to the foundation of this Idealism, the proper consideration of the problem of transcendental solipsism or of transcendental intersubjectivity, of the essential relationship of the objective world, that is valid for me, to others which are valid for and with me. The completing developments should have been furnished in a Second Volume which the author had hoped to be able to supply very soon after the first, as a sequel that had been planned at the same time with it.

The objections raised against this Idealism and its alleged Solipsism seriously impeded the reception of the work, as though its essential significance lay in any way in this sketch of its philosophical import: whereas this was no more than a means devised in the interest of the problem of a possible objective knowledge, for winning this necessary insight: that the very meaning of that problem refers us back to the Ego that is in and for itself; and that this Ego, as the presupposition of the knowledge of the world, cannot be and remain presupposed as having the existence of a world, and must therefore, in respect of the world's being, be brought to its pure state through phenomenological reduction, that is, through "Epoché." I might have been better advised if, without altering the essential connexions of the exposition, I had left open the final decision in favour of transcendental Idealism, and contented myself with making clear that trains of thought of crucial philosophical significance with a trend that is towards Idealism necessarily arise here, and must by all means be thought out; so that to this end one needs in any case to make sure of the ground of transcendental subjectivity.

I must not hesitate, however, to state quite explicitly that in regard to transcendental-phenomenological Idealism, I have nothing whatsoever to take back, that now as ever I hold every form of current philosophical realism to be in principle absurd, as no less every idealism to which in its own arguments that realism stands contrasted, and which in fact it refutes. Given a deeper understanding of my exposition, the solipsistic objection should never have been raised as an objection against phenomenological idealism, but only as an objection to the incompleteness of my exposition. Still, one should not overlook what is the radical essential in all philosophizing to which, in this book, a path will be opened. Over against the thinking, rich in presuppositions, which has as its premises the world, science, and sundry understandings bearing on method, and rooted in the scientific tradition as a whole, a radical form of the autonomy of knowledge is here active, in which form of datum given in advance, and all Being taken for granted, is set out as invalid, and there is a reversion to that which is already presupposed *implicite* in all presupposing and in all questioning and answering, and herewith of necessity exists already, immediate and persistent. This is the first to be freely and expressly posited, and with a self-evidence which precedes all conceivable instances of self-evidence, and is contained implicitly in them all. Although it is only with the phenomenological reduction which would convert this radicalism into conscious work, that genuine work-performing philosophizing begins, the whole preparatory reflexion has already been carried through, and precisely in this spirit. It is phenomenological, though still unconsciously so. It follows, therefore, that it is a piece of pure self-reflexion revealing original self-evident facts; and, moreover, when it exhibits in these facts (though incompletely) the outlines of Idealism, it is as far as can be from being one of the usual balancings between Idealism and Realism, and cannot be affected by the arguments involved in any of their objections. Such essential connexions of a phenomenological kind, and such motivations in an "idealistic" direction as are in fact revealed, hold firm under all the improvements and completions that may eventually prove necessary, even as the reality of rivers and mountain ranges, which the first explorer has really seen and described, remains standing despite the improvements and additions to which his descriptions are subjected by later explorers. The first preliminary steps towards a fresh formulation of the transcendental problem (to subserve mere purposes of motivation) must then be taken in accord with its phenomenological content, and in accord with what from this point of departure forecasts with objective necessity the true meaning of an objective being that is subjectively knowable. Moreover, transcendental phenomenology is not a theory, devised merely as a reply to the historic problem of Idealism, it is a science founded in itself, and standing absolutely on its own basis; it is indeed the one science that stands absolutely on its own ground. Only in such wise, however, that when consistently carried forward, it leads, as is already apparent in the important concluding portions of the book, to the "constitutive" problems, which take in all the conceivable objects we could ever meet with in experience, briefly the whole real world spread out before us together with all its categories of the object, and likewise all "ideal" worlds, and makes these all intelligible as transcendental correlates. Whence it clearly follows that transcendental phenomenological Idealism is not a special philosophical thesis, a theory among others; that transcendental phenomenology, rather, as concrete science, is, in itself, even when no word is spoken concerning Idealism, universal Idealism worked out as a science. And it proves it through its own meaning as transcendental science in each of its special constitutive domains. But we also need to make clearly explicit the fundamental and essential difference between transcendental-phenomenological Idealism and that form of Idealism which in popular realism is opposed to it as its incompatible opposite. And in the very first place let this be said: Our phenomenological idealism does not deny the positive existence of the real (*realen*) world and of Nature—in the first place as though it held it to be an illusion. Its sole task and service is to clarify the meaning of this world, the precise sense in which everyone accepts it, and with undeniable right, as really existing (*wirklich seiende*). *That* it exists—given as it is as a universe out there (*daseiendes*) in an experience that is continuous, and held persistently together through a thread of widespread unanimity—that is quite indubitable. It is quite another consideration, although in the light of the discussions in the text of this work one of great philosophical importance, that the continuance of experience in the future under such form of universal agreement is a mere (although reasonable) presumption, and that accordingly the non-existence of the world although, and whilst it is in point of fact the object of a unanimous experience, always remains *thinkable*. The result of the phenomenological clarification of the meaning of the manner of existence of the real world (and, eidetically, of a real world generally) is that only transcendental subjectivity has ontologically the meaning of Absolute Being, that it only is non-relative, that is relative only to itself; whereas the real world indeed exists, but in respect of essence is relative to transcendental subjectivity, and in such a way that it can have its meaning as existing (*seiende*) reality only as the intentional meaning-product of transcendental subjectivity. But that first attains its full meaning when the phenomenological disclosure of the transcendental Ego is so far advanced that the experience of fellow-subjects implicit in it has won its reduction to transcendental experience; in other words, when the self-interpretation carried out purely on the basis of transcendental experience had led to the knowledge of the real and whole meaning of the transcendental subjectivity, which, for the Ego reflecting at the time means this: "I, the transcendental, absolute I, as I am in my own life of transcendental consciousness; but besides myself, the fellow-subjects who in this life of mine reveal themselves as co-transcendental, within the transcendental society of 'Ourselves,' which simultaneously reveals itself." It is thus within the intersubjectivity, which in the phenomenological reduction has reached empirical givenness on a transcendental level, and is thus itself transcendental, that the real (*reale*) world is constituted as "objective," as being there for everyone.

The world has this meaning, whether we are aware of it or not. But how could we ever be aware of it prior to the phenomenological reduction which first brings the transcendental subjectivity as our absolute Being into the focus of experience? So long as it was only the psychological subjectivity that was recognized, and one sought to posit it as absolute, and to understand the world as its correlate, the result could only be an absurd Idealism, a psychological Idealism—the very type which the equally absurd realism has as its counterpart. Now by such as have won their way to the genuine transcendental subjectivity it can assuredly be seen that the great idealists of the eighteenth century, Berkeley and Hume on the one side, Leibniz on the other, had, properly speaking, already reached beyond psychological subjectivity in the sense it bears within the natural world. But since the contrast between psychological and transcendental subjectivity remained unexplained, and the all-dominant sensationalism of the school of Locke could not render intelligible the constituting of what is real as a performance giving to subjectivity meaning and true being, the unfruitful and unphilosophical conflict fought out on the field of nature remained in vogue for the times that followed, and there prevailed a perverse interpretation of the meaning which the great idealists had really intended, yet to be sure without making that meaning scientifically clear.

The new publications which the author began to issue in 1929 (the first since the *Ideen*) will contribute far-reaching advances, clarifications, and completions of what, for the rest, had already been begun in the *Logische Untersuchungen* (1900–1901), and then in the *Ideen,* so that the claim to have set going the necessary beginnings of a philosophy, "which can present itself as a science," cannot well be regarded as self-deception. In any case, he who for decades instead of speculating concerning a New Atlantis has really wandered in the trackless wilds of a new continent and undertaken bits of virgin cultivation, will not allow himself to be diverted by the refusals of geographers who judge the reports in the light of their own experiences and habits of thought, and on the strength of this exempt themselves from all the trouble of making a journey into the land proclaimed to be new.

There is still one point that calls for a remark. In the eyes of those who set aside the phenomenological reduction as a philosophically irrelevant eccentricity (whereby, to be sure, they destroy the whole meaning of the work and of my phenomenology), and leave nothing remaining but an *a priori* psychology, it often happens that this residual psychology is identified as to its main import with Franz Brentano's psychology of intentionality. Great indeed as is the respect and gratitude with which the author remembers this gifted thinker as his teacher, and strongly convinced as he is that his conversion of the scholastic concept of intentionality into a descriptive root-concept of psychology constitutes a great discovery, apart from which phenomenology could not have come into being at all; none the less we must distinguish as essentially different the author's pure psychology implicitly contained in this transcendental phenomenology and the psychology of Brentano. This holds good also of his "psychognosis" limited to pure description in the region of inner experience. It is indeed "phenomenological" psychology if, as has often happened at the present time, we are to give the title "phenomenological" to every psychological inquiry conducted purely within the framework of "inner experience," and, grouping all such studies together, to speak further of a phenomenological psychology. For this latter discipline, quite apart from its name, takes us back, naturally, to John Locke and to his school, including John Stuart Mill. One can then say that David Hume's *Treatise* gives the first systematic sketch of a pure phenomenology, which, though under the name of psychology, attempts to supply a philosophical transcendental philosophy. Like his great predecessor, Berkeley, it is as a psychologist that he is regarded and has exercised his influence. Thus, excluding all transcendental questions, it is this whole "phenomenological" school which alone calls here for our consideration. Characteristic of it and of its psychology is the conception set forth in Locke's "white paper" simile of the pure soul as a complex or heap of temporally co-existing and successive data, which run their course under rules partly their own, partly psychophysical. It would thus be the function of descriptive psychology to distinguish and classify the main types of these "sense-data," data of the "inner sense," of inner experience, and likewise the elementary basic forms of the psychical complex; that of explanatory psychology to seek out the rules of genetic formations and transformations, much as in the case of natural science, and on similar lines of method. And quite naturally so, since the pure psychical being or the psychical life is regarded as a nature-resembling flow of events in a quasi-space of consciousness. On grounds of principle, we may say that it obviously makes no difference whether we let the psychic "data" be blown along in a collective whole "atomistically," though in accordance with empirical laws, like heaps of sand, or regard them as parts of wholes which by necessity, whether empirical or *a priori,* can alone operate as such parts, and principally perhaps within the whole of consciousness fettered as that is to a rigid form of wholeness. In other words, atomistic and Gestalt-psychology alike participate in that intrinsic meaning of psychological "naturalism," as defined in terms of what we have stated above, which, having regard to the expression "inner sense," may also be termed "sensationalism" (*Sensualismus*). Clearly Brentano's psychology of intentionality also remains fettered to this inherited naturalism, though in virtue of its having introduced into psychology as a main concept, descriptive in type and universal in scope, that of Intentionality, it has worked therein as a reforming factor.

The essentially new influence which in transcendentally directed phenomenology becomes active for descriptive psychology, and is now completely changing the whole aspect of this psychology, its whole method, the setting of its concrete aims, is the insight that a concrete description of the sphere of consciousness as a self-contained sphere of intentionality (it is never otherwise concretely given), a concrete description, for instance, of perceptions or recollections, and so forth, also calls, of necessity, for a description of the object as such, referred to in intentional experiences, as such, we say, indicating thereby that they belong inseparably to the current experience itself as its objectively intended or "objective meaning." Furthermore, that one and the same intentional object as such, from the viewpoint of descriptive psychology, is an ideal indicator of a group of ways of being conscious that are proper to it, whose system of typical differences tallies essentially with the typical articulation of the intentional object. It does not suffice to say that every consciousness is a consciousness-of on the lines, perhaps, of Brentano's classification (to which I cannot subscribe) into "presentations," "judgments," "phenomena of love and of hate"; but one must question the different categories of objects in their pure objectivity as objects of possible consciousness, and question back to the essential configurations of possible "manifolds" to be synthetically connected, through which an object of the relevant category can alone be known as the same, that is, as that which can be known through experiences of very differing description, differing and always differing still again, but always restricted to the descriptive types of such ways of consciousness as belong to it essentially and *a priori*. The reference to the fact that every object is either experienced or thought or sought after as an end, and so forth, is only a first step, and still tells us very little. The task of a phenomenological "constitution" of objects referred to at the close of this book, in a transcendental setting, it is true, finds its place here, only that now it is conceived as projected back upon the natural psychological standpoint.

Unfortunately, the necessary stressing of the difference between transcendental and psychological subjectivity, the repeated declaration that transcendental phenomenology is not in any sense psychology, not even phenomenological psychology has had this effect upon the majority of professional psychologists (who are wont to be very frugal, moreover, in all that concerns philosophy), that they failed to notice at all the radical psychological reform which was involved in the transcendental; they interpreted my utterances as an intimation that as psychologists they were not concerned in any way with phenomenology, or with any part of it. Even the few who noticed here that it was very relevant to psychology, and sought to make it accessible, have not grasped the whole meaning and scope of an intentional and constitutive phenomenology, and have not seen that here for the first time, in contrast with naturalistic psychology from an outer standpoint, a psychology comes to words and deeds, a psychology in which the life of the soul is made intelligible in its most intimate and originally intuitional essence, and that this original intuitional essence lies in a "constituting" of meaning-formations in modes of existential validity, which is perpetually new and incessantly organizing itself afresh—briefly, in the system of intentional actions, whereby existential (*seiende*) objects of the most varied grades right up to the level of an objective world are there for the Ego as occasion demands.

It was, moreover, not without reason that the psychological reform made its first entry as the concealed implication of a transcendental reform. For only a compulsion grounded on the philosophically transcendental problem, an urge towards extreme radicalism in the clearing up of the modes in which knowledge and object stand to each other in the conscious life itself, necessarily led to a universal and concrete phenomenology of consciousness, which received its primary orientation from the intentional object. In the transition to the psychology of the natural standpoint, it is then obvious that an intentional psychology has a quite different meaning from that of the traditions of the school of Locke or of that of Brentano. A. von Meinong also, although, in writings that appeared subsequently to my *Logical Studies,* his teaching comes here and there into touch with my own, is in no way to be regarded here as an exception: he remains bound to Brentano's leading conceptions, or to psychological sensationalism, as does the entire psychology of the modern tradition and the whole psychology of the present day.

The present work, however, as a philosophical treatise does not include psychological reform among its themes, although it should not be wholly lacking in indications bearing on a genuine intentional psychology. Even as philosophical, moreover, its task is limited. It does not claim to be anything more than an attempt that has been growing through decades of meditation exclusively directed to this one end: to discover a *radical beginning* of a philosophy which, to repeat the Kantian phrase, "will be able to present itself as science." The ideal of a philosopher, to think out sooner or later a logic, an ethic, a metaphysic, and so forth, which he can at all times justify to himself and others with an insight that is absolutely cogent—this ideal the author had early to abandon, and has not resumed it to this day. And for no reason other than the following, seeing that at any rate this insight was and remained for him indubitable, that a philosophy cannot start in a naïve straightforward fashion—not then as do the positive sciences which take their stand on the previously given ground of our experience of a world, presupposed as something that exists as a matter of course. That they do it causes them all to have problems in respect of their foundations, and paradoxes of their own, a condition which a subsequent and belated theory of knowledge first seeks to remedy. For this very reason the positive sciences are unphilosophical, they are not ultimate, absolute sciences. A philosophy with problematic foundations, with paradoxes which arise from the obscurity of the fundamental concepts, is no philosophy, it contradicts its very meaning *as* philosophy. Philosophy can take root only in radical reflexion upon the meaning and possibility of its own scheme. Through such reflexion it must in the very first place and through its own activity take possession of the absolute ground of pure pre-conceptual experience, which is its own proper preserve; then, self-active again, it must create original concepts, adequately adjusted to this ground, and so generally utilize for its advance an absolutely transparent method. There can then be no unclear, problematic concepts, and no paradoxes. The entire absence of this procedure, the overlooking of the immense difficulties attaching to a correct beginning, or the covering up of the same through the haste to have done with them, had this for its consequence, that we had and have many and ever new philosophical "systems" or "directions," but not the *one* philosophy which as Idea underlies all the philosophies that can be imagined. Philosophy, as it moves towards its realization, is not a relatively incomplete science improving as it goes naturally forward. There lies embedded in its meaning as philosophy a radicalism in the matter of foundations, an absolute freedom from all presuppositions, a securing for itself an absolute basis: the totality of presuppositions that can be "taken for granted." But that too must itself be first clarified through corresponding reflexions, and the absolutely binding quality of its requirements laid bare. That these reflexions become more and more interwoven as thought advances, and lead eventually to a whole science, to a science of Beginnings, a "first" philosophy; that all philosophical disciplines, the very foundations of all sciences whatsoever, spring from its matrix—all this must needs have remained implicit since the radicalism was lacking without which philosophy generally could not be, could not even make a start. The true philosophical beginning must have been irretrievably lost in beginning with presuppositions of a positive kind. Lacking as did the traditional schemes of philosophy the enthusiasm of a first beginning, they also lacked what is first and most important: a specifically philosophical groundwork acquired through original self-activity, and therewith that firmness of basis, that genuineness of root, which alone makes real philosophy possible. The author's convictions on such lines have become increasingly self-evident as his work progressed. If he has been obliged, on practical grounds, to lower the ideal of the philosopher to that of a downright beginner, he has at least in his old age reached for himself the complete certainty that he should thus call himself a beginner. He could almost hope, were Methuselah's span of days allotted him, to be still able to become a philosopher. He has always been able to follow up the problems that issue from the Beginning, and primarily from what is first for a descriptive phenomenology, the beginning of the beginning, and to develop it concretely in what to him have been instructive pieces of work. The far horizons of a phenomenological philosophy, the chief structural formations, to speak geographically, have disclosed themselves; the essential groups of problems and the methods of approach on essential lines have been made clear. The author sees the infinite open country of the true philosophy, the "promised land" on which he himself will never set foot. This confidence may wake a smile, but let each see for himself whether it has not some ground in the fragments laid before him as phenomenology in its beginnings. Gladly would he hope that those who come after will take up these first ventures, carry them steadily forward, yes, and improve also their great deficiencies, defects of incompleteness which cannot indeed be avoided in the beginnings of scientific work.

But when all is said, this work of mine can help no one who has already fixed his philosophy and his philosophical method, who has thus never learnt to know the despair of one who has the misfortune to be in love with philosophy, and who at the very outset of his studies, placed amid the chaos of philosophies, with his choice to make, realizes that he has really no choice at all, since no one of these has taken care to free itself from presuppositions, and none has sprung from the radical attitude of autonomous self-responsibility which the meaning of a philosophy demands. He who believes that he can appeal to the "fruitful βάθος " (*bathos*—depth)—of experience in the current sense of that term, or to the "assured results" of the exact sciences, or to experimental or physiological psychology, or to a constantly improved logic and mathematics, and so forth, and therein find premises for his philosophy, cannot have much susceptibility for the contents of this book. He is unable to bring to his reading an intensive interest, nor can he hold that the time and effort have been well spent which the sympathetic understanding of such a way of beginning demands. Only he who is himself striving to reach a beginning will herein behave otherwise, since he must say to himself: *tua res agitur.*

Those who are interested in the author's continued work and progress since 1913 may be referred to the recently published writing entitled "Formale und transzendentale Logik, Versuch einer Kritik der logischen Vernunft" (in the *Jahrbuch f. Phänomenologie und phänomenologische Forschung*, Bd. X, 1929). Also to his *Cartesianischen Meditationen*, an extended elaboration of the four lectures which he had the pleasure of giving first in the spring of 1922 at the University of London, and in this last year in an essentially maturer form at the Sorbonne in Paris. They furnish once again, though merely in outline an Introduction to phenomenological philosophy, but contain an essential supplement in the detailed treatment of the fundamental problem of transcendental intersubjectivity, wherewith the solipsistic objection completely collapses. They will presumably appear simultaneously with this English edition of the *Ideen* in a French rendering in the *Bulletin de la Société de Philosophie*. In the same year a German edition should be appearing, published by Niemeyer of Halle a.d.S, containing as additional matter a second Introduction, in which the clarification of the idea of a personal (on the lines of a mental science) and natural anthropology and psychology, and lastly of a pure intuitional psychology, is undertaken as an initial problem. At a later stage only is it shown how, starting from this discussion, which, like all that has preceded, remains on natural ground, the Copernican reversal to the transcendental standpoint finds its motive. At the same time a series of publications is being started in my *Jahrbuch:* the concrete phenomenological studies which I have drafted as the years went by, to clear up my own mind, and for the safeguarding of the structure of phenomenology.

In conclusion, let me thank my own honoured friend, Professor W. R. Boyce Gibson, for the disinterested labour involved in this translation. It fills me with some hope when so thorough and so earnest a thinker takes so great an interest in my efforts to furnish philosophy with a scientific beginning as to take upon himself the translating of this extensive work, the language of which is so difficult, even for Germans.

# Translator's Preface

THE *Ideen zu einer reinen Phänomenologie und phänomenologischen Philosphie*, of which this is a translation, first appeared as the leading Article of the first issue of the *Jahrbuch für Philosophie und Phänomenologische Forschung*[1] in 1913, and has been twice reprinted, in 1922 and in 1928. It furnishes the groundwork and starting-point of the phenomenological movement now so active in Germany, and is the "classic" of that reform movement in philosophy which, in the words of the Author's stirring article in *Logos* (Bd. I), 1910, conceives philosophy as a "rigorous science," and aims at a radical reconstruction of its basis and method. Since the year 1900, which saw the first edition of Husserl's *Logical Studies,* the Author has been known as a profound and penetrating logical thinker, but in these same Studies, more particularly in the Second Edition (1913–1921), we have not only logic, but the transition from logic to phenomenology, and the growing conviction that a radical or "transcendental" logic is possible only on a phenomenological basis. The present work supplies that basis in a form at once general and fundamental, special problems, such as those of Intersubjectivity, the Pure Ego, and the relation of phenomenology to Metaphysics being reserved for later treatment. It is, as expressly stated on the front page of the third impression of the *Ideen* (Halle, Max Niemeyer, 1928), the "First Book," and, *as such,* bears the title *Allgemeine Einführung in die reine Phänomenologie,* or *General Introduction to Pure Phenomenology*—the title adopted for this English version.

The translation from the German covers the Author's Preface, the Text of the *Ideen,* and the Index. It has had its difficulties, and the sincerest effort has been made to straighten these out, and present a faithful rendering—in somewhat modified style, maybe—of the terse and compact original. I have had important help towards the elucidating of the meaning of the text from Professor Husserl himself, for whose generous kindness to me during my stay in Freiburg in 1928 I cannot be

---

[1] Edited by E. Husserl. Freiburg-i-B. Published by Max Niemeyer, Halle, a.d.S.

too grateful, and from Professor Oskar Becker of the same University. In particular, Professor Husserl has laid all readers of this translation under a special debt by his important and illuminating "Preface to the English Edition," which not only sheds a most helpful light on the author's own thought and writings, but supplements most usefully the discussion of the meaning of Transcendental Phenomenology, and its distinction from phenomenological psychology given in his Article on "Phenomenology" in the Fourteenth Edition of the *Encyclopædia Britannica*. I owe also many helpful suggestions to my own students of the Metaphysics Class, and in particular to Norman Porter, now Lecturer in Philosophy in the University of Sydney, who read through the whole work in MS. To my proof-reader, Dr. C. V. Salmon of Belfast University, I am quite specially indebted. He has taken on himself that burden of final revision, which writers ordinarily assume in their own person, but must carry by proxy when, as in my own case, they are ten thousand miles away. Dr. Salmon is himself an expert phenomenologist, one of Professor Husserl's own pupils, a contributor of the tenth volume of the *Jahrbuch*, and the translator of the Encyclopædia Article on Phenomenology, to which I have just referred. His services in scrutinizing the translated terminology have therefore been of exceptional value, and the fact that he has co-operated with the translator in the search after terminological precision should be most reassuring to the reader.

It is hoped that the elaborate Analytical Index, which essentially, and in its present form, is the work of Dr. Ludwig Landgrebe of Freiburg, and has simply been put into English and English order by the translator, will prove a real and constant help to the student in his effort to follow the thought of one who always says what he sees, and never sacrifices a significant insight to the simplifying and obliterating conveniences of generalized statement.

The translator is deeply indebted to his publishers, George Allen & Unwin Ltd., of Ruskin House, and especially to the Editor of the Library of Philosophy, Professor J. H. Muirhead, for the interest and care they have taken in the publishing of this English version of Edmund Husserl's fundamental work. Professor Muirhead greeted the venture from the outset with genuine and discerning sympathy, and his suggestions for the improvement of the English text, ever since the first MS. came into his hands, have been most helpful.

It has been a constant satisfaction to realize that the editorship of the present translation was in the competent hands of so distinguished a scholar.

In conclusion, I owe to my wife not only the typing of the MS. of the complete text, but many happy suggestions and improvements in the wording. The translation owes much to her scholarly care.

If, with the interests of the reader in mind, the translator may venture on a word of advice, it would be this: Should the first chapter of the first Section—which treats of logical preliminaries, and forms the link of connexion with the later *Logical Studies*—prove by reason of its compression difficult or unsatisfying to the uninitiated, let him pass on to the Second Chapter, and make that the starting-point of his reading, reserving to himself, of course, the privilege of returning to the omitted chapter when he has become more familiar with the drift of the main argument, and feels the need for further light on its logical basis.

W. R. Boyce Gibson

# Contents

27

## Chapter 2

## PART TWO

## THE FUNDAMENTAL PHENOMENOLOGICAL OUTLOOK

## Chapter 3

## Chapter 4

## Chapter 5

The Region of Pure Consciousness ... 133

## Chapter 8

### General Structures of Pure Consciousness 194

## Chapter 9

### Noesis and Noema 235

## Chapter 10

Theory of the Noetic-Noematic Structures: Elaboration of the Problems                                      260

PART FOUR
REASON AND REALITY (*WIRKLICHKEIT*)

Chapter 11

## Chapter 12

Phenomenology of the Reason                          350

## Chapter 13

Grades of Generality in the Ordering of the Problems of
the Theoretic Reason                                 373

# Introduction

PURE PHENOMENOLOGY, to which we are here seeking the way, whose unique position in regard to all other sciences we wish to make clear, and to set forth as the most fundamental region of philosophy, is an essentially new science, which in virtue of its own governing peculiarity lies far removed from our ordinary thinking, and has not until our own day therefore shown an impulse to develop. It calls itself a science of "phenomena." Other sciences, long known to us, also treat of phenomena. Thus one hears psychology referred to as a science of psychical, and natural science as a science of physical "appearances" or phenomena. So in history we hear speak occasionally of historical, and in the cultural sciences of cultural phenomena, and similarly for all sciences that deal with realities. Now differently as the word "phenomenon" may be used in such contexts, and diverse as may be the meanings which it bears, it is certain that phenomenology also deals with all these "phenomena" and in all their meanings, but from a quite different point of view, the effect of which is to modify in a determinate way all the meanings which the term bears in the old-established sciences. Only as thus modified do these meanings enter the phenomenological sphere. To understand these modifications, or, to speak more accurately, to reach the phenomenological standpoint, and through reflexion to fix its distinctive character, and that also of the natural viewpoints, in a scientific way, this is the first and by no means easy task which we must carry out in full, if we would gain the ground of phenomenology and grasp its distinctive nature scientifically.

In the last decade there has been much talk of phenomenology in German philosophy and psychology. In presumed agreement with the *Logical Studies*,[1] phenomenology is conceived as a sub-domain of empirical psychology, as a region containing "immanent" descriptions of psychical events (*Erlebnisse*), which—such is their understanding of this immanence—remains strictly within the framework in inner

---

[1] E. Husserl, *Logische Untersuchungen*, 2 vols., 1900 and 1901. Republished (3rd ed.) in three vols. 1922. The references in this translation are to the three vols. of this third edition.

*experience (Erfahrung)*. My protest against this interpretation[2] has apparently been of small use, and the accompanying elucidations, which sharply delineate some at least of the main points of the difference, have not been understood or have been heedlessly set aside. Thence also the completely empty replies—empty because the plain *meaning* of my statement was missed—to my criticism of the psychological method, a criticism which in no way denied the value of modern psychology, and in no sense depreciated the experimental work carried out by men of distinction, but exposed certain, in the literal sense of the term, radical defects of method on the removal of which, in my opinion, the raising of psychology to a higher scientific level and an extraordinary extension of its field of work must depend. There will still be occasion to deal briefly with the superfluous defences of psychology against my presumed "attacks." I mention this dispute here that I may state from the outset most emphatically, in face of prevailing and far-spreading misinterpretations, *that the pure phenomenology*, to which in what follows we would prepare a way of approach, the same which emerged for the first time in the *Logical Studies*, and has revealed an ever richer and deeper meaning to me as my thought has dwelt on it through the last ten years, *is not psychology*, and that it is not accidental delimitations and considerations of terminology, but grounds *of principle*, which forbid its being counted as psychology. Great as is the importance which phenomenology must claim to possess for psychology in the matter of method, whatever the essential "bases" it provides for it, it is itself (if only as Science of ideas) as little identifiable with psychology as is geometry with natural science. Indeed, the difference is more marked, and reaches deeper than this comparison would itself suggest. It makes no difference that phenomenology has to do with "consciousness," with all types of experience, with acts and their correlates; though in view of the prevailing habits of thought, it demands no small effort to see this. That

[2] In the article "Philosophy as Strict Science" ("Philosophie als strenge Wissenschaft"), *Logos*, vol. i. pp. 316–318 (observe more particularly my treatment of the concept of experience (*Erfahrung*), p. 316). Cf. the detailed discussion which already in my *Review of German Writing on Logic* between the years 1895–99 (*Archiv. I. system. Philosophie*, Bd. X (1903), pp. 307–400, is devoted to the relation between phenomenology and descriptive psychology. I could not change a word of this to-day.

we should set aside all previous habits of thought, see through and break down the mental barriers which these habits have set along the horizons of our thinking, and in full intellectual freedom proceed to lay hold on those genuine philosophical problems still awaiting completely fresh formulation which the liberated horizons on all sides disclose to us—these are hard demands. Yet nothing less is required. What makes the appropriation of the essential nature of phenomenology, the understanding of the peculiar meaning of its form of inquiry, and its relation to all other sciences (to psychology in particular) so extraordinarily difficult, is that in addition to all other adjustments *a new way of looking at things* is necessary, one that contrasts *at every point* with the natural attitude of experience and thought. To move freely along this new way without ever reverting to the old viewpoints, to learn to see what stands before our eyes, to distinguish, to describe, calls, moreover, for exacting and laborious studies.

It will be the chief task of this *First* Book to search out ways in which the excessive difficulties of penetrating into this new world can be overcome as it were bit by bit. We shall start from the standpoint of everyday life, from the world as it confronts us, from consciousness as it presents itself in psychological experience, and shall lay bare the presuppositions essential to this viewpoint. We shall then develop a method of "phenomenological Reductions," according to which we may set aside the limitations to knowledge essentially involved in every nature-directed form of investigation, deflecting the restricted line of vision proper to it, until we have eventually before us the free outlook upon "transcendentally" purified phenomena, and therewith the field of phenomenology in our own special sense of that term.

Let us trace the lines of this anticipatory sketch somewhat more firmly, and in conformity with the bias of the times, as also with inner affinities of the subject-matter, connect them with psychology.

*Psychology* is a science of experience. Keeping to the customary sense of the word experience (*Erfahrung*), this has a twofold meaning:

1. Psychology is a science of *facts* (*Tatsachen*), of "matters of fact"—in Hume's sense of the word.

2. Psychology is a science of *realities* (*Realitäten*). The "phenomena" which it handles as psychological "phenomenology" are real events which as such, in so far as they have

real existence (*Dasein*), take their place with the real Subjects to which they belong in the one spatio-temporal world, the *omnitudo realitatis*.

As over against this psychological "phenomenology," *pure or transcendental phenomenology will be established not as a science of facts, but as a science of essential Being* (as *"eidetic"* Science); a science which aims exclusively at establishing "knowledge of essences" (*Wesenserkenntnisse*) and *absolutely no "facts."* The corresponding Reduction which leads from the psychological phenomenon to the pure "essence," or, in respect of the judging thought, from factual ("empirical") to "essential" universality, is the *eidetic Reduction*.

*In the second place, the phenomena of transcendental phenomenology will be characterized as non-real* (*irreal*). Other reductions, the specifically transcendental, "purify" the psychological phenomena from that which lends them reality, and therewith a setting in the real "world." Our phenomenology should be a theory of essential Being, dealing not with real, but with transcendentally reduced phenomena.

What this all affirms when more closely considered will first become plain in the developments that follow. In an anticipatory way it gives an outline sketch of the preliminary series of studies. I consider it necessary at this point to add only one remark: It will surprise the reader that in the two foregoing passages in italics, in place of the single division of sciences into realistic and idealistic (or into empirical and *a priori*) which is universally adopted, two divisions are preferred, corresponding to the two pairs of opposites: Fact and Essence, Real and not-Real. The distinction conveyed by this twofold opposition replacing that between real and ideal will find a thoroughgoing justification in the later course of our inquiries (as a matter of fact, in the Second Book). It will be shown that the concept of reality requires a fundamental limitation in virtue of which a difference must be set up between real Being and individual (purely temporal) Being. The transition to the pure Essence provides on the one side a knowledge of the essential nature of the Real, on the other, in respect of the domain left over, knowledge of the essential nature of the non-real (*irreal*). It will transpire further that all transcendentally purified "experiences" are non-realities, and excluded from every connexion within the "real world." These same non-realities are studied by phenomenology, but not as singular particularities (*Einzelheiten*), rather in their "essential being."

The extent, however, to which transcendental phenomena as singular *facta* are at all available for study, and the question of the relation which a factual study of such a kind may bear to the idea of a Metaphysic, can be considered only in the concluding series of investigations.

In the *first* Book we shall treat not only of the general theory of the phenomenological Reductions which make the transcendentally purified consciousness with its essential correlates perceptible (*sichtlich*) and accessible; we shall also seek to win definite ideas of the most general structures of this pure consciousness, and through their agency of the most general groups of problems, directions of study and methods which pertain to the new science.

In the *second* Book we make a thorough inquiry into certain specially important sets of problems the systematic formulation of which and solution under types is the precondition for bringing into real clearness the difficult relations of phenomenology to the physical sciences of nature, to psychology, and to the sciences of the mind, and on another side also to the *a priori* sciences as a collective whole. The phenomenological sketches here traced in outline offer also the welcome means of considerably deepening the understanding of phenomenology reached in the *first* Book, and of winning from its immense circle of problems a far richer content of knowledge.

A *third* and concluding Book is dedicated to the Idea of Philosophy. The insight will be awakened that genuine philosophy, the idea of which is to realize the idea of Absolute Knowledge, has its roots in pure phenomenology, and this in so earnest a sense that the systematically rigorous grounding and development of this first of all philosophies remains the perpetual precondition of all metaphysics and other philosophy "which would aspire to be a *science.*"

Since phenomenology is here to be established as a science of Essential Being—as an *a priori*, or, as we also say, eidetic science—it will be useful to preface the labours devoted to phenomenology itself with a series of fundamental discussions upon Essence (*Wesen*) and the Science of Essential Being, and with a defence as against naturalism of the original and intrinsic authority of this Knowledge of Essence.

We bring to a close these introductory words with a short terminological discussion. Following my custom in the *Logical Studies*, I avoid as far as possible the expressions *a priori* and *a posteriori*, partly on account of the confusing obscurities and ambiguities which infect their ordinary use, but also because of the notorious philosophical theories which as an evil heritage from the past are interwoven with them. Only in contexts which lend them singleness of sense, and only as the equivalent of other concomitant terms to which we have assigned clear and univocal meanings, should they be used, especially when we are concerned to note the sympathetic accord with historical parallels.

The expression *Idea* and *Ideal* are not quite in such evil odour as regards confusing ambiguities, though they suffer on the whole pretty badly in this respect, as the frequent misinterpretations of my *Logical Studies* have made me feel often painfully enough. As a further incentive to a change of terminology, I may mention the need to keep the highly important *Kantian concept of the Idea* free from all contact with the general concepts of (the formal or material) essence. I therefore make use, as a foreign expression, of the terminologically unspent *Eidos,* and as a German expression of a term whose equivocations are harmless, though at times vexatious, the word *Wesen* (Essence or Essential Being).

I would also have been pleased to dispense with the heavily laden word *Real,* if only I could have found a suitable substitute.

I add this further general remark: Since it is not advisable to choose technical expressions which fall wholly outside the framework of tradition philosophical speech, and, above all, since the fundamental concepts of philosophy cannot be defined through stable concepts that can be identified at any time by reference to a directly accessible intuitional basis; since rather it is only, as a rule, after protracted inquiries that they can be finally cleared up and determined: it is often indispensable to make use of a set of speech-forms which group together in an orderly way a *number* of current expressions bearing closely equivalent meanings, the individual members of the group being terminologically distinguished one from the other. Definition cannot take the same form in philosophy as it does in mathematics; the imitation of mathematical procedure is invariably in this respect not only unfruitful, but perverse and most harmful in its consequences. Moreover, the foregoing terminological expressions should by means of obvious and determinate indications maintain their fixed meaning throughout the course of the inquiry, whilst all close critical comparisons with philosophical tradition in this or other respects, if only to prevent the undue expansion of this work, must be omitted.

# PART ONE

# THE NATURE AND KNOWLEDGE OF ESSENTIAL BEING

# Chapter 1

## Fact and Essence

### 1. Natural Knowledge and Experience

NATURAL KNOWLEDGE begins with experience (*Erfahrung*) and remains *within* experience. Thus in that theoretical position which we call the "natural" standpoint, the total field of possible research is indicated by a *single* word: that is, the *World*. The sciences proper to this original[1] standpoint are accordingly in their collective unity sciences of the World, and so long as this standpoint is the only dominant one, the concepts "true Being," "real (*wirkliches*) Being," i.e., real empirical (*reales*) Being, and—since all that is real comes to self-concentration in the form of a cosmic unity—"Being in the World" are meanings that coincide.

Every science has its own object-domain as field of research, and to all that it knows, i.e., in this connexion, to all its correct assertions, there correspond as original sources of the reasoned justification that support them certain intuitions in which objects of the region appear as self-given and in part at least as *given in a primordial* (*originärer*) *sense*. The *object-giving* (or *dator*) intuition of the first, "natural" sphere of knowledge and of all its sciences is natural experience, and the *primordial* dator experience is *perception* in the ordinary sense of the term. To have something real primordially given, and to "become aware" of it and "perceive" it in simple intuition, are one and the same thing. In "outer perception" we have primordial experience of physical things, but in memory or anticipatory expectation this is no longer the case; we have primordial experience of ourselves and our states of conscious-

[1] We are not talking here in terms of history. In this reference to originality there need not be, and should not be, any thought of genesis along the lines either of psychological causality or of evolutionary history. What other meaning is intended will become clear only in the sequel and in the light of scientific reflexion. But everyone feels at once that the priority of empirically concrete knowledge of facts to all other knowledge, to all knowledge on ideal mathematical lines, for instance, must not be taken in any temporal sense, though intelligible in non-temporal terms.

ness in the so-called inner or self-perception, but not of others and their vital experiences in and through "empathy." We "behold the living experiences of others" through the perception of their bodily behaviour. This beholding in the case of empathy is indeed intuitional dator, yet no longer a *primordially* dator act. The other man and his psychical life is indeed apprehended as "there in person," and in union with his body, but, unlike the body, it is not given to our consciousness as primordial.

The World is the totality of objects that can be known through experience (*Erfahrung*), known in terms of orderly theoretical thought on the basis of direct present (*aktueller*) experience. This is not the place to discuss in greater detail the method proper to a science of experience or to consider how such a science justifies its claim to transcend the narrow framework of direct empirical givenness. Under sciences of the World, that is sciences developed from the natural standpoint, are included not only all so-called *natural sciences*, in the more extended as well as in the narrower sense of that term, the sciences of *material* nature, but also the sciences of animal beings (*Wesen*), with their *psychophysical nature*, physiology, psychology, and so forth. All so-called *mental sciences* also come under this head—history, the cultural sciences, the sociological disciplines of every kind, whereby we provisionally leave it an open question whether they are to be held similar to the natural sciences or placed in opposition to them, be themselves accepted as natural sciences or as sciences of an essentially new type.

## 2. Fact. Inseparability of Fact and Essence

Sciences of experience are *sciences of "fact."* The acts of cognition which underlie our experiencing posit the Real in *individual* form, posit it as having spatio-temporal existence, as something existing in *this* time-spot, having this particular duration of its own and a real content which in its essence could just as well have been present in any other time-spot; posits it, moreover, as something which is present at this place in this particular physical shape (or is there given united to a body of this shape), where yet the same real being might just as well, so far as its own essence is concerned, be present at any other place, and in any other form, and might likewise change whilst remaining in fact unchanged, or change otherwise than the way in which it actually does. Individual Being of every kind is, to speak quite generally, "*accidental.*" It is so-and-so, but essentially it could be other than it is. Even if definite laws of nature obtain according to which such and such definite consequences must in fact follow when such and such real conditions are in fact present, such laws express only orderings that do in fact obtain, which might run quite differently, and already presuppose, as pertaining *ab initio* to the *essence* of objects of possible experience, that the objects thus ordered by them, when considered in themselves, are accidental.

But the import of this contingency, which is there called matter-of-factness (*Tatsächlichkeit*), is limited in this respect that the contingency is correlative to a *necessity* which does not carry the mere actuality-status of a valid rule of connexion obtaining between temporo-spatial facts, but has the character of *essential necessity,* and therewith a relation to *essential universality.* Now when we stated that every fact could be "essentially" other than it is, we were already expressing thereby *that it belongs to the meaning of everything contingent that it should have essential being and therewith an Eidos to be apprehended in all its purity;* and this Eidos comes under *essential truths of varying degrees of universality.* An individual object is not simply and quite generally an individual, a "this-there" something unique; but being constituted thus and thus "*in itself*" it has *its own proper mode of being,* its own supply of *essential* predicables which must qualify it (*qua* "Being as it is in itself"), if other secondary relative determinations are to qualify it also. Thus, for example, every tone in and for itself has an essential nature, and at the limit the universal meaning-essence "tone in general," or rather the acoustic in general—understood in the pure sense of a phase or aspect intuitively derivable from the individual tone (either in its singleness, or through comparison with others as a "common element"). So too every material thing has its own essential derivatives, and at the limit the universal derivative "material thing in general," with time-determination-in-general, duration-, figure-, materiality-in-general. *Whatever belongs to the essence of the individual can also belong to another individual can also belong to another individual,* and the *broadest* generalities of essential being, of the kind we have been indicating through the help of examples, delimit "*regions*" or "*categories*" of individuals.

## 3. Essential Insight and Individual Intuition

*At first* "essence" indicated that which in the intimate self-being of an individual discloses to us *"what"* it is. But every such What can be "set out as Ideas." *Empirical or individual intuition* can be transformed into *essential insight* (ideation) —a possibility which is itself not to be understood as empirical but as essential possibility. The object of such insight is then the corresponding *pure* essence or eidos, whether it be the highest category or one of its specializations, right down to the fully "concrete."

This insight which *gives* the essence and in the last resort in *primordial* form can be *adequate;* and as such we can easily procure it, for instance, from the essential nature of a sound; but it can also be more or less imperfect, *"inadequate,"* and that not only in respect of its greater or lesser *clearness* and *distinctness.* It belongs to the type of development peculiar to certain categories of essential being that essences belonging to them *can* be given only *"one-sidedly,"* whilst in succession more "sides," though never "all sides," can be given; so correlatively the individual concrete particularities corresponding to these categories can be experienced and represented only in inadequate "one-sided" empirical intuitions. This holds for every essence related to the *thing-like,* and indeed for all the essential components of extension and materiality respectively; it even holds good, if we look more closely (subsequent analyses will make that evident) for *all realities* generally, whereby indeed the vague expressions "one-sidedness" and "more-sidedness" receive determinate meanings, and different kinds of inadequacy are separated out one from the other.

Here the preliminary indication will suffice that already on grounds of principle the spatial shape of the physical thing can be given only in some single perspective aspect; also that apart from this inadequacy which clings to the unfolding of any series of continuously connected intuitions and persists in spite of all that is thereby acquired, every physical property draws us on into infinities of experience; and that every multiplicity of experience, however lengthily drawn out, still leaves the way open to closer and novel thing-determinations; and so on, *in infinitum.*

Of whatever kind the individual intuition may be, whether adequate or not, it can pass off into essential intuition, and the latter, whether correspondingly adequate or not, has the character of a dator act. And this means that—

*The essence (Eidos) is an object of a new type. Just as the datum of individual or empirical intuition is an individual object, so the datum of essential intuition is a pure essence.*

Here we have not a mere superficial analogy, but a radical community of nature. *Essential insight is still intuition,* just as the eidetic object is still an object. The generalization of the correlative, mutually attached concepts "intuition" and "object" is not a casual whim, but is compellingly demanded by the very nature of things.[2] Empirical intuition, more specifically sense-experience, is consciousness of an individual object, and as an intuiting agency "brings it to givenness": as perception, to primordial givenness, to the consciousness of grasping the object in "a primordial way," in its *"bodily"* selfhood. On quite similar lines essential intuition is the consciousness of something, of an "object," a something towards which its glance is directed, a something "self-given" within it; but which can then be "presented" in other acts, vaguely or distinctly thought, made the subject of true and false predications—as is the case indeed with every *"object" in the necessarily extended sense proper to Formal Logic.* Every possible object, or to put it logically, *"every subject of possibly true predications,"* has indeed *its own* ways, that of predicative thinking above all, of coming under a glance that presents, intuits, meets it eventually in its "bodily selfhood" and "lays hold of" it. Thus essential insight *is* intuition, and if it is insight in the pregnant sense of the term, and not a mere, and possibly a vague, representation, it is a *primordial* dator Intuition, grasping the essence in its "bodily" selfhood.[3] But, on the other hand, it is

---

[2] The surprising polemic of O. Külpe against my theory of categorical intuition in the work entitled *Die Realisierung* (1912, I. p. 127) illustrates the difficulty felt by psychological experts in our time of assimilating this simple and quite fundamental insight. I regret being misunderstood by this excellent scholar. But a critical reply becomes impossible where the misconception is so complete that there remains no vestige of the *meaning* of the positions originally laid down.

[3] In my *Logical Studies* I used to employ the word *Ideation* to represent the primordial dator insight into essential being, and even then chiefly of the adequate type. Yet we clearly need a more plastic concept which shall include every consciousness plainly

an intuition of a fundamentally *unique* and *novel* kind, namely in contrast to the types of intuition which belong as correlatives to the object-matters of other categories, and more specifically to intuition in the ordinary narrow sense, that is, individual intuition.

It lies undoubtedly in the intrinsic nature of essential intuition that it should rest on what is a chief factor of individual intuition, namely the striving for this, the visible presence of individual fact, though it does not, to be sure, presuppose any apprehension of the individual or any recognition of its reality. Consequently it is certain that no essential intuition is possible without the free possibility of directing one's glance to an individual *counterpart* and of shaping an illustration; just as contrariwise no individual intuition is possible without the free possibility of carrying out an act of ideation and therein directing one's glance upon the corresponding essence which exemplifies itself in something individually visible; but that does not alter the fact that *the two kinds of intuition differ in principle*, and in assertions of the kind we have just been making it is only the essential relations between them that declare themselves. Thus, to the essential differences of the intuitions correspond the essential relations between "existence" (here clearly in the sense of individual concrete being) and "essence," between *fact* and *eidos*. Pursuing such connexions, we grasp *with intelligent insight* the conceptual essence attached to these terms, and from now on firmly attached to them, and therewith *all* thoughts *partially mystical in nature* and clinging chiefly to the concepts Eidos (Idea) and Essence remain *rigorously excluded*.[4]

## 4. Essential Insight and the Play of Fancy. Knowledge of Essences Independent of All Knowledge of Facts

The Eidos, the *pure essence*, can be exemplified intuitively in the data of experience, data of perception, memory, and so forth, but just as readily *also in the mere data of fancy* (*Phantasie*). Hence, with the aim of grasping an essence itself in its *primordial* form, we can set out from corresponding

and straightly directed to an essence which it also grasps and fixes; and in addition also includes every obscure consciousness which no longer intuits at all.

[4] Cf. my article in *Logos,* I. p. 315.

empirical intuitions, *but we can also set out just as well from non-empirical intuitions, intuitions that do not apprehend sensory existence, intuitions rather "of a merely imaginative order."*

If in the play of fancy we bring spatial shapes of one sort or another to birth, melodies, social happenings, and so forth, or live through fictitious acts of everyday life, of satisfaction or dissatisfaction, of volition and the like, we can through "ideation" secure from this source primordial and even on occasion adequate insight into pure essences in manifold variety: essences, it may be, of spatial shape *in general*, of melody *as such*, of social happening *as such*, and so forth, or of the shape, melody, etc., of the relevant special *type*. It is a matter of indifference in this connexion whether such things have ever been given in actual experience or not. Could free make-believe through some sort of psychological miracle lead to the imagining of something fundamentally new in kind (sensory data, for instance) which never occurred in anyone's experiences, nor ever will, that would not affect in any way the primordial giveness of the corresponding essences, although imagined data are never under any circumstances real data.

It follows essentially from all this that *the positing of the essence*, with the intuitive apprehension that immediately accompanies it, *does not imply any positing of individual existence whatsoever; pure essential truths do not make the slightest assertion concerning facts*; hence from them *alone* we are not able to infer even the pettiest truth concerning the fact-world. Just as to think a fact or to express it needs the grounding of experience (so far as the *essential relevancy* of such thinking *necessarily* demands it), so thought concerning pure essence—the unmixed thought, not that which connects essence and facts together—needs for its *grounding* and support an insight into the essences of things.

## 5. Judgments about Essence and Judgments of Eidetic Generality

We have still to consider the following point: Judgments *about* essences and essential relationships on the one hand, and on the other hand eidetic judgments in general, in the broad sense in which we must consider them, are not the same thing; *eidetic knowledge has not essences as its object-matter in all its propositions*; and what is closely connected

with this: intuition of the Essence—as we have so far understood it—as a consciousness analogous to natural experience,
to the apprehension of concrete existence (*Dasein*); and
wherein an essence is *objectively* grasped, as is an individual
in the experience of nature, is not the only consciousness
which includes the essence whilst excluding the positing of
any *concrete existence*. We can be intuitively aware of essences and can apprehend them after a certain fashion without
their becoming "objects *about* which."

Let us start from judgments. Speaking more accurately, our
concern is with the difference between judgments *about* essences and judgments which in an indeterminate universal
way, and unmixed with any positing of what is individual,
still judge *about the individual, but purely as an instance of
essential being*, and in accordance with the rubric "*in general.*"
Thus, in pure geometry, we judge as a rule not about the
eidos "straight," "angle," "triangle," or "conic section," etc.,
but about the straight line and angle in general or "as such,"
about individual triangles in general, conic sections in general.
Such universal judgments have the character of *essential
generality*, of "pure," or, as one also says, of "*rigorous*,"
absolutely "*unconditioned*" *generality*.

For the sake of simplicity, let us assume that we are dealing
with "axioms," with judgments immediately obvious, to which
all other judgments lead back as their ground of mediation.
Such judgments—so far as they treat of individual instances
in the way just indicated, as we here assume that they do—
require for their noetic grounding, that is their being made
open to insight, a certain essential vision which (in a *modified*
sense) could also be designated as essential apprehension; and
even the latter, as well as the essential intuition which confers
objectivity, rests on having an awareness of individual instances of the essence, but not on their being experienced as
empirically real. Moreover, mere presentations of fancy or
rather fancy-'warenesses suffice to give us these instances; of
that concerning which we are aware we are conscious as such;
it "appears," but is not grasped as concretely existing. When,
for instance, we judge in an essentially general way (with a
generality that is "unconditioned" and "pure") that "a colour
in general is different from a sound in general," the judgment
confirms what we have just been saying. An instance of the
essence "colour" and an instance of the essence "sound" are
intuitively "present," and indeed *as* instancing their own

essences; fancy-intuition (not involving the positing of concrete existence) and essential intuition are present at the same time and in a certain way, though the latter does not function as an intuition which *objectifies* the essence. But it belongs to the essence of the situation that we are free at time to pass over to the corresponding standpoint from which the essence is objectified, and that the possibility of doing this is in fact an essential one. In keeping with the changed standpoint the judgment would also suffer change, and would run as follows: The essence (the "genus") Colour is other than the essence (the "genus") Sound. And so in all cases.

Conversely *every judgment treating of Essences can be transformed equivalently into an unconditionally universal judgment concerning instances of this essence as such*. In this respect *pure judgments relating to Essences* (pure eidetic judgments) have a *common* affinity, *whatever their logical form* may happen to be. What is common to them is that they posit no individual being even when in pure essential generality they judge about what is individual.

## 6. Some Fundamental Concepts.
### Generality and Necessity

Eidetic *judging*, eidetic *judgment* or eidetic *proposition*, eidetic *truth* (or true proposition)—these ideas manifestly belong to the same system. Connected with them is also the correlate of the third of these ideas: the plain eidetic *fact* (*Sachverhalt*) as subsisting within eidetic truth): and the correlate of the first two ideas: the eidetic *fact* in the *modified* sense of that which it is merely *presumed to be*; in the sense of the judged content as such; and this may or may not prove reliable.

Every eidetic division and individuation of an eidetically general fact is called, just *in so far as* it is this, an *essential necessity*. *Essential generality and essential necessity are thus correlates*. The use of the term "necessity" here vacillates somewhat so as to conform to the attached correlations: the corresponding judgments are also termed "necessary." But it is important to take note of the distinctions, and above all not to refer to essential generality (as is ordinarily done) as itself necessity. The consciousness of a necessity, or more specifically a consciousness of a judgment, in which we become aware of a certain matter as the specification of an eidetic generality, is called *apodeictic*, the judgment itself, the proposition, an *apodeictic* (also apodeictically—"necessary") *consequent* of the general proposition to which it is related. The propositions we have stated concerning the relations between generality, necessity, apodeicticity can also be conceived in a more general way, so as to hold good for any realm of discourse, and not only for such as are purely eidetic. But with the eidetic limitation they obviously win a distinctive and specially important meaning.

The connexion of *eidetic* judging about the individual in general with the *positing* of the individual as a *concrete existent* is also very important. The essential generality is transferred to an individual, or to an indeterminately general range of individuals, posited as concretely existing. Every "application" of geometrical truths to cases in nature (posited as real) has its place here. The subject-matter set down as real is then *fact*, so far as its real content is individual, but it is *eidetic necessity*, in so far as it is the instancing (*Vereinzelung*) of an essential generality.

One should not confuse the *unrestricted generality of natural laws* with *essential generality*. The proposition "all bodies are heavy" does not indeed take any determinate potential thing within the universe to be a concrete existent. And yet it has not the unconditional generality of eidetically general propositions in so far as, in accordance with its meaning as a natural law, it continues to carry with it a reference to concrete existence (*Daseinssetzung*), to that, namely, of Nature itself, of temporo-spatial reality: all bodies—*in Nature*, all "real" bodies are heavy. On the other hand, the proposition "all material things are extended" has eidetic validity and can be taken as *purely* eidetic if the reference to concrete existence conveyed by the subject is excluded as irrelevant. It states that which has its pure ground in the essence of a material thing, and in the essence of extension, that which we can bring home to insight, as "unconditioned" generality. This is done by bringing the essence of a material thing (any fictitious image of a thing of this type will here serve as a basis) to primordial givenness, and then in this object-giving consciousness completing the mental steps required for the "insight," for the primordial givenness, that is, of the essential content which the foregoing proposition openly expressed. That the *real* in space corresponds to truths of such a kind is not a mere fact (*Faktum*), but as a special development of essential laws an *essential necessity*. The element of fact in this connexion is only the reality itself which serves as basis for the application.

## 7. Sciences of Facts and Sciences of Essence

The connexion (itself eidetic) which holds between individual object and essence, and which is such that to each individual object a state of essential being belongs as *its* essence, just as conversely to each essence there corresponds a series of possible individuals as its factual instancings (*Vereinzelungen*), is the ground for a corresponding reciprocal relationship between sciences of fact and sciences of the essence. There are *pure sciences of essential being* such as pure logic, pure mathematics, pure time-theory, space-theory, theory of movement, etc.

These, in all their thought-constructions, are free throughout from any positings of actual fact; or, what comes to the same thing, *in them no experience qua experience*, i.e., *qua* consciousness that apprehends or sets up reality or concrete being, *can take over the function of supplying a logical ground*. Where experience functions in them, it is not *as* experience. The *geometer* who draws his figures on the blackboard produces in so doing strokes that are actually there on a board that is actually there. But his experience of what he thus produces, *qua* experience, affords just as little *ground* for his sight and thought of the geometrical essence as does the physical act of production itself. Whether or no he thereby suffers hallucination, and whether instead of actually drawing the lines he draws his lines and figures in a world of fancy, does not really matter. The *student of nature* behaves quite differently. He observes and experiments, i.e., he fixes *what is concretely there* just as he experiences it; *experience for him is an act that supplies grounds*, and for which mere imagining could never be a substitute. For this very reason science of *fact* and science of *experience* (*Erfahrung*) are equivalent concepts. But for the geometer, who studies not actualities, but "ideal possibilities," not actual but essential relationships, *essential insight* and not experience is *the act that supplies the ultimate grounds*.

So it is with all the eidetic sciences. Essential contents which are mediated, which emerge as data in and through the mediating insight of thought, and indeed on principles that are throughout immediately transparent, are grounded in essential contents (or eidetic axioms) which come under the grasp of immediate insight. *Every step of mediated grounding is accordingly apodeictically and eidetically necessary*. Thus the essential nature of pure eidetic science consists in this, that its procedure is *exclusively eidetic*, that from the beginning and in all that follows further it makes known no factual meaning that is not eidetically valid, in the sense that it could either be brought without mediation to primordial givenness (as being immediately grounded in essences of which we have primordial insight), or could be "inferred" through pure consequential reasoning from "axiomatic" factual meanings of this type.

Closely connected with the foregoing considerations is the *practical Ideal of exact eidetic science*, which in truth the more recent mathematics first taught us to realize: To confer the highest grade of rationality on every eidetic science by reducing all the mediated mental steps to mere subsumptions under the definitively systematized axioms of the eidetic field concerned, and in so far as "formal" or "pure" logic (in the broadest sense of a *mathesis universalis*)[5] was not itself the science primarily in question, with the co-operation of all the axioms of this latter discipline.

In close connexion once again with the foregoing is the *Ideal of "mathematization,"* which, alike in this to the Ideal just characterized, is, on cognitive lines, of great practical importance for all "exact" eidetic disciplines, whose whole store of knowledge (as in geometry, for instance) is wrapped up in a scheme of pure deductive necessity within the broad generality of some few axioms. This is not the place to go into such matters more closely.[6]

## 8. Interdependence of the Sciences of Fact and of Essence

Following what we have said, it is clear that the *meaning* of eidetic science *excludes in principle every assimilation of the theoretical results of empirical sciences*. The references to reality which appear in the immediately valid premises of these sciences reappear in all the mediated positions. From facts follow always nothing but facts.

If, however, all eidetic science is intrinsically independent

[5] On the idea of pure Logic as *mathesis universalis,* cf. the concluding chapter of the first volume of the *Logical Studies.*

[6] For further discussion under this head, cf. *infra*, § 70.

of all science of fact, the opposite obtains, on the other hand, in respect of *the science of fact* itself. *No fully developed science of fact could subsist unmixed* with eidetic knowledge, and in consequent *independence of eidetic sciences formal or material*. For *in the first place* it is obvious that an empirical science, wherever it finds grounds for its judgments through mediate reasoning, must proceed according to the *formal* principles used by formal logic. And generally, since like every science it is directed towards objects, it must be bound by the laws which pertain to the essence of *objectivity in general. Thereby it enters into relation with the group of formal-ontological* disciplines, which, besides formal logic in the narrower sense of the term, includes the disciplines which figured formerly under the formal *"mathesis universalis"* (thus arithmetic also, pure analysis, theory of manifolds). Moreover, and *in the second place*, every fact includes an essential factor of a *material* order, and every eidetic truth pertaining to the pure essence thus included must furnish a law that binds the given concrete instance and generally every possible one as well.

## 9. Region and Regional Eidetics

Every concrete empirical objectivity, together with its material essence, finds its proper place within a *highest* material genus, a *"region"* of empirical objects. To the pure regional essence belongs then a *regional eidetic science*, or, as we can also say, a *regional ontology*. We assume herewith that in the regional essence, or in the different genera which enter into it as components, there are grounded systems of knowledge so rich and so ramified that it is worth while, having regard to their systematic development, to speak of a science or of a whole connected group of ontological disciplines corresponding to the several generic components of the region. We shall be able to convince ourselves very fully of the great extent to which this presupposition is actually fulfilled. In accordance herewith every empirical science which finds its ordered place within the scope of a (given) region will be essentially related to the regional as well as to the formal ontological disciplines. We can express this also in this way: *Every factual science* (empirical science) *has essential theoretical bases in eidetic ontologies*. For it is quite self-evident (supposing that the assumption we have made holds good) that the rich supply of knowledge which refers in a pure, *unconditionally* valid way to all possible objects of the region—so far as it pertains in part to the empty form of objectivity in general, in part to the eidos of the region which presents as it were a *necessary material form* of all regional objects—cannot be void of significance for the study of the empirical facts.

In this way, for instance, the eidetic science of physical nature in general (the *Ontology of nature*) corresponds to all the natural science disciplines, so far indeed as an Eidos that can be apprehended in its purity, the "essence" *nature in general*, with an infinite wealth of included essential contents, corresponds to actual nature. If we construct the *Idea of a completely rationalized empirical science* of nature, i.e., of a science that has progressed so far on its theoretical side that every particular incorporated in the same is referred back to its most universal and most fundamental grounds, it is then clear *that the realization of this Idea is essentially dependent on the cultivation of the corresponding eidetic sciences*; not only then on that of the *formal mathesis* which is related similarly to all the sciences, but, in particular, on that of the *material-ontological disciplines* which analyse out the *essential being* of Nature, and consequently also all essential articulations of Nature's objectivities as such, in rational purity, i.e., after the eidetic pattern. And this holds good, of course, for all regions indifferently.

From the viewpoint of *practical knowledge*, also, we might expect in advance that the more an empirical science approximates to the "rational" stage, the stage of "exact" monological science, i.e., the greater the extent to which its structure is ordered on the basis of well-developed eidetic disciplines, and to its own advantage draws upon them for the grounding of its own propositions, the greater will be the increase in scope and power of those practical services which are the fruits of knowledge.

In support we may appeal to the development of the rational sciences of Nature, the physical sciences. Their era of greatness takes its rise in the modern age precisely from this, that the geometry which in the ancient world (and in its essentials in the school of Plato) had already been developed on pure eidetic lines to a high pitch of perfection was at one sweep and in the grand style made fruitful for physical method. It is clearly realized that it is the *essence* of a material thing to be a *res extensa*, and that consequently *geometry is an ontological discipline relating to an essential phase of such thinghood, the spatial form.* But it is further realized that the universal (as we would say, the regional) essence of the Thing reaches much farther. The evidence for this is that forthwith development took the line of shaping a *series of new disciplines* to be set alongside geometry and *called to discharge the same function of rationalizing the empirical.* The splendid outburst of the mathematical sciences formal and material springs from this impulse. With passionate zeal they were founded or organized as *pure* "rational" sciences (*eidetic ontologies*, as we would say) and indeed (in the dawn of the modern world and much beyond that) not on their own account, but for the sake of the empirical sciences. They then bore abundantly the hoped-for fruits in the parallel development of the rational physics we admire so much.

## 10. Region and Category. The Analytic Region and its Categories

If we place ourselves in imagination within any eidetic science, e.g., in the Ontology of Nature, we find ourselves directed normally, at any rate, not towards essences as objects, but towards the objects of the essences which in the case we have selected are subordinate to the Region we call Nature. But we observe thereby that "*object*" is a title for diverse though connected formations, such as "thing," "property," "relation," "substantive meaning" (fact), "group," "order" and so forth, which are clearly not equivalent but refer back at times to a type of *objectivity* which has, so to speak, the prerogative of being primarily *original*, and in respect of which all others pose in a certain sense as mere differentiations. In the instance chosen the *Thing itself* has naturally this prerogative as against the property of a thing, relation, and so forth. But this is precisely a fragment of that formal order which must be cleared up if our talk about object and object-region is not to remain in confusion. From this clarification to which we devote the following reflexions, the important *concept of the category* as related to the concept of region will spontaneously emerge.

Category is a word which on the one hand and in the combination "*category of a region*" refers us precisely to the relevant region, e.g., to the region of physical nature; but on the other hand sets the *material region* specified in relation to the *form of region in general*, or, which comes to the same thing, to the *formal essence: object in general* and the "*formal categories*" belonging to it.

Let us first make this not unimportant remark: Formal and material ontologies appear at first sight to belong to the same series, in so far as the formal essence of an object in general and the regional essence appear on both sides to play the same part. One is therefore inclined to speak of material regions rather than of regions *simpliciter* as heretofore, and to set the "*formal region*" in alignment with them. If we adopt this form of words, we need to be a little cautious. On the one side stand the *material*, which in a certain sense are the *essences "properly so-called."* But on the other side stands what is still eidetic but none the less fundamentally and essentially different: a *mere essential form*, which is indeed an essence, but a completely "*empty*" one, an essence which *in the fashion of an empty form fits all possible essences*, which in its formal universality has even the highest material generalities subordinated to it, and prescribes *laws* to these through the formal truths which belong to it. The so-called "*formal region*" is thus not something co-ordinate with the material regions (the regions pure and simple), *it is properly no region at all, but the pure form of region in general*; it has all regions with all their essential diversities of content *under* (though indeed only *formaliter*) rather than side by side with itself. Now this subordination of the material under the formal proclaims itself in this, that at the same time *formal Ontology conceals in itself the forms of all possible ontologies in general* (i.e., of all in the "proper," "material" sense); and that it prescribes to the material ontologies *a formal constitution common to all of them*—including therein also those which we have still to study in respect of the distinction between region and category.

We take our start from formal ontology (conceived always as pure logic in its full extension so as to cover the *mathesis universalis*), which, as we know, is the eidetic science of object in general. In the view of this science, object is everything and all that is, and truths in endless variety and distributed among the many disciplines of the *mathesis* can in fact be set down to fix its meaning. But as a whole they lead back to a small set of immediate or basic truths, which in the pure logical disciplines function as "axioms." Now we define the *pure logical basic concepts* which figure in these axioms as *logical categories*, or *categories of the logical region* "object-in-

*general*." Through these concepts as they figure in the total system of axioms the logical essence of object-in-general is determined, and the unconditionally necessary and constitutive determinations of an object as such, a something or other —so far as it should permit of being Something at all—are expressed. Since the pure logical in the sense we have marked out with absolute precision determines the concept of the "*analytical*" as opposed to the "*synthetical*," a concept which alone is philosophically (and indeed fundamentally) important, we are wont to designate these categories as analytical.

As examples of logical categories we may cite such concepts as property, relative quality, substantive meaning (fact), relation, identity, equality, group (collection), number (*Anzahl*), whole and part, genus and species, etc. But the "*meaning-categories*" also, the fundamental concepts of the various kinds of propositions, of their elements and forms, which belong to the essence of the proposition (*apophansis*), have their proper place here, and they have it, following our definition, with reference to the essential truths which link together "object-in-general" and "meaning-in-general," and link them moreover in such a way that pure truths concerning meaning can be transformed into pure truths concerning the object. It is precisely for this reason that "*apophantic logic*," even when its statements concern meanings exclusively, belong in the full inclusive sense to formal Ontology. None the less the meaning-categories must be separated off as a group having its own distinctive character, and the remaining ones set over against them as the *formal objective categories in the pregnant sense of the term.*[7]

We add here this further remark, that by "categories" we can understand, on the one hand, concepts in the sense of meanings, but on the other also, and to better effect, the

[7] Concerning division of logical categories into meaning-categories and formal-ontological categories, *vide Logical Studies,* Vol. I, § 67. The whole third study of the second volume treats specifically of the categories of Whole and Part. On historical grounds I had at that time not yet dared to make use of the alienating expression Ontology, and I described their study (*loc. cit.,* p. 222, of the first edition) as a fragment of an "*a priori theory of objects as such,*" which A. v. Meinong has brought more compactly under the title "Theory of the Object" (*Gegenstandstheorie*). In opposition to this arrangement, I now hold it to be more correct, in sympathy with the changed condition of the time, to make the old expression Ontology current once again.

formal essences themselves which find their expression in these meanings. For instance, the "category" substantive meaning, plurality and the like, ultimately mean the formal eidos substantive meaning generally, plurality generally and the like. The equivocation is dangerous only so long as one has not learnt to separate clearly what must here be separated on all occasions: "meaning," and that which *in virtue of* its meaning permits of being expressed; and again: meaning and objectivity meant. In the terminological interest one can expressly distinguish between *categorical concepts* (as meanings) and *categorical essences*.

## 11. Syntactical Objectivities and Ultimate Substrata. Syntactical Categories

We have still to draw an important distinction in the domain of objectivities generally, which reappears reflected within the formal theory of meanings as the distinction (derived from "pure-grammar") between "syntactical forms" and "syntactical substrata" or "elements" (*Stoffen*). Concomitantly with this distinction there appears a division of formal ontological categories into *syntactical categories* and *substrative categories*, which must now be more closely considered.

By *syntactical objectivities* we understand such as are derived from other objectivities by means of "*syntactical forms*." The categories which correspond to these forms we call *syntactical categories*. To the latter belong, for example, the categories: substantive meaning, relation, constitutive quality, unity, plurality, numerical quantity (*Anzahl*), order, ordinal number, and so forth. In its essential aspect we can describe the situation here existing as follows: Every object, so far as it can be rendered more explicit and related to other objects, and is in brief logically determinable, takes on different syntactical forms; as correlates of the thinking in its determining function objectivities of a higher grade are constituted: qualities and qualitatively determined objects, relations between such and such objects, pluralities of unities, members of ordered series, objects as bearers of determinations through ordinal numbering, and so forth. If the thinking is predicative, there gradually emerge expressions and corresponding apophantic complexes of meaning which reflect the syntactical objectivities according to all their forms and divisions in series of meanings that exactly correspond with them. All these "categorical objectivities"[8] can function as objectivities in general, and again as substrata of categorical constructions, the latter [as substrata] once again [for further constructions], and so forth. Conversely every such construction points back in a self-evident way to *ultimate substrata*, to objects of a first or lowest grade; thus to objects *which are no longer constructions of a syntactico-categorical kind*, which contain in themselves no further vestige of those ontological forms which are mere correlates of the functions of thought (to attribute, cancel, relate, connect, count, etc.). The formal region of objectivity in general divides up accordingly into ultimate substrata and syntactical objectivities. The latter we call *syntactic derivatives* of the corresponding substrata, to which also, as we shall presently learn, all "Individuals" belong. When we speak of individual property, individual relation, and so forth, these derived objects are naturally being called after the substrata from which they are derived.

We would add the following remark: We can also reach the ultimate syntactically formless substrata from the side of the formal theory of meanings: every proposition and every possible member of it contains the so-called "terms" as substrata of its apophantic forms. They can be terms in a merely relative sense, they can themselves contain forms (e.g., the plural form, attributes, and the like). But in any case we reach back and necessarily so to *ultimate terms*, ultimate substrata, which no longer contain in themselves any vestige of syntactical formation.[9]

## 12. Genus and Species

We now need to draw within the realm of essences as a whole a new set of categorical distinctions. Every essence, whether it has content or is empty (and therefore purely logical), has its proper place in a graded series of essences, in

[8] Cf. *Logical Studies,* Vol. III, Sixth Study, Second Section, esp. §§ 46 ff.

[9] I reserve the more detailed discussion of the theory of "syntactical forms" and "syntactical matter," very important in respect of the formal theory of meanings—this basic portion of an *"a priori* grammar"—till I have occasion to publish the lectures on Pure Logic which I have been giving for many years. On the subject of "pure" grammar and the general programme of a formal theory of meanings, cf. *Logical Studies,* Vol. II, Fourth Study.

a graded series of *generality* and *specificity*. The series necessarily possesses two limits that never coalesce. Moving downward we reach the *lowest specific differences* or, as we also say, the *eidetic singularities*; and we move upwards through the essences of genus and species to a *highest genus*. Eidetic singularities are essences, which indeed have necessarily "more general" essences as their genera, but no further specifications in relation to which they themselves might be genera (proximate or mediate, higher genera). Likewise that genus is the highest which no longer has any genus above it.

In this sense, in the pure logical realm of meanings, "meaning in general" is the highest genus; every determinate form of proposition or of its components an eidetic singularity; proposition in general a mediating genus. Numerical quantity in general (*Anzahl*) is likewise a highest genus. Two, three, and so forth are its lowest differences or eidetic singularities. In the sphere of positive content, thing in general, for instance, or sensory quality, spatial shape, experience (*Erlebnis*) in general are highest genera; the essential elements pertaining to determinate things, determinate sensory qualities, spatial shapes, vital experiences as such, are eidetic singularities, possessing thereby positive content.

It is a mark of *these* essential relations (not class, i.e., group relations) indicated by the terms genus and species, that in the more specific essence the more general is "immediately or mediately *contained*"—in a definite sense to be understood in and through eidetic intuition and in accordance with the specific type of Being intended. For this very reason many inquiries would bring the relation of eidetic genus and species to eidetic division under the relation of the "part" to the "whole." Here "whole" and "part" bear indeed the widest conceptual meaning of "containing" and "contained," and of this the eidetic relation of kind to kind is a specification. Thus the eidetic singular implies all the generalities which lie above it, and these on their side "lie one in the other" in graded order, the higher always within the lower.

## 13. Generalization and Formalization

A sharp distinction must be drawn between the relations of generalization and specialization on the one hand, and on the other the *reduction of what has material content to a formal generality of a purely logical kind,* or conversely the *process of filling in with content* what is logically formal. In other words: generalization is something wholly different from *formalization*, which plays so marked a part, for instance, in mathematical analysis. Specialization is also something entirely different from *deformalization*, the "filling out" of an empty logico-mathematical form, or of a formal truth.

In sympathy with this distinction, the subordination of an *essence* under the formal generality of a *pure logical* essence should not be confused with the subordination of an essence under its higher *generic essences*. Thus, for example, the essence triangle is subordinated to the highest genus, spatial shape; the essence red to the highest genus, sensory quality. On the other hand, red, triangle, and all essences homogeneous, are subordinated under the categorical title "essence," which in relation to them all has in no sense the character of a generic essence, rather *lacks* this character in respect of them *all*. To regard "essence" as generically related to essence with a positive content would be just as perverse as to misinterpret object in general (empty somewhat) as the genus of all objects indiscriminately, and then naturally without more ado as the one and only highest genus, as the genus of all genera. One should rather designate all formal-ontological categories as eidetic singularities, which have their highest genus in the essence "formal-ontological-category-in-general." On similar grounds it is clear that every definite inference, it may be one that is serving the interests of physics, is the instancing of a definite pure-logical form of inference, every definite proposition of physics the instancing of a propositional form, and so forth. But pure forms are not genera to propositions or inferences with a positive content, but are themselves only the lowest differentiations of the pure logical genera proposition, inference respectively, which like all similar genera have as their summum genus "meaning-in-general." The filling out of empty forms of a logical nature (and in *mathesis universalis* there are no forms that are not empty) is thus an "operation" which is totally different from the genuine specialization which extends to the limits of differentiation. The assertion holds good universally; thus, for instance, the transition from space to the "Euclidean manifold" is no generalization, but a reduction to "formal" generality.

For the justification of this radical division, as in all such cases, we must fall back on essential intuition, which at once teaches us that essential forms of a logical character (the categories for instance) do not "lie" within the material content of *infimæ species* as does red in its unspecified generality within the different shades of red, or as "colour" in red or blue, and that they are not at all "within" them in that strict sense which might claim sufficient community with a part-relation in the ordinary narrow sense of the term to justify us in speaking of its *being contained in it*.

No lengthy disquisition is needed to indicate that the *subsumption* of an individual, in general of a this-there, under an essence (a process which has a different character according as we are dealing with an *infima species* or with a genus) is not to be confused with the *subordination* of an essence under its higher species or under a genus.

We would likewise do no more than indicate the topic of *extensions* with its varied aspects relating more particularly to the function of essences in universal judgments and clearly requiring to be adjusted to the differences we have been considering. Every essence which is not an *infima species* has an *eidetic extension*, an extension of specific differences, and in the last resort at any rate of eidetic singularities. Every formal essence has on the other hand its formal or *"mathematical"* extension. Further, every essence as such has its extension of *individual* units, an ideal conceptual totality of possible particulars to which it can be related through a thought that is both eidetic and universal. The topic of *empirical extension* has something more to add: the limitation to a sphere of *concrete existence* through a reference to concrete existence woven in with it and annulling the *pure universality*. All this transfers itself naturally from essences to "concepts" as meanings.

## 14. Substrative Categories. The Substrative Essence and the τόδε τι

We consider further the distinction between "full" *substrata "with positive content"* (*Sachhaltigen*), together with the corresponding "full" "content-laden" syntactical objectivities, and the empty *sub-strata* together with the syntactical objectivities shaped out of them, the modifications of the empty Somewhat. This last class is in no sense itself empty or poor; it has a fixed content, namely, as the totality of the positive contents belonging to the structure of pure Logic as *mathesis universalis* with all the categorical objectivities out of which the same build themselves up. Thus every subject-matter which expresses any syllogistic or arithmetical axiom or theorem, every form of inference, every numerical digit, every number-complex, every function of pure analysis, every Euclidean or non-Euclidean manifold properly defined through the analysis, has its place here.

We now turn our attention to the class of objectivities with positive content. Here we reach *ultimate content-laden substrata* as the nucleus of all syntactical constructions. To these nuclei belong the *substrative categories*, which sort themselves out under the two main alternative headings: "ultimate substantitive (*Sachhaltiges*) essence," and "this-there," or pure syntactically formless individual unit. The term "individual" which suggests itself so readily is here unsuitable just because the indivisibility, as always still to be made definite, which the word's meaning conveys, should not be taken up into the concept, but reserved rather for the special and quite indispensable concept "individual." We therefore take over the Aristotelean expression τόδε τι (*tode ti*—this-there) which verbally at any rate does not include this meaning.

We have contrasted the formless ultimate essence and the "this-there"; we must now fix the essential connexion obtaining between them, which consists in this, that every "this-there" has *its* essential substantive quality possessing the character of a formless substrative essence in the sense we have assigned.

## 15. Independent and Dependent Objects. Concretum and Individual

We still need a further basic distinction, that between *independent* and *dependent objects*. A categorical form, for instance, is dependent in so far as it necessarily refers to a substratum of which it is the form. Substratum and form are essences which point the one to the other and are not thinkable "apart." In this broadest sense, the pure logical form, e.g., the categorical form Object in respect of all objective material, the category Essence in respect of all determinate essences, and so forth, is dependent. Let us disregard these relations of dependence, and connect a fruitful concept of dependence or independence with systems that show genuine content, with relations of *"being contained in," being one with*, and, on occasion, *being connected with* in the stricter sense of the term.

Of special interest to us here is the position as it concerns the ultimate substrata, and, to narrow the field still farther, the substrative substantive (*Sachhaltigen*) essences. Two possibilities remain open, that an essence of this kind in conjunction with another shall be the foundation of the unity of a *single* essence, or that it shall not do so. In the first case there arise relations which remain to be described more closely, possibly of one-sided or mutual dependence, and in respect of the eidetic and individual members that fall under the united essences there results the apodeictically necessary consequence that there can be no members of the one essence that are not determined through essences which have at least generic community with the other essence.[10] Sensory quality, for instance, points necessarily to some sort of difference in extensity. Extensity again is necessarily the spread of some quality united with it and "enveloping" it. A phase of "increase" relating, shall we say, to the category of intensity is possible only as immanent in a qualitative content, and a content of such a kind is in turn not thinkable apart from some degree of increase. An appearing as a realized experience of a certain definite kind is impossible except as the appearing of an "appearing agency as such," and likewise conversely. And so forth!

From all this there result important determinations of the formal-categorical concepts Individual, Concretum and Abstractum. A dependent essence is called an *Abstractum*, an absolutely self-sustaining [independent] essence a *Concretum*. A this-there, of which the substantive (*Sachhaltiges*) essence is a Concretum, is called an *Individual*.

If we bring the "operation" of generalization under the concept of logical "modification," we may say: the Individual is the primordial object demanded on purely logical grounds, the logical Absolute to which all logical modifications refer us back.

It goes without saying that a concretum is an eidetic singularity, since species and genera (expressions which ordinarily exclude the lowest differentiations) are in principle dependent. *Eidetic singularities* fall accordingly into *abstract* and *concrete*.

---

[10] Cf. the detailed analysis in the *Logical Studies*, Vol. II, Third Study, especially in the somewhat improved account in the later editions.

Eidetic singularities which are contained in a *concretum* as alternatives are necessarily "heterogeneous," having regard to the formal-ontological law, that two eidetic singularities of one and the same genus cannot be bound together within the unity of a *single* essence, or as we also say: the lowest differentiations of a genus are mutually "incompatible." Accordingly every singularity which finds its place within a concretum leads, when regarded as a differentiation, to a separate system of species and genera, and thus also to separate summa genera. For instance, within the unity of a thing as phenomenon the definite shape leads to the summum genus spatial shape in general, the definite colour to visual quality in general. Meanwhile the lowest differentiations within a concretum, instead of being mutually exclusive, can also overlap each other; as, for instance, physical properties both presuppose and include in themselves spatial determinations. Then the summa genera also are not mutually exclusive.

As a further development genera divide in a characteristic and fundamental way into such as have concreta and such as have abstracta subordinated to them. We speak more conveniently of *concrete* and *abstract genera*, despite the ambiguity which now attaches to the adjectives. For no one can entertain the thought of holding concrete genera themselves for concreta in the original sense of that term. Where accuracy demands, we must fall back on the clumsy expression: genera of concretes or of abstracts respectively. As examples of concrete genera we have real thing, visual phantom (visual shape appearing with sensory fullness), vital experience, and so forth. In contrast with these, spatial shape, visual quality, and the like, are examples of abstract genera.

## 16. Region and Category in the Sphere of Substantive Meaning. Synthetic Cognitions *a priori*

With the concepts "Individual" and "Concretum," the concept also of *Region*, so fundamental for scientific theory, is defined in a strict "analytic" way. Region is just the *highest and most inclusive generic unity belonging to a concretum*, that is, the essential unitary connexion of the summa genera which belong to the lowest differences within the concretum. The eidetic scope of the Region includes the ideal totality of the concretely unified systems of differences of these genera, the individual scope the ideal totality of possible individuals answering to such concrete essences.

Every regional essence determines *"synthetic" essential truths, i.e., such as are grounded in it as this generic essence, but are not mere specifications of formal-ontological truths.* The regional concept and its regional subdivisions are thus not free to vary in these synthetical truths; the replacing of the relatively constant terms by variables gives no formal logical law, of the kind which has a place in characteristic fashion in the case of all "analytic" necessities. The system of synthetic truths which have their ground in the regional essence constitutes the content of the regional ontology. The totality of the *fundamental* truths among these, of the *regional axioms,* limits—and *defines* for us—*the system of regional categories.* These concepts express not merely, as do concepts generally, specifications of purely logical categories, but are distinguished by this, that by means of regional axioms they express the features *peculiar to* the regional essence, or *express in eidetic generality what must belong "a priori" and "synthetically" to an individual object of the region.* The application of such (not pure logical) concepts to given individuals is apodeictic and unconditionally necessary, and regulated, moreover, through the regional (synthetic) axioms.

If, despite notable differences in fundamental outlook which are not incompatible however with an inner affinity, one wishes to maintain approval of Kant's Critique of the Reason, one has only to interpret the regional axioms as *synthetic cognitions a priori,* and we should then have as many irreducible classes of such forms of knowledge as there are regions. The *"synthetic primary concepts"* or *categories* would be the regional primary concepts (related essentially to the region in question and its synthetic principles), and we should have as many *different groups of categories as there are regions* to be distinguished.

On this understanding *formal Ontology* takes its place, *outwardly,* in the same series as the regional (the strictly "material," "synthetic" ontologies). Its regional concept "object" determines (cf. *supra,* § 10) the formal system of axioms, and thereby the system of formal ("analytic") categories. Therein lies, in fact, a justification of the parallelism, despite all the essential differences which have been brought forward.

## 17. Conclusions of the Logical Considerations

We have so far been concerned entirely with pure logical considerations, keeping clear of every "material" sphere, or, as we equivalently put it, every *determinate* region; we have spoken in general terms of regions and categories, and this generality, according to the sense of our successive definitions, is purely logical in kind. The precise task was to draw up *a scheme on the foundations of pure Logic, as a sample of the logically originated fundamental constitution of all possible knowledge, or of the objectivities proper to such knowledge, according to which individuals must be determinable in terms of concepts and laws and under the leading of "synthetic a priori principles,"* and *all empirical sciences grounded in their own regional ontologies,* and not merely on the pure logic which is common to all sciences.

From this position there emerges also *the idea of a task that is set us*: To determine within the circuit of our individual intuitions the *highest genera of concreta,* and in this way to effect a *distribution of all intuitable individual existence according to existential regions, each of which,* since the distinction rests on the most radical essential groups, *marks off on lines of principle an eidetic and an empirical science* (or group of sciences). Moreover, the radical distinction in no way bars out intercrossing and partial overlapping. Thus, for instance, "material thing" and "soul" are different existential regions, and yet the latter has its grounds in the former, and there follows therefrom the grounding of the theory of the soul in the theory of the body.

The problem of a radical "classification" of the sciences is in the main the problem of the separating of the regions, and for this again we need, as a preliminary, pure logical studies of the kind we have here been briefly outlining. But, of course, we need also, on the other hand, Phenomenology—about which we still know nothing.

# Chapter 2

# Naturalistic Misconstructions

## 18. Introduction to the Critical Discussions

THE GENERAL DISCUSSION concerning essence and the science of essences in contrast with fact and the science of facts, which we have undertaken by way of prelude, concerned essential foundations for our construction of the idea of a pure phenomenology (which, indeed, as was noted in the Introduction, should become a science of the Essential Being of things), and for understanding its position in regard to all empirical sciences, and thus also to psychology. But —and much depends on this point—all determinations of principle must be correctly understood. In developing them, and we would stress the point firmly, we have not been arguing academically from a philosophical standpoint fixed in advance, we have not made use of traditional or even of generally recognized philosophical theories, but on lines which are in the strictest sense *fundamental* have *shown up* certain features, i.e., given true expression to distinctions which are directly given to us in *intuition*. We have taken them exactly as they there present themselves, without any admixture of hypothesis or interpretation, and without reading into them anything that might be suggested to us by theories handed down from ancient or modern times. Positions so laid down are real "beginnings"; and when, as in our own case, they are of a generality that covers the all-enveloping regions of Being, they are surely fundamental in a philosophical sense, and belong, themselves, to philosophy. But we do not need to presuppose even the last-named; our previous reflexions have been, as all that are to follow should be, free from every relation of dependence on a "science" so contentious and contemptible as is philosophy. In the fundamental positions we have set up we have presupposed nothing, not even the concept of philosophy, and we intend to hold on to this policy henceforth. The *philosophic* ἐποχή, which we propose to adopt, should consist, when explicitly formulated, in this, that *in respect of the theoretical content of all previous philosophy, we shall abstain from passing any judgment at all, and that our whole discussion shall respect the limits imposed by this abstention.* On the other hand, we do not need on that account to avoid (and indeed we could not avoid) speaking of philosophy at all, of philosophy as a historical fact, of philosophical movements that have once existed, and in good though often also in a bad sense have determined the general scientific convictions of mankind, most markedly indeed in respect of the fundamental positions of which we have treated.

It is precisely in this connexion that we must engage in a contest with empiricism, a contest which we can readily fight out within the limits of our ἐποχή, since the points at issue here permit of being established on a basis of immediacy. If philosophy possesses "fundamental" principles in the genuine sense of the term, principles which can therefore be grounded in their essential character only through what intuition immediately gives, a contest which concerns such intuition does not depend for its decision on any philosophical *science*, on the possession of the idea of philosophy, and the professedly grounded content of its theory. The circumstances which compels us to give battle is this, that "Ideas," "Essence," and "knowledge of Essential Being" are denied by empiricism. It is not the place here to unfold the historical grounds which should show us just why the victorious advance of the natural sciences, however greatly indebted for their high scientific level, as "mathematical," to eidetic grounding, has favoured philosophical empiricism, and has made it the dominating, and indeed in the circles of empirical science the almost exclusively dominating, conviction. In any case, within these circles, and therefore also among the psychologists, there prevails a hostility to Ideas which must eventually prove dangerous to the empirical sciences themselves; since thereby the eidetic grounding of these sciences, which is in no sense already completed, the establishing—which must eventually prove necessary—of new sciences dealing with Essential Being, and indispensable for the further advance of the empirical sciences themselves, is definitely hindered. What is said here, as will later come clearly to light, directly concerns phenomenology, a discipline which furnishes the essential eidetic basis of psychology and the sciences of mind. Thus we need to take certain steps to defend our position.

## 19. The Empiricist's Identification of Experience and Primordial Dator Act

Empiricistic Naturalism springs, as we must recognize, from the most praiseworthy motives. It is an intellectually practical radicalism, which in opposition to all "idols," to the powers of tradition and superstition, to crude and refined prejudices of every kind, seeks to establish the right of the self-governing Reason to be the only authority in matters that concern truth. Now to pass rational or scientific judgment upon facts (*Sachen*) means being guided by the *facts themselves*, getting away from talk and opinion back to the facts, questioning them in their self-givenness, and laying aside all prejudices alien to their nature. *It is only another way of expressing the very same thing—so the empiricist thinks*—to say that all science must spring from *experience*, that its mediated knowledge must be *grounded* in immediate experience. Thus to the empiricist genuine science and the science of experience mean just the same thing. "Ideas," "Essence" as opposed to facts, what else might they be than scholastic entities, metaphysical ghosts? To have saved mankind from such philosophical spooks as these is precisely the chief service of the natural science of modern times. Science is alone concerned with the experienceable real fact-world. What is not fact-world is imagination, and a science based on imaginations is simply imaginary science. Imaginations as psychical facts have of course their *raison d'être*, they belong to psychology. But—as we sought to explain in the previous chapter—that there should spring from our imaginings, through a so-called essential vision grounded upon them, new data, "eidetic" in nature, objects which are non-real, this—so the empiricist will conclude—is indeed "ideological extravagance," a "reversion to scholasticism," or to that sort of "speculative construction *a priori*," whereby the Idealism of the first half of the nineteenth century, unfamiliar as it was with the scientific knowledge of nature, so greatly impeded the course of true science.

Meanwhile, all that the empiricist here says rests on misunderstandings and prejudices—however good or well meant the motive which originally inspired him. The fundamental defect of the empiricist's argument lies in this, that the basic requirement of a return to the "facts themselves" is identified or confused with the requirement that all knowledge shall be grounded in *experience*. Accepting the intelligible naturalistic limitation of the field of knowable "facts," he takes for granted without further question that experience is the only act through which facts themselves are given. But *facts* (*Sachen*) are *not* necessarily *facts of nature*, the fact-world in the ordinary sense, not necessarily the fact-world (*Wirklichkeit*) in general, and it is *only with the fact-world of nature* that the primordial dator act which we call *experience* is concerned. To trace identifications here, and to take them for granted as matters of course, is simply to wave aside unnoticed distinctions in respect of which the clearest insight is available. Thus the question arises, On *which* side do the prejudices lie? Genuine lack of prejudice does not call for the downright rejection of "judgments foreign to experience," except when the judgments' *own proper meaning demands* a grounding in experience itself. To *maintain* straight away that *all* judgments permit of being grounded in experience, and even demand such grounding, without previously submitting to *study* the essential nature of judgments with due regard to their fundamentally distinct types, and without considering at the same time whether this declaration may not in the long run be *absurd,* that is a "speculative construction *a priori,*" which is none the better for proceeding in this instance from the empiricist side. Genuine science, and the genuine absence of bias which inwardly distinguishes it, demands as the foundation of all proofs judgments which as such are immediately valid, drawing their validity directly from *primordial dator intuitions*. These again are divided as the *meaning* of the judgments, or *the proper essential nature of the objects and contents of the judgments,* prescribes. The fundamental regions of objects, and, correlatively, the regional types of object-giving intuitions, the types of judgment belonging to these, and finally the noetic standards, which for the grounding of such types may *demand* just this kind of intuition and no other—all this cannot be postulated or decreed *ex cathedra*; it can be established only through insight; and that again means: shown up in and through the primordial dator intuition, and fixed through judgments which faithfully fit the intuitively given data. We cannot but think that a procedure that is really free from bias or purely matter-of-fact must take this form, and no other.

*Immediate "seeing"* (*Sehen*), not merely the sensory seeing of experience, but *seeing in general as primordial dator consciousness of any kind whatsoever,* is the ultimate source of justification for all rational statements. It has this right-conferring function only because and in so far as its object-giving is primordial. If we see an object standing out in complete clearness, if purely on the basis of the seeing, and within the limits of what we grasp through really seeing, we have carried out processes of discrimination and conceptual comprehension, if then we see (as a new way of "seeing") how the object is constituted, the statement faithfully expressing this has then its justification. If we ask why the statement is justified, and ascribe no value to the reply "I see that it is so," we fall into absurdity, as will later become clear to us. Moreover, this does not exclude the possibility, as we may here add so as to prevent misconstructions that may arise, that under certain circumstances one "seeing" can very well conflict with another, and likewise one *legitimate* statement with another. For the implication in this case is not that seeing is no ground of legitimacy, any more than the outweighing of one force by another means that it is no force at all. What it does tell us is that perhaps in a certain category of intuitions (those of sensory experience would just fit the suggestion), seeing in its very essence is "imperfect": it can on lines of principle be strengthened or weakened, and hence an assertion which has an immediate and therefore a genuine ground of legitimacy in experience must none the less be given up in the course of experience under the pressure of a counterclaim which exceeds and annuls it.

## 20. Empiricism and Scepticism

Thus for "experience" (*Erfahrung*) we substitute the more general "intuition," therefore decline to identify science in general and science of experience. Moreover, it is easy to see that he who supports this identification and contests the validity of pure eidetic thinking is led into a scepticism which, genuine, cancels itself through its own absurdity.[1] It is sufficient to question empiricists concerning the source of the validity of their general thesis (e.g., that "all valid thought has its ground in experience as the sole object-giving intuition") to get them involved in demonstrable absurdities.

[1] Cf. concerning the characteristic concept of Scepticism the "Prolegomena to Pure Logic," *Logical Studies,* Vol. I, § 32.

Direct experience gives only singular elements and no generalities, and is thus insufficient. It can make no appeal to the intuition of essence, since it denies such intuition; it must clearly rely on induction, and so generally on the system of mediate modes of inference through which the science of experience wins its general propositions. How fares it now, we ask, with the truth of mediated conclusions, be these deductively or inductively inferred? Is this *truth* (indeed, we could even say, the truth of a singular judgment) itself something experienceable, and thus in the last resort perceptible? And how fares it with the *principles* on which modes of inference depend, to which we appeal in cases of doubt or conflict, as, e.g., with the principles of the syllogism, the law of "mediated equality," and so forth, upon which as to ultimate sources, we here fall back for justification of all modes of inference? Are these themselves in their turn empirical generalizations, or is not the very conception of such a thing involved in radical absurdity?

Without allowing ourselves to be led into any further discussions, thereby merely repeating what has been said elsewhere,[2] this at any rate should have become clear, that the fundamental tenets of empiricism need first and foremost to be set out with greater distinctness, clearness, and precision, and to have their grounds better specified; and the grounding itself must follow the very standard to which the tenets give expression. But at the same time it is manifest that here at least there arises a serious suspicion whether in this falling back upon fundamentals an absurdity may not be concealed; whilst in the literature of empiricism it is hard to find any suggestion of a serious attempt being made to bring real clearness and a scientific grounding into these basic relations. Scientific grounding on empirical lines would demand here, as elsewhere, a start from single instances fixed with theoretical rigour, and an advance to general positions in accordance with rigorous methods lit up throughout with insight into principle. Empiricists appear to have overlooked the fact that the scientific demands which in their own theses they exact from all knowledge are equally addressed to these theses themselves.

Whereas these philosophers, holding characteristically to an adopted standpoint, and in open contradiction with their principle of freedom from bias, start out from unclarified,

[2] Cf. *Logical Studies*, Vol. I, esp. chs. 4 and 5.

ungrounded preconceptions; we start out from that which *antedates* all standpoints: from the totality of the intuitively self-given which is prior to any theorizing reflexion, from all that one *can* immediately see and lay hold of, provided one does not allow oneself to be blinded by prejudice, and so led to ignore whole classes of genuine data. If by "*Positivism*" we are to mean the absolute unbiased grounding of all science on what is "positive," i.e., on what can be primordially apprehended, then it is *we* who are the genuine positivists. In fact we permit *no* authority to deprive us of the right of recognizing all kinds of intuition as equally valuable sources for the justification of knowledge, not even that of "modern natural science." When it is really natural science that speaks, we listen willingly and as disciples. But the language of the natural scientists is not always that of natural science itself, and is assuredly *not* so when they speak of "natural philosophy" and the "theory of knowledge of natural science." And it is above all not so when they would have us believe that general truisms such as all axioms express (propositions such as $a + 1 = 1 + a$, that a judgment cannot be coloured, that of every two sounds that differ in quality one is lower and the other higher, that a perception *in itself* is a perception of something and the like) are expressive of facts of experience, whereas we know in the *fullness of insight* that propositions of this type bring to developed expression data of eidetic intuition. But just on this account it is clear to us that the "positivists" confuse at one time the cardinal disinctions between the types of intuition, and at another, though they se them as opposed types, are yet *not willing*, being bound by their prejudices, to recognize more than one of these as valid, or indeed even as present at all.

## 21. Obscurities on the Idealistic Side

Obscurity prevails to be sure, on the opposite side also. There indeed one accepts pure thought, an *"a priori,"* and thereby discards the thesis of the empiricist; but does not bring to clear consciousness, through reflexion, the fact that there is such a thing as pure intuition, a mode of being presented in which essences are primordially given as objects, just as individual realities are given in empirical intuition; nor does one know that *every process of insight involving judgment,* and in particular the insight into unconditionally *universal* truths, falls *under the concept "dator intuition," which has indeed differentiations of diverse sorts, above all, those that run parallel to the logical categories.*[3] It is true that there is talk about self-evidence, but instead of its being brought as a process of insight *into essential relations* with ordinary seeing, one hears of a *"feeling of self-evidence,"* which like a mystical *Index veri* lends to the judgment a feeling-colouring. Such interpretings are possible only so long as one has not learnt to analyse types of consciousness, viewing them purely and in respect of their essence, instead of making theories about them from somewhere up above. These so-called feelings of self-evidence, of intellectual necessity, and however they may otherwise be called, are just *theoretically invented feelings.*[4] Everyone will recognize this who has brought some case of self-evidence into view as a really given object of vision, and has compared it with a case in which evidence of the same content of judgment is lacking. It is at once noticed that the tacit presupposition of the "feelings of evidence" theory, namely, that psychologically a judgment may remain constant except in this one circumstance, that at one time it is coloured with feeling and at another not, is radically erroneous; that rather the self-same upper stratum, that of one and the same statement considered as mere expressed *meaning,* is at one time adjusted point for point to "clear-seeing" intuition of fact, whereas at another time, and at this lower level, a quite different phenomenon is taking place which is not intuitive (*intuitives*), but, maybe, a consciousness of fact that is wholly confused and inarticulate. With *the same* right, indeed, in the empirical realm one might grasp the difference between the clear and faithful judgment of perception and some vague judgment concerning the same subject-matter as consisting simply in this, that the former is endowed with a *"feeling of clearness,"* and the other not.

[3] Cf. *Logical Studies,* Vol. III, Sixth Study, § 45 f. Likewise *supra,* § 3.

[4] Presentations such as, for instance, Elsenhans gives in his *Textbook of Psychology,* p. 289 f., are, in my opinion, psychological fictions having no basis whatsoever in the phenomena themselves.

## 22. The Reproach of Platonic Realism. Essence and Concept

It has ever and anon been a special cause of offence that as "Platonizing realists" we set up Ideas or Essence as objects, and ascribe to them as to other objects true Being, and also correlatively the capacity to be grasped through intuition, just as in the case of empirical realities. We here disregard that, alas! most frequent type of superficial reader who foists on the author his own wholly alien conceptions, and then has no difficulty in reading absurdities into the author's statements.[5] If *object* and *empirical object, reality* and *empirical reality* mean one and the same thing, then no doubt the conception of Ideas as objects and as realities is perverse "Platonic hypostatization." But if, as has been done in the *Logical Studies,* the two are sharply separated, if Object is defined as anything whatsoever, e.g., a subject of a true (categorical, affirmative) statement, what offence then can remain, unless it be such as springs from obscure prejudices? Also, I did not discover the general concept of Object, but only set up in a new form something which all pure logical propositions demanded, and at the same time pointed out that it is in principle indispensable, and therefore also determinative of general scientific speech. In this sense, indeed, the tone-quality *c,* which is a numerically unique member in the tone-scale, or the digit *2* in the series of numbers, or the figure of a circle in the ideal world of geometrical constructions, or any proposition in the "world" of propositions—in brief, the ideal in all its diversity *is* an "object." Blindness to ideas is a kind of psychic blindness, which through prejudices renders us incapable of bringing into the field of judgment what we have already in our field of intuition. Our critics in truth see, and so to speak continuously see, "ideas," "essences"—make use of them in thought, formulate judgments concerning essences —only from their epistemological "standpoints" they explain the same away. Self-evident data are patient, they let theories chatter about them, but remain what they are. It is the business of theories to conform to the data, and the business of theories of knowledge to discriminate the funda-

[5] The polemics directed against the *Logical Studies* and my *Logos* article, even those that are well-intentioned, move in the main, alas! on this level.

mental types, and to describe them in accordance with their distinctive nature.

Prejudices in theoretical matters give remarkable self-assurance. There *cannot* be any such thing as essence or, therefore, intuition of essence (Ideation), and thus, where common speech contradicts this, it *must* be an affair of *"grammatical hypostatizations,"* and one should not allow oneself to be driven by these on to *"metaphysics."* What lies before us, in fact, can be only the empirically real mental products of *"abstraction,"* which tack themselves on to experiences or presentations in their natural reality. Accordingly theories of Abstraction are now zealously constructed, and here, *as well as in all the sections that treat of intentionality* (which are indeed leading chapters in Psychology), this experience-proud Psychology is made rich with *invented phenomena* and with *psychology analyses that are no analyses at all*. Thus ideas or essences, they say, are *"concepts,"* and concepts are *"mental constructions,"* *"products of abstraction,"* and as such they surely play a great part in our thought. "Essence," "Idea," or "Eidos," such are only grand "philosophical" names for "sober psychological facts" (*Fakta*). Dangerous names on account of the metaphysical suggestions they convey!

We reply: certainly essences are "concepts," if, as the ambiguous word permits, we take "concepts" to mean "essences." Only we must be quite clear in our mind that the talk about mental products is *in that case* mere nonsense, and so too all talk about the *formation* of concepts, in so far as it is to be understood in a rigorous and proper sense. One may read in a treatise that the number-series is a series of concepts, and then a little farther on: concepts are mental constructs. Thus the numbers themselves, the essences, were being referred to at the outset as concepts. But, we ask, are not the numbers what they are whether we "construct" them or not? Certainly I perform the counting, I construct my number-presentations, "adding unit to unit." These number-presentations are now such as they are, but even when I repeat their construction identically, they are something different. In this sense we may have at one time no number-presentations of one and the same number, at other times many such presentations, as many as we like. But in saying this we have already (and how could we avoid it?) drawn a distinction; number-presentation is not number itself: it is not the digit *Two,* this unique member of the number series, which like all such members, is a non-temporal being. To refer to it as a mental construct is thus an absurdity, an offence against the perfectly clear meaning of arithmetical speech which can at any time be perceived as valid, and *precedes* all theories concerning it. If concepts are mental constructs, then such things as pure numbers are no concepts. But if they are concepts, then concepts are no mental constructs. Thus fresh terms are *needed* if only to resolve ambiguities so perilous as these.

## 23. Spontaneity of Ideation, Essence, and Fiction

But, comes the retort, is it not true and self-evident that concepts, or, if you prefer, essences, such as red house, and so forth, originate through abstraction from individual intuitions? And do we not *construct* concepts at pleasure out of concepts already formed? We have then clearly, to deal here with psychological products. The case is similar, so one will perhaps add, to that of *arbitrary fictions*: the flute-playing centaur which we freely imagine is certainly a presentation we have ourselves constructed. We reply: "conceptual construction" certainly takes place spontaneously, and free fancy likewise, and what is spontaneously produced is of course a product of mind. But so far as the flute-playing centaur is concerned, it is a presentation in the sense in which that which is presented is called presentation, but not in the sense in which presentation stands verbally for a mental experiencing. Naturally the centaur itself is not mental, it exists neither in the soul, nor in consciousness, nor anywhere else, it is in fact "nothing," mere "imagination"; or, to be more precise, the living experience of imagination is the imagining *of* a centaur. To this extent, indeed, "the centaur as meant," the centaur as fancied, belongs to the experience itself as lived. But we must also beware of confusing this lived experience of imagination with that in the experience which is imagined, *qua* object imagined.[6] So also what is engendered in the spontaneous act of abstracting is not the *essence*, but the consciousness of the essence, and the position here is as follows: that a *primordial dator* consciousness of an essence (Ideation)—we are here clearly concerned with essential relations—is in itself and necessar-

---

[6] Cp. on this point the phenomenological analyses of the later sections of this work.

ily spontaneous, whereas to the empirical consciousness which gives us sensory objects spontaneity is non-essential: the individual object can "appear," one may be aware of it as apprehended, but without being spontaneously "busied with" it at all. Thus there are no motives discoverable unless it be those of mistaken identity which could demand the identification of the consciousness of the essence with the essence itself, and therefore the reduction of the latter to psychological terms.

The comparison with our fiction-constructing consciousness might raise still another doubt, in respect namely of the "existence" of essences. Is not the essence a fiction, as the sceptics indeed would have it? It is true that as the co-ordinating of fiction and perception under the more general concept "intuiting consciousness" casts a doubt on the existence of objects given in perception, so the comparison drawn above renders suspect the "existence" of essences. [But it is with essences as it is with things.] Things can be perceived and remembered, and therewith recognized as "real"; or again, in modified acts, as doubtful or null (illusory); finally also, in acts quite differently modified, as "mere apparition," or appearing *as if* real or null, and so forth. So too, precisely, with essences; whence it also follows that even they, like other objects, have meanings given them that are sometimes right, but, as in the case of false geometrical thinking, sometimes wrong as well. But the apprehension and intuition of essences is an act that has many forms. In particular *essential insight is a primordial dator act*, and as such *analogous to sensory perception*, and *not to imagination*.

## 24. The Principle of All Principles

But enough of such topsy-turvy theories! No theory we can conceive can mislead us in regard to the *principle of all principles*: that *very primordial dator Intuition is a source of authority* (Rechtsquelle) *for knowledge, that whatever presents itself in "intuition" in primordial form* (as it were in its bodily reality), *is simply to be accepted as it gives itself out to be, though only within the limits in which it then presents itself*. Let our insight grasp this fact that the theory itself in its turn could not derive its truth except from primordial data. Every statement which does nothing more than give expression to such data through merely unfolding their meaning and adjusting it accurately is thus really, as we have put it in the introductory words of this chapter, an *absolute beginning,* called in a genuine sense to provide foundations, a *principium.* But this holds in a special measure of the essential judgments of this class that are general in form, and it is to these that the term "principle" is normally limited.

In this sense the natural scientist is perfectly justified in following the "principle" that in respect of all assertions relating to facts of nature we must look for the experiences upon which they are grounded. For that *is* a principle, an assertion drawn immediately from sources of general insight, as we can at any time convince ourselves by clearing up to our own satisfaction the meaning of the expressions used in formulating the principle, and bringing out in their pure givenness the essences that attach to these. Now *the worker in the field of essences,* and whosoever uses and expresses universal propositions, must follow a parallel principle; and such a principle must exist, since already indeed the principle, just admitted to be such, of the grounding of all knowledge of facts in experience is not itself open to empirical insight, as is indeed true of every principle, and in general of all knowledge concerning essences.

## 25. The Positivist at Work as Natural Scientist, the Natural Scientist in Reflective Thought as Positivist

*De facto* the positivist rejects knowledge of essences only when he reflects "philosophically" and allows himself to be deceived through the sophisms of empiricist philosophers, but not when as a natural scientist he thinks himself into the normal viewpoint of natural science and gives grounds for his convictions. For then, as is obvious, he lets himself be guided to a very large extent by his essential insights. As is well known, the pure mathematical disciplines, whether material like geometry or kinematics, or formal (purely logical) like arithmetic, analysis, and so forth, are the basic means used by natural science in its theoretical work. And it is open to all to observe that these disciplines do not proceed empirically, and are not grounded in observations and experiments on figures, movements, and so forth as presented in experience.

Empiricism indeed, will not see this. But should we take its contention seriously, that so far from there being too few experiences to serve as grounds, an infinity of experiences is at our service; that in the collective experience of all races of mankind, even of the races of beasts that preceded them, an immense store of impressions, arithmetical and geometrical, has been accumulating, and been integrated in the shape of habits of apprehension, and that it is from this source that our geometrical insight now draws its inspiration? But whence then the knowledge of these alleged accumulated stores when no one observes them scientifically or faithfully reports them? Since when have long-forgotten and entirely hypothetical experiences supplanted actual experiences that have been most carefully tested in their proper empirical action and scope as the grounds of a science, and of the most exact science at that? The physicist observes and experiments, and on good grounds will not be satisfied with pre-scientific experiences, let alone instinctive apprehensions and hypotheses concerning experiences which are said to have been intuited.

Or should we say, as from another quarter has in fact been said, that we owed the insights of geometry to the *"experiences of our fancy,"* drawing them as *inductions from experiments on the functioning of fancy?* But how then is it, so runs our counterquery, that the physicist makes no use of such wonderful experiences through fancy? For this reason, no doubt, because experiments conducted in imagination would be imagined experiments, just as figures, movements, and groups in fancy are not real but imagined.

We take the most correct course, however, in regard to all such interpretations, when, instead of adopting the position they stand for and arguing from that basis, we point to the *intrinsic meaning* of mathematical assertions. In order to know, and to know indubitably, what a mathematical axiom states, we must not turn to the philosophical empiricists, but to consciousness, wherein, as mathematicians, we grasp axiomatic matter with complete insight into its axiomatic character. If we hold purely to this intuition, it is quite certain that in the axioms pure connexions between essences find expression without the slightest assistance from facts of experience. Instead of philosophizing and psychologizing about geometrical thought and intuition from an outside standpoint, we should enter vitally into these activities, and through direct analyses determine their immanent meaning. It may well be that we have inherited dispositions for knowledge from the knowledge of past generations; but for the question concerning the meaning and value of what we know, the genetic story of this heritage is as indifferent as is that of our gold currency to its real value.

## 26. Sciences of the Dogmatic and Sciences of the Philosophic Standpoint

Thus the natural scientists *speak* about mathematics and everything eidetic in a *sceptical* vein, but through their eidetic method they *behave dogmatically*. And to their own benefit! Natural science has grown to greatness by pushing ruthlessly aside the rank growth of ancient scepticism and *renouncing* the attempt to conquer it. Instead of toiling over such vexed problems as that concerning the general possibility of a knowledge of "external" nature, or asking how all the difficulties which the ancients had already discovered in this possibility were to be solved, it preferred to busy itself with the question of the *right method* for a science of nature if it is to be carried really through and as perfectly as possible in the form of *exact* natural science. But this direction of effort, whereby it cleared a free path for its inquiry into *facts*, has been *half nullified* by the consideration *that once again it is giving scope for sceptical reflexions, and lets itself be limited in its possibilities of work by sceptical tendencies*. In consequence of the surrender to empiricist prejudices, scepticism at present is blocked in respect only of the *sphere of experience*, and no longer in respect of the *realm of essences*. For it is not sufficient here to draw the eidetic into the circle of inquiry only under false empiricist colours. Those eidetic disciplines which, like the mathematical, are of ancient origin, and have become unassailable through the sanctions of habit, these alone can tolerate such misvaluations; whereas (as already indicated) when it comes to the establishing of new disciplines, empirical prejudices must exercise their full power of obstruction. *The right attitude* to take in the *prephilosophical* and, in a good sense, *dogmatic* sphere of inquiry, to which all the empirical sciences (but not these alone) belong, is in full consciousness *to discard all scepticism together with all "natural philosophy" and "theory of knowledge,"* and find the data of knowledge there where they actually face you, whatever difficulties epistemological reflexion may *subsequently* raise concerning the possibility of such data being there.

There is indeed an unavoidable and important division to be drawn in the field of scientific inquiry. On the one side stand the *sciences of the dogmatic standpoint,* facing the facts and unconcerned about all problems of an epistemological kind. They take their start from the primordial givenness of the facts they deal with (and in the testing of their ideas return always to these facts), and they ask what the nature of the immediately given facts may be, and what can be mediately inferred from that natural ground concerning these name facts and those of the domain as a whole. On the other side we have the rigorous inquiries of the epistemological, the *specifically philosophical standpoint.* They are concerned with the sceptical problems relating to the possibility of knowledge. Their object is finally to solve the problems in principle and with the appropriate generality, and then, when applying the solutions thus obtained, to study their bearing. on the critical task of determining the eventual meaning and value for knowledge of the results of the dogmatic sciences. *Having regard to the present situation,* and so long as a highly developed critique of knowledge that has attained to complete rigour and clearness is lacking, it is at any rate *right to fence off the field of dogmatic research from all "critical" forms of inquiry.* In other words, it seems right to us at present to see to it that epistemological (which as a rule are sceptical) prejudices upon whose validity as right or wrong philosophical science has to decide, but which do not necessarily concern the dogmatic worker, shall not obstruct the course of his inquiries. But it is precisely the way with scepticisms that they favour such unseasonable obstructions.

Herewith indeed we find indicated the special situation, to develop which the theory of knowledge is needed as a science having a direction of inquiry peculiar to itself. However self-contained the knowledge may be that is directed towards pure fact and rests on insight, none the less, as the knowledge is bent reflectively back upon itself, the possibility of any type of knowledge being valid, including its intuitions and insights, appears beset with baffling obscurities, and with difficulties that are almost insoluble, more particularly with reference to the transcendence which the *objects* of knowledge claim to possess in relation to knowledge itself. On this very ground *scepticisms* arise which force their way in the face of all intuition, experience, and insight, and in the sequel might develop into factors *that obstruct the working of the practical sciences.* We get rid of these difficulties that concern the form of *"dogmatic"* natural *science* (a term, therefore, which should not express here any depreciation whatsoever); *just through clearly grasping the most general principle of all method, that of the original right of all data,* and holding it vividly in mind, whilst we ignore the rich and varied problems relating to the possibility of the different kinds of knowledge and their respective correlatives.

PART TWO

THE FUNDAMENTAL
PHENOMENOLOGICAL OUTLOOK

# Chapter 3

## The Thesis of the Natural Standpoint and its Suspension

### 27. The Word of the Natural Standpoint: I and My World About Me

OUR FIRST OUTLOOK upon life is that of natural human beings, imaging, judging, feeling, willing, *"from the natural standpoint."* Let us make clear to ourselves what this means in the form of simple meditations which we can best carry on in the first person.

I am aware of a world, spread out in space endlessly, and in time becoming and become, without end. I am aware of it, that means, first of all, I discover it immediately, intuitively, I experience it. Through sight, touch, hearing, etc., in the different ways of sensory perception, corporeal things somehow spatially distributed are *for me simply there,* in verbal or figurative sense "present," whether or not I pay them special attention by busying myself with them, considering, thinking, feeling, willing. Animal beings also, perhaps men, are immediately there for me; I look up, I see them, I hear them coming towards me, I grasp them by the hand; speaking with them, I understand immediately what they are sensing and thinking, the feelings that stir them, what they wish or will. They too are present as realities in my field of intuition, even when I pay them no attention. But it is not necessary that they and other objects likewise should be present precisely in my *field of perception.* For me real objects are there, definite, more or less familiar, agreeing with what is actually perceived without being themselves perceived or even intuitively present. I can let my attention wander from the writing-table I have just seen and observed, through the unseen portions of the room behind my back to the verandah, into the garden, to the children in the summer-house, and so forth, to all the objects concerning which I precisely "know" that they are there and yonder in my immediate co-perceived surroundings —a knowledge which has nothing of conceptual thinking in it, and first changes into clear intuiting with the bestowing of

91

attention, and even then only partially and for the most part very imperfectly.

But not even with the added reach of this intuitively clear or dark, distinct or indistinct *co-present* margin, which forms a continuous ring around the actual field of perception, does that world exhaust itself which in every waking moment is in some conscious measure "present" before me. It reaches rather in a fixed order of being the limitless beyond. What is actually perceived, and what is more or less clearly co-present and determinate (to some extent at least), is partly pervaded, partly girt about with a *dimly apprehended depth or fringe of indeterminate reality*. I can pierce it with rays from the illuminating focus of attention with varying success. Determining representations, dim at first, then livelier, fetch me something out, a chain of such recollections takes shape, the circle of determinacy extends ever farther, and eventually so far that the connexion with the actual field of perception as the *immediate* environment is established. But in general the issue is a different one: an empty mist of dim indeterminacy gets studded over with intuitive possibilities or presumptions, and only the "form" of the world as "world" is foretokened. Moreover, the zone of indeterminacy is infinite. The misty horizon that can never be completely outlined remains necessarily there.

As it is with the world in its ordered being as a spatial present—the aspect I have so far been considering—so likewise is it with the world in respect to its *ordered being in the succession of time*. This world now present to me, and in every waking "now" obviously so, has its temporal horizon, infinite in both direction, its known and unknown, its intimately alive and its unalive past and future. Moving freely within the moment of experience which brings what is present into my intuitional grasp, I can follow up these connexions of the reality which immediately surrounds me. I can shift my standpoint in space and time, look this way and that, turn temporally forwards and backwards; I can provide for myself constantly new and more or less clear and meaningful perceptions and representations, and images also more or less clear, in which I make intuitable to myself whatever can possibly exist really or supposedly in the steadfast order of space and time.

In this way, when consciously awake, I find myself at all

times, and without my ever being able to change this, set in relation to a world which, through its constant changes, remains one and ever the same. It is continually "present" for me, and I myself am a member of it. Therefore this world is not there for me as a mere *world of facts and affairs,* but, with the same immediacy, as a *world of values,* a *world of goods,* a *practical world.* Without further effort on my part I find the things before me furnished not only with the qualities that befit their positive nature, but with value-characters such as beautiful or ugly, agreeable or disagreeable, pleasant or unpleasant, and so forth. Things in their immediacy stand there as objects to be used, the "table" with its "books," the "glass to drink from," the "vase," the "piano," and so forth. These values and practicalities, they too belong to *the constitution of the "actually present" objects as such,* irrespective of my turning or not turning to consider them or or indeed any other objects. The same considerations apply of course just as well to the men and beasts in my surroundings as to "mere things." They are my "friends" or my "foes," my "servants" or "superiors," "strangers" or "relatives," and so forth.

## 28. The "Cogito." My Natural World-about-me and the Ideal Worlds-about-me

It is then to this world, *the world in which I find myself and which is also my world-about-me,* that the complex forms of my manifold and shifting *spontaneities* of consciousness stand related: observing in the interests of research the bringing of meaning into conceptual form through description; comparing and distinguishing, collecting and counting, presupposing and inferring, the theorizing activity of consciousness, in short, in its different forms and stages. Related to it likewise are the diverse acts and states of sentiment and disapproval, joy and sorrow, desire and aversion, hope and fear, decision and action. All these, together with the sheer acts of the Ego, in which I become acquainted with the world as *immediately* given me, through spontaneous tendencies to turn towards it and to grasp it, are included under the one Cartesian expression: *Cogito.* In the natural urge of life I live continually in *this fundamental form of all "wakeful" living,* whether in addition I do or do not assert the *cogito,* and whether I am or am not "reflectively" concerned with the Ego and the *cogitare.* If I am so concerned, a new *cogito* has become livingly active, which for its part is not reflected upon, and so not objective for me.

I am present to myself continually as someone who perceives, represents, thinks, feels, desires, and so forth; and *for the most part* herein I find myself related in present experience to the fact-world which is constantly about me. But I am not always so related, not every *cogito* in which I live has for its *cogitatum* things, men, objects or contents of one kind or another. Perhaps I am busied with pure numbers and the laws they symbolize: nothing of this sort is present in the world about me, this world of "real fact." And yet the world of numbers also is there for me, as the field of objects with which I am arithmetically busied; while I am thus occupied some numbers or constructions of a numerical kind will be at the focus of vision, girt by an arithmetical horizon partly defined, partly not; but obviously this being-there-for-me, like the being there at all, is something very different from this. *The arithmetical world is there for me only when and so long as I occupy the arithmetical standpoint.* But the *natural* world, the world in the ordinary sense of the word, is *constantly there for me,* so long as I live naturally and look in its direction. I am then at the *"natural standpoint,"* which is just another way of stating the same thing. And there is no need to modify these conclusions when I proceed to appropriate to myself the arithmetical world, and other similar "worlds," by adopting the corresponding standpoint. The natural world *still remains "present,"* I am at the natural standpoint after as well as before, and in this respect *undisturbed by the adoption of new standpoints.* If my *cogito* is active *only* in the worlds proper to the new standpoints, the natural world remains unconsidered; it is now the background for my consciousness as act, but it is *not the encircling sphere within which an arithmetical world finds its true and proper place.* The two worlds are present together but *disconnected,* apart, that is, from their relation to the Ego, in virtue of which I can freely direct my glance or my acts to the one or to the other.

## 29. The "Other" Ego-subject and the Intersubjective Natural World-about-me

Whatever holds good for me personally, also holds good,

as I know, for all other men whom I find present in my world-about-me. Experiencing them as men, I understand and take them as Ego-subjects, units like myself, and related to their natural surroundings. But this in such wise that I apprehend the world-about-them and the world-about-me objectively as one and the same world, which differs in each case only through affecting consciousness differently. Each has his place whence he sees the things that are present, and each enjoys accordingly different appearances of the things. For each, again, the fields of perception and memory actually present are different, quite apart from the fact that even that which is here intersubjectively known in common is known in different ways, is differently apprehended, shows different grades of clearness, and so forth. Despite all this, we come to understandings with our neighbours, and set up in common an objective spatio-temporal fact-world as *the world about us that is there for us all, and to which we ourselves none the less belong.*

## 30. The General Thesis of the Natural Standpoint

That which we have submitted towards the characterization of what is given to us from the natural standpoint, and thereby of the natural standpoint itself, was a piece of pure description *prior to all "theory."* In these studies we stand bodily aloof from all theories, and by "theories" we here mean anticipatory ideas of every kind. Only as facts of our environment, not as agencies for uniting facts validly together, do theories concern us at all. But we do not set ourselves the task of continuing the pure description and raising it to a systematically inclusive and exhaustive characterization of the data, in their full length and breadth, discoverable from the natural standpoint (or from any standpoint, we might add, that can be knit up with the same in a common consent). A task such as this can and must—as scientific—be undertaken, and it is one of extraordinary importance, although so far scarcely noticed. Here it is not ours to attempt. For us who are striving towards the entrance-gate of phenomenology all the necessary work in this direction has already been carried out; the few features pertaining to the natural standpoint which we need are of a quite general character, and have already figured in our descriptions, and been sufficiently *and fully clarified.* We even made a special point of securing this full measure of clearness.

We emphasize a most important point once again in the sentences that follow: I find continually present and standing over against me the one spatio-temporal fact-world to which I myself belong, as do all other men found in it and related in the same way to it. This "fact-world," as the world already tells us, I find to *be out there,* and also *take it just as it gives itself to me as something that exists out there.* All doubting and rejecting of the data of the natural world leaves standing the *general thesis of the natural standpoint.* "The" world is as fact-world always there; at the most it is at odd points "other" than I supposed, this or that under such names as "illusion," "hallucination," and the like, must be struck *out of it,* so to speak; but the "it" remains ever, in the sense of the general thesis, a world that has its being out there. To know it more comprehensively, more trustworthily, more perfectly than the naïve lore of experience is able to do, and to solve all the problems of scientific knowledge which offer themselves upon its ground, that is the goal of the *sciences of the natural standpoint.*

## 31. Radical Alteration of the Natural Thesis "Disconnexion," "Bracketing"

*Instead now of remaining at this standpoint, we propose to alter it radically.* Our aim must be to convince ourselves of the possibility of this alteration on grounds of principle.

The General Thesis according to which the real world about me is at all times known not merely in a general way as something apprehended, but as a fact-world *that has its being out there,* does *not* consist of course *in an act proper,* in an articulated judgment *about existence.* It is and remains something all the time the standpoint is adopted, that is, it endures persistently during the whole course of our life of natural endeavour. What has been at any time perceived clearly, or obscurely made present, in short everything out of the world of nature through experience and prior to any thinking, bears in its totality and in all its articulated sections the character "present" "out there," a character which can function essentially as the ground of support for an explicit (predicative) existential judgment which is in agreement with the character it is grounded upon. If we express that same judgment, we know quite well that in so doing we have simply put into the form of a statement and grasped as a predication what already lay somehow in the original experience, or lay there as the character of something "present to one's hand."

We can treat the potential and unexpressed thesis exactly as we do the thesis of the explicit judgment. A procedure of this sort, *possible at any time,* is, for instance, *the attempt to doubt everything* which *Descartes,* with an entirely different end in view, with the purpose of setting up an absolutely indubitable sphere of Being, undertook to carry through. We link on here, but add directly and emphatically that this attempt to doubt everything should serve us *only as a device of method,* helping us to stress certain points which by its means, as though secluded in its essence, must be brought clearly to light.

The attempt to doubt everything has its place in the realm of our *perfect freedom.* We can *attempt to doubt* anything and everything, however convinced we may be concerning what we doubt, even though the evidence which seals our assurance is completely adequate.

*Let us consider what is essentially involved in an act of this kind.* He who attempts to doubt is attempting to doubt "Being" of some form or other, or it may be Being expanded into such predicative forms as "It is," "It is this or thus," and the like. The attempt does not affect the form of Being itself. He who doubts, for instance, whether an object, whose Being he does not doubt, is constituted in such and such a way doubts *the way it is constituted.* We can obviously transfer this way of speaking from the doubting to the *attempt* at doubting. It is clear that we cannot doubt the Being of anything, and in the same act of consciousness (under the unifying form of simultaneity) bring what is substantive to this Being under the terms of the Natural Thesis, and so confer upon it the character of "being actually there" (*vorhanden*). Or to put the same in another way: we cannot at once doubt and hold for certain one and the same quality of Being. It is likewise clear that the *attempt* to doubt any object of awareness in respect of it *being actually there necessarily conditions a certain suspension (Aufhebung) of the thesis*; and it is precisely this that interests us. It is not a transformation of the thesis into its antithesis, of positive into negative; it is also not a transformation into presumption, suggestion, indecision, doubt (in one or another sense of the word);

such shifting indeed is not at our free pleasure. *Rather is it something quite unique. We do not abandon the thesis we have adopted, we make no change in our conviction,* which remains in itself what it is so long as we do not introduce new motives of judgment, which we precisely refrain from doing. And yet the thesis undergoes a modification— whilst remaining in itself what it is, *we set it as it were "out of action," we "disconnect it," "bracket it."* It still remains there like the bracketed in the bracket, like the disconnected outside the connexional system. We can also say: The thesis is experience as lived (*Erlebnis*), *but we make "no use" of it,* and by that, of course, we do not indicate privation (as when we say of the ignorant that he makes no use of a certain thesis); in this case rather, as with all parallel expressions, we are dealing with indicators that point to a definite but *unique form of consciousness,* which clamps on to the original simple thesis (whether it actually or even predicatively *posits* existence or not), and transvalues it in a quite peculiar way. *This transvaluing is a concern of our full freedom, and is opposed to all cognitive attitudes* that would set themselves up as co-ordinate with the *thesis,* and yet within the unity of "simultaneity" remain incompatible with it, as indeed it is in general with all attitudes whatsoever in the strict sense of the word.

In *the attempt to doubt* applied to a thesis which, as we presuppose, is certain and tenaciously held, the "disconnexion" takes place in and with a modification of the antithesis, namely with the "*supposition*" (*Ansetzung*) *of Non-Being,* which is thus the partial basis of the attempt to doubt. With Descartes this is so markedly the case that one can say that his universal attempt at doubt is just an attempt at universal denial. We disregard this possibility here, we are not interested in every analytical component of the attempt to doubt, nor therefore in its exact and completely sufficing analysis. *We extract only the phenomenon of "bracketing" or "disconnection,"* which is obviously not limited to that of the attempt to doubt, although it can be detached from it with special ease, but can appear *in other contexts also,* and with no less ease *independently.* In relation to every thesis and wholly uncoerced we can use this *peculiar ἐποχή, (epokhe —abstention), a certain refraining from judgment which is compatible with the unshaken and unshakable because self-*

*evidencing conviction of Truth.* The thesis is "put out of action," bracketed, it passes off into the modified status of a "bracketed thesis," and the judgment *simpliciter* into *"bracketed judgment."*

Naturally one should not simply identify this consciousness with that of "mere supposal," that nymphs, for instance, are dancing in a ring; for thereby *no disconnecting* of a living conviction that goes on living takes place, although from another side the close relation of the two forms of consciousness lies clear. Again, we are not concerned here with supposal in the sense of *"assuming"* or *taking for granted,* which in the equivocal speech of current usage may also be expressed in the words: "I suppose (I make the assumption) that it is so and so."

Let us add further that nothing hinders us *from speaking bracketing correlatively* also, in respect of *an objectivity to be posited,* what ever be the region or category to which it belongs. What is meant in this case is that *every thesis related to this objectivity* must be *disconnected* and changed into its bracketed counterpart. On closer view, moreover, the "bracketing" image is from the outset better suited to the sphere of the object, just as the expression "to put out of action" better suits the sphere of the Act or of Consciousness.

## 32. The Phenomenological ἐποχή

We can now let the universal ἐποχή, (*epokhe*—abstention) in the sharply defined and novel sense we have given to it step into the place of the Cartesian attempt at universal doubt. But on good grounds we *limit* the universality of this ἐποχή. For were it as inclusive as it is in general capable of being, then since every thesis and every judgment can be modified freely to any extent, and every objectivity that we can judge or criticize can be bracketed, no field would be left over for unmodified judgments, to say nothing of a science. But our design is just to discover a new scientific domain, such as might be won precisely *through the method of bracketing,* though only through a definitely limited form of it.

The limiting consideration can be indicated in a word. *We put out of action the general thesis which belongs to the essence of the natural standpoint,* we place in brackets whatever it includes respecting the nature of Being: *this entire natural world therefore* which is continually "there for us," "present to our hand," and will ever remain there, is a "fact-world" of which we continue to be conscious, even though it pleases us to put it in brackets.

If I do this, as I am fully free to do, I do *not* then *deny* this "world," as though I were a sophist, *I do not doubt that it is there* as though I were a sceptic; but I use the "phenomenological" ἐποχή, which *completely bars me from using any judgment that concerns spatio-temporal existence (Dasein).*

Thus *all sciences which relate to this natural world,* though they stand never so firm to me, though they fill me with wondering admiration, though I am far from any thought of objecting to them in the least degree, *I disconnect them all, I make absolutely no use of their standards, I do not appropriate a single one of the propositions that enter into their systems, even though their evidential value is perfect, I take none of them, no one of them serves me for a foundation* —so long, that is, as it is understood, in the way these sciences themselves understand it, as a truth *concerning the realities* of this world. *I may accept it only after I have placed it in the bracket.* That means: only in the modified consciousness of the judgment as it appears in disconnexion, and *not as it figures within the science as its proposition, a proposition which claims to be valid and whose validity I recognize and make use of.*

The ἐποχή here in question will not be confined with that which positivism demands, and against which, as we were compelled to admit, it is itself an offender. We are not concerned at present with removing the preconceptions which trouble the pure positivity (*Sachlichkeit*) of research, with the constituting of a science "free from theory" and "free from metaphysics" by bringing all the grounding back to the immediate data, nor with the means of reaching such ends, concerning whose value there is indeed no question. What *we* demand lies along another line. The whole world as placed within the nature-setting and presented in experience as real, taken completely "free from all theory," just as it is in reality experienced, and made clearly manifest in and through the linkings of our experiences, has now no validity for us, it must be set in brackets, untested indeed but also uncontested. Similarly all theories and sciences, positivistic or otherwise, which relate to this world, however good they may be, succumb to the same fate.

# Chapter 4

## Consciousness and Natural Reality

### 33. Intimation Concerning "Pure" or "Transcendential Consciousness" as Phenomenological Residuum

We have learnt to understand the meaning of the phenomenological ἐποχή (epokhe—abstention), but we are still quite in the dark as to its serviceability. In the first place it is not clear to what extent the limitation of the total field of the ἐποχή, as discusssed in the previous pages, involves a real narrowing of its general scope. *For what can remain over when the whole world is bracketed, including ourselves and all our thinking (cogitare)?*

Since the reader already knows that the interest which governs these "Meditations" concerns a new eidetic science, he will indeed at first expect the world as fact to succumb to the disconnexion, but not *the world as Eidos,* nor any other sphere of Essential Being. The disconnecting of the world does not as a matter of fact mean the disconnecting of the number series, for instance, and the arithmetic relative to it.

However, we do not take this path, nor does our goal lie in its direction. That goal we could also refer to as *the winning of a new region of Being, the distinctive character of which has not yet been defined,* a region of *individual* Being, like every genuine region. We must leave the sequel to teach us what that more precisely means.

We proceed in the first instance by showing up simply and directly what we see; and since the Being to be thus shown up is neither more nor less than that which we refer to on essential grounds as "pure experiences (*Erlebnisse*)" "pure consciousness" with its pure "correlates of consciousness," and on the other side its "pure Ego," we observe that it is from *the Ego, the* consciousness, *the* experience as given to us from the natural standpoint, that we take our start.

I, the real human being, am a real object like others in the natural world. I carry out *cogitationes,* "acts of consciousness" in both a narrower and a wider sense, and these acts, as belonging to this human subject, are events of the same natural world. And all my remaining experiences (*Erlebnisse*) likewise, out of whose changing stream the specific acts of the Ego shine forth in so distinctive a way, glide into one another, enter into combinations, and are being incessantly modified. Now in its *widest connotation* the expression "*consciousness*" (then indeed less suited for its purpose) includes *all* experiences (*Erlebnisse*), and entrenched in the natural standpoint as we are even in our scientific thinking, grounded there in habits that are most firmly established since they have never misled us, we take all these data of psychological reflexion as real world-events, as the experiences (*Erlebnisse*) of animal beings. So natural is it to us to see them only in this light that, though acquainted already with the possibility of a change of standpoint, and on the search for the new domain of objects, we fail to notice that it is from out these centres of experience (*Erlebnisse*) themselves that through the adoption of the new standpoint the new domain emerges. Connected with this is the fact that instead of keeping our eyes turned towards these centres of experience, we turned them away and sought the new objects in the ontological realms of arithmetic, geometry, and the like, whereby indeed nothing truly new has to be won.

Thus we fix our eyes steadily upon the sphere of Consciousness and study what it is that we find immanent in *it*. At first, without having yet carried out the phenomenological suspensions of the element of judgment, we subject this sphere of Consciousness in its essential nature to a systematic though in no sense exhaustive analysis. What we lack above all is a certain general insight into the essence of *consciousness in general,* and quite specially also of consciousness, so far as in and through its essential Being, the "natural" fact-world comes to be known. In these studies we go so far as is needed to furnish the full insight at which we have been aiming, to wit, *that Consciousness in itself has a being of its own which in its absolute uniqueness of nature remains unaffected by the phenomenological disconnexion.* It therefore remains over as a *"phenomenological residuum,"* as a region of Being which is in principle unique, and can become in fact the field of a new science—the science of Phenomenology.

Through this insight the "phenomenological" ἐποχή will for the first time deserve its name; to exercise it in full consciousness of its import will turn out to be the necessary operation which *renders "pure" consciousness accessible to us, and subsequently the whole phenomenological region.* And thus we shall be able to understand why this region and the new science attached to it was fated to remain unknown. From the natural standpoint nothing can be seen except the natural world. So long as the possibility of the phenomenological standpoint was not grasped, and the method of relating the objectivities which emerge therewith to a primordial form of apprehension had not been devised, the phenomenological world must needs have remained unknown, and indeed barely divined at all.

We would add yet the following to our terminology: Important motives which have their ground in epistemological requirements justify us in referring to "pure" consciousness, of which much is yet to be said, also as *transcendental consciousness,* and the operation through which it is acquired as *transcendental ἐποχή.* On grounds of method this operation will split up into different steps of "disconnexion" or "bracketing," and thus our method will assume the character of a graded reduction. For this reason we propose to speak, and even preponderatingly, of *phenomenological reductions* (though, in respect of their unity as a whole, we would speak in unitary form of *the* phenomenological reduction). From the epistemological viewpoint we would also speak of transcendental reductions. Moreover, these and *all* our terms must be understood exclusively in accordance with the sense which *our* presentations indicate for them, but not in any other one which history or the terminological habits of the reader may favour.

## 34. The Essence of Consciousness as Theme of Inquiry

We start with a series of observations within which we are not troubled with any phenomenological ἐποχή. We are directed to an "outer world," and, without forsaking the natural standpoint, reflect psychologically on our Ego and its experience (*Erleben*). We busy ourselves, precisely as we have done if we had never heard of the new viewpoint, with *the essential nature of "the consciousness of something,"* following, for instance, our consciousness of the existence of material things, living bodies and men, or that of technical and literary works, and so forth. We adhere to our general principle that each individual event has its essence that can be grasped in its eiditic purity, and in this purity must belong to a field available to eidetic inquiry. In accordance herewith the universal fact of nature conveyed by the words "I am," "I think," "I have a world over against me," and the like, has also its essential content, and it is on this exclusively that we now intend to concentrate. Thus we rehearse to ourselves by way of illustration certain conscious experiences chosen at random, and in their individuality just as they are in their natural setting as real facts of human life, and we make these present to ourselves through memory or in the free play of fancy. On the ground of illustrations such as these, which we assume to be presented with perfect clearness, we grasp and fix in adequate ideation the pure essences that interest us. The individual facts, the fact-character of the natural world in general, thereby escapes our theoretical scrutiny—as in all cases where our inquiry is purely eidetic.

We limit still further the theme of our inquiry. Its title ran: Consciousness, or more distinctly *Conscious experience* (*Erlebnis*) *in general*, to be taken in an extremely wide sense about whose exact definition we are fortunately not concerned. Exact definitions do not lie at the threshold of analysis of the kind we are here making, but are a later result involving great labour. As starting-point we take consciousness in a pregnant sense which suggests itself at once, most simply indicated through the Cartesian *cogito,* "I think." As is known Descartes understood this in a sense so wide as to include every case of "I perceive, I remember, I fancy, I judge, feel, desire, will," and all experiences of the Ego that in any way resemble the foregoing, in all the countless fluctuations of their special patterns. The Ego itself to which they are all related, spontaneous, in receptive or any other "attitude," and indeed the Ego in any and every sense, we leave at first out of consideration. We shall be concerned with it later, and fundamentally. For the present there is sufficient other material to serve as support for our analysis and grasp of the essential. And we shall find ourselves forthwith referred thereby to enveloping connexions of experience which compel us to widen our conception of a conscious experience beyond this circle of specific *cogitationes*.

We shall consider conscious experiences *in the concrete*

*fullness and entirety* with which they figure in their concrete context—the *stream of experience*—and to which they are closely attached through their own proper essence. It then becomes evident that every experience in the stream which our reflexion can lay hold on has *its own essence open to intuition,* a "content" which can be considered in its *singularity in and for itself.* We shall be concerned to grasp this individual content of the *cogitatio* in its *pure* singularity, and to describe it in its general features, excluding everything which is not to be found in the *cogitatio* as it is in itself. We must likewise describe the *unity of consciousness* which is demanded *by the intrinsic nature of the cogitationes,* and so necessarily demanded that they could not be without this unity.

## 35. The Cogito as "Act." The Modal Form of Marginal Actuality

Let us start with an example. In front of me, in the dim light, lies this white paper. I see it, touch it. This perceptual seeing and touching of the paper as the full concrete experience *of* the paper that lies here as given in truth precisely with this relative lack of clearness, with this imperfect definition, appearing to me from this particular angle—is a *cogitatio,* a conscious experience. The paper itself with its objective qualities, its extension in space, its objective position in regard to that spatial thing I call my body, is not *cogitatio,* but *cogitatum,* not perceptual experience, but something perceived. Now that which is perceived can itself very well be a conscious experience; but it is evident that an object such as a material thing, this paper, for instance, as given in perceptual experience, is in principle other than an experience, a being of a completely different kind.

Before pursuing this point farther, let us amplify the illustration. In perception properly so-called, as an explicit awareness (*Gewahren*), I am turned towards the object, to the paper, for instance, I apprehend it as being this here and now. The apprehension is a singling out, every perceived object having a background in experience. Around and about the paper lie books, pencils, ink-well, and so forth, and these in a certain sense are also "perceived," perceptually there, in the "field of intuition"; but whilst I was turned towards the paper there was no turning in their direction, nor any apprehending of them, not even in a secondary sense. They appeared and yet were not singled out, were not posited on their own account. Every perception of a thing has such a zone of *background intuitions* (or background awarenesses, if "intuiting" already includes the state of being turned towards), and this also is a *"conscious experience,"* or more briefly a "consciousness *of*" all indeed that in point of fact lies in the co-perceived objective "background." We are not talking here of course of that which is to be found as an "objective" element in the objective space to which the background in question may belong, of all the things and thing-like events which a valid and progressive experience may establish there. What we say applies exclusively to that zone of consciousness which belongs to the model essence of a perception as "being turned towards an object," and further to that which belongs to the proper essence of this zone itself. But it is here implied that certain modifications of the original experience are possible, which we refer to as a free turning of the "look"—not precisely nor merely of the physical but of the *"mental look"*—from the paper at first *descried* to objects which had already appeared before of which we had been "implicitly" aware, and whereof *subsequent* to the directing of one's look thither we are explicitly aware, perceiving them "attentitively," or "noticing them near by."

We are aware of things not only in perception, but also consciously in recollections, in representations similar to recollections, and also in the free play of fancy; and this in "clear intuition" it may be, or without noticeable perceptibility after the manner of "dim" presentations; they float past us in different "characterizations" as real, possible, fancied, and so forth. All that we have stated concerning perceptual experiences holds good, obviously, of these other experiences, essentially different as they are. We shall not think of confusing the *objects of which we are aware* under these forms of consciousness (the fancy-shaped nymphs, for instance) with the conscious experiences themselves which are a consciousness *of* them. Then, again, we know that it is the essence of all such experiences—taking the same, as always, in their concrete fullness—to show that remarkable modification which transfers consciousness in the *mode of actual orientation* to consciousness in the *mode of non-actuality* and conversely. At the one time the experience is, so to speak *"explicitly"* aware of its objective content, at the other implicitly and merely *potentially*. The objective factor, whether in perception, memory, or fancy, may already be appearing to us, but *our mental gaze is not yet "directed" towards it*, not even in a secondary sense, to say nothing of being "busied" with it in some special way.

Similar remarks apply to all and any of the *cogitationes* in the sense illustrated by Descartes' use of the term, to all experiences of thought, feeling and will, except that, as will be emphasized (in the next paragraph), the "directedness towards," the "being turned towards," which is the distinctive mark of focal actuality, does not coincide, as in the favourite because simplest examples of sensory presentations, with singling out and noting the objects we are aware of. It is also obviously true of all such experiences that the focal is girt about with a "zone" of the marginal; *the stream of experience can never consist wholly of focal actualities*. These indeed determine, in a very general sense which must be extended beyond the circle of our illustrations, and through the contrast with marginal actualities already drawn, the *pregnant* meaning of the expression "cogito," "I have *consciousness* of something," "I perform an *act* of consciousness." In order to keep this well-established concept purely separate, we propose to reserve for it exclusively the Cartesian expressions *cogito* and *cogitationes*, unless through some addition, such as "marginal" or the like, we expressly indicate the modified use we are making of the term.

We can define a *"wakeful" Ego* as one that within its stream of experience is continually conscious in the specific form of the *cogito;* which, of course, does not mean that it can and does bring these experiences persistently or in general to predicative expression. Ego-subjects include animals. But, according to what we have said above, it belongs to the essence of the stream of experience of a wakeful Self that the continuously prolonged chain of *cogitationes* is constantly enveloped in a medium of dormant actuality (*Inaktualität*), which is ever prepared to pass off into the wakeful mode (*Aktualität*), as conversely the wakeful into the dormant.

## 36. Intentional Experience. Experience in General

However drastic the change which the experiences of a wakeful Consciousness undergo in their transition into the dormant state, the experiences as modified share the essential nature of the original experiences in an important respect. It belongs as a general feature to the essence of every actual *cogito* to be a consciousness *of* something. But according to what we have already said, the *modified cogitatio is likewise and in its own way Consciousness,* and *of the same* something as with the corresponding unmodified consciousness. Thus the essential property of Consciousness in its general form is preserved in the modification. All experiences which have these essential properties in common are also called "*internal experiences*" (acts in the *very wide sense* of the *Logical Studies*); in so far as they are a consciousness of something they are said to be "*intentionally related*" to this something.

We must, however, be quite clear on this point that *there is no question here of a relation between a psychological event—called experience* (Erlebnis)—*and some other real existent* (Dasein)—*called Object—or of a psychological connexion obtaining between the one and the other in objective reality.* On the contrary, we are concerned with experiences in their essential purity, with *pure essences,* and with that which is *involved in* the essence "*a priori,*" in *unconditioned necessity.*

That an experience is the consciousness of something: a fiction, for instance, the fiction of this or that centaur; a perception, the perception of its "real" object; a judgment, the judgment concerning it subject-matter, and so forth, this does not relate to the experimental fact as lived within the world, more specifically within some given psychological context, but to the pure essence grasped ideationally as pure idea. In the very essence of an experience lies determined not only *that,* but also *whereof* it is a consciousness, and in what determinate or indeterminate sense it is this. So too in the essence of consciousness as dormant lies included the variety of wakeful *cogitationes,* into which it can be differentiated through the modification we have already referred to as "the noticing of what was previously unnoticed."

Under *experiences* in the *widest sense* we understand whatever is to be found in the stream of experience, not only therefore intentional experiences, *cogitationes* actual and potential taken in their full concreteness, but all the real (reellen) phases to be found in this stream and in its concrete sections.

For it is easily seen that *not every real phase* of the concrete unity of an intentional experience has itself the *basic character of intentionality,* the property of being a "consciousness of something." This is the case, for instance, with all sensory data, which play so great a part in the perceptive intuitions of things. In the experience of the perception of this white paper, more closely in those components of it related to the paper's quality of whiteness, we discover through properly directed noticing the sensory datum "white." This "whiteness" is something that belongs inseparably to the essence of the concrete perception, as a *real (reelles)* concrete constitutive portion of it. As the content which presents the whiteness of the paper as it appears to us it is the *bearer of* an intentionality, but not itself a consciousness of something. The same holds good of other data of experience, of the so-called *sensory feelings,* for instance. We shall be speaking of these at greater length in a later context.

## 37. The "Directedness" of the Pure Ego in the *Cogito,* and the Noticing that Apprehends

Though we are unable at this point to proceed farther with our descriptive analysis of intentional experiences in their essential nature, we would single out certain aspects as noteworthy in relation to further developments. If an intentional experience is actual, carried out, that is, after the manner of the *cogito,* the subject "directs" itself within it towards the intentional object. To the *cogito* itself belongs an immanent "glancing-towards" the object, a directedness which from another side springs forth from the "Ego," which can therefore never be absent. This glancing of the Ego towards something is in harmony with the act involved, perceptive in perception, fanciful in fancy, approving in approval, volitional in will, and so forth. This means, therefore, that this having in one's glance, in one's mental eye, which belongs to the *essence* of the *cogito,* to the act as such, is not in itself in turn a proper act, and in particular should not be confused with a perceiving (in however wide a sense this term be used), or with any other types of act related to perceptions. It should be noticed that *intentional* object of a consciousness (understood as the latter's full correlate) is by no means to be identified with *apprehended* object. We are accustomed without further thought to include the being apprehended in the concept of the object (of that generally which stands over against the subject), since in so far as we think of it and say something *about* it, we have made it into an object in the sense of something apprehended. In the widest sense of the world, apprehending an object (*Erfassen*) coincides with mindfully heeding it (*achten*), and noting its nature (*bemerken*), whether attentively as a special case, or cursorily, provided at least that these expressions are used in their customary sense. *This heeding or apprehending is not to be identified with the modus of "cogito" in general,* that of actuality, but seen more closely, with a *special act-modus* which every consciousness or every act which does not yet possess it can assume. Should it do this, its intentional object is not only known in a general way and brought within the directed glance of the mind, but is an apprehended and noted object. A turning towards a Thing, to be sure, cannot take place otherwise than in the way of apprehension, and the same holds good of all *objectivities that are "plainly presentable"*: here a turning towards (be it even in fancy) is *eo ipso* an "apprehending" and a "heeding." But in the act of valuation we are turned towards values, in acts of joy to the enjoyed, in acts of love to the beloved, in acting to the action, and *without* apprehending all this. The intentional object rather, that which is valued, enjoyed, beloved, hoped as such, the action as action, first becomes an apprehended object through a distinctively *"objectifying" turn of thought.* If one is turned towards some matter absorbed in appreciation, the apprehension of the matter is no doubt included in the total attitude; but it is not the *mere* matter in general, but the matter *valued* or the *value* which is (and the point will concern us more in detail later on) *the complete intentional correlate of the act of valuation.* Thus *"to be turned in appreciation* towards some matter" does not already imply *"having"* the value *"for object"* in the special sense of object apprehended, as indeed we must have the object if we are to predicate anything of it; and similarly in regard to all logical acts which are related to it.

Thus in acts like those of appreciation we have an *intentional object in a double sense*: we must distinguish between the *"subject matter" pure and simple* and the *full intentional object*, and corresponding to this, a *double intentio*, a twofold directedness. If we are directed towards some matter in an act of appreciation, the direction towards the matter in question is a noting and apprehending of it; but we are "directed"—only not in an apprehending way—also to the value. Not merely the *representing of the matter* in question, but also the *appreciating* which includes this representing, has the modus of actuality.

But we must hasten to add that it is only in respect of simple acts of valuation that the matter stands so simply. In general, acts of sentiment and will are consolidated upon a higher level, and the intentional objectivity also differentiates itself accordingly: there is also a complicating of the ways in which the objects included in the unitary total objectivity come under the directed mental glance. But in any case the following main propositions hold good:

*In every act some mode of heeding* (*Achtsamkeit*) *holds sway. But wherever it is not the plain consciousness of a subject-matter,* wherever some further "attitude towards" the subject-matter is grounded in such consciousness, *subject-matter and full intentional object* ("subject-matter" and "value," for instance), likewise *heeding the object and mentally scrutinizing it, separate out the one from the other.* But at the same time the possibility of a modification remains an essential property of these grounded acts, a modification whereby their full intentional objects become noticed, and in this sense *"represented"* objects, which now, from their side, become capable of serving as bases for explanations, relations, conceptual renderings, and predications. Thanks to this objectification we find facing us in natural setting, and therefore *as members of the natural world,* not natural things merely, but values and practical objects of every kind, cities, streets with street-lighting arrangements, dwellings, furniture, works of art, books, tools and so forth.

## 38. Reflexions on Acts. Immanent and Transcendent Perceptions

We add the following: Living in the *cogito* we have not got the *cogitatio* consciously before us as intentional object; but it can at any time become this: to its essence belongs in principle the possibility of a *"reflexive"* directing of the mental glance towards itself naturally in the form of a new *cogitatio* and by way of a simple apprehension. In other words every *cogitatio* can become the object of a so-called "inner perception," and eventually the object of a *reflexive* valuation, an approval or disapproval, and so forth. The same holds good in correspondingly modified ways, not only of real acts in the sense of acts of perception (*Aktimpressionen*), but also of acts of which we are aware "in" fancy, "in" memory, or "in" empathy, when we understand and relive the acts of others. We can reflect "in" *memory, empathy,* and so forth, and in these various possible modifications make the acts we are "therein" aware of into objects of our apprehending and of the attitude-expressing acts which are grounded in the apprehension.

We connect with the foregoing the distinction between *transcendent* and *immanent* perceptions and acts generally. We avoid talking about inner and outer perception as there are serious objections to this way of speaking. We give the following explanations:

Under *acts immanently directed*, or, to put it more generally, under *intentional experiences immanently related*, we include those acts which are *essentially* so constituted *that their intentional objects, when these exist at all, belong to the same stream of experience as themselves*. We have an instance of this wherever an act is related to an act (a *cogitatio* to a *cogitatio*) of the same Ego, or likewise an act to a given sensible affect of the same Ego, and so forth. Consciousness and its object build up an individual unity purely set up through experiences.

Intentional experiences for which this does *not* hold good are *transcendently directed*, as, for instance, all acts directed towards essences, or towards the intentional experiences of other Egos with other experience-streams; likewise all acts directed upon things, upon realities generally, as we have still to show.

In the case of an immanently directed, or, more briefly, *immanent* (the so-called "inner") *perception, perception and perceived essentially* constitute *an unmediated unity, that of a single concrete cogitatio*. The perceiving here so conceals its objects in itself that it can be separated from it only through abstraction, and as something *essentially incapable of subsisting alone*. If the perceived is an intentional experience, as when we reflect upon some still lively conviction (expressed, it may be, in form: I am convinced that—) we have a nexus of two intentional experiences, of which at least the superimposed one is dependent, and, moreover, not merely grounded in the deeper-lying, but at the same time intentionally directed towards it.

This type of *real* (*reellen*) *"self-containedness"* (in strictness a similitude only) is a *distinctive characteristic of immanent perception and the mental attitudes founded upon it*; it is lacking in most of the other cases of immanent relationship between intentional experiences, as, for instance, in the remembering of remembering. The remembered remembering of yesterday does not belong to the present remembering as a real constituent of its concrete unity. The present remembering could still retain its *own* full essential nature, even though yesterday's in truth never took place, whilst the latter, on the other hand, *assuming that* it really happened, belongs necessarily with it to one and the same unbroken stream of experience, which through manifold concrete experiences mediates continuously between the two. In this respect transcendent perceptions and other transcendently related intentional experiences are clearly ordered very differently. The perception of a thing not only does not contain in itself, in its real (*reellen*) constitution, the thing itself, it is also without *any essential unity with it,* its existence naturally presupposed. *A unity determined purely by the proper essence of the experiences themselves can be only the unity of the stream of experience,* or, which is the same thing, it is only with experiences that an experience can be bound into one whole of which the essence in its totality envelops these experiences' own essences and is grounded within them. This proposition will become still clearer in the sequel and its great significance will become apparent.

## 39. Consciousness and Natural Reality. The View of the "Man in the Street"

All the essential characteristics of experience and consciousness which we have reached are for us necessary steps towards the attainment of the end which is unceasingly drawing us on, the discovery, namely, of the essence of that *"pure" consciousness* which is to fix the limits of the phenomenological field. Our inquiries were eidetic; but the individual instances of the essences we have referred to as experience, stream of experience, "consciousness" in all its senses, belonged as real events to the natural world. To that extent we have not abandoned the ground of the natural standpoint. Individual consciousness is interwoven with the *natural world* in a twofold way: it is some *man's* consciousness, or that of some *man* or *beast,* and in a large number at least of its particularizations it is a consciousness of this world. *In respect now of this intimate attachment with the real world, what is meant by saying that consciousness has an essence "of its own,"* that with other consciousness it constitutes a self-contained *connexion determined purely through this, its own essence,* the connexion, namely, of the stream of consciousness? Moreover, since we can interpret consciousness in the widest sense to cover eventually whatever the concept of experience includes, the question concerns the experience-stream's own essential nature and that of all its components. To what extent, in the first place, must the *material world* be fundamentally different in kind, *excluded from the experience's own essential nature*? And if it is this, if over against all consciousness and the essential being proper to it, it is that which is "*foreign*" and "*other*," how can consciousness be *interwoven* with it, and consequently with the whole world that is alien to consciousness? For it is easy to convince oneself that the material world is not just any portion of the natural world, but its fundamental stratum to which all other real being is *essentially* related. It still fails to include the souls of men and animals; and the new factor which these introduce is first and foremost their "experiencing" together with their conscious relationship to the world surrounding them. *But here consciousness and thinghood form a connected whole*, connected within the particular psychological unities which we call *animalia*, and in the last resort within the *real unity of the world as a whole*. Can the unity of a whole be other than made one through the essential proper nature of its parts, which must therefore have some *community of essence* instead of a fundamental heterogeneity?

To be clear, let us seek out the ultimate sources whence the general thesis of the world which I adopt when taking up the natural standpoint draws its nourishment, thereby enabling me as a conscious being to discover over against me an existing world of things, to ascribe to myself in this world a body, and to find for myself within this world a proper place. This ultimate source is obviously *sensory experience*. For our purpose, however, it is sufficient to consider *sensory perception*, which in a certain proper sense plays among experiencing acts the part of an original experience, whence all other experiencing acts draw a chief part of their power to serve as a ground. Every perceiving consciousness has this peculiarity, that it is the consciousness of *the embodied* (*leibhaftigen*) *self-presence of an individual object*, which on its own side and in a pure logical sense of the term is an individual or some logico-categorical modification of the same.[1] In our own

---

[1] Cf. *supra*, § 15.

instance, that of sensory perception, or, in distincter terms, perception of a world of things, the logical individual is the Thing; and it is sufficient for us to treat the perception of things as representing all other perceptions (of properties, processes, and the like).

The natural wakeful life of our Ego is a continuous perceiving, actual or potential. The world of things and our body within it are continuously present to our perception. How then does and can *Consciousness itself* separate out as a *concrete thing in itself,* from that within it, of which we are conscious, namely, the *perceived being, "standing over against"* consciousness *"in and for itself"*?

I meditate first as would the man "in the street." I see and grasp the thing itself in its bodily reality. It is true that I sometimes deceive myself, and not only in respect of the perceived constitution of the thing, but also in respect of its being there at all. I am subject to an illusion or hallucination. The perception is not then "genuine." But if it is, if, that is, we can "confirm" its presence in the actual context of experience, eventually with the help of correct empirical thinking, then the perceived thing *is real* and itself really given, and that bodily in perception. Here perceiving considered simply as consciousness, and apart from the body and the bodily organs, appears as something in itself essenceless, an empty looking of an empty "Ego" towards the object itself which comes into contact with it in some astonishing way.

## 40. "Primary" and "Secondary" Qualities. The Bodily Given Thing "Mere Appearance" of the "Physically True"

If as a "man in the street" misled by sensibility I have indulged the inclination to spin out such thoughts as these, now, as a "man of science," I call to mind the familiar distinction between *secondary* and *primary* qualities, according to which the specific qualities of sense should be "merely subjective" and only the geometrico-physical qualities "objective." The colour and sound of a thing, its smell, its taste, and so forth, though they appear to cleave to the thing "bodily" as though belonging to its essence, are not themselves and as they appear to be, real, but mere "signs" of certain primary qualities. But if I recall familiar theories of Physics, I see at once that the meaning of such much-beloved propositions can hardly be the one which the words warrant: as though really only the "specific" sensory qualities of the perceived thing were mere appearance; which would come to saying that the "primary" qualities which remain after the *subtraction* of these same sensory qualities belonged to the same thing as it objectively and truly is, together with other such qualities which did not show forth as appearance. So understood, the old Berkeleian objection would hold good, namely, that extension, this essential nucleus of corporeality and all primary qualities, is unthinkable apart from the secondary qualities. Rather *the whole essential content of the perceived thing*, all that is present in the body, with all its qualities and all that can ever be perceived, *is "mere appearance," and the "true thing" is that of physical science*. When the latter defines the given thing exclusively through concepts such as atoms, ions, energies, and so forth, and in every case as space-filling processes whose sole *characteristica* are mathematical expressions, its reference is to *something that transcends the whole content of the thing as present to us in bodily form*. It cannot therefore mean even the thing as lying in natural sensible space; in other words, its physical space cannot be the space of the world of bodily perception: otherwise it would also fall under the Berkeleian objection.

The "*true Being*" would therefore be entirely and *fundamentally something that is defined otherwise than as that which is given in perception as corporeal reality*, which is given exclusively through its sensory determinations, among which must also be reckoned the sensori-spatial. *The thing as strictly experienced gives the mere "this," an empty X which becomes the bearer of mathematical determinations, and of the corresponding mathematical formulæ* and exists not in perceptual space, but in an "*objective space*," of which the former is the mere "symbol," *a Euclidean manifold of three dimensions that can be only symbolically represented*.

Let us then accept this. Let that which is given bodily in any perception be, as is taught there, "mere appearance," in principle "merely subjective," and yet no empty illusion. Yet that which is given in perception serves in the rigorous method of natural science for the valid determination, open to anyone to carry out and to verify through his own insight of that transcendent being whose "symbol" it is. The sensory content of that which is given in perception itself continues indeed to be reckoned as other than the true thing as it is in itself, but the *substratum*, the bearer (the empty X) of the perceived determinations still continues to count as that which is determined through exact method in the form of physical predicates. *All physical knowledge serves accordingly, and in the reverse sense, as an indicator of the course of possible experiences with the sensory things found in them and the occurrences in which they figure.* Thus it helps us to find our way about in the world of actual experience in which we all live and act.

## 41. The Real Nature of Perception and its Transcendent Object

All this being presupposed, *what is it, we ask, that belongs to the concrete real nature (reellen Bestande) of the perception itself, as cogitatio?* Not the physical thing, as is obvious: radically transcendent as it is, transcendent over against the whole "world of appearance." But *even the latter,* though we refer to it habitually as "merely subjective," does not belong in all its detail of things and events to the real nature of perception, but is opposed to it as "transcendent." Let us consider this more closely. We have indeed already spoken of the transcendence of the thing, but only in passing. It concerns us now to win a deeper insight into *the relation of the transcendent to the Consciousness* that knows it, and to see how this mutual connexion, which has its own riddles, is to be understood.

We shut off the whole of physics and the whole domain of theoretical thought. We remain within the framework of plain intuition and the syntheses that belong to it, including perception. It is then evident that intuition and the intuited, perception and the thing perceived, though essentially related to each other, are in principle and of necessity *not really (reell) and essentially one and united.*

We start by taking an example. Keeping this table steadily in view as I go round it, changing my position in space all the time, I have continually the consciousness of the bodily presence out there of this one and self-same table, which in itself remains unchanged throughout. But the perception of the table is one that changes continuously, it is a continuum of changing perceptions. I close my eyes. My other senses are inactive in relation to the table. I have now no perception of it. I open my eyes, and the perception returns. The perception? Let us be more accurate. Under no circumstances does it return to me individually the same. Only the table is

the same, known as identical through the synthetic consciousness which connects the new perception with the recollection.
The perceived thing can be, without being perceived, without
my being aware of it even as potential only (in the way of
inactuality, as previously[2] described), and perhaps without
itself changing at all. But the perception itself is what it is
within the steady flow of consciousness, and is itself constantly in flux; the perceptual now is ever passing over into
the adjacent consciousness of the just-past, a new now simultaneously gleams forth, and so on. The perceived thing in
general, and all its parts, aspects, and phases, whether the
quality be primary or secondary, are necessarily transcendent
to the perception, and on the same grounds everywhere. The
colour of the thing seen is not in principle a real phase of the
consciousness of colour; it appears, but even while it is appearing the appearance can and *must* be continually changing, as experience shows. The *same* colour appears "in" continuously varying patterns of *perspective colour-variations*.
Similarly for every sensory quality and likewise for every
spatial shape! One and the same shape (given *as* bodily the
same) appears continuously ever again "in another way," in
ever-differing perspective variations of shape. That is a necessary state of things, and it has obviously a more general bearing. For it is only in the interests of simplicity that we have
illustrated our point by reference to a thing that appears unchanged in perception. The transfer to changes of any other
sort is a perfectly simple proceeding.

*An empirical consciousness of a self-same thing that looks
"all-round" its object, and in so doing is continually confirming the unity of its own nature, essentially and necessarily
possesses a manifold system of continuous patterns of appearance and perspective variations, in and through which all objective phases of the bodily self-given which appear in perception manifest themselves perspectively in definite continua.*
Every determinate feature has *its own* system of perspective
variations; and for each of these features, as for the thing as
a whole, the following holds good, namely, that it remains one
and the same for the consciousness that in grasping it unites
recollection and fresh perception synthetically together, despite interruption in the continuity of the course of actual
perception.

[2] Cf. *supra*, § 35.

We now see also what it is that really and indubitably belongs to the real nature of the concrete intentional experiences which we refer to here as perceptions of things. Whilst the thing is the intentional unity, that which we are conscious of as one and self-identical within the continuously ordered flow of perceptual patterns as they pass off the one into the other, these patterns themselves have always their *definite descriptive nature* (*Bestand*), which is *essentially* correlated with that unity. To every phase of perception there necessarily belongs, for instance, a definite content in the way of perspective variations of colour, shape, and so forth. They are counted among the "*sensory data*," data of a particular region with determinate divisions, which within every such division gather together into concrete unities of experience *sui generis (sensory "fields")* which, further, in ways we cannot here describe more closely, are ensouled within the concrete unity of perception through "*apprehensions*," and, in this ensouling, exercise the "*exhibitive* (*darstellende*) *function*," or in unison with it constitute that which we call the "appearing of" colour, shape, and so forth. This, after interweaving itself with still further features, constitutes the real nature (*Bestand*) of perception, which is the consciousness of one identical thing derived through the confluence into one *unity of apprehension,* a confluence grounded in the *essential Being* of the apprehensions unified, and again through the possibility, grounded in the very *essence* of different unities of this kind, of *syntheses of identification.*

We must keep this point clearly before our eyes, that the sensory data which exercise the function of presenting colour, smoothness, shape, and so forth perspectively (the function of "exhibiting"), differ wholly and in principle from colour, smoothness, shape *simpliciter,* in short, from all the generic aspect which *a thing* can show. *The perspective variation (the "Abschattung"), though verbally similar to the perspected variable (the "Abgeschattetes"), differs from it generically and in principle.* The perspective variation is an experience. But experience is possible only as experience, and not as something spatial. The perspected variable, however, is in principle possible only as spatial (it is indeed spatial in its essence), but not possible as experience. In particular it is also nonsense to take the perspective shape-variation (that of a triangle, for instance) for something spatial and capable of being in space, and whoever does this is confusing it with the perspected variable, the shape that manifests itself through the appearances. How further we are to separate with systematic thoroughness the different real (*reellen*) phases of the perception as *cogitatio* (as contrasted with the phases of the *cogitatum* which transcends it), and to characterize them in accordance with their natural divisions, very difficult to trace, in part, that is a theme for inquiries on a large scale.

## 42. Being as Consciousness and Being as Reality. Intrinsic Difference between the Modes of Tuition

The studies we have just completed left us with the transcendence of the thing over against the perception of it, and as a further consequence, over against every consciousness generally which refers to the thing; not merely in the sense that the thing as a real (*reelles*) constituent part of consciousness is as a matter of fact not to be found—the whole situation rather concerns eidetic insight: in *absolutely unconditioned* generality or necessity, a thing cannot be given as really immanent in any possible perception or, generally, in any possible consciousness. Thus a basic and essential difference arises between *Being as Experience* and *Being as Thing*. In principle it is a property of the regional essence experience (more specifically of the regional subdivision *cogitatio*), that it is perceivable through immanent perception, but it is of the essence of a spatial thing that this is not possible. When, as a deeper analysis teaches, it belongs to the essence of every thing-giving intuition that in unity with the given thing other data analogous to things can be apprehended through looking in the appropriate direction, detachable strata, and stages in the makeup of what appears as a thing—"*visual illusions*," for instance, in their various specifications—precisely the same holds good for them too: they are in principle transcendent entities.

Before pursuing somewhat farther this opposition between immanence and transcendence, we insert the following remark: Apart from perception, we find a variety of intentional experiences which essentially exclude the real immanence of their intentional objects, whatever for the rest the nature of these objects may be. This holds, for instance, of every representative activity: of every recollection, of the apprehension through empathy of the consciousness of others, and so forth. Naturally we should not confuse this transcendence with that which is here concerning us. The inability to be perceived immanently, and therefore, generally, to find a place in the system of experience belongs in essence and "in principle" [3] altogether to the thing as such, to every reality in that genuine sense which we have still to fix and make clear. Thus the Thing itself, *simpliciter*, we call transcendent. In so doing we give voice to the most fundamental and pivotal difference between ways of being, that between *Consciousness* and *Reality*.

This opposition between immanence and transcendence, as our exposition has further brought out, is accompanied by a *fundamental difference in the mode of being given*. Immanent and transcendent perception do not only differ generally in this, that the intentional object which has its lodgment in the character of the bodily self is in the one case really immanent in the perceiving, but not so in the other case; they differ much more through a mode of being given which embodies the difference in its essential form, and conveys it *mutatis mutandis* into all the representational modifications of perception, and into the correlated intuitions of memory and fancy. We perceive the Thing through the "perspective" manifestations of all its determinate qualities which in any given case are "real," and strictly "fall" within the perception. *An experience has no perspectives* (*Ein Erlebnis schattet sich nicht ab*). It is not an accidental caprice of the Thing nor an accident of "our human constitution" that "our" perception can reach the things themselves only and merely through their perspective modifications. On the contrary, it is evident, and it follows from the essential nature of spatial thinghood (and in the widest sense inclusive of "visual illusion") that Being of this species can, in principle, be given in perceptions only by way of perspective manifestation; and it follows likewise from the essential nature of *cogitationes*, of experiences in general, that they exclude these perspective shadings; or, otherwise stated, when referring to that which has being in this region, any-

[3] We use the term "in principle" (*prinzipiell*) here, as in this work generally, in a rigorous sense, with reference to the highest and therefore most radical generalities or necessities of an essential character.

thing of the nature of "appearing," or self-revealing through perspective variations, has simply no meaning. Where there is no Being in space, it is senseless to speak of seeing from different standpoints with a changing orientation, and under the different aspects thereby opened up, or through varying appearances and perspective shadings; on the other hand, it is an essential necessity to be apprehended as such with apodeictic insight that spatial Being in general can be perceived by an Ego actual or possible only when presented in the way described. It can "appear" only with a certain "orientation," which necessarily carries with it sketched out in advance the system of arrangements which makes fresh orientations possible, each of which again corresponds to a certain "way of appearing," which we perhaps express as a being presented from this or that "aspect," and so forth. If we take the reference to ways of appearing to apply to ways of *experiencing* (it can also, as is clear from the description we have just given, bear a correlative ontic meaning), it comes to saying this, that it belongs to the essential nature of certain peculiarly constructed *types of experience,* or, more specifically, peculiarly constructed concrete perceptions, that the intentional element in them is known as a spatial thing; and that the ideal possibility of passing over into determinate, ordered, continuous perceptual patterns, which can always be continued, and are therefore never exhausted, belongs to their very essence. It lies then in the essential structure of these pattern-groups that they establish the unity of a *singly intentional* consciousness: the consciousness of a *single* perceptual thing appearing with ever-increasing completeness, from endlessly new points of view, and with ever-richer determinations. On the other hand, a spatial thing is no other than an intentional unity, which, in principle, can be given only as the unity of such ways of appearing.

## 43. Light on a Fundamental Error

It is thus a fundamental error to suppose that perception (and every other type of the intuition of things, each after its own manner) fails to come into contact with the thing itself. We are told that the thing in itself and in its itselfness is not given to us; that what every existent (*Seienden*) in principle possesses is the possibility of seeing things as they plainly are, and, more specifically, of perceiving them in an adequate perception which gives us the bodily self *without any mediation through "appearances."* God, the Subject of absolutely perfect knowledge, and therefore also of every possible adequate perception, naturally possesses what to us finite beings is denied, the perception of things in themselves.

But this view is nonsensical. It implies that there is no *essential difference* between transcendent and immanent, that in the postulated divine intuition a spatial thing is a real (*reelles*) constituent, and indeed an experience itself, a constituent of the stream of the divine consciousness and the divine experience. The thought that the transcendence of the thing is that of an *image* or sign has proved misleading here. The image-theory is often zealously attacked and a sign-theory substituted for it. But the one and the other alike are not only incorrect but nonsensical. The spatial thing which we see is, despite all its transcendence, perceived, we are consciously aware of it as given in its *embodied form.* We are not given an image or a sign *in its place.* We must not substitute the consciousness of a sign or an image for a perception.

Between *perception* on the one hand and, on the other, *the presentation of a symbol in the form of an image or meaning* there is an unbridgeable and essential difference. With these types of presentation we intuit something, in the consciousness that it copies something else or indicates its meaning; and though we already have the one in the field of intuition, we are not directed towards it, but through the medium of a secondary apprehension are directed towards the other, that which is copied or indicated. There is nothing of all this in perception, as little as in plain recollection or fancy.

Through acts of immediate intuition we intuit a "self." No apprehensions at a higher level are built up on the basis of these apprehending acts of intuition; nothing is therefore known *for which* the intuited might serve as a "sign" or "image." And for this reason, therefore, it is said to be immediately intuited as "self." The same, in perception, is still uniquely characterized as "bodily" as contrasted with the modified character of "hovering before the mind," or being "presented to it" in memory or free fancy.[4] We collapse into nonsense when, as is ordinarily done, we completely mix up these modes of presentation with their essentially different constructions, and correlatively the data correspondingly presented: thus plain presentation with symbolic interpretation (whether on the basis of image or sign) and downright plain perception with both of these. The perception of things does not present something that is not present as though it were a recollection of a fancy; it presents and apprehends a Self in this bodily presence. It does this in accordance with the apprehended object's *own meaning,* and to suppose that it acts otherwise is just to run counter to its own proper sense. Moreover, if it is a question, as it is here, of these perception of things, its essential nature is to be a perception that works through perspectives; and correlatively it belongs to the meaning of its intentional object of the thing *as* given within it, to be perceivable, in principle, only through perceptions of such a kind, perceptions that imply perspectives.

## 44. The Merely Phenomenal Being of the Transcendent, the Absolute Being of the Immanent

A certain *inadequacy* belongs, further to the perception of things, and that too is an essential necessity. In principle a thing can be given only "in one of its aspects," and that only means incompletely, in some sense or other imperfectly, but precisely that which presentation through perspectives prescribes. A thing is necessarily given in mere *"modes of appearing,"* and the necessary factors in this case are *a nucleus of what is "really presented,"* an outlying zone of

---

[4] In my lectures delivered at Göttingen (and indeed since the summer term of 1904) I have substituted an improved version of the inadequate exposition which I gave in the *Logical Studies* (an exposition still influenced overmuch by the views of the dominant Psychology) dealing with the relations between these simple intuitions and those that are grounded in them, and have made detailed communications covering the researches that are leading me forward, and in the interval, moreover, have been influencing literary thought both in point of terminology and of literary substance. In the coming volumes of the *Jahrbuch* I hope to publish these and other studies which have for long been utilized in lectures.

apprehension consisting of *marginal "co-data" of an accessory kind* (*uneigentlicher*), and a more or less vague *indeterminacy*. And the meaning of this indeterminacy is once again foreshadowed by the general meaning of the thing perceived as such, or by the general and essential nature of this type of perception which we call thing-perception. The indeterminacy necessarily means the *determinability of a a rigorously prescribed mode* (*Stils*). It *points forward to* possible patterns of perception, which continually passing off into one another, coalesce in the unity of a single perception in which the continuously enduring thing in ever new series of perspectives reveals ever again new "aspects" (or retraces the old.) Meanwhile the subsidiary co-apprehended phases of the thing come gradually into the focus of real presentation as real data, the indeterminacies define themselves more clearly to turn at length into clear data themselves; contrariwise, what is clear passes back into the unclear, the presented into the non-presented, and so forth. *To remain for ever incomplete after this fashion is in ineradicable essential of the correlation Thing and Thing-perception.* If the meaning of Thing gets determined through what is given in Thing-perception (and what else could determine the meaning?), it must require such incompleteness, and we are referred of necessity to unified and continuous series of possible perceptions which, developed from any one of these, stretch out in an infinite number of directions in *systematic strictly ordered ways,* in each direction endlessly, and always dominated throughout by some unity of meaning. In principle a margin of determinable indeterminacy always remains over, however far we go along our empirical way, and however extended the continua of actual perceptions of the same thing which we may have treasured. No God can alter this in any way, any more than He can the equation $1 + 2 = 3$, or the stability of any other essential truth.

On broad lines we can always see that transcendent Being in general, whatever its genus may be, when understood as Being *for* an Ego, can become a datum only in a way analogous to that in which a thing is given, thus only through appearances. Otherwise it would really be a Being which could also become immanent; whereas what is immanently perceivable is this and *nothing more.* Only when we fall into the confusions we have indicated above, and have now cleared up, can we hold it possible that one and the same could at one time be given through appearance, in the form of transcendent perception, and at another through immanent perception.

Still, let us first develop from the other side also the specific contrast between Thing and Experience (*Erlebnis*). *Experience,* we said, does not present itself. This implies that the perception of experience is plain insight into something which in *perception is given* (or to be given) *as "absolute,"* and not as an identity uniting modes of appearance through perspective continua. All that we have stated concerning the givenness of things here loses its meaning, and we must bring this home to ourselves in detail with full clearness. The experience of a feeling has no perspectives. If I look upon it, I have before me an absolute; it has no aspects which might present themselves now in this way, and now in that. In thought I can think truly or falsely about it, but that which is there at the focus of mental vision is there absolutely with its qualities, its intensity, and so forth. Contrariwise, the tone of a violin with its objective identity is given through perspectives, it has its changing forms of appearance. They differ according as I approach the violin or recede from it, according as I am in the concert hall itself or listen through its closed doors, and so forth. No way of appearing claims to rank as giving its data absolutely, although a certain type, appearing as normal within the compass of my practical interests, has a certain advantage; in the concert hall, at the "right" spot, I hear the tone "itself" as it "really" sounds. So likewise we say of everything in its visual relations that it has a normal appearance; we say of the colour, the form, and the thing as a whole which we see in ordinary daylight, and normally oriented in regard to us, so the thing really looks, that is its real colour, and the like. But that points only to *a kind of secondary objectification* within the compass of the total objectification of the thing, as we can easily convince ourselves. It is indeed clear that, if we were to hold fast to the "normal" form of appearance as the one and only form, and cut away all other varieties of appearance and the essential connexions with them, no vestige of the meaning of the givenness of the thing would be left over.

We therefore maintain: whereas it is an essential mark of what is given through appearances that no one of these gives the matter in question in an "absolute" form instead of presenting just one side of it, it is an essential mark of what is immanently given precisely to give an absolute that simply cannot exhibit aspects and vary them perspectively. It is also indeed self-evident that the perspectively varying sensory contents themselves, which, as real (*reell*), belong to our experience of the perception of the thing, function, no doubt, for something other as perspective variations, but are not themselves manifested in turn through perspective variation.

We must note the following distinction also: Even an experience (*Erlebnis*) is not, and never is, perceived in its completeness, it cannot be grasped adequately in its full unity. It is essentially something that flows, and starting from the present moment we can swim after it, our gaze reflectively turned towards it, whilst the stretches we leave in our wake are lost to our perception. Only in the form of retention or in the form of retrospective remembrance have we any consciousness of what has immediately flowed past us. And in the last resort the whole stream of my experience is a unity of experience, of which it is in principle impossible "swimming with it" to obtain a complete perceptual grasp. But *this* incompleteness or "imperfection" which belongs to the essence of our perception of experience is fundamentally other than that which is of the essence of "transcendent" perception, perception through a presentation that varies perspectively through such a thing as appearance.

All the ways of being given, and the differences between these which we find in the sphere of perception, reappear, in modified form, in the *modifications connected with reproduction*. The presentings of things are set out through presentations whereby the perspective variations themselves, the apprehensions, and thus the phenomena in their entirety and *through and through*, are modified *in reproduction*. We have also reproductions of experiences and acts of reproductive intuition in the manner of presentation and of reflexion in presentation. Here naturally there is no hint of reproduced perspective variations.

We now add the following case of contrast: It is of the essence of presentations to show gradual differences of relative clearness or dimness. Obviously also this difference in degree of perfection has nothing to do with that which relates to the conditions under which perspectively varying appearances are given to us. A presentation that is more or less clear does not in its graded changes of clearness pass through changes of perspective in the same sense as that which has shaped our own terminology, when we say that a spatial configuration, every quality that clothes it, and so the whole "appearing thing as such," changes perspectively in manifold ways, whether the presentation is clear or obscure. The reproduced presentation of a thing has its different possibilities of graded clearness, and this indeed for every form of perspective variation. As one sees, the question concerns differences in different dimensions. It is also obvious that the differences which we make in the sphere of perception itself under the headings clear and unclear, distinct and indistinct vision, show indeed a certain analogy with the differences in clearness just referred to, so far, that is, as we are concerned in either case with gradual increases and decreases in the fullness with which the presented material is given, but that even these differences belong to different dimensions.

## 45. Unperceived Experience, Unperceived Reality

If we live ourselves into these positions, we shall understand also the following essential difference in the way in which experiences (*Erlebnisse*) and things stand to one another in respect of their perceivability.

It is a mark of the type of Being peculiar to experience that perceptual insight can direct its immediate, unobstructed gaze upon every real experience, and so enter into the life of a primordial presence. This insight operates as a "reflexion," and it has this remarkable peculiarity that that which is thus apprehended through perception is, in principle, characterized as something which not only is and endures within the gaze of perception, but *already was before* this gaze was directed to it. "All experiences are conscious experiences": this tells us specifically with respect to intentional experiences that they are not only the consciousness of something, and as such present not merely when they are objects of a reflective consciousness, but that when unreflected on they are already there as a "background," and therefore in principle, and at first in an analogical sense, *available for perception*, like unnoticed things in our external field of vision. These can be available only in so far as they are already, as unnoticed, objects of consciousness in a certain sense, and that means, in their case, when they appear. *Not all* things fulfil this condition: the field of view of my attention which includes all that appears is not endless. On the other hand, unreflective experience must also fulfil certain conditions of preparedness, although in a quite different way more in conformity with its nature. It cannot "appear." It fulfils these conditions none the less at all times through the mere manner of its existence, and indeed for that same Ego to which it belongs whose pure personal gaze on occasion lives "in" it. It is only because reflexion and experience have the *essential* peculiarities which are here only hinted at that we can know anything about experiences that we do not reflect on, and therefore also about the reflexions themselves. And it goes without saying that the modifications of experiences in reproduction (and retention) run, *mutatis mutandis,* on similar lines.

Let us carry the contrast farther. We see that *it is the intrinsic nature of an experience to be perceivable through reflextion.* Things also are *perceivable,* on principle, and in perception they are apprehended as things of the world that surround me. Also they belong to this world without being perceived, they are thus *there for the Ego even then.* Still, in general, not so that a glance noting their presence could be sent in their direction! The background area, taken as the field of sheer noticeability, includes indeed only a small portion of the world that surrounds me. The statement "It is there" means rather that from actual perceptions and their background of real appearances *possible* series of perceptions lead up under *motives* that are constant and continuous and girt about (as unnoticed backgrounds) with ever-changing fields of things; and so further till we reach those systems of perceptions in which the Thing in question appears and is apprehended. In principle we make no essential alteration here when in the place of a single Ego we consider a plurality of Egos. Only through the relation of a possible reciprocity of understanding can I identify the world of my experience with that of others, and at the same time enrich it through the overflowings of their experience. A transcendence which dispensed with the aforesaid systematically motived connexion with my existing sphere of actual perception would be a completely groundless assumption; a transcendence which dispensed with the same, *on principle,* would be *nonsense.* The presence of what is actually not perceived in the world of things is then of this type, and is essentially different from that mode of Being of which we are intrinsically sensible, the Being of our own inward experiences.

## 46. Indubitability of Immanent, Dubitability of Transcendent Perception

From all this important consequences follow. Every immanent perception necessarily guarantees the existence (*Existenz*) of its object. If reflective apprehension is directed to my experience, I apprehend an absolute Self whose existence (*Dasein*) is, in principle, undeniable, that is, the insight that it does not exist is, in principle, impossible; it would be nonsense to maintain the possibility of an experience *given in such a way not* truly existing. The stream of experience which is mine, namely, of the one who is thinking, may be to ever so great an extent uncomprehended, unknown in its past and future reaches, yet so soon as I glance towards the flowing life and into the real present it flows through, and in so doing grasp myself as the pure subject of this life (what that means will expressly concern us at a later stage), I say forthwith and because I must: *I am*, this life is, I live: *cogito*.

To every stream of experience, and to every Ego as such, there belongs, in principle, the possibility of securing this self-evidence: each of us bears in himself the warrant of his absolute existence (*Daseins*) as a fundamental possibility. But is it not conceivable, one might ask, that an Ego might have only fancies in its stream of experience, that the latter might consist of nothing beyond fictive intuitions? Such an Ego would thus discover only fictive *cogitationes;* its reflexions, by the very nature of this experiential medium, would be exclusively reflexions within the imagination. But that is obvious nonsense. That which floats before the mind may be a mere fiction; the floating itself, the fiction-producing consciousness, is not itself imagined, and the possibility of a perceiving reflexion which lays hold on absolute existence belongs to its essence as it does to every experience. No nonsense lies in the possibility that all alien consciousness which I posit in the experience of empathy does not exist. But *my* empathy and my consciousness in general is given in a primordial and absolute sense, not only essentially but existentially. This privileged position holds only for oneself and for the stream of experience to which the self is related; here only is there, and must there be, anything of the nature of immanent perception.

In contrast to this, it is, as we know, an essential feature of the thing-world that no perception, however perfect it may be, gives us anything absolute within its domain; and with this the following is essentially connected, namely, that every experience (*Erfahrung*), however far it extends, leaves open the possibility that what is given, despite the persistent consciousness of its bodily self-presence, does *not* exist. It is an essentially valid law that *existence in the form of a thing is never demanded as necessary by virtue of its givenness*, but in a certain way is always *contingent*. That means: It can always happen that the further course of experience will compel us to abandon what has already been set down and justified *in the light of empirical canons of rightness*. It was, so we afterwards say, mere illusion, hallucination, merely a coherent dream, and the like. Moreover, in this sphere of given data the open possibility remains of changes in apprehension, the turning of an appearance over into one which cannot unite with it harmoniously, and therewith an influence of later empirical positions on early ones whereby the intentional objects of these earlier positings suffer, so to speak, a posthumous reconstruction—eventualities which in the sphere of subject-experience (*Erlebnis*) are essentially excluded. In the absolute sphere, opposition, illusion, and being-otherwise have no place. It is a sphere of the absolutely established (*absoluter Position*).

In every way, then, it is clear that everything which is there for me in the world of things is on grounds of principle *only a presumptive reality*; that *I myself*, on the contrary, for whom it is there (excluding that which is imputed to the thing-world "by me"), I myself or my experience in its actuality am *absolute* Reality (*Wirklichkeit*), given through a positing that is unconditioned and simply indissoluble.

*The thesis of my pure Ego and its personal life, which is "necessary" and plainly indubitable, thus stands opposed to the thesis of the world which is "contingent." All corporeally given thing-like entities can also not be, no corporeally given experiencing can also not be*: that is the essential law, which defines this necessity and that contingency.

Obviously then the ontic necessity of the actual present experiencing is no pure essential necessity, that is, no pure eidetic specification of an essential law; it is the necessity of a fact (*Faktum*), and called "necessity" because an essential law is involved in the fact, and here indeed in its existence as such. The ideal possibility of a reflexion which has the essential character of a self-evident unshakeable *existential* thesis has its ground in the essential nature of a pure Ego *in general* and of an experiencing *in general*.[5]

The reflexions in which we have been indulging also make it clear that no proofs drawn from the empirical consideration of the world can be conceived which could assure us with absolute certainty of the world's existence. The world is not doubtful in the sense that there are rational grounds which might be pitted against the tremendous force of unanimous experiences, but in the sense that a doubt is *thinkable,* and this is so because the possibility of non-Being is in principle never excluded. Every empirical power, be it ever so great, can be gradually outweighed and overcome. Nothing is thereby altered in the absolute Being of experiences, indeed these remain presupposed in all this all the time.

With this conclusion our study has reached its climax. We have won the knowledge we needed. In the essential connexions it has revealed to us already involved the most important of the premises on which depend those inferences we would draw concerning the detachability in principle of the whole natural world from the domain of consciousness, the sphere in which experiences have their being; inferences in which, as we can readily convince ourselves, a central, though not fully developed, thought of the quite otherwise oriented meditations of Descartes comes at last to its own. To reach our final goal we shall need indeed to add in the sequel a few supplementary discussions, which for the rest will not trouble us too much. Meanwhile let us draw our conclusions provisionally within a compass of limited bearing.

[5] It concerns a *quite outstanding* case of the empirical necessities which are considered in § 6 at the conclusion of the second paragraph of this treatise. Cf. on this point also the Third Study of the Second Book in the new edition of the *Logical Studies.*

# Chapter 5

# The Region of Pure Consciousness

## 47. The Natural World as Correlate of Consciousness

In connexion with the results of the last chapter we add the following consideration: In point of fact the course of our human experiences (*Erfahrungen*) is such that it compels our reason to pass beyond intuitively given things (those of the Cartesian *imaginatio*) and place at their basis a "physical truth." But it might also have been differently ordered. Not only might human development have never overstepped the pre-scientific stage and been doomed never to overstep it so that the physical world might indeed retain its truth whilst we should know nothing about it; the physical world might have been other than it is with systems of law other than those actually prevailing. It is also conceivable that our intuitable world should be the last, and "beyond" it no physical world at all, i.e., that the things as perceived should lack mathematical and physical determinacy, that the data of experience should exclude every type of physics similar to ours. The connexions within experience would then be correspondingly other than they actually are, and of a different type, inasmuch as the empirical motives which are basic for the formation of physical concepts and judgments would then have lapsed. Yet on the whole, within the compass of the dator *intuitions* included under the title "simple experience" (perception, remembrance, and so forth), "things" might still present themselves as similar to the things we know, maintaining themselves continuously in appearance-patterns as intentional unities.

But we can go farther in this direction; when we mentally destroy the objectivity of things—as correlate of empirical consciousness—there is nothing to limit us. We must always bear in mind that *what things are* (the things about which alone we ever speak, and concerning whose being or non-being, so being or not so being, we can alone contend and reach rational decisions), *they are as things of experience.* Experience alone prescribes their meaning, and indeed, when we are dealing with things that are founded on fact, it is actual experience in its definitely ordered expirical connexions which does the prescribing. But if we can subject the forms under which our experience is inwardly lived, and in particular the basic experience of the perception of things to an *eidetic* study, looking out for their essential necessities and possibilities (as we can obviously do), and on these lines also eidetically track down the modifications of empirical connexions that are essentially possible with their motivations: *"the real world,"* as it is called, the correlate of our factual experience, then presents itself as *a special case of various possible worlds and non-worlds,* which, on their side, are no other than *correlates of the essentially possible variations of* the *idea "empirical consciousness,"* with its more or less orderly empirical connexions. We must therefore not let ourselves be deceived by any talk about the transcendence of the thing over against consciousness or about its "Being in itself." The genuine concept of thing-transcendence, which is the standard whereby all rational statements about transcendence are measured, cannot be extracted from any source other than the perception's own essential content, or the definitely *articulated* connexions which we call evidential (*ausweisenden*) experience. The idea of this transcendence is thus the eidetic correlate of the pure idea of this evidential experience.

This holds of every conceivable kind of transcendence which might be treated as real or possible. *An object that has being in itself (an sich seiender) is never such as to be out of relation to consciousness and its Ego.* The thing is thing of *the world about me,* even the thing that is not seen and the really possible thing, not experienced, but experienceable or perhaps-experienceable. *Experienceability never betokens an empty logical possibility,* but one that has its *motive* in the system of experience. The latter is itself through and through a system of *"motivation,"*[1] constantly taking up new motivations and transforming such as have already taken shape.

---

[1] It is to be noticed that this fundamental phenomenological concept of motivation, which suggested itself to me so early as in the *Logical Studies* I had isolated the pure phenomenological sphere (as a contrast indeed to the concept of causality which was related to the transcendent sphere of reality), is a *generalization* of that concept of motivation according to which we could say,

Motivations differ in respect of the contents which mark our apprehension of them or their own definition, being more or less richly organized, more or less restricted or vague in content accordingly as they concern things already "known" or "wholly unknown" and "still undiscovered," or else, in regard to the seen thing, concern what we know or still ignore about it. Our exclusive concern is with the *essential configurations* of such systems which underlie pure eidetical research in all its possible development. It is an essential requirement that what exists already *realiter,* but it is not yet actually experienced, can come to be given, and that that then means that it belongs to the undetermined but *determinable* marginal field of my factual experience at the time being. But this marginal field is the correlate of the components of indeterminacy which essentially depend on the thing-experiences themselves, and these components—always on essential grounds—leave open possibilities of a filling out which are in no sense arbitrary, but *predesignated in accordance with their essential type,* and are, in brief, motivated. All actual experiences refers beyond itself to possible experiences, which themselves again point to new possible experiences, and so *in infinitum*. And all this takes place according to essentially definite specifications and forms of order which conform necessarily to *a priori* types.

Every hypothetical construction of practical life and of empirical science is related to this shifting but ever-present horizon through which the world-thesis receives its essential meaning.

## 48. Logical Possibility and Real Absurdity of a World Outside Our Own

The hypothetical assumption of a Real Something outside this world is indeed a "logically" possible one, and there is clearly no formal contradiction in making it. But if we question the essential conditions of its validity, the kind of evidence (*Ausweisung*) demanded by its very meaning and

---

for instance, of the willing of an end that it motivated the willing of the means. For the rest, the concept of motivation undergoes on essential grounds various modifications, but the ambiguities that arise therefrom are not dangerous, and even appear to be inevitable, as soon as the phenomenological positions are cleared up.

the nature of the evidential generally as determined in principle through the thesis of a transcendent—however we may generalize correctly its essential nature—we perceive that the transcendent must needs be *experienceable*, and not merely by an Ego conjured into being as an empty logical possibility but by any *actual* Ego, as the demonstrable (*ausweisbare*) unity of its systematic experience. But we can see (we are indeed not yet far enough advanced here to be able to give detailed grounds for the view) that what is perceivable by *one* Ego must *in principle* be conceivable by *every* Ego. And though *as a matter of fact* it is not true that everyone stands or can stand in a relation of empathy of inward understanding with every other one as we ourselves, for instance, are unable to stand with the spirits that may frequent the remotest starry worlds, yet in point of principle there exist *essential possibilities for the setting up of an understanding*, possibilities, therefore, that worlds of experience sundered in point of fact may still be united together through actual empirical connexions into a single intersubjective world, the correlate of the unitary world of minds (of the universal extension of the human community). If we think this over, the logical possibility on formal grounds of realities outside the world, the *one* spatio-temporal world which is fixed through our *actual* experience is seen to be really nonsense. If there are worlds or real things at all, the empirical motivations which constitute them must *be able to* reach into my experience, and that of every single Ego in the manner which in its general features has been described above. Things no doubt exist and worlds of things which cannot be definitely set out in any *human* experience, but that has its purely factual grounds in the factual limits of this experience.

## 49. Absolute Consciousness as Residuum after the Nullifying of the World

What we have said does not imply, on the other hand, that there *must* be a world or thing of some sort. The existence of a world is the correlate of certain experience-patterns marked out by certain essential formations. But it is *not* at all clear that actual experiences can run their course *only* when they show these patterns: we cannot extract such patterns purely from the essence of perception in general, and from the varieties of empirical intuitions which play their part in the perceptual function. On the contrary, it is quite conceivable that it is not only in single instances that experience through conflict dissolves into illusion, and that every illusion does not as it were *de facto* proclaim a deeper truth, and every conflict in its proper place be precisely what is demanded by more widely connected systems for maintaining the harmony of the whole; it is conceivable that our experiencing function swarms with oppositions that cannot be evened out either for us or in themselves, that experience shows itself all at once obstinately set against the suggestion that the things it puts together should persist harmoniously to the end, and that its connectedness, such as it is, lack the fixed order-schemes of perspectives, apprehensions, and appearances—that a world, in short, exists no longer. It might happen, moreover, that, to a certain extent still, rough unitary formation might be constituted, fleeting concentration-centres for intuitions which were the mere analogues of thing-intuitions, being wholly incapable of constituting self-preserving "realities," unities that endure and "exist in themselves whether perceived or not perceived."

Let us now bring in the results we reached at the close of the last chapter; let us think of the possibility of non-Being which belongs essentially to every Thing-like transcendence: it is then evident *that the Being of consciousness,* of every stream of experience generally, *though it would indeed be inevitably modified by a nullifying of the thing-world, would not be affected thereby in its own proper existence.* Modified certainly! For the nullifying of the world means, correlatively, just this, that in every stream of experience (the full stream, both ways endless, of the experiences of an Ego) certain ordered empirical connexions, and accordingly also systems of theorizing reason which take their bearings from these, would be excluded. But this does not involve the exclusion of other experiences and experiential systems. *Thus no real thing,* none that consciously presents and manifests itself through appearances, *is necessary for the Being of consciousness* (in the widest sense of the stream of experience).

*Immanent Being is therefore without doubt absolute in this sense, that in principle nulla 're' indiget ad existendum.*

*On the other hand, the world of the transcendent "res" is related unreservedly to consciousness, not indeed to logical conceptions, but to what is actual.*

That has already been made clear in a very general way in the analyses already carried out (in the foregoing paragraphs). What is transcendent is *given* through certain empirical connexions. Given directly and with increasing completeness through perceptual continua harmoniously developed, and through certain methodic thought-forms grounded in experience, it reaches ever more fully and immediately theoretic determinations of increasing transparency and unceasing progressiveness. Let us assume that consciousness with its *experimental content* and its *flux* is really so articulated in itself that the subject of consciousness in the free theoretical play of empirical activity and thought *could* carry all such connexions to completion (wherewith we should have to reckon in the help given through mutual understanding with other Egos and streams of experience); let us further assume that the proper arrangements for conscious-functioning are in fact satisfied, and that as regards the courses of consciousness itself there is nothing lacking which might in any way be required for the appearance of a unitary world and the rational theoretical knowledge of the same. We ask now, presupposing all this, is it still *conceivable*, is it not on the contrary absurd, that the corresponding transcendental world should *not be*?

We thus see that consciousness (inward experience) and real Being are in no sense co-ordinate forms of Being, living as friendly neighbours, and occasionally entering into "relation" or some reciprocal "connexion." Only that which is essentially related to an other, each related element having its own proper essence, and on the same lines as the other, can in a true sense be said to form a connexion with that other or build up a whole with it. Both immanent or absolute Being and transcendent Being are indeed "being" (*seiend*) and "object," and each has, moreover, its objective determining content; but it is evident that what then on either side goes by the name of object and objective determination bears the same name only when we speak in terms of the empty logical categories. Between the meanings of consciousness and reality yawns a veritable abyss. Here a Being which manifests itself perspectively, never giving itself absolutely, merely contingent and relative; there a necessary and absolute Being, fundamentally incapable of being given through appearance and perspective-patterns.

It is thus clear that in spite of all talk—well-grounded no doubt in the meaning intended—of a real Being of the *human Ego*, and its conscious experiences *in* the world and of all that belongs thereto in any way in respect of "psychophysical connexions"—that in spite of all this, Consciousness, considered in its "purity," must be reckoned as a *self-contained system of Being*, as a system of *Absolute Being*, into which nothing can penetrate, and from which nothing can escape; which has no spatio-temporal exterior, and can be inside no spatio-temporal system; which cannot experience causality from anything nor exert causality upon anything, it being presupposed that casuality bears the normal sense of natural causality as a relation of dependence between realities.

On the other side, the whole *spatio-temporal world*, to which man and the human Ego claim to belong as subordinate singular realities, is *according to its own meaning mere intentional Being*, a Being, therefore, which has the merely secondary, relative sense of a Being *for* a consciousness. It is a Being which consciousness in its own experiences (*Erfaurungen*) posits, and is, in principle, intuitable and determinable only as the element common to the [harmoniously]² motivated appearance-manifolds, but *over and beyond* this, is just nothing at all.

## 50. The Phenomenological Viewpoint and Pure Consciousness as the Field of Phenomenology

Thus the meaning which "Being" bears in common speech is precisely inverted. The being which for us is first, is in itself second, i.e., it is what it is only in "relation" to the first. It is not as though a blind legal decree had ordained that the *ordo et connexio rerum* (nature of the universe) must direct itself according to the *ordo et connexio idearum* (nature of ideas). Reality, that of the thing taken singly as also that of the whole world, essentially lacks independence. And in speaking of essence we adopt here our own rigorous use of the term. Reality is not in itself something absolute, binding itself to another only in a secondary way, it is, absolutely speaking, nothing at all, it has no "absolute essence" what-

---

² [TR. NOTE.—"Einstimmig." This word appears in the 1922 reprint of the first issue of the *Jahrbuch*, but neither in the first issue itself nor in the reprint of the *Ideen* published in 1928.]

soever, it has the essentiality of something which in principle is *only* intentional, *only* known, consciously presented as an appearance.

Now let us turn our thoughts back again to the first chapter, to our reflexions upon phenomenological reduction. It is now clear in point of fact that over against the natural theoretical standpoint, whose correlate is the world, a new standpoint must be available which in spite of the switching off of this psycho-physical totality of nature leaves something over—the whole field of absolute consciousness. Thus, instead of living naïvely in experience (*Erfahrung*), and subjecting what we experience, transcendent nature, to theoretical inquiries, we perform the "phenomenological reduction." In other words: instead of naïvely *carrying out* the acts proper to the nature-constituting consciousness with its transcendent theses and allowing ourselves to be led by motives that operate therein to still other transcendent theses, and so forth—we set all these theses "out of action," we take no part in them; we direct the glance of apprehension and theoretical inquiry to *pure consciousness in its own absolute Being*. It is this which remains over as the "phenomenological residuum" we were in quest of: remains over, we say, although we have "Suspended" the whole world with all things, living creatures, men, ourselves included. We have literally lost nothing, but have won the whole Absolute Being, which, properly understood, conceals in itself all transcendences, "constituting" them within itself.

Let us make this clear to ourselves in detail. At the natural standpoint we simply *carry out* all the acts through which the world is there for us. We live naïvely unreflective in our perceiving and experiencing, in those thetic acts in which the unities of things appear to us, and not only appear but are given with the stamp of "presentness" and "reality." When we pursue natural science, we *carry out* reflexions ordered in accordance with the logic of experience, reflexions in which these realities, given and taken alike, are determined in terms of thought, in which also on the ground of such directly experienced and determined transcendences fresh inferences are drawn. At the phenomenological standpoint, acting on lines of general principle, we *tie up* the *performance* of all such cogitative theses, i.e., we "place in brackets" what has been carried out, "we do not associate these theses" with our new inquiries; instead of living *in* them and carrying *them* out, we carry out acts of *reflexion* directed towards them, and these we apprehend as the *absolute* Being which they are. We now live entirely in such acts of the second level, whose datum is the infinite field of absolute experiences—*the basic field of Phenomenology*.

## 51. The Import of the Transcendental Preliminary Reflexions

We can all perform acts of reflexion, to be sure, and bring them within the apprehending glance of consciousness; but such reflexion is not yet *phenomenological*, nor is the apprehended consciousness pure consciousness. Radical discussions of the kind we have undertaken are therefore necessary in order to penetrate to the knowledge that there is, indeed can be, any such thing as the field of pure consciousness, which is not a portion of nature itself; and this it is so little that Nature is possible only as an intentional unity within this field and grounded in immanent organizations. They are necessary that we may further know that a unity such as this is given adjusted to the theoretical research in a quite different setting from that in which the consciousness which "constitutes" this unity, and so every absolute consciousness whatsoever is presented and made an object of inquiry. They are necessary that in face of the philosophic poverty in which we waste our energies, covering it with the fine name of a worldview grounded in natural science, it shall become clear that the transcendental study of consciousness does not mean nature-research, and may not presuppose this as a premise, since from its transcendental standpoint Nature is in principle placed within the bracket. They are necessary in order that we should know that this detachment from the whole world in the form of a phenomenological reduction is something totally different from the mere abstraction of certain components of an embracing organization, whether the connexions be necessary or merely factual. If conscious experiences were inconceivable apart from their interlacing with Nature in the *very way* in which colours are inconceivable apart from extension, we could not look on consciousness as an absolute region for itself alone in the sense in which we must actually do so. But we must see that through such "abstraction" from Nature we could win only what was natural, never pure transcendental consciousness. And again, phenomenological reduction does not betoken a mere restriction of the judgment to a connected portion of the totality of real Being. In all the particular sciences of reality the theoretical interest is confined to special domains of the real universe, the others remaining unconsidered except in so far as real threads of connexion crossing to and fro compel inquiries of a mediating kind. In this sense mechanics "abstracts" from optical events, physics in general and in the widest sense of the term from the psychological. For this reason, as every man of science knows, no domain of reality is isolated, the whole world is in the last resort a single "Nature," and all the natural sciences articulations of one Natural Science. With the realm of experience as absolute essences the case is radically and essentially different. It is shut off fast within itself, and yet has no boundaries which might separate it from other regions. For that which it would bound off from itself would need to be in essential community with it. But it is the whole of Absolute Being in the definite sense stressed by our analyses. It is *essentially* independent of all Being of the type of a world or Nature, and it has no need of these for its *existence* (*Existenz*). The existence of what is natural *cannot* condition the existence of consciousness since it arises as the correlate of consciousness; it *is* only in so far as it constitutes itself within ordered organizations of consciousness.

## Note

In passing we note the following: Let it be stated to prevent misunderstandings. If the element of fact (*Faktizität*) in the given order of the course of consciousness, in its differentiation into individuals and the *teleology* immanent in them gives legitimate occasion for the question covering the grounds of this same order, the *theological principle* which might rationally be presupposed here *cannot*, for essential reasons, be accepted *as a transcendence in the sense of world-transcendence*, for as is self-evident in advance from the positions we have already established, that would be an absurd circle. The governing principle of the Absolute must be found in the Absolute itself and through pure and absolute reflexion. In other words, since a world-God is evidently impossible, and since, on the other hand, the immanence of God in the absolute Consciousness cannot be grasped as immanence in the sense of Being as experience (*Erlebnis*) (which would be no less absurd), there must be in the absolute stream of consciousness and its infinities other ways of manifesting the transcendent than the constituting of thing-like realities as unities of appearances that agree together; and finally there must be intuitive manifestations to which theorizing thought can adjust itself, and by following the indication of which in a reasonable spirit we might come to understand the single rule of the assumed theological principle. It is then also evident that this rule could not be taken as causal, in the sense of the natural concept of causality, which is lowered to the pitch suited to realities and to the functional systems proper to their peculiar essence.

However, that does not concern us here any further. Our immediate aim concerns not theology but phenomenology, however important the bearing of the latter on the former may indirectly be. The fundamental considerations we have raised, so far as they were indispensable, have served to open up the realm of the Absolute as the research-domain proper to Phenomenology.

## 52. Supplementary Remarks. The Physical Thing and the "Unknown Cause of Appearances"

But we still need to add something by way of supplement. Our last reflexions bore chiefly on the thing of the sensory *imaginatio*, and we paid inadequate attention to the physical thing, for which the thing that appears to sense (what is given in perception) must function as "mere appearance," much as though it were something "purely subjective." Meanwhile it follows from our previous studies that this mere subjectivity should not be confused (as it is so frequently) with an experiential subjectivity, as though the perceived things in their perceptual qualities were themselves experiences. Moreover, it cannot be the intended meaning of scientific workers (especially when we do not judge them by what they say but by the real significance of their method) that the thing that appears is an illusion or a faulty *image* of the "true" physical thing. Similarly the statement that the apparent determinations are "*signs*" of the true determinations is misleading.[3]

Should we then say on the lines of the "*Realism*" so fashionable in our day: what is really perceived (and, in the first sense of the term, appears) is to be regarded from its side as appearance or instinctive basis of something else inwardly alien to it and separated from it? And must the later be

[3] Cf. what is said about the image-and-sign theory in § 43.

reckoned on theoretical grounds as a reality which for the purposes of explaining the way in which we experience these appearances must be accepted hypothetically as something wholly unknown, as a concealed *cause* of these appearances, to be characterized only indirectly and analogically through mathematical concepts?

Already on the ground of our general exposition (which the analyses that follow should tend greatly to deepen and to confirm more stably) it is clear that theories of this kind are possible only so long as we fail to keep persistently in mind and to justify scientifically the meaning of thing-givenness which lies in the *essential* nature of experience, and therefore also of "thing in general" the meaning which supplies the absolute standard of all rational statements concerning things. Whatever conflicts with this meaning is even absurd in the strictest sense of that term,[4] and this holds undoubtedly of all epistemological theories of the type described.

It can be easily shown that, if the unknown cause we have assumed *exists* (*ist*) at all, it must be *in principle* perceptible and experienceable, if not by us, at least for other Egos who see better and farther than we do. We are not concerned here with any empty, psychological possibility, but with an essential possibility possessing content and validity. Further, we should need to show that the possible perception itself again, and with essential necessity, must be a perception through appearances, and that we have therefore fallen into an inevitable *regressus in infinitum*. Again, we should need to point out that an explanation of the perceptually given events through causal realities hypothetically assumed, through unknown entities of the nature of a thing (as, for instance, the explanation of certain planetary disturbances through the assumption of a still unknown new planet, Neptune), is something that differs in principle from explanation in the sense of a physical determination of experienced things and through physical means of explanation after the style of atoms, ions, and the like. So too on similar lines much else could be discussed and developed.

---

[4] In this work Absurdity is a term of *logical* import, and expresses no extralogical valuation in terms of feeling. Even the greatest of the men of science have occasionally lapsed into absurdity, and when it is our scientific duty to point this out that does not in any way prejudice our respect for them.

It is not our duty to enter into a systematically exhaustive discussion of all such relations. It is enough for our purpose to bring certain main points into clear relief.

Returning then, let us take the position, easily tested, that in physical method the *perceived thing itself* is always and in principle *precisely the thing which the physicist studies and scientifically determines.*

This assertion appears to contradict the statements expressed[5] on an earlier page, in which we sought to determine more closely the meaning of current phrases used by the physicists, and in particular the sense of the traditional separation between primary and secondary qualities. After excluding obvious misinterpretations, we said that "the thing we strictly experience" gives us "the mere this," an "empty $x$," which becomes the bearer of the exact physical determinations which do not themselves fall within experience properly-so-called. The "physically true thing" is thus "in principle differently determined" from that which is given "bodily" in perception itself. The latter displays purely sensory features which are precisely not physical.

None the less, the two expositions are compatible enough, and we do not need to challenge that interpretation of the physical viewpoint at all seriously. We have only to understand it correctly. On no account should we fall into the fundamentally perverse copy-and-sign-theories which, without taking the physical thing specially into account, we considered at an earlier stage and likewise disposed of in its most general form.[6] An image or sign points to something that lies beyond it, which, could it but pass over into another form of presentation, into that of a dator intuition, might "itself" be apprehended. A sign and copy does not "announce" in its self the self that is signified (or copied). But the physical thing is nothing foreign to that which appears in a sensory body, but something that manifests itself in it and in it *alone* indeed in a primordial way, a way that is also *a priori* in that it rests on essential grounds which cannot be annulled. Moreover, even the sensory determining-content of the $x$ which functions as bearer of the physical determinations does not clothe the latter in an alien dress that conceals them: rather it is only in so far as the $x$ is the subject of the sensory determinations that

5 Cf. *supra*, § 40.
6 Cf. *supra*, § 43.

it is also subject of the physical, which on its side *announces itself in* the sensory. In principle a thing, the precise thing of which the physicist speaks, can in accordance with what has been already set out in detail be given only sensorily, in sensory "ways of appearance," and it is the identical element which appears in the shifting continuity of these ways of appearance which the physicist in relation to all experienceable (thus perceived or perceivable) systems which can come under consideration as "conditioning circumstances," subjects to a causal analysis, to an inquiry into real necessary connexions. The thing which he observes, with which he experiments, which he sees continually, handles, places on the scales, "brings to the fusing-furnace," this and no other thing is the subject of physical predicates, since it is it that has the weight, mass, temperature, electrical resistance, and so forth. So too it is the perceived processes and connexions themselves which are defined through concepts such as force, acceleration, energy, atom, ion, and so forth. The thing that appears to sense, which has the sensory properties of shape, colour, smell, and taste, is therefore far from being a sign for *something else*, though to a certain extent a sign *for itself*.

Only so much can be said: The thing that appears with such and such sensory properties under the given phenomenal conditions is, *for the physicist*, who for such things generally, and in the form of relevant connexion between the appearances, has *already fixed the physical determinations on general lines*, the sign and symbol for a wealth of causal properties of this same thing, which as such declare their presence in specific and familiar relations of dependence among appearances. What is there declared—even when revealed in intentional unities of conscious experiences—is clearly, in principle, transcendent.

It is clear from the foregoing that *even the higher transcendence of the physical thing does not imply any reaching out beyond the world for consciousness*, or shall we say, for any Ego that functions as the subject of knowledge (singly or in the relation of empathy).

The situation as generally indicated, that physical thought builds itself up on the basis of natural experience (*Erfahren*) (or of the natural theses, which it establishes). *Following the rational motives* which the connexions of experience suggest, it is compelled to adopt certain forms of apprehending its material, to construct such intentional systems as the reason of the case may require, and to utilize them for the *theoretical determination* of things as experienced through sense. Out of this springs up the opposition between the Thing of the plain sensory *imaginatio* and the Thing of the physical *intellectio*, and on the latter side grow up all the ideal ontological thought-constructions which express themselves in physical concepts, and derive their meaning as they should de exclusively from the method of natural science.

If the empirical logical reason, under the rubric Physics, thus works into shape an intentional correlate of a higher level—physical nature *out of* nature as it plainly appears—it is pure mythology to set up what the reason so *transparently* puts into our hands, which is no more than the *determination* of the nature given to us in simple intuition in terms of the *logic of experience*, as an *unknown* world of thing-realities in themselves, a hypothetical substructure devised to subserve the *causal* explanation of appearances.

Sensory things are thus connected with physical things, and that most absurdly, through *causality*. But in so doing ordinary Realism confuses, by reason of their "mere subjectivity" sensory appearances, i.e., the appearing objects as such (which are in fact already transcendent) with the absolute experiences which constitute them—confuses them, that is, with experiences of the appearing, of the empirical (*erfahrenden*) consciousness generally. The confusion is rife in *this* form, at any rate, that one speaks as though objective physics were concerned to explain not the "appearances of things" in the sense of the appearing things, but in the sense of the constituting *experiences* of the experiencing consciousness. Causality which belongs in principle to the system of the constituted intentional world, and has no meaning except in this world, is not only made into a mythical bond of union between "objective" physical Being and the "subjective Being" which appears in immediate experience—the "merely subjective" things of sense with the "secondary qualities"—but through the unjustified transition from the latter to the consciousness that constitutes it, causality is made into a bond between physical Being on the one hand and absolute Consciousness, more specifically the pure experiences of the experiencing (*des erfahrenden*) consciousness on the other. Thereby Physical Being is made to rest on a mythical absolute reality, whilst that which is truly absolute, the pure consciousness as such, is not even seen. Thus the implied absurdity, that of turning physical nature, this intentional correlate of logically determining thought, into an absolute, passes unnoticed; with the result that this Nature which defines the directly determined world of things in terms of the logic of experience, and in this function is fully *known*, this Nature—to seek behind which for something else is senseless—is made into an unknown reality which can never be *itself* apprehended, nor through any distinctive quality of its own, to which now is ascribed the rôle of a *causal* reality in relation to the flux of subjective appearances and empirical experiences.

In these misunderstandings, no doubt, the fact that a false interpretation has been put upon the *sensory unintuitability* characteristic of all categorical unities of thought, more particularly, of course, of those whose construction is highly mediated, exercises an influence that is anything but slight; and it is none the less true that the misconception of the tendency so useful to practical knowledge of supplying sensory pictures, or "models" to these unities of thought, has also exercised considerable influence. What is unintuitable to sense has been taken as *symbolically representing* a concealed entity which could be made simply sense-intuitable through improvements in the organization of our ideas, and the models have served as intuitable schematic pictures of this hidden thing; their function was therefore similar to that of those problematic drawings of antediluvian forms of life which the palæontologist sketches on the strength of some meagre data. The *transparent* meaning of the constructive forms of thought *as such* is disregarded, as is also the fact that the hypothetical element is bound up with the work of synthetic thinking. Even a divine physics cannot make categorical thought-determinations of realities intuitable in the plain, ordinary way, as little as divine omnipotence can bring it about that elliptic functions should be painted or played on the fiddle.

Much as the foregoing stands in need of deeper development, much as it may have induced in us a sensitive need for a complete classifying of all the relevant relationships, we now see clearly at any rate, and our own purposes require this, that the transcendence of the physical thing is, in principle, the transcendence of an existent (*Seins*) which constitutes itself within consciousness and remains fettered to consciousness, and the regard we pay to the mathematically grounded science of Nature (whatever the special enigmas may be to which its knowledge gives rise) does not affect our results in the least.

It needed no particular discussion to show us that all that we have brought home to ourselves in respect to the objectivities of Nature, considered as "mere facts" (*Sachen*), must hold good for all the *axiological* and *practical* objectivities, æsthetic objects, cultural creations, and so forth which are grounded on them. And finally likewise for all the transcendences generally constituted in accordance with the requirements of consciousness.

## 53. Animalia and Psychological Consciousness

There is a further extension of the scope of our studies which is very important. We have drawn the whole of material nature within the ambit of our established conclusions, both that which appears to us through sense, and the physical nature which is grounded in it as a higher level of knowledge. But how fares it with *animal realities*, with men and beasts? And in respect of their souls and *psychical experiences*? The world in its fullness is in fact not merely physical but psychological. All streams of consciousness bound up with animated bodies should belong to it, undeniably. Thus *on the one hand consciousness should be the Absolute*, within which everything transcendent is constituted, and in the last resort the whole psychological world; and *on the other hand* consciousness should be *a subordinate real event within this world*. How does this tally?

Let us make clear to ourselves how consciousness, so to speak, enters into the real world, how that which is absolute in itself can abandon its immanence and put on the character of transcendence. We see at once that it can do this only in virtue of a certain participation in transcendence in its first and primordial sense, and that obviously is the transcendence of material Nature. Only through the empirical relation to the body does consciousness become real in a human and animal sense, and only thereby does it win a place in Nature's space and time—the time which is physically measured. We recollect also that it is only through the connecting of consciousness and body into a natural unity that can be empirically intuited that such a thing as mutual understanding between the animal natures that belong to one world is possible, and that only thereby can every subject that knows find before it a full world containing itself and other subjects, and at the same time know it for one and the same world about us belonging in common to itself and all other subjects.

A peculiar type of apprehending or experiencing, a peculiar type of "apperception," completes what is brought about by this so-called "linking-on," this realization of consciousness. Whatever this apperception may consist of, whatever special type of manifestation it may demand, so much is quite obvious, that consciousness itself in these apperceptive interweavings, in this psychological relation to the corporeal, forfeits nothing of its own essential nature, and can assimilate nothing that is foreign to its own essence, which would indeed be absurd. Corporeal Being is in principle a Being that appears, declaring itself through sensory perspectives. The consciousness that is naturally apperceived, the stream of experiences, given as human and animal at once, in close empirical connexion with corporeality, does not itself become of course through this apperception something that appears perspectively.

And yet it has become something other than it was: a very part of Nature. In itself it is what it is, its essential nature is absolute. But it is not grasped in its absolute essence, in its flowing thisness, but "as something apprehended"; and in this quite distinctive form of apprehension, a quite distinctive *transcendence* shapes itself: a *state* of consciousness appears which is the state of a self-identical *real* ego-subject. This ego-subject declares in and through this state of consciousness its *individual real properties*, and it is *as* properties which manifest this unity through conscious states that we become aware of the ego-subject as united with the bodily appearance. Thus *on the plane of appearance* the psychophysical natural unity, man or beast, is constituted as a unity that rests on bodily *foundations* and corresponds to the grounding function of apperception.

As with every transcendence-instituting apperception, so here also we are presented with an essentially *twofold point of view*. In the *one*, the apprehending glance is turned towards the apperceived object through the very act of apprehending, as it were, through which the transcendent object is set up; in the *other*, the apprehending look passes back in reflection to the pure apprehending consciousness itself. We have then, to take our own case, on the one side the psychological point of view in which the glance is directed upon experience as the natural standpoint dictates, upon an experience of joy, for instance, as an *inner state* of feeling of a man or an animal. On the other side we have woven together with this, as an essential possibility, the *phenomenological point of view*, according to which, all transcendences having been disconnected, the glance is directed in reflection upon the absolute pure consciousness, giving us the apperception of an absolute experience in its intimate subjective flow; so it is, to revert to our previous example, with the affective experience of joy as an absolute phenomenological datum, yet under the influence of a function of apprehension which animates it, the function, namely, of "making manifest" the state of consciousness of a human ego-subject linked to the appearance we call a body. The "pure" experience "lies" in a certain sense in what is psychologically apperceived, in the experience as subjective human condition; with its own essence it takes on the form of psychical subjectivity, and therewith the intentional relation to man's Ego and man's body. If the experience in question— the feeling of joy in the example selected—loses this intentional form (and it might quite conceivably do so), it suffers a change, certainly, but only one which simplifies it *into pure consciousness*, so that it loses all its meaning as a natural event.

## 54. The Same Continued. The Transcendent Psychological Experience Contingent and Relative, the Transcendental Experience Necessary and Absolute

Let us suppose that we have been apperceiving according to the natural pattern, but that our apperceptions have been continually invalid, so that all coherent (*einstimmige*) connexions in which empirical unities might take shape have become impossible; in other words, let us imagine in the spirit of the foregoing exposition[7] that the whole of nature—and the physical in the first instance—has been "annulled," there would then be no more bodies and therefore no men. As a man I should no longer be, and again I should have no neighbours. But my consciousness, however its states of experience might vary, would remain an absolute stream of experience with its own distinctive essence. Were something still left over enabling us to grasp the experiences as "states" of a personal Ego, in and through whose changes self-identical

[7] Cf. § 49.

personal properties were manifested, we could break up these apprehensions also, do away with the intentional forms which bring them into shape, and reduce them to pure experiences. *Even psychical states* point to the ordering conditions of absolute experiences in which they are constituted and take on the intentional and in its way *transcendent* form "*state of consciousness.*"

Certainly an incorporeal and, paradoxical as it may sound, even an inanimate and non-personal consciousness is conceivable, i.e., a stream of experience in which the intentional empirical unities, body, soul, empirical ego-subject do not take shape, in which all these empirical concepts, and therefore also that of *experience in the psychological sense* (as experience of a person, an animal ego), have nothing to support them, and at any rate no validity. *All* empirical unities, and therefore psychological experiences also, are *indicators of absolute systems of experience*, and show a quite distinctive essential formation, besides which still other formations are conceivable; all are in the same sense transcendent, merely relative, contingent. We must bring ourselves to see that in taking for granted that every experience of oneself or another has empirical validity as the psychological and psychophysical state of consciousness of animal subjects, we are indeed fully justified, but only within the relevant limits; that over against the empirical experience, and *as the assumption on which it depends for its very meaning*, stands the *absolute* experience, and that this is not a metaphysical construction but with appropriate shifting of the standpoint indubitably manifest in all its absoluteness and immediately given in intuition. We must convince ourselves that *the psychical in general in the psychological sense*, that psychical personalities, psychical properties, experiences or states are *empirical* unities, and are therefore as realities of every kind and degree, mere unities of an intentional "constitution"—in their own sense truly existing (*wahrhaft seiend*); intuitable, experienceable, and on empirical grounds scientifically determinable—and yet "merely intentional," and therefore merely "relative." To hold that they exist in an absolute sense is therefore absurd.

## 55. Conclusion. All Reality Exists through "The Dispensing of Meaning." No "Subjective Idealism"

In a certain sense and with proper care in the use of words we may even say that *all real unities are "unities of meaning."*

Unities of meaning presuppose (let me repeat it with emphasis: not through deduction from metaphysical postulates of any description, but because we can point to it in our intuitive wholly doubt-free procedure) *a sense-giving consciousness*, which, on its side, is absolute and not dependent in its turn on sense bestowed on it from another source. If the concept of reality is derived from *natural* realities, from the unities of possible experience, then "universe," "Nature as a whole," means just so much as the totality of realities; but to identify the same with the totality of *Being*, and therewith to make it absolute, is simply nonsense. *An absolute reality is just as valid as a round square.* Reality and world, here used, are just the titles for certain valid *unities of meaning*, namely, unities of "meaning" related to certain organizations of pure absolute consciousness which dispense meaning and show forth its validity in certain *essentially* fixed, specific ways.

If anyone objects, with reference to these discussions of ours, that they transform the whole world into subjective illusion and throw themselves into the arms of an "idealism such as Berkeley's," we can only make answer that he has not grasped the *meaning* of these discussions. We subtract just as little from the plenitude of the world's Being, from the totality of all realities, as we do from the plenary geometrical Being of a square when we deny (what in this case indeed can plainly be taken for granted) that it is round. It is not that the real sensory world is "recast" or denied, but that an absurd interpretation of the same, which indeed contradicts its *own* mentally clarified meaning, is set aside. It springs from making the world absolute in a *philosophical* sense, which is wholly foreign to the way in which we naturally look out upon the world. This outlook is altogether natural, it pervades our unsophisticated action as we exhibit in practice the general thesis already described, it can therefore never be absurd. Absurdity first arises when one philosophizes and, in probing for ultimate information as to the meaning of the world, fails to notice that the whole being of the world consists in a certain "meaning" which presupposes[8] absolute consciousness as the field from which the meaning is derived; and further, when in support of this attitude, one fails to notice that this field, *this*

---

[8] I allow myself here in passing, and for the purposes of impressive contrast, the use of an unusual and yet in its own way trustworthy extension of the concept of "meaning."

*existential realm of absolute origins, is open to research on an intuitional basis,* and contains an infinite wealth of insight-rooted knowledge of the highest scientific worth. It is true that we have not yet shown that this is so, it will first become clear to us in the course of our inquiries.

We would remark in conclusion that the generality with which we have stated these last reflexions concerning the con-stituting of the natural world in absolute consciousness should give no offence. The scientific reader will be able to gather from the conceptual precision of the expositions that we have not been airing philosophical fancies, but, on the basis of systematic work among the fundamentals in this field, have been focusing in the form of descriptive statements consist-ently general in character items of knowledge that have been carefully and cautiously acquired. The need for closer develop-ment and the filling of vacant gaps may very well be left, and should be so felt. The further exposition will contribute sub-stantially to the more concrete shaping and filling out of the previous outlines. But we must note that our aim has not been to present a detailed theory of such transcendental consti-tuting, and therewith to sketch a new "Theory of Knowledge" in respect of the spheres of reality so constituted, but only to clarify certain general thoughts which may help us in acquir-ing the idea of a pure transcendental consciousness. What is essential for our purpose is to see upon evidence that the phenomenological reduction, as a means of disconnecting us from the natural standpoint and its general thesis, is possible, and that, when carried out, the absolute or pure transcendental consciousness is left over as residuum, to which it is then absurd to ascribe reality (*Realität*).

# Chapter 6

## The Phenomenological Reductions

### 56. The Question Concerning the Extension of the Phenomenological Reduction. The Natural and the Mental Sciences

THE DISCONNEXION from Nature was for us the methodological means whereby the direction of the mental glance upon the pure transcendental consciousness becomes at all possible. Now that we have brought it within the focus of mental vision, it still remains useful to consider, conversely, what in general, in the interests of an inquiry into the nature of pure consciousness, must remain disconnected, and whether the necessary disconnexion concerns the sphere of Nature only. From the side of the phenomenological science which we propose to establish, this amounts to the query, "*Which sciences* does it *draw from* whilst leaving its pure meaning unimpaired? Which should it depend on *as already given*, and which should it not depend on? Which then need to be bracketed?" It lies in the peculiar and essential nature of phenomenology as a science of "origins" that such questions of method which lie remote from the interest of every unsophisticated ("dogmatic") science must in its own case be a matter of careful reflexion.

In the first place it goes without saying that with the suspending of the natural world, physical and psychological, all individual objectivities which are constituted through the functional activities of consciousness in valuation and in practice are suspended—all varieties of cultural expression, works of the technical and of the fine arts, of the sciences also (so far as we accept them as cultural facts and not as validity-systems) æsthetic and practical values of every shape and form. Natural in the same sense are also realities of such kinds of state, moral custom, law, religion. Therewith *all the sciences natural and mental*, with the entire knowledge they have accumulated, *undergo disconnexion* as sciences which require for their development the natural standpoint.

## 57. The Question of the Suspension of the Pure Ego

Difficulties arise just at one limiting point. Man as a natural being and as a person linked with others in a personal bond, the uniting bond of "society," is suspended, so too whatever possesses an animal nature. But how fares it then with the *pure Ego*? Is even the phenomenological Ego which finds things presented to it brought through the phenomenological reduction to transcendental nothingness? Let us reduce till we reach the stream of pure consciousness. In reflexion every *cogitatio* on being carried out takes the explicit form *cogito*. Does it lose this form when we make use of a transcendental reduction?

So much is clear from the outset, that after carrying this reduction through, we shall never stumble across the pure Ego as an experience among others within the flux of manifold experiences which survives as transcendental residuum; nor shall we meet it as a constitutive bit of experience appearing with the experience of which it is an integral part and again disappearing. The Ego appears to be permanently, even necessarily, there, and this permanence is obviously not that of a stolid unshifting experience, of a "fixed idea." On the contrary, it belongs to every experience that comes and streams past, its "glance" goes "through" every actual *cogito*, and towards the object. This visual ray changes with every *cogito*, shooting forth afresh with each new one as it comes, and disappearing with it. But the Ego remains self-identical. In principle, at any rate, every *cogitatio can* change, can come and go, even though it may be open to doubt whether each is *necessarily* perishable, and not merely, as we find it, perishable *in point of fact*. But in contrast the pure Ego appears to be *necessary* in principle, and as that which remains absolutely self-identical in all real and possible changes of experience, it can *in no sense* be reckoned *as a real part or phase* of the experiences themselves.

In every actual *cogito* it lives out its life in a special sense, but all experiences also within the mental background belong to it and it to them, and all of them, as belonging to *one* single stream of experience, that, namely, which is mine, *must* permit of being transformed into actual *cogitationes* or of being inwardly absorbed into such; in the words of Kant, "The *'I think' must be able to accompany all my presentations*."

If as residuum of the phenomenological suspension of the world and the empirical subjectivity that belongs to it there remains a pure Ego (a fundamentally different one, then, for each separate stream of experiences), a *quite peculiar* transcendence simultaneouly presents itself—a non-constituted transcendence—*a transcendence in immanence*. Given the immediately essential part which this transcendence plays in every *cogito*, we should not be free to suspend it, although for many inquiries the problem of the pure Ego can remain *in suspenso*. But we will count the pure Ego as a phenomenological datum only so far as the immediate and clearly ascertainable peculiarity of its essential nature reaches, and it is given together with pure consciousness, whereas all theories concerning it which reach out beyond these limits should be disconnected. We shall find occasion, moreover, to devote a special chapter in the Second Book of this whole work to the difficult questions raised by the pure Ego and also by the need to render secure the provisional position which we have here adopted.[1]

## 58. The Transcendence of God Suspended

After abandoning the natural world, we strike in our course another transcendence, which is not given like the pure Ego immediately united to consciousness in its reduced state, but comes to knowledge in a highly mediated form, standing over against the transcendence of the world as if it were its polar opposite. We refer to the transcendence of God. The reduction of the natural world to consciousness in its absoluteness gives *factual* (*faktische*) systems of conscious experiences of certain kinds splendidly ordered and regulated, within which, as intentional correlate, there is constituted, in the sphere of empirical intuition, a *morphologically ordered world*, a world, that is, in respect of which classificatory and descriptive sciences can be supplied. This very world, so far as its

[1] In the *Logical Studies* I took up on the question of the pure Ego a sceptical position which I have not been able to maintain as my studies progressed. The criticism which I directed against Natorp's stimulating *Introduction to Psychology* (Vol. II, pp. 340 ff.) ceases therefore to be relevant on one of the main issues. (I regret that I have not been able to read and consider any further the revised edition of Natorp's work which has recently appeared.)

material basis is concerned, permits at once of being determined in the theoretical thought of the mathematically grounded natural sciences as the "appearance" of a *physical nature* that conforms to exact natural laws. And since *the rationality* which the fact-world shows is not in any sense such as the essence demands, there lies concealed in all this a wonderful *teleology*.

Further: the systematic study of all teleologies which are to be found in the empirical world itself, the concrete evolution of the series of organisms, for instance, up to man, and within the evolution of humanity, the growth of culture with its care for the spirit and so forth, is not exhausted by the explanations of all such creations by the natural sciences out of the given concrete environment and in conformity with natural laws. On the contrary, the transition to pure consciousness through the method of transcendental reduction leads necessarily to the question concerning the ground of what now presents itself as the intuitable actuality (*Faktizität*) of the corresponding constituting consciousness. It is not concrete actuality (*Faktum*) in general, but concrete actuality as the source of possible and real values extending indefinitely, which compels us to ask after the "ground"—which of course has not then the meaning of a substantive cause. We pass by all that might lead to the same principle from the side of the religious consciousness, even though its argument rests on rationally grounded motives. What concerns us here, after merely touching on the different groupings of such rational grounds for the existence of a "divine" Being beyond the world, is that this existence should not only transcend the world, but obviously also the "absolute" Consciousness. It would thus be an *"Absolute"* in a totally different sense from the Absolute of Consciousness, as on the other hand it would be a *transcendent in a totally different sense* from the transcendent in the sense of the world.

We naturally extend the phenomenological reduction to this "Absolute" and to this "Transcendent." It should remain disconnected from the field of research still to be created, so far as this is to be a field of pure Consciousness.

## 59. The Transcendence of the Eidetic. The Suspending Pure Logic as *Mathesis Universalis*

As we have suspended individual realities in every sense, so now we seek to suspend all other varieties of the "transcendent." This affects the series of the "general" objects, the essences. They too are in a certain way "transcendent" to pure consciousness, and not to be really found in it. Meanwhile we cannot disconnect transcendents indefinitely, transcendental purification cannot mean the disconnecting of *all* transcendents, since otherwise a pure consciousness might indeed remain over, but no possbility of a science of pure consciousness.

We proceed to make this clear. Let us attempt the most extensive disconnecting of the eidetic conceivable, and with it therefore that of all eidetic sciences. To every sphere of individual Being which can be separated off as a region—the term "Being" is here given its widest logical meaning—there belongs an ontology; to physical nature, for instance, an ontology of nature, to animality an ontology of animality—all these, whether maturely developed or disciplines set up for the first time, succumb to the reduction. Over against the material ontologies stands the "formal" ontology (in unison with the formal logic of thought-meanings), and belonging to it the quasi-region "object in general." If we try to disconnect this also, we are met by doubts which will at the same time affect the possibility of a limitless disconnecting of the eidetic.

The following line of thought impresses itself on us. The purposes of science demand that we should tack on to every domain of being certain eidetic spheres, not precisely as fields of research, but as places where the knowledge of essential forms can be ordered, places to which the workers in the domain in question must always penetrate whenever their interest lies in the theoretical motives which are linked together within the essence proper to this domain. Above all, every scientific worker must be free to make appeal to formal logic (or formal ontology). For whatever he inquires into will always have the character of an object, and that which holds good *formaliter* for objects in general (properties, contents generally, and the like), that also is his concern. And however he conceives concepts and propositions, draws inferences, and so forth, that which formal logic decrees with formal generality concerning meanings of this type and classes of such meanings concerns him in the same way as it does every special worker. Therefore it concerns the phenomenologist also. Every pure experience also finds its place under the widest logical meaning of object. Thus—so it would seem—

we cannot suspend formal logic and formal ontology. So too, and for obviously similar reasons, we cannot suspend general Noetics, which expresses our essential insight into the rationality or irrationality of the judging activity generally, the meaning-content of which is determined only in its formal generality.

But if we look at the matter more closely, there opens up the possibility under certain provisos of placing formal logic in "brackets," and therewith all the disciplines of formal Mathesis (algebra, theory of numbers, theory of manifolds, and so forth). For if we may take for granted that the inquiry of phenomenology into Pure Consciousness sets itself and needs set itself no other task than that of making such descriptive analyses as can be resolved into pure intuition, the theoretical framework of the mathematical disciplines and all the theorems which develop within it cannot be of any service. Where the formation of concepts and judgments does not proceed constructively, where no systems of mediated deduction are built up, the formal theory of deductive systems generally, as we have it in mathematics, cannot function as the instrument of material research.

Now phenomenology, in point of fact, is a *pure descriptive* discipline which studies the whole field of pure transcendental consciousness in the light of *pure intuition*. The logical propositions to which it might find occasion to refer would thus throughout be logical *axioms* such as the principle of contradiction, whose universal and absolute validity, however, it could make transparent by the help of examples taken from the data of its own domain. We can therefore expressly include formal logic and the entire field of Mathesis generally in our disconnecting ἐποχή (*epokhe*—abstention), and in this respect convince ourselves of the legitimacy of the *standard* which, as phenomenologists, we wish to follow. *To claim nothing that we cannot make essentially transparent to ourselves by reference to Consciousness* and on purely immanental lines.

With this understanding we attain at once the explicit knowledge that a descriptive phenomenology is in principle independent of all those disciplines. This conclusion is not without its importance in respect to the philosophic appreciation of the value of phenomenology, and it therefore serves our purpose to record it here straight away.

## 60. The Suspending of the Material-Eidetic Disciplines

As regards the eidetic fields of study on their material side, *one* of these is of such outstanding significance for us that the impossibility of disconnexion can be taken for granted: that is, the essential domain of the phenomenologically purified consciousness itself. Even when we set ourselves the task of studying pure consciousness in its particularized specifications, after the manner therefore of a science of facts, though not in an empirico-psychological sense (since we are moving within the limits imposed upon us by our phenomenological disconnexion from the world), we could not dispense with the *a priori* consciousness. A science of facts cannot alienate the right of making use of the essential truths which relate to the individual objectivities *of its own* domain. Now it is our direct intention, as follows from what we have already said in the Introduction to this work, to establish phenomenology itself as an *eidetic* science, as the theory of the essential nature of the transcendentally purified consciousness.

If we do this, phenomenology brings under its own ægis all *"immanental essences,"* i.e., those which within the individual happenings of a stream of consciousness, and nowhere else, get particularized influx-conditioned experiences of some sort or other. Now it is of fundamental importance to see that *by no means all essences* belong to this special circle, that, on the contrary, the distinction between *immanent* and *transcendent* which holds good for individual objectivities holds on precisely similar lines for the corresponding *essences.* Thus "thing," "spatial shape," "movement," "colour of a thing," and so forth; also "man," "human feeling," "soul," and "psychical experience" (experience in the psychological sense), "person," "quality of character," and the like, are transcendent essences. If we wish to construct a phenomenology as a *pure descriptive theory of the essential nature of the immanent formations of Consciousness,* of the events which under the limitations of the phenomenological suspension can be grasped within the stream of experiences, we must exclude from this limited field everything that is transcendently individual, therefore also *all* the *transcendent essences,* whose logical position lies rather in the theory of the essential nature of the relevant transcendent objectivities.

Thus in its immanence it must admit *no postings of such*

*essences in the form of Being,* no statements touching their validity or nonvalidity, or concerning the ideal possibility of objectivities that shall correspond to them; nor may it establish any *laws* bearing on their *essential* nature.

To phenomenology that proposes really to limit itself to the region of pure experience, no transcendent-eidetic regions and disciplines can contribute, in principle, any premises at all. Since, then, it is our purpose, in conformity with the standard already referred to above, to give to phenomenology precisely this purity of construction, and since issues of the greatest philosophical import depend on deliberately preserving this purity throughout, we *expressly* sanction *an extension of the original reduction* to all transcendent-eidetic domains and the *ontologies* which belong to them.

So, just as we disconnect the real Nature of physical science and the empirical natural sciences, we disconnect also the eidetic sciences, i.e., the sciences which study what belongs essentially to the physical objectivity of Nature as such. Geometry, kinematics, the "pure" physics of matter enter the bracket. Similarly, just as we have suspended all empirical sciences dealing with the nature of animals and all mental sciences concerning personal beings in personal relationships, concerning men as subjects of history, as bearers of culture, and treating also the cultural institutions themselves, and so forth, we also suspend now the eidetic sciences which correspond to these objectivities. We do so, in advance and in idea; for, as everyone knows, these eidetic sciences (rational psychology, sociology, for instance) have not as yet received a proper grounding, at any rate none that is pure and free from all objection.

With reference to the philosophic functions which phenomenology is called to undertake, it is also advisable here again to state explicitly that in the investigations carried out above the *absolute independence of phenomenology* of all sciences, including *the eidetic sciences in their material bearing,* has been firmly established.

The given extensions of the phenomenological reduction have obviously not the fundamental importance which attaches to the original plain disconnexion from the natural world and the sciences which relate to it. Through this prior reduction it first became possible to focus attention on the phenomenological field and the apprehending of its data. The remaining reductions, as presupposing the first, are thus secondary, but by no means therefore of *small* importance.

## 61. The Methodological Importance of the Systematic Theory of Phenomenological Reductions

A systematic theory of the phenomenological reductions as a whole such as we have here attempted to outline has great importance for phenomenological method (and in the sequel for the method of transcendental philosophical research generally). Its explicit "bracketings" have this bearing on method that they continually remind us that the relevant spheres of Being and Knowledge lie, *in principle*, outside those which require to be studied in the way proper to transcendental phenomenology, and that every intrusion of premises belonging to those bracketed domains is a sign pointing to a nonsensical confusion, a genuine μετάβασις. If the phenomenological domain could but be taken immediately for granted, as is the case with domains that possess a natural empirical setting, or could we but reach it through a mere transition from the empirical to the eidetic standpoint, as the geometrical domain can be reached, shall we say, starting from the empirically spatial, it would not then stand in need of any elaborate reductions with the difficult considerations arising therefrom. Moreover, if persistent temptations to a fallacious metabasis did not exist, more particularly in the interpretation of the objectivities of the eidetic disciplines, we should not have needed to separate so carefully the single steps in the process. But the temptations are so strong that they even threaten those who in certain particular domains have freed themselves from all general misconceptions.

We note in the first place the extraordinarily widespread disposition of our time to *interpret the eidetic psychologically*. Even many who call themselves idealists have yielded to it; and indeed, generally speaking, the influence of empiricist views on idealist thinkers has been a strong one. Those who take ideas or essences for "mental constructions," who with respect to the operations of consciousness through which "concepts" of colour and shape are acquired, drawn from intuited examples of things with colours and shapes, confuse the consciousness of these essences, colour and shape resulting from the momentary intuition, with these essences themselves, ascribe to the flow of consciousness as a real part of it what is in principle transcendent to it. But that is on the one hand a corruption of psychology, for it affects the purity of the empirical consciousness; on the other hand (and that is what here concerns us), it is a corruption of phenomenology. If then the region we are seeking is to be really discovered, it is most important that we should reach a clear understanding on this point. But we compass this most naturally when we follow our own track, in the first instance by a general justification of the eidetic generally, and then, as a more specific step in connexion with the theory of phenomenological reduction, by the suspending of the eidetic. This suspension had indeed to be confined to the eidetics of the transcendent individual objectivities in all the meanings which these transcendences bear. A new and fundamental phase of this whole question must here be considered. Granted that we have already freed ourselves from the tendency to interpret essences and essential contents psychologically, it is a new and big step farther forward which does not by any means follow the earlier step as a matter of course, when the fruitful distinction which we have briefly indicated as that between *immanent* and *transcendent essence* is perceived and consistently observed on all occasions. On the one side essences of the formations of consciousness itself, on the other essences of individual events which transcend consciousness, essences therefore of that which only "declares" itself in formations of consciousness; "constituting" itself, for instance, through sensory appearances, as indeed Consciousness requires.

In my own case, at any rate, the second step, though the first had been taken before it, gave me great difficulty. No attentive reader of the *Logical Studies* could now miss this. The first step is there carried out with unhesitating decision: the right of the eidetic to be its own self as against the attempt to interpret it psychologically is justified in detail—very much against the sense of the time which reacted so vehemently against "Platonism" and "Logical Absolutism." But as regards to the second step, in certain theories, as in those concerning the logico-categorical objectivities and the object-giving consciousness *of* these, it is quite decisively taken, whereas in other developments of the same volume there is obvious oscillation, in so far, namely, as the concept of the logical proposition is referred now to the logico-categorical objectivity, and now to the corresponding essence immanent in the judging thought. It is indeed hard for the beginner in phenomenology to learn to master in reflexion the different standpoints of consciousness with their different objective correlates. But that holds for all essence-domains which do not themselves belong to the immanence relationships of consciousness. This insight must be won not only in respect of the formal-logical and the ontological essences and essence-contents (thus for essences such as "proposition," "conclusion," and the like, as well as "number," "order," "manifold," and so forth), but also in respect of the essences which are taken from the sphere of the natural world (such as "thing," "bodily shape," "man," "person," and so forth). An indication of this insight is the phenomenological reduction in its extended form. The controlling practical thought which this extension brings with it, that, as a matter of principle, not only the sphere of the natural world but all these eidetic spheres as well should, in respect of their true Being, provide no data for the phenomenologist; that as a guarantee for the purity of its region of research they should be bracketed in respect of the judgments they contain, that not a single theorem, not even an axiom, should be taken from any of the related sciences, nor be allowed as premises for phenomenological purposes—now assumes great methodological importance. Let us therefore protect ourselves methodically from those confusions which are too deeply rooted in us, as born dogmatists, for us to be able to avoid them otherwise.

## 62. Epistemological Preliminaries. "Dogmatic" and Phenomenological Standpoints

I have just made use of the term "dogmatist." We shall see that no merely analogical use of that word is here intended, but that an affinity with the Theory of Knowledge is implied in the very nature of the case. There is good reason at this point for thinking of the epistemological opposition between dogmatism and criticism, and for designating as *dogmatic* all the sciences which yield to the reduction. For it is clear from essential sources that the sciences which are bracketed are really just those and all those which stand in need of "criticism," and indeed of a criticism which they are not able on principle to supply themselves, and that, on the other hand, the science which has the unique function of criticizing all the others and itself at the same time is none

other than phenomenology.[2] To put it more precisely: It is
the distinctive peculiarity of phenomenology to include all
sciences and all forms of knowledge in the scope of its eidetic
universality, and indeed in respect of all that which is *immediately transparent* in them, or at least would be so, if they
were genuine forms of knowledge. The meaning and legitimacy
of all the immediate starting-points possible and of all immediate steps in possible method come within its jurisdiction.
Therefore all eidetic (all unconditionally and universally valid)
forms of knowledge lie enclosed in phenomenology, and
through them the root-problems of "possibility," as bearing
on any science or form of knowledge one may care to consider, receive an answer. As applied, phenomenology supplies
the definitive criticism of every fundamentally distinct science,
and in particular there with the final determination of the
sense in which their objects can be said to "be." It also clarifies
their methodology in the light of first principles. It is therefore not surprising that phenomenology is as it were the
secret longing of the whole philosophy of modern times. The
fundamental thought of Descartes in its wonderful profundity
is already pressing towards it; Hume again, a psychological
philosopher of the school of Locke, almost enters its domain,
but his eyes are dazzled. The first to perceive it truly is Kant,
whose greatest intuitions first become quite clear to us after
we have brought the distinctive features of the phenomenological field into the focus of full consciousness. It then becomes evident to us that Kant's mental gaze rested on this
field, although he was not yet able to appropriate it and recognize it as the centre from which to work up on his own line
a rigorous science of Essential Being. Thus the Transcendental
Deduction of the first edition of the *Critique of Pure Reason*,
for instance, already moves strictly on phenomenological
ground; but Kant misinterprets the same as psychological,
and therefore eventually abandons it of his own accord.

Meanwhile we are anticipating subsequent developments
(those of the Third Book of this whole work). The anticipatory statement may serve to justify us in referring to the group
of sciences subject to reduction as dogmatic and opposing
phenomenology to them as a science of a wholly different
dimension. At the same time we draw a parallel contrast be-

[2] Cf. on this point § 26. Phenomenology is then the natural
ground for the so-called specific philosophical sciences.

tween a *dogmatic* and a *phenomenological standpoint*, in which case the natural standpoint obviously comes under the dogmatic as a special case.

## Note

The fact that the specific phenomenological suspensions which we have put forward are independent of the eidetic suspension of individual existence suggests the query whether within the compass of the former an empirical science (*Tatsachenwissenschaft*) of the transcendentally reduced experiences may not be possible. Like every fundamental question bearing on possibility, this question can be decided only on the ground of eidetic phenomenology. It is answered in a way when we come to see why it is that every attempt to begin naïvely with a phenomenological science on a basis of fact *before* completing the phenomenological theory of essential being is mere nonsense. It can be shown that there cannot be *by the side of* the extra-phenomenological sciences of fact a phenomenological science of fact that runs parallel to them and is co-ordinate with them, and that on the ground that the final appraisement of all sciences of fact leads to the uniting within a single system of the phenomenological connexions corresponding to all these sciences, connexions that have a concrete reference and function as possibilities with a concrete bearing; and that this interconnected unity is no other than the field of the phenomenological science of fact that was felt to be lacking. This science in one of its main aspects is thus the "phenomenological transformation" of the ordinary sciences of fact, made possible through eidetic phenomenology, and the only question that remains over is the extent to which something further can be done from the position thus achieved.

# PART THREE

# THE PROCEDURE OF PURE PHENOMENOLOGY IN RESPECT OF METHODS AND PROBLEMS

# Chapter 7

# Preliminary Considerations of Method

## 63. The Special Importance for Phenomenology of Considerations of Method

IF WE OBSERVE the rules (*Normen*) which the phenomenological reductions prescribe for us; if, as they require us to do, we strictly suspend all transcendences; if we take experiences pure, in accordance with their own essential nature, then after all we have set down there opens up before us a field of eidetic knowledge. Once the difficulties of the first beginnings have been overcome, we perceive it stretching endlessly in every direction. The variety of the species and forms of experience with their essential natures real and intentional is indeed inexhaustible; and correspondingly endless is the variety of the essential connexions and apodeictically necessary truths that have their ground in these. Thus this infinite field of the *a priori* of consciousness which in its unique singularity has never yet come to its own, never strictly been seen at all, must now be brought under cultivation and the full value of fruitage drawn from it. But how find the right beginning? In point of fact, the beginning is here the most difficult thing of all and the situation out of the ordinary. The new field does not lie spread before our gaze crowded with given products, so that we could simply grasp them, confident of being able to make them objects of a science; nor can we be sure of the method we need for our advance.

For when we seek to press forward on our own account and increase our knowledge of this new field, we lack the data of the natural standpoint, natural objects in particular, which through long-standing experience and the thought-practice of millenniums have become thoroughly familiar through their various distinctive properties, their elements, and their laws. Here the unknown still borders on the known. All methodical labour attaches itself to fact, all improvements of method to methods already in use; our concern generally is merely with the developing of special methods which fit in

171

with the already prescribed and well-established requirements of an approved scientific canon of method in general, and in the work of discovery they take their lead from these requirements.

How different in phenomenology! It is not only that *prior to* all matter-determining method it stands already in need of a method, so as to bring into the focus of apprehension the content of the pure transcendental consciousness; not only that it calls furthermore for a wearisome diversion of mind from natural data of which we are constantly conscious and with which the newly intended object is as it were interwoven, so that we are always in danger of confusing the one with the other; there is also lacking all that helps us so much in the sphere of natural objects, the familiarity won from practised intuitions, the favour conferred by ways of thinking left ready to one's hand and traditional methods grown smooth to their task. Even a well-established method in this field will lack the hopeful confidence which derives its nourishment from various successful and approved applications in the recognized sciences and the practice of life.

The phenomenology which has recently come forward has therefore to reckon with a radical sceptical temper. It has not only to develop its method, to win new forms of knowledge from new kinds of material, it has to reach the completest clearness concerning the meaning and the validity of the method which is to enable it to hold its own against all serious criticisms.

Whence it follows—and this is very much more important as it relates to a matter of principle—that phenomenology is bound by its essential nature to make the claim of being "first" philosophy and to provide the means for all the rational criticism that needs to be performed; that it therefore demands the completest freedom from all assumptions and absolute reflexive insight in relation to itself. It is its own essential nature to realize the completest clearness concerning its own essence, and therefore also concerning the principles of its own method.

For these reasons the painstaking efforts spent in winning insight into the basic grounds of the method, into *that* which right from the outset and continuously throughout its whole development is decisive for the new science, have a significance for phenomenology which is quite different from that which analogous efforts could ever have for other sciences.

## 64. The Self-suspending of the Phenomenologist

Let us consider first a doubt as to method which might at once check the first steps we take.

We disconnect the whole natural world and all eidetic spheres of the transcendent order, and should thereby reach a "pure" consciousness. But did we not say just now "we" disconnect, and *can* we as phenomenologists set *ourselves* out of action, we who still remain members of the natural world?

We may soon convince ourselves that there is no real difficulty, provided we have not shifted the meaning of the "disconnecting." We can even continue undisturbed to speak as in our capacity as natural human beings we have to speak; for as phenomenologists we should not cease to remain natural human beings and to set ourselves down as such also in our speech. But as a piece of method, and in respect of the set propositions which are to find their place in the fundamental work of Phenomenology still to be brought out, we apply to ourselves the rule of phenomenological reduction which bears on our own empirical *existence* as well as on that of other beings, forbidding us to introduce a proposition which contains, implicitly or explicitly, such references to the natural Order. So far as the reference to individual existence is concerned, the phenomenologist proceeds like any other eidetic worker, e.g., the geometer. In their scientific treatises geometers frequently speak of themselves and their work; but the subject who thinks out mathematics does not enter as such into the eidetic content of the mathematical propositions themselves.

## 65. The Reference of Phenomenology Back to its Own Self

Again, it might be a stumbling-block to someone that whereas from the phenomenological standpoint we direct our mental glance towards this or that pure experience with a view to studying it, the experiences of this inquiry itself, of this adoption of a standpoint and this direction of the mental glance, taken in their phenomenological purity, should belong to the domain of what is to be studied.

That too is not a difficulty. It is precisely the same in psychology, and the case is similar in logical noetics. The thinking of the psychologist is itself something psychological, the thinking of the logician something logical, namely, as coming itself within the scope of the logical norms. This back-reference upon oneself would be a matter for concern only if upon the phenomenological, psychological, and logical knowledge of this momentary thinking of this momentary thinker depended the knowledge of all other matters in the relevant spheres of study, which is, as anyone can see, an absurd presupposition.

It is true that a certain difficulty attaches to all disciplines that are referred back upon themselves, and in this respect that the first introduction to them, as also the first serious inquiry into their import, must operate with certain accessories of method which they have first in the sequel to shape in a scientifically adequate way. Without preliminary and preparatory considerations both of matter and method, the sketch of a new science could never be outlined. But the concepts and the other methodic elements with which psychology, phenomenology, and so forth, in their beginnings, operate in such preparatory treatises, are themselves psychological, phenomenological, and so forth, and first acquire their scientific impress within the system of the science already grounded.

Obviously no really serious doubts which might hinder the real development of such sciences and of phenomenology in particular need disturb us in this direction. If it figures as a science *within the limits of mere immediate intuition,* a pure *"descriptive"* science of Essential Being, the general nature of its procedure is given in advance as something that needs no further explanation. It has to place before its own eyes as instances certain pure conscious events, to bring these to complete clearness, and within this zone of clearness to subject them to analysis and the apprehension of their essence, to follow up the essential connexions that can be clearly understood, to grasp what is momentarily perceived in faithful conceptual expressions, of which the meaning is prescribed purely by the object perceived or in some way transparently understood. If this procedure in its unsophisticated form serves at first only to make one at home in a new domain, to practise seeing, apprehending, analysing generally within it, and to encourage some acquaintance with its data, scientific reflection upon the essential nature of the procedure itself, upon the essential nature of the types of presentation which play their part within it, upon essence, performance, conditions of complete clearness and insight, as well as of completely true and steady conceptual expression, and more of the same kind, undertakes the function of a general and logically rigorous methodic grounding. Followed up deliberately, it takes on the character and rank of scientific method; and this, in any given case, in the application of rigorously formulated methodic standards, permits of the practice of a limiting and improving criticism. The essential relation of phenomenology to its own self here reveals itself in this, that what there in methodic reflexion under the rubrics: clearness, insight, expression, and the like, is considered and established, itself belongs on its own side to the phenomenological domain, that all the reflexive analyses are phenomenological analyses of the essential nature of things, and the methodological insights obtained in respect of their establishment come under the very norms which they formulate. Thus it must be possible through fresh reflexions to convince oneself on every occasion that statements in the methodological propositions can be given with complete clearness, that the concepts utilized really and truly answer to what is given, and so forth.

What has just been said obviously holds good for all methodological inquiries which relate to phenomenology, however widely we might extend their limits, and so we can understand that this whole work which aims at preparing the way for phenomenology is itself through and through phenomenological in content.

## 66. Faithful Expression of the Clearly Given. Unambiguous Terms

Let us follow up a little farther the most general of all the methodological thoughts which have figured in the previous paragraphs. In phenomenology which claims to be nothing beyond a Theory of Essential Being developed within a medium of pure intuition, let us carry through by the help of given examples of pure transcendental consciousness cases of insight into such Being and fixate them *conceptually* or *terminologically*. The words we use may be derived from common speech, they may be ambiguous, and in respect of their shifting sense also vague. In so far as in the way of actual expression they are "congruent" with the intuitively given data, they take on a definite meaning as their *hic et nunc* actual and clear meaning; and from this point they can be rendered scientifically determinate.

Everything indeed is not done when we have settled how

the word is to be applied so as to fit faithfully the intuitively apprehended essence, even supposing that in regard to this intuitive apprehension everything is exactly as it should be. Science is possible only when the results of thought can be preserved in the form of knowledge and remain available for further thinking as a system of propositions distinctly stated in accordance with logical requirements but lacking the clear support of presentations, and so, understood without insight, or else actualized after the manner of a judgment. It requires, of course, special provisions, both subjective and objective, for setting up at will (and on an intersubjective basis) the appropriate grounds and the actual insight.

Germane to all this is also the requirement that the same words and propositions shall be unambiguously correlated with certain essences that can be intuitively apprehended and constitute their completed "meaning." On the ground of intuition and illustrative single data to which we have grown familiar, they will be furnished with distinct and unique meanings ("cancelling" as it were other meanings which under certain circumstances thrust themselves forward through the force of habit), and in such a way that in all the possible contexts in which thought may be active they maintain their developed concepts, whilst they lose the capacity to adapt themselves to other intuitive data with other completed essences. And since in the languages in general use foreign technical terms are, so far as possible, avoided and on good grounds, it is a constant necessity, in face of the existing ambiguities of ordinary speech, to be cautious and frequently test whether a word fixed for use in a previous context may be employed in some new context in a sense which is really the same as before. But this is not the place to go more closely into these and similar rules (into such, for instance, as relate to science as shaped through intersubjective intercourse.

## 67. Method of Clarification. The "Nearness" and "Remoteness" of Given Data

Of greater interest to us are certain considerations of method which, instead of relating to the verbal expression, relate to the essence and the essential connexions which they once fixated and now express. If the glance of inquiry is turned towards experiences, these will generally be presented with a certain *emptiness* of content and *vague* sense of *dis-*

*tance* which prevents their being employed in reaching conclusive results, whether singular or eidetic. The matter would stand otherwise if, interested not so much in the experiences for their own sake as in the manner of their presentation, we wished to study the essential nature of emptiness and vagueness themselves, for these on their side are not vague but are presented with fullest clearness. But if that itself which is vaguely known, the unclear floating image, shall we say, of memory or fancy, produces its own essence, that which it produces can only be something imperfect; i.e., where the *single intuitions* which underlie our apprehension of the essence are on a lower plane of clearness, so *also* are the *apprehensions of the essence*, and correlatively the *object apprehended* has an *"unclear"* meaning, it has its disorderly mixtures, its lack of proper distinctions both within and without. It is impossible or "only roughly" possible to decide whether what is apprehended now here and now there is the same (the same Being) or something different; it cannot be determined what components are really present, and what the components which already show themselves in vague relief, and give but a wavering indication of their own presence, "properly are."

We must then *bring* to the normal distance, *to complete clearness,* what at any time floats before us shifting and unclear and more or less far removed, intuitionally, so that our intuitions of the essence may be given a corresponding value in which the intended essences and essential relations are given to the fullest possible advantage.

Apprehension of the essence has accordingly its own *grades of clearness,* just as in the case of the particular which floats before our gaze. But for every essence, just as for the corresponding phase of its individual counterpart, there exists, so to speak, an *absolute nearness,* in which its givenness is in respect of this graded series absolute, i.e., *pure* self-givenness. The objective element does not only meet one's gaze as "itself" in general, and we are not only aware of it as "given," but it confronts us as a self given *in its purity, wholly and entirely as it is in itself.* So far as a vestige of unclearness remains over, so far too does a factor of obscurity enter into the "self-"given phase, which therefore does not pass within the circle of light reserved for that which is given pure. In the case of *full unclearness,* the polar opposite of full clearness, the phase of givenness, is not reached at all, consciousness is "obscure," *intuits no longer,* in the strict sense it no longer "gives objects" at all. We must accordingly state the matter as follows:

*Dator consciousness in the pregnant sense of the term* and the *intuitable* over against the *unintuitable,* the *clear* over against the *obscure,* these are parallel oppositions. Similarly: *Grades of givenness, of intuitability, of clearness.* The zero-limit is obscurity, the unity-limit is full clearness, intuitability, givenness.

But givenness in this connexion is not to be understood as primordial givenness, therefore not as givenness of the perceptual type. We do not identify the *"self-given"* with the *"primordially given,"* with the "embodied." Understood in a strict sense, "given" and "self-given" may be used indifferently for each other, and the use of the super-sufficient expression should serve only to exclude *givenness in that wider sense* in which it is said of everything presented that it is given in presentation (though maybe emptily).

Our distinctions apply further, as is forthwith apparent, to *intuitions of any and every kind,* including *empty* presentations; therefore, too, *without restriction in respect of the objects referred to,* although we are here interested only in the ways in which experiences are given and in their phenomenological constituents (real (*reellen*) and intentional).

But with reference to future analyses we must also take care that what is most essential to the matter is retained, whether the glance of the pure Ego searches through the whole of the relevant conscious experience, or, to put it more clearly, whether the pure Ego *"turns towards"* a "given matter" and eventually *"grasps"* it, or does not do so. Thus, for instance, "given percept-wise," instead of being tantamount to "perceived" in the strict and normal sense of the apprehensions of this given object as it is, may mean no more than "ready to be perceived"; likewise "given fancy-wise" need not mean so much as "grasped through a movement of fancy," and so generally, and indeed with respect also to all grades of clearness or obscurity. We may refer thus in advance to the "readiness," which at a later stage we will discuss more closely, but let it be also noted that under the heading "givenness," where no contrary indication is added or obviously implied by the context, we *understand as an included factor the being apprehended,* and, where the givenness of the essence is concerned, the being apprehended primordially.

## 68. Genuine and Counterfeit Grades of Clearness. The Essence of Normal Clarifying

But we must continue our descriptions. If we speak of grades of givenness or clearness, we must distinguish between *genuinely* graded increases of clearness, to which one should also add *graded increases in obscurity,* and *ungenuine increases of clearness,* namely, *enlargements extensive in kind of the scope of the clearness,* with an accompanying rise, maybe, in its intensity.

A phase already given, already really intuited, can be given with greater or lesser clearness—a tone or a colour, for instance. Let us exclude all apprehensions which reach beyond the intuitively given. We have then to deal with serial gradations that develop within the framework in which the intuitable can really be intuited; intuitability as such under the rubric clearness admits of continuous differences of the intensive type, the intensities starting from zero, but closing at the upper end with a fixed limiting value. To this, one might say, the lower grades, in a certain sense, point forward; when we look at a flower in some mode of imperfect clearness, we "mean" the colour as it is "in itself," and this is precisely that which is given when the clearness is perfect. And yet we must not allow ourselves to be led astray by the metaphor of "pointing"—as though one thing were a sign for another—and one should be just as chary of speaking here (we recall what we have already noted once before)[1] of exhibiting the clear "in itself" through the unclear: as the property of a things, maybe, "exhibits" in intuition through sensory phases, namely, through perspective appearances. *The graded differences of clearness are proper throughout to the mode of being given.*

It is quite otherwise when an apprehension that reaches *beyond* what is intuitively given weaves empty apprehensions into the real intuitive apprehension, for now, by degrees as it were, an increasing amount of what is emptily presented can become intuitable, or of what is already intuitable emptily presented. Thus the procedure of *making clear to oneself* consists here in two interconnected sets of processes: *rendering intuitable,* and *enhancing the clearness of what is already intuitable.*

[1] Cf. *supra,* § 44.

In these words we have described *the essential nature of the normal process of making something clear*. For as a rule no pure intuitions are present, and there are no pure empty presentations passing over into pure intuitions; it is the *impure intuitions* which, as intermediate grades maybe, play the chief part, bringing their objective matter on certain sides or in certain phases intuitively before us, and on other sides or in other phases yielding mere empty presentations.

## 69. The Method of Apprehending Essences with Perfect Clearness

*Perfectly clear apprehension* has this advantage, that in virtue of its own essential nature it permits us with absolute certainty to identify and distinguish, to relate and make explicit, enables us, briefly, to carry out "with insight" all "logical" acts. Under this class come the *acts of apprehending the essence*, to whose objective correlates, as already stated above, the distinctions of clearness, now more familiar to us, are transferred, just as on the other side the methodological knowledge we have just gained is transferred to the objective of securing that the essence shall be perfectly presented.

Thus in general the method which is *a basic part of the method of eidetic science generally* is one of going forward step by step. The particular intuitions which minister to the apprehension of the essence may be already sufficiently clear to render possible a completely clear grasp of some essential generality, and yet not so adequate as to satisfy the main intention; there is a lack of clearness as regards the closer definitions of the interwoven essences; thus we need to scrutinize our illustrative instances more closely or to contrive others that are better suited, in which the pertinent single features left confused and obscure stand out and can then be transformed into data of the clearest kind.

We can always bring the data nearer to us even in *the zone of obscure aprehension*. What is obscurely presented comes closer to us in its own peculiar way, eventually knocking at the door of intuition, though it need not for that reason pass over the threshold (and perhaps cannot do so "on account of psychological resistances").

We have further to consider that *what is given to us at the moment has a determinable margin, not yet determinate*, and possessing its own way of effecting the transition through a process of *"unfolding,"* of separating out into series of presentations at first; it may be passing once more into obscurity, then emerging once again in the presentational sphere, until the object referred to (*das Intendierte*) passes into the brightly lit circle of perfect presentation.

Further, we would draw attention to the point that it would be *going too far to say that all self-evident apprehension of the essence demands that the subsumed particulars in their concrete fullness should be fully clear*. It is quite sufficient when grasping essential differences of the most general kind, as those between colour and sound, perception and will, that the exemplifying instances should show a lower grade of clearness. It is as though the most general character, the genus (colour in general, sound in general), were *fully* given, but not as yet the difference. That's a shocking way of putting it, but I could not see how to avoid it. Let the reader figure the situation for himself in vivid intuition.

## 70. The Role of Perception in the Method for Clarifying the Essence. The Privileged Position of Free Fancy

Let us, as a further step, accentuate some of the specially important features of the method of apprehending essence.

It belongs to the general and essential nature of immediate, intuitive essence-apprehension (and the point is one that we have already stressed)[2] that it can be carried out on the basis of *the mere present framing* of particular illustrations. But such presenting under the form of fancy, for instance, can, as we have just been showing, be so perfectly clear as to enable us to see and apprehend perfectly the essential nature of things. In general, *perception* with its primordial dator quality, and external perception, of course, in particular, has advantages of its own as compared with all forms of representation. And this, moreover not merely as the empirical act whereby we fix the content of an objective experience—such fixing does not at present concern us—but as the basis for firmly establishing the essential being of things on phenomenological lines. Outer perception has its perfect clearness in respect of all objective phases which reach their mode of givenness really within it and on pri-

[2] Cf. § 4.

mordial lines. But it also offers, with the eventual assistance of the reflexion directed back upon it, clear and steady details for general analyses of a phenomenological kind, directed towards essences, and even, on closer inspection, for analyses of acts as well. Anger reflected upon may dissipate, quickly modifying its content. It is also not always available like perception, not producible at pleasure with the help of convenient experimental apparatus. To study it reflectively in its primordiality would be to study an anger in process of dissipation, which has its own meaning, no doubt, but perhaps not that which was to be studied. Outer perception, on the contrary, so much more accessible as it is, does not "dissipate" under reflexion, and we are able, without special trouble in fixing the conditions of clearness and keeping within the limits of primordiality, to study in general its essential nature, and that also of its own components and essential correlates. If one says that perceptions also have their differences of clearness (in relation, namely, to the cases of perception), e.g., in the dark, in fog, and so forth, we will not let ourselves be drawn into further discussion as to whether these differences are quite so similar to those already referred to as they are here assumed to be. Let it suffice that perception is not ordinarily conditioned by fog, and that clear perception, as it is needed, is always at our disposal.

Now if for purposes of method the advantages of primordiality were very marked, we should have to consider where and how and to what extent it could be realized in the different types of experience; which of these types come specially near in this respect to the pre-eminently privileged domain of sensory perception, and many similar questions. But as it is we can disregard all this. There are reasons why, in phenomenology as in all eidetic sciences, representations, or, to speak more accurately, *free fancies*, assume *a privileged position over against perceptions*, and that *even in the phenomenology of perception itself, excepting of course that of the sensory data*.

The geometer when he thinks geometrically operates with imagery vastly more than he does with percepts of figures or models; and this is true also of the "pure" geometer, who dispenses with the methods of algebra. In fancy it is true he must toil to secure clear intuitions, and from this labour the drawing and the model sets him free. But in actual drawing and modelling he is restricted; in fancy he has perfect freedom in the arbitrary recasting of the figures he has imagined, in running over continuous series of possible shapes, in the production therefore of an infinite number of new creations; a freedom which opens up to him for the first time an entry into the spacious realms of essential possibility with their infinite horizons of essential knowledge. The drawings therefore follow normally *after* the constructions of fancy and the pure eidetic thought built upon these as a basis, and serve chiefly to fix stages in the process already previously gone through, thereby making it easier to bring it back to consciousness once again. Even where the thinker "meditates" over the figure, the new processes of thought which link themselves on to it have fancy-processes as their sensory basis, and it is the results of this work of fancy which fix the new lines on the figure.

Keeping to the most general considerations, the position for the phenomenologist, who has to deal with experiences as reduced and with the correlates which essentially belong to them, is substantially the same. There is also an infinite number of essential forms of the phenomenological kind. The worker in phenomenology, as in other fields, can make only a limited use of the help supplied through the primordial order of givenness. He has indeed at his disposal as primordial data all the main types of perception and representation. He has them as perceptual illustrations for a phenomenology of perception, of fancy, of memory, and so forth. For the most part he has likewise at his disposal in the sphere of the primordial examples for judgments, supposals, feelings, volitions. But naturally not for all possible special forms, just as little as the geometer depends on drawings and models for the infinite variety of his corporeal types. Here too at all events the freedom of research in the region of the essence necessarily demands that one should operate with the help of fancy.

It is naturally important, on the other hand (once again as in geometry, which has recently and not idly been attaching great value to collections of models and the like), to make rich use of fancy in that service of perfect clearness which we are here demanding, to use it in the free transformation of the data of fancy, but previously also to fructify it through the richest and best observations possible in primordial intuition; noting, of course, that this fructifying does not imply that experience as such can be the ground of validity. We can draw extraordinary profit from what history has to offer us, and in still richer measure from the gifts of art and particularly of poetry. These are indeed fruits of imagination, but in respect of the originality of the new formations, of the abundance of detailed features, and the systematic continuity of the motive forces involved, they greatly excel the performances of our own fancy, and moreover, given the understanding grasp, pass through the suggestive power of the media of artistic presentation with quite special ease into perfectly clear fancies.

Hence, if anyone loves a paradox, he can really say, and say with strict truth if he will allow for the ambiguity, that the *element* which *makes up the life of phenomenology as of all eidetical science* is *"fiction,"* that fiction is the source whence the knowledge of "eternal truths" draws its sustenance.[3]

## 71. The Problem of the Possibility of a Descriptive Eidetic of Experiences

In the preceding pages we have repeatedly described phenomenology quite frankly as a descriptive science. A fundamental question of method is again raised, and with it a doubt which checks us as we press eagerly forward into the new territory. *Is it right to set phenomenology the aims of pure description? A descriptive eidetic*: is that not *something altogether perverse?*

The motives to such questioning are sufficiently familiar to all of us. He who, like ourselves, is feeling his way, so to speak, in a new eidetic, asking what researches are here possible, what points to start from, what methods to adopt, glances involuntarily towards the old, highly developed eidetic disciplines, towards the mathematical therefore, and in particular towards geometry and arithmetic. But we notice at once that in our own case these disciplines cannot be appealed to for guidance, that the conditions in their case are essentially different. There is indeed some danger here that

[3] A sentence which should be particularly appropriate as a quotation for bringing ridicule from the naturalistic side on the eidetic way of knowledge!

the novice who has not yet come across any bit of genuine phenomenological essence-analysis may be misled as to the possibility of a phenomenology. Since the mathematical disciplines are the only ones at the present time which could effectively represent the idea of a scientific eidetic, the thought at first does not suggest itself that there may be still other types of eidetic disciplines, non-mathematical in character, and in their whole theoretical cast radically different from the type already known. Hence, if someone has allowed himself, on the strength of general considerations, to be won over to the demand for a phenomenological eidetic, the attempt, doomed to miscarry from the outset, to establish such a thing as a mathematics of phenomena, may mislead him into abandoning the very idea of a phenomenology. But that again would be perverse.

So let us in the most general way make clear to ourselves *the distinctive uniqueness of the mathematical disciplines in opposition to that of a theory of experiences in their essential aspect,* and at the same time be clear as to the precise aims and methods which should in principle be unsuited for the sphere of experience.

## 72. Concrete, Abstract, "Mathematical" Sciences of Essential Being

Let use start from the distinction of essences and essential sciences into material and formal. We can exclude the formal and therewith the whole group of formal, mathematical disciplines, since phenomenology obviously belongs to the material eidetic sciences. If analogy can give any guidance at all in matters of method, its influence should be felt most strongly when we restrict ourselves to material mathematical disciplines such as geometry, and therefore ask in more specific terms whether a phenomenology must be built up, or can be built up, as a *"geometry" of experiences.*

In order to win at this point the requisite insight, we must not lose sight of some important distinctions drawn from the general theory of science.[4]

Every theoretical science binds an ideally limited whole of being together by relating it to a domain of knowledge which on its side is determined through a higher genus. We first

---

[4] Cf. with subsequent developments the first chapter of the first section, esp. §§ 12, 15, and 16.

reach a radical unity through reverting to the highest genus of all, to the relevant region and the regional components of the genus, that is, to the highest genera which unite within the regional genus and are eventually grounded mutually the one in the other. The construction of the highest concrete genus (the region) out of genera that are partly alternative, partly grounded in one another (and in this way enveloping one another), corresponds to the construction of the concreta that belong to it out of lowest differences that are partly alternative, partly grounded in one another; as obtains with temporal, spatial, and material determinations, for instance, in the case of the Thing. To each region there corresponds a regional Ontology with a series of self-limited regional sciences, which eventually rest on one another and correspond to the highest genera which have their unity in the region. To subordinate genera correspond mere disciplines or so-called theories, to the genus conic "section," for in-instance, the discipline of the conic sections. Such a discipline, as will be readily grasped, has no complete independence so long as, in its forms of knowledge and its assignings of grounds to knowledge, it has naturally to adapt itself to the whole basic group of forms of knowledge concerning the essence which have their unity in the summum genus.

According as the highest genera are regional (concrete) or mere components of such genera, are *sciences concrete* or *abstract*. The division corresponds obviously to that between concrete and abstract genera.[5] There belong then to the domain at one time concrete objects, as in the eidetic science of nature, at another, abstract objects like the configurations of space, time, and motion. The essential relation of all abstract genera to concrete, and in the last resort regional genera, gives to all abstract disciplines and full-fledged sciences essential connexion with those that are concrete and regional.

Precisely parallel with the division of eidetic sciences there runs, moreover, a corresponding division of empirical sciences. They divide again according to regions. We have, for instance, just *one* physical science of nature, and all single natural sciences are strictly speaking mere disciplines: the impressive balance not only of eidetic but of empirical laws also, which stands to the credit of physical nature gen-erally prior to any division into natural spheres, gives these

[5] Cf. *supra*, § 15.

single sciences their unity. Moreover, different regions can show interconnexion through empirical rules, as, for instance, the region of the physical and that of the psychical.

If we now glance at the familiar eidetic sciences, we are struck by the fact that they do *not* proceed *by description*, that geometry, for instance, does not grasp in single intuitions, describe and classify in order the lowest eidetic differences, the numberless spatial figures that can be drawn in space, as do the descriptive natural sciences in respect of empirical natural formations. Geometry gives, rather, a few types of fundamental constructs, the ideas of body, surface, point, angle, and the like, the same which play the controlling part in the "axioms." With the help of axioms, i.e., of primitive laws of Essential Being, it is now in the position to infer deductively, and in the form of exact determining concepts which represent essences that remain as a rule estranged from our intuition, *all* forms that "exist" in space, i.e., all spatial forms that are ideally possible and all the essential relations that concern them. The essential generic nature of the domain of geometry, and in relation thereto the pure essential nature of space, is so ordered that geometry can be fully certain of being able to control, through its method, with exact precision really all the possible cases. In other words, the variety of spatial formations generally has a remarkable logical basic property, to indicate which we introduce the name *"definite" manifold* or *"mathematical manifold in the pregnant sense of the term."*

It has the following distinctive feature, that a *finite number of concepts and propositions*—to be drawn as occasion requires from the essential nature of the domain under consideration—*determines completely and unambiguously on lines of pure logical necessity the totality of all possible formations in the domain,* so that *in principle,* therefore, *nothing further* remains *open* within it.

We can also put it thus: A manifold of this type has the distinctive property of being *"mathematically, exhaustively definable."* The "definition" lies in the system of axiomatic concepts and axioms, and the "mathematically-exhaustive" herein that the defining assertions in relation to the manifold imply the greatest conceivable prejudgment—nothing further is left undetermined.

An equivalent of the concept of a definite manifold lies also in the following propositions:

Every proposition constructed out of the designated axiomatic concepts, and in accordance with any logical form
whatsoever, is either a pure formal implication of the axioms,
or formally derivable from these as the opposite of what they
imply, that is, formally contradicting the axioms; the con-
tradictory opposite would then be a formal implication of the
axioms. *In a mathematically definite manifold the concepts
"true" and "formal implication of the axioms" are equivalent,*
and likewise also the concepts "false" and "formally implied
as the opposite of a formal implication of the axioms."

I also refer to a system of axioms which on purely analytic lines "exhaustively defines" a manifold in the way
described as a *definite system of axioms;* every deductive
discipline which rests on such a system is a *definite discipline,*
or one that is *mathematical in the pregnant sense of the term.*

The definitions remain as a system even when we leave the
material specification of the manifold fully undetermined,
thus making a generalization of the formalizing type. The
system of axioms is thereby transformed into a system of
axiomatic forms, the manifold into a form of manifoldness,
and the discipline relating to the manifold into a form of
discipline.[6]

## 73. Application to the Problem of Phenomenology. Description and Exact Determination

How fares it then with *phenomenology* as compared with
geometry, as the representative of a material mathematics in

[6] Cf. on this point *Logische Untersuchungen,* Vol. I. §§ 69, 70.
I had already made use of the concepts here introduced towards
the beginning of 1890 (in the *Studies in the Theory of the Formal
Mathematical Disciplines,* which I had thought of as a sequel to
my *Philosophy of Arithmetic*), and indeed chiefly with the purpose of finding a solution, on lines of principle, of the problem
of imaginary quantities (cf. the brief indication, *Log. Unters.,*
Vol. I. p. 250). I have had many an opportunity since then in
lectures and practice-classes of developing the related concepts
and theories, sometimes in full detail, and in the winter term
1900–01 I treated of the same in two addresses given before
the "Mathematical Society" in Göttingen. Certain points out of
this circle of ideas have found their way into current literature
without any reference to the original source. The close relation
of the concept of definiteness to the "Axiom of Completeness"
introduced by D. Hilbert for the Foundations of Arithmetic will
be apparent without further remark on my part to every mathematician.

general? It is clear that it belongs to the concrete-eidetic disciplines. *Experimental essences* (*Erlebniswesen*) which are not abstracta but concreta constitute its scope. These, as such, have many varieties of abstract phases, and the question now is: Do the highest genera which belong to these abstract phases form here too domains for definite disciplines, for "mathematical" disciplines after the pattern of geometry? Have we then here also to seek after a definite system of axioms and to erect deductive theories upon it? In other words, have we here also to seek for "fundamental constructs" and to derive from these constructively, i.e., deductively, through applying the axioms consistently to all other essential formations of the domain and their essential determinations? Now it belongs to the very essence of such derivation, and this also is to be observed, to be a determining form that is logically mediated, and its results, even if they are "shown on the figure," cannot in principle be grasped in immediate intuition. We can also set our question in these words: Is the stream of consciousness a genuine mathematical manifold? Does it in its actuality (*Faktizität*) resemble physical nature, which indeed, if the ideal which leads the physical in the last resort is valid and is grasped through rigorous concepts, we should have to designate as a concrete definite manifold?

It is a very important problem of theoretical science how to reach fully clear conclusions concerning all the questions of principle which have here been mooted; thus, after the fixing of the concept of the definite manifold, to consider the necessary conditions which a materially determined domain must satisfy if it is to correspond to this idea. One condition for this is the *exactness* of the *"conceptual construction,"* which is in no sense a matter of our arbitrary choice and of logical dexterity, but in respect of the assumed axiomatic concepts, which must however be presentable in immediate intuition, presupposes *exactness in the apprehended essence itself*. But to what extent "exact" essences can be found in an essence-domain, and whether exact essences figure in the substructure of all essences apprehended in real intuition, and therefore also of all the components of the essence, these are matters that depend throughout on the peculiar nature of the domain.

The problem we have just been glancing at is inwardly bound up with the fundamental and still unsolved problems of setting out clearly on grounds of principle the relation of *"description"* with its *"descriptive concepts,"* to *unambiguous,"* *"exact determination"* with its *"ideal concepts"*; and running parallel to this, of clearly setting out the relation so little understood between "descriptive" and "explanatory" sciences. An attempt bearing in this direction will be communicated in the sequel to these studies. At this point we should not postpone too long the main train of our reflections, and we are moreover not sufficiently prepared to treat such questions at present in an exhaustive way. Let it suffice if in what follows we just hint at some points which in a general way we may perhaps bring more closely home to ourselves.

## 74. Descriptive and Exact Sciences

Let us connect our observations with the contrast we have been drawing between geometry and descriptive natural science. The geometer is not interested in actual forms intuitable through sense, as is the descriptive student of nature. He does not, like the latter, construct *morphological concepts* of vague types of configuration, which on the basis of sensory intuition are directly apprehended, and, vague as they are, conceptually or terminologically fixed. The *vagueness* of the concepts, the circumstances that they have mobile spheres of application, is no defect attaching to them; for they are flatly indispensable to the sphere of knowledge they serve, or, as we may also say, they are within this sphere the only concepts justified. If it behoves us to bring to suitable conceptual expression the intuitable corporeal data in their intuitively given essential characters, we must indeed take them as we find them. And we do not find them otherwise than in flux, and typical essences can in such case be apprehended only in that essential intuition which can be immediately analysed. The most perfect geometry and its most perfect practical control cannot help the descriptive student of nature to express precisely (in exact geometrical concepts) that which in so plain, so understanding, and so entirely suitable a way he expresses in the words: notched, indented, lens-shaped, umbelliform, and the like—simple concepts which are *essentially and not accidentally inexact,* and are *therefore* also unmathematical.

Geometrical concepts are *"ideal"* concepts, they express something which one cannot "see"; their "origin," and therefore their content also, is essentially other than that of the *descriptive concepts* as concepts which express the essential nature of things as drawn directly from simple intuition, and not anything "ideal." Exact concepts have their correlates in essences, which have the character of *"Ideas" in the Kantian sense.* Over against these Ideas or ideal essences stand the *morphological essences,* as correlates of descriptive concepts.

That ideation which gives ideal essences as *ideal "limits,"* which cannot on principle be found in any sensory intuition, to which on occasion morphological essences "approximate" more or less, without ever reaching them, this ideation is something essentially and radically different from the apprehension of the essence through simple "abstraction," in which a selected "phase" in the world of essences is set up as something intrinsically vague, as simply typical. The *constancy and clear-cut distinguishability of generic concepts* or generic essences, which have their scope within the flux of things, *should not be confused with the exactness of the ideal concepts,* and the genera whose scope includes an ideal element throughout. We must further realize that *exact* and *purely descriptive sciences* can indeed unite their efforts, but can never take each other's place; that however far the development of exact science, the science, that is, that operates with an ideal ground-work, is pushed, it cannot discharge the original and authentic tasks of pure description.

## 75. Phenomenology as Descriptive Theory of the Essence of Pure Experiences

As concerns Phenomenology, it aims at being a *descriptive* theory of the essence of pure transcendental experiences from the phenomenological standpoint, and like every descriptive discipline, neither idealizing nor working at the substructure of things, it has its own justification. Whatever there may be in "reduced" experiences to grasp eidetically in pure intuition, whether as a real portion of such experience or as intentional correlate, that is its province, and is a vast source of absolute knowledge for it.

Still, let us see more clearly to what extent really scientific descriptions can be set up on the phenomenological field, with its infinite number of eidetic concreta, and to what services they can be put.

It is part of the peculiarity of consciousness generally to be continually fluctuating in different dimensions, so that there can be no talk of fixing any eidetic concreta or any of the phases which enter immediately into their constitution with conceptual exactness. Let us take, for instance, an experience of the genus "imagery of a thing" as it is given us either in phenomenologically immanent perception or in some other (of course reduced) intuition. The phenomenologically particular object (the eidetic singularity) is then just this imagery of the thing in the whole wealth of of its concreteness, precisely as it participates in the flow of experience, with the precise determinacy or indeterminacy with which it lets its thing appear, now in this aspect, now in that, and with just that distinctness or mistiness, that fluctuating clearness and intermittent obscurity, and so forth, which is peculiar to it. It is *only the individual* element which phenomenology ignores, whilst it raises the whole essential content in its concrete fullness into eidetic consciousness, and takes it as an ideally selfsame essence, which like every essence could particularize itself not only *hic et nunc* but in numberless instances. We can see at once that a conceptual and terminological *fixation* of this and every similar flowing *concretum* is not to be thought of, and that this applies to each of its immediate and no less flowing parts and abstract aspects.

If now there is no question of an unambiguous determination of *eidetic singularities* in our realm of description, it is quite otherwise with the essences at a *higher specific level*. These are susceptible of stable distinction, unbroken self-identity, and strict conceptual apprehension, likewise of being analysed into component essences, and accordingly they may very properly be made subject to the conditions of a comprehensive scientific description.

Thus we describe and determine with *rigorous* conceptual precision the generic essence of perception generally or of subordinate species such as the perception of physical thinghood, of animal natures, and the like; likewise of memory, empathy, will, and so forth, in their generality. But the highest generalities stand foremost: experience in general, *cogitatio* in general, and these make it possible to give comprehensive descriptions of the essential nature of things. Moreover, it belongs to the very nature of a general apprehension of essences and of general analysis and description that there is no corresponding dependence of what is done at higher grades on what is done at the lower. In point of method we cannot insist, for instance, on a systematic inductive procedure, on a gradual ascent, rung by rung, up the step-ladder of generality.

We now note a further consequence. It follows from what we have said that all deductive theorizing is excluded from phenomenology. *Mediate inferences* are not positively denied it; but seeing that all its knowledge is descriptive and must be purely adjusted to immanent requirements, it follows that inferences, unintuitable ways and means of every description, have only the methodological meaning of leading us toward the facts which it is the function of an ensuing direct essential insight to set before us as given. Analogies which press upon us may, prior to real intuition, supply us with conjectures as to the essential relations of things, and from these may be drawn inferences that lead us farther forward; but in the end the conjectures must be redeemed by the real vision of the essential connexions. So long as this is not done we have no result that we can call phenomenological.

The pressing question whether within the eidetic domain of reduced phenomena (in the domain as a whole or in some one or other of its subdivisions) an idealizing procedure may be adopted *side by side with* the descriptive, substituting for the intuitable data pure and rigorously conceived ideals, which might then indeed serve as the fundamental nexus for a mathesis of experiences and as a counterpart to *descriptive* phenomenology, is indeed not settled by the foregoing considerations.

Much as the studies we have just completed must leave open to inquiry, they have considerably furthered our quest, and not only through bringing into our field of view a series of important problems. We are now quite clear that for the grounding of phenomenology there is nothing to be gained from mere analogies. It is only a misleading prejudice to suppose that the historical methods of the *a priori* sciences, which are *exact* ideal sciences throughout, must be accepted without question as the pattern for every new method of science, and especially for our transcendental phenomenology —as though all eidetic sciences must show one type of method only, that of "exactness." Transcendental phenomenology as descriptive science of Essential Being belongs in fact to *a main class of eidetic science wholly other* than that to which the mathematical sciences belong.

# Chapter 8

## General Structures of Pure Consciousness

### 76. The Theme of the Following Studies

THE REALM of transcendental consciousness had proved, as a result of phenomenological reduction, to be, in a certain definite sense, a realm of "absolute" Being. It is the original category of Being generally (or, as we would put it, the original region), in which all other regions of Being have their root, to which they are *essentially* related, on which they are therefore one and all dependent in an essential way. The doctrine of Categories must take its start unreservedly from this the most radical of all distinctions of Being—Being *as Consciousness* and Being as "*declaring*" itself in consciousness, or as "transcendent" Being, a distinction which, as is clearly apparent, can be drawn in all its purity and properly justified only through the method of phenomenological reduction. The relations between phenomenology and all other sciences, a topic we have frequently touched on, but must go into more deeply at a later stage, have their ground in this essential relation between *transcendental* and *transcendent* Being. Their very meaning implies that the domain over which phenomenology rules extends in a certain remarkable way over all the other sciences from which it has none the less disconnected itself. *The disconnexion has also the character of a change of indicator which alters the value of that to which the indicator refers, but if this change of indicator be reckoned in, that whose value it serves to alter is thereby reinstated within the phenomenological sphere.* Or to put it metaphorically: the bracketed matter is not wiped off the phenomenological slate, but only bracketed, and thereby provided with a sign that indicates the bracketing. Taking its sign with it, the bracketed matter is reintegrated in the main theme of the inquiry.

It is most necessary to get a thorough understanding of this position, together with the different points of view intrinsic to it. To take a pertinent illustration: physical nature suffers disconnexion, whilst notwithstanding we continue to have not only a phenomenology of the natural scientific consciousness on the side of its thought and experience, but also a phenomenology of nature itself as correlate of the natural scientific consciousness. Similarly, although psychology and mental science are affected by the disconnexion, we have a phenomenology of man, his personality, personal qualities, and his conscious course (as a human being); a phenomenology, further, of the mind of the community, its social institutions, its cultural creations, and so forth. Whatever is transcendent, in so far as it comes to be consciously presented, is an object of phenomenological study not only on the side of the *consciousness* of it, of the various conscious ways, for instance, in which it comes to be given as transcendent, but also, although essentially bound up with the viewpoint just noted, as the given and that which is experienced in it.

There are in this way immense fields of phenomenological research which have been quite overlooked by those who have started out from the idea of experience—especially when we start, as we all do, with the psychological viewpoint, and have at first allowed ourselves to take over the concept of experience from the psychology of our own time—fields of inquiry which at first, under the influence of inner resistances, one is apt to be little inclined to recognize as phenomenological at all. Through this inclusion of bracketed matter, quite peculiar and at first confusing situations are created in the case of psychology and the science of mind. To restrict oneself to the case of psychology, we may set it down that consciousness, as a given datum of psychological experience, and as human or animal, is an object of psychology, of empirical psychology in the investigations of empirical science, of eidetic psychology in those of the science of Essences. On the other hand, the whole world, with its psychic individuals and its psychic experiences—all this as correlate of the absolute consciousness—falls in modified bracketed form within phenomenology. Thus consciousness figures under different forms of apprehension and in different connexions, even within phenomenology itself: first in itself as absolute consciousness, then in its correlate as psychological consciousness, which now finds its place in the natural world, with its value altered in a certain way and yet without loss of its own content as consciousness. These are complicated connexions and extraordinarily important ones. It also depends on them that every phenomenological position concerning absolute consciousness can be reinterpreted in terms of eidetic psychology (which, strictly considered, is itself in no sense phenomenological), though the phenomenological outlook is, of the two, the more comprehensive, and as absolute the more radical. To see all this clearly, and then further to clarify fully and inwardly the essential relations between pure phenomenology, eidetic and empirical psychology, and in the last resort mental science, is of deep concern to the disciplines here involved and to general philosophy. In particular, the psychology which is being so energetically developed in our own day can win the radical foundation which it still lacks only when, in respect of the essential connexions that have been indicated, it commands far-reaching insight into their nature.

The indications that have just been given make us feel how far removed we still are from an understanding of phenomenology. We have learnt how to make use of the phenomenological standpoint, we have set aside a whole series of deflecting misgivings concerning method, we have defended the claims of pure description: the field of research lies free before us. But we do not yet know *what* its *main themes* are, or, more specifically, *what main types of description are prescribed by the most general division of experiences in their essential aspect*. To bring clearness into these relations, let us try in the chapters that follow to describe this most general division among essences by reference to some of its specially important features.

With these new reflexions we do not really leave behind us the problem of method. The discussions on method which we have so far undertaken were determined by the most general insight into the essential nature of the sphere of phenomenology. It goes without saying that a deeper-reaching knowledge of this sphere—not in its details, but in its sweeping generalities—must also furnish us with standards of method of richer capacity, with which all special methods will have to link themselves up. We do not and cannot bring method to any field from beyond its boundaries. Formal Logic, or Noetics, does not give method, but the *form* of possible method, and, useful as the knowledge of form can be in methodological matters, *determinate* method—not after the pattern of mere technical specialization, but after the general type of method—is a norm which springs from the main regional division of the sphere in question and its general structural forms, and therefore, in its epistemological aspect, is essentially dependent on the knowledge of these structures.

## 77. Reflexion as the Basic Peculiarity of the Sphere of Experience. Studies on Reflexion

Under the most general peculiarities of the essential nature of the pure sphere of experience we treat in the first place of "*Reflexion.*" We do this on account of its *universal* methodological function: phenomenological method proceeds entirely through acts of reflexion. There are, however, as bearing on the functional capacity of reflexion, and therefore on the possibility of a phenomenology generally, certain sceptical doubts, which we would first of all dispose of in a radical way.

We have already had to refer to Reflexion in our previous discussions. The conclusions we there reached, before we had passed on to phenomenological ground, we can now, under the strictest conditions of phenomenological reduction, simply take over, since those results merely concerned what is inwardly essential to the experiences, and therefore, as we know, such matter as remains a sure possession to us, transcendentally purified only in regard to the way in which we apprehend it. We will first of all recapitulate what we already know, and seek at once to penetrate deeper into the facts of the case, as well as into that type of phenomenological study which reflexion renders both possible and imperative.

Every Ego lives its own experiences, and in these is included much that is real (*reell*) and intentional. The phrase "It lives them" does not mean that it holds them and whatever is in them "in its glance," and that it apprehends them after the manner of immanent experience (*Erfahrung*), or any other immanent intuition or presentation. It is ideally possible for every experience not included in the glance to be "brought under it"; a reflective act of the Ego is directed towards it, and it now becomes an object *for* the Ego. It is just the same as regards the possible glances which the Ego may direct towards the component elements of the experience and towards their intentionalities (towards that *of which* they are in the last resort the consciousness). Again, the reflexions are experiences, and as such can furnish the basis for new reflexions, and so on *ad infinitum*, with a generality that is grounded on principle.

The experience as really lived at the moment, as it first

enters the focus of reflexion, presents itself *as* really lived, as being "now"; but not only that, it presents itself as just *having been*, and so far as it was unnoticed as precisely such, as not having been reflected on. At the natural standpoint we take it for granted, without thinking about it, that experiences do not exist only when we turn to greet them and grasp them in immanent experience (*Erfahrung*); and that if in immanent reflexion and as *retained* (in "primary"'" memory) they are still "objects of awareness," as having "just" been, then they really (*wirklich*) existed and were indeed really lived by us.

We are further convinced that it is also reflexion which "in" the process of recall, and as grounded within it, informs us concerning our former experiences, which were "then" present, "then" immanently perceptible, although not immanently perceived. The same holds good, according to the naïvely natural view, in respect of *anticipation* (*Vorerinnerung*), or previsional expectation. At first there comes in the immediate "*protention*" (as we might put it), the exact counterpart of immediate retention, and then the anticipation (*r*eproductive in the more proper sense of the term) which re-presents in quite another way, and is the counterpart of *recall*. Here the intuitively expected whereof, thanks to the reflexion possible "in" anticipation, we are aware through prevision as "presently coming," has at the same time the meaning of what will be perceived, just as the recalled has the meaning of what has been perceived. Thus we can reflect in anticipation also, and bring to consciousness experiences of ours for the enjoyment whereof the anticipation itself did not offer the proper standpoint, as none the less belonging to the anticipated as such: as we do each time we say that we *shall see* what is coming, when, in so saying, the reflecting glance has turned towards the "coming" perceptual experience.

Reflecting from the natural standpoint we make all this clear to ourselves, maybe as psychologists, and follow it out into its further connexions.

Now let us set in action the phenomenological reduction. Established results (within their bracket) are transformed into cases that illustrate essential generalities, and we can now make them our own within the framework of pure intuition and sympathetically study them. For instance, in vivid intuition (imaginative, if you like it) we picture ourselves as involved in this or that act, in joy, it may be over a theoretical train of thought that is running its free and fruitful course.

We perform all the reductions and see what lies in the pure essential nature of the phenomenological material. We turn then first towards the passing train of thought. We develop further the phenomenon in its illustrative aspect. During the course of the enjoyment we cast a reflective glance on the joy itself. It becomes the experience glanced at and immanently perceived, fluctuating thus and thus in the focus (*Blick*) of reflexion, then sinking away. The free flow of thought suffers thereby, we are now aware of it in the modified way, the joyousness which is an element in its flux is essentially and sympathetically affected; we can verify this, and in so doing must redirect our gaze thither once again. But let us set all this aside for the present and consider the following:

The first reflexion upon the joy finds it actually present, *but not as just beginning*. It is already there as a *going* concern, previously experienced but not held before the eye. It is evidently open to us to look into the past duration and mode of givenness of the joy-producing factor, to pay attention to the earlier stretches of the theoretical course of thinking which engendered it, and also to the vision (*Blick*) previously directed to it; to note, on the other hand, how joy turned in its direction, and thus, through the contrast, appreciate the lack of any glance directed towards the joy during the preceding phases of the phenomenon. We may also in respect of the joy, that subsequently became an object of reflexion, reflect on the act of reflexion that objectified it, and so render more effectively clear the difference between what is *experienced* but not noticed, and the joy that is *noticed*; likewise the modifications which come about through the acts of apprehending, unfolding, and so forth, which emerge with the redirecting of the vision.

We can examine all this from a phenomenological standpoint and *eidetically*, whether at a higher level of generality or following the essential conditions which hold for special types of experience. The whole stream of experience with its experiences lived after the *mode of unreflecting consciousness* can be made the subject of a scientific study of the nature of the essence which should aim at systematic completeness, with reference, moreover, to all the possibilities of *intentional* aspects of experience included in them, with reference also more specifically to the experiences of modified consciousness which may be in them and *their* intentional aspects. In regard to the latter we have become acquainted with examples in the shape of modifications of experience that are involved as intentional phases in all representations, and can be brought out through reflexions carried on "within" them: that of "having been perceived" which lies in every memory, that of "about to be perceived" which lies in every expectation.

The study of the stream of consciousness takes place, on its own side, through various acts of reflexion of peculiar structure, which themselves, again, belong to the stream of experience, and in corresponding reflexions of a higher grade can be and indeed must be made into objects for phenomenological analyses. For it is through analyses of this kind that the foundations of a general phenomenology are laid, and the methodological insight so indispensable to its development is grounded. Similar considerations obviously apply to psychology. No headway is made through vague talk concerning the study of experiences through reflexion or—what is ordinarily identified with this—recollection; to say nothing of much erroneous stuff which (precisely because all serious analysis of the essence is lacking) is wont to intrude itself very soon, as, for instance, that nothing of the nature of immanent perception and observation can possibly be.

Let us go into these matters somewhat more closely.

## 78. Phenomenological Study of Reflexion upon Experience

Reflexion, as the foregoing analysis will have shown us, is an expression for acts in which the stream of experience (*Erlebnis*), with all its manifold events (phases of experience, intentionalities) can be grasped and analysed in the light of its own evidence. It is, as we may also express it, the name we give to consciousness' own method for the knowledge of consciousness generally. But in this very method it becomes itself the object of possible studies. Reflexion is also the title for types of experience which belong essentially together, and therefore the theme of a leading chapter of phenomenology, whose function it is to distinguish the different "reflexions" and to analyse them completely in systematic order.

In this connexion we must first of all be clear on this point, that *every variety of "reflexion" has the character of a modification of consciousness*, and indeed of such a modification as every consciousness can, in principle, experience.

We speak of modifications here just in so far as every reflexion has its essential origin in changes of standpoint, whereby a given experience or unreflective experience-datum undergoes a certain transformation—into the mode, that is, of reflective consciousness (consciousness of which we are aware). The given experience can itself already possess the character of a reflective consciousness of something, in which case the modification is of a higher grade; but we are thrown back at last on absolutely irreflective experiences and the real (*reellen*) or intentional data implicit in them (*Dabilien*). *Every* experience can now be translated in accordance with essential laws into reflective modifications, and that along different directions which we shall learn to know more accurately still.

The fundamental methodological importance for phenomenology, and no less for psychology, of the study of reflexions in their essential nature is manifest in this, that under the concept of reflexion must be included all modes of immanent apprehension of the essence, and on the other hand all modes of immanent experience (*Erfahrung*). So, for instance, the immanent perception, which in point of fact is a reflexion, in so far as it presupposes a shifting of the glance from something we are conscious of objectively to the subjective consciousness of it. Likewise, as we have mentioned (in the preceding paragraph) when discussing what the natural standpoint takes for granted, every memory not only admits a reflective directing of the glance upon itself, but also that peculiar reflexion which takes place "in" the recollection itself. At first we are unreflectively aware in memory of the flow of a piece of music, it may be, in the mode of what is "past." But to the *essence* of what we are thus aware of belongs the possibility of reflecting on what has been perceived. Similarly in the case of expectation, of the consciousness that looks forward to "what is coming," there is always the essential possibility of diverting the glance from this coming event to its coming perceivedness. It is a consequence of these essential connexions that the propositions "I remember A" and "I have perceived A"; "I look forward to A," and "I shall see A," are equivalent *a priori* and immediately; but only equivalent, for the meaning is a different one.

Here the task of phenomenology is to make a systematic study of all the experimental modifications which fall under the heading of "reflexion," together with all the modifications with which they stand in essential relation and which they *presuppose*. The latter concern the totality of essential modifications which *every* experience must undergo during its primordial phase, and in addition the different kinds of transformation which can be thought of as carried out on every experience ideally in the way of "operations."

Every experience is in itself a flow of becoming, it is what it is within an *original engendering* (*Erzeugung*) of an essential type that never changes: a constant flow of retentions and protentions mediated by a primordial phase which is itself in flux, in which the living now of the experience comes to consciousness contrasting with its "before" and "after." On the other hand, every experience has its parallels in different forms of reproduction which can be regarded as ideal "operative" transformations of the original experience; each has its "exactly corresponding" and yet radically modified counterpart in a recollection, as also in a possible anticipation, in a possible fancy, and again in repetitions of such transformations.

Naturally we think of all experiences that run parallel to others as belonging to a common essence-stock: the parallel members should also be conscious of the same intentional objects of reference and conscious of them in identical modes of givenness—identical, provided that they share these common elements, though remaining in other respects open to variation.

Since the modifications we have been considering belong to *every* experience as ideally possible changes, and therefore in a certain sense indicate operations of thought which can be conceived as carried out on every such experience, they can be repeated *in infinitum*, and can also be performed on the experiences in their modified form. Conversely, starting from any experience which has already the character of such a modification, and remains then always so characterized *in itself*, we are led back to certain original experiences, to *"impressions"* which exhibit experiences that in the phenomenological sense are *absolutely primordial*. Thus *perceptions* of things are primordial experiences in relation to all memories, fancy presentations, and so forth. They are primordial in the sense in which concrete experiences can be that at all. For closer inspection reveals in their concreteness only *one*, but that always a continuously flowing *absolute primordial phase*, that of the living *now*.

We can relate these modifications in primary instance to actual experiences of which we are unreflectively aware, since we can see at once that all such as we are reflectively aware of must participate *eo ipso* in these primary modifications, inasmuch as they are *reflexions* upon experiences, and, when taken in their full concreteness, themselves experiences of which we are unreflectively aware, and as such take on all modifications. Now reflexion itself is assuredly a general modification of a new type—this self-*directing* of the Ego upon its experiences, and in agreement therewith the functioning of acts of the *cogito* (of such acts in particular as belong to the lowest, most fundamental stratum, that of the simple presentations) "in" which the Ego directs itself upon its experiences; but precisely the interweaving of reflexion with intuitive or empty apprehensions, or comprehensions, makes it necessary that the study of the reflective modification should be combined with the study of the modifications indicated above.

Only through acts of *experiencing* as reflected on do we know anything of the stream of experience and of its necessary relationship to the pure Ego; e.g., that it is a field for the free consummation of the conscious processes of one and the same pure Ego; and that all the experiences of the stream are its own just in so far as it can glance at them or "through them" at what is other than and foreign to the Ego. We convince ourselves that these experiences retain their meaning and their right even in their *reduced* form, and in a general and essentially universal way we grasp the *right* of such kinds of experiences generally, just as, parallel therewith, we grasp the right of *essential insights* relating to experiences in general.

Thus, for instance, we grasp the *absolute right* of immanent *perceiving* reflexion, i.e., of immanent perception *simpliciter*, and indeed in respect of that which it brings in its flow to real primordial givenness; likewise the *absolute right of immanent retention*, in respect of that in it of which we are conscious as "still" living and having "just" happened, but of course no further than the content of what is thus characterized reaches; right, for instance, in respect of the fact that it was the perception of a sound and not of a colour. We likewise grasp the *relative* right of immanent recollection, which extends just so far as the content of this memory, taken by itself, shows the genuine character of recollection (this is by no means shown, in general, by every aspect of the remembered), a right which in this precise sense cleaves to *every* recollection. But it is of course a merely "relative" right, one that permits of our asking how far the right extends. And so forth.

We thus see with completest clearness and with the consciousness of unconditional validity that it would be absurd to suppose that experiences are epistemologically guaranteed only in so far as they are given to us in the reflective consciousness of immanent perception; or that we can be sure of them indeed only in the actual now of the present moment; that it would be absurd to doubt whether that which we discover as "still" consciously there when we give a glance backwards (the immediately retained) ever existed; or again, to doubt whether in the end experiences which pass into the field of vision are not precisely for this reason transformed into something *entirely* different from what they were, and so forth. It is important only that we should not allow ourselves to be confused by arguments which, despite all their formal precision, show no sense of adjustment to the primitive sources of validity, those of pure intuition; we must abide by the "principle of all principles," that complete clearness is the measure of all truth, and that statements which give faithful expression to their data need fear nothing from the finest arguments.

## 79. Critical Excursus. Phenomenology and the Difficulties of "Self-observation"

It is clear from what we have just said that phenomenology is not affected by the methodological scepticism which in empirical psychology has led so often in parallel case to the denial or improper restriction of the value of inner experience. Recently H. J. Watt[1] has none the less believed that he could maintain this scepticism as against phenomenology, though he has quite failed to grasp the distinctive meaning of pure phe-

[1] Cf. Sammelbericht II: "Über die neueren Forschungen in der Gedächtnisund Assoziationspsychologie aus dem Jahre 1905," *Archiv. f. d. ges. Psychologie*, Bd. IX (1907). H. J. Watt criticizes exclusively the position of Th. Lipps. Though my name is not mentioned, I believe myself justified in regarding his criticism as directed against me as well, since a great part of his exposition where he is reporting the views of others might be referred just as well to my *Logical Studies* (1900–01) as to the writings of Th. Lipps, which appeared later.

nomenology to which the *Logical Studies* have sought to provide an introduction, and has not seen how the pure phenomenological differs from the empirico-psychological situation. Related as the difficulties on both sides may be, it remains a real difference whether there is raised the question concerning the range and the intrinsic value for knowledge of the *existential* states through which the data of our inner (human) experience are brought to expression—the question advanced by psychological method; or, on the other side, the question proper to a phenomenological method, concerning the intrinsic possibility and range of *essential* states, which, on the ground of pure reflexion, should concern experiences as such, considered from the standpoint of their own essence as liberated from all natural apperception. Yet between the two there subsist inner relationships, congruences, indeed, in no small measure, which justify our paying attention to Watt's objections, in particular to remarkable statements such as the following:

"It is scarcely possible even to form opinions concerning the way in which one comes to a knowledge of immediate experience. For it is neither knowledge nor the object of knowledge, but something different. One cannot see how a record concerning the experience of experience, even if it has been taken, could be put on paper." "But this is always the final question of the fundamental problem of self-observation." "It is now customary to refer to this absolute description as phenomenology."[2]

Resuming Th. Lipps's expositions, Watt says further: "In contrast to the *known* reality of the objects of self-observation we have the reality of the present Ego and the present conscious experiences. This reality is experienced (merely lived, that is, not "known," not reflectively apprehended). It is therefore absolute reality." "Very different opinions may be held," he now adds as his own comment, "as to what one is to do with this absolute reality. . . . Moreover, it is only a question here of results of self-observation. If now this observation which is always retrospective is always a knowledge about experiences we have just *had* as objects, how should we set up mental states of which we can know nothing, of which we are only aware? The importance of the whole discussion turns, in fact, round this point, the origin, namely, of the notion of an

[2] *Loc. cit.*, p. 5.

immediate experience which is not knowledge. It must be possible to observe. Everyone in the last resort experiences, only he doesn't *know* this. Even if he knew it, how could he know that his experience is really as absolute as he thinks it to be? Out of whose head should Phenomenology spring up into life ready-fashioned? Is a phenomenology possible, and, if so, in what sense? All these questions press for an answer. Perhaps a discussion of the question of self-observation undertaken by experimental psychology will shed new light on the topic. For the problem of phenomenology is one which necessarily arises for experimental psychology also. Perhaps the latter's solution will be more cautious since it lacks the supporting zeal of the discoverer of phenomenology. In any case it has a natural and spontaneous bias towards inductive method."[3]

In view of the pious belief in the omnipotence of inductive method which breathes from the lines last quoted (a belief Watt should hardly be cherishing when he is meditating upon the conditions of the possibility of this method), it is truly surprising to hear him confess "that a functional analytic psychology will never be able to explain the fact of knowledge."[4]

In opposition to these assertions, so characteristic of the psychology of the present day, and just so far as they are psychologically intended, we should in the first place have to justify the separation above referred to between the psychological and the phenomenological questions, and in this connexion to stress the point that a phenomenological doctrine of the essence is as little called on to take an interest in the methods which might enable the phenomenologist to certify the *existence* of those experiences which serve as a basis for his phenomenological findings, as the geometer is expected to be interested in determining on methodical lines how the existence of the figures on the board or the models in the cupboard is to be rendered convincing. Geometry and phenomenology, as sciences of the pure essence, know nothing positive concerning real existence. It hangs together with this, that clear fictions do not only serve these sciences for a foundation as well as do data of actual perception and experience, but to a certain extent even better.[5]

Now if phenomenology also has no existential judgments to make concerning experiences (*Erlebnisse*), thus no "experi-

[3] *Loc cit.*, p. 7.
[4] *Loc. cit.*, p. 12.
[5] Cf. *supra*, § 70.

mentings" (*Erfahrungen*) and "observings" in the natural sense in which a science of facts must find support in such acts, it makes none the less, as a fundamental condition of its possibility, positive affirmations concerning unreflective experiences. These it owes to reflexion, or, more accurately, to reflective intuition of the essence. Consequently the sceptical doubts concerning self-observation, in so far as these doubts spread in a way easy to understand, from reflexion as immanent to every reflexion generally, come under the ken of phenomenology also.

And, indeed, what could we make of phenomenology if we "cannot see how a record concerning the experiencing of experience, even if it has been taken, could be put on paper?" What could we make of it if it had to make statements concerning the essence of "known" reflective experiences, but not concerning the essence of experiences as such? What could be done if it were "scarely possible even to hold opinions concerning the way in which one comes to a knowledge of immediate experience," or to a knowledge of one's essence? It may be that the phenomenologist has no existential judgments to pass on the experiences which come before him as the examples on which his ideal formations depend. Yes, one might object, but he sees in these ideal formations only ideas of that which at the moment he has before him as an illustration. As his glance turns towards the experience, it first becomes that which now offers itself to his gaze; as he looks away, it becomes something else. The essence apprehended is essence only of the reflective experience, and the supposition that through reflexion one can win absolutely valid knowledge which is valid for experiences generally, reflective or unreflective, is wholly ungrounded. "How can we set up mental states," though it be only as essential possibilities, "of which we can know nothing?"

Clearly this concerns every kind of reflexion, although in phenomenology each separate kind claims to be a source of absolute knowledge. In fancy a thing, it may even be a centaur, hovers before my eyes. I believe myself to know that it manifests itself under certain "modes of appearance," and in certain "sensory variations of the perspective kind," apprehensions and the like. I believe myself to have the *essential* insight that an object of this kind *can* be viewed only under modes of appearance of this particular kind, only through these functions of perspective manifestation, and whatever else may play a part here. But as I keep my centaur in view, I have not in view its modes of appearance, its perspective data, its apprehended meanings; and when I comprehend its essence, I do not comprehend these and their essence. For this there is needed a certain turn of reflective insight, and this renders fluid the whole experience with modifying effect; thus in the new ideal formation I have something new before my eyes, and should not maintain that I have reached essential components of the unreflective experience. I should not maintain that it belongs to the essence of a thing as such to exhibit itself in the form of "appearances," manifesting itself in the indicated way in perspective and through sensory data, which on their side must submit to apprehension, and so forth.

The difficulty obviously bears on the analyses of consciousness also in respect of the "meaning" of the intentional experiences, of all that which belongs to the supposed, to the object intentionally referred to, as such, to the meaning of a statement, and the like. For these also are analyses conducted with a scheme of specially directed reflexions. Watt himself goes even so far as to say: "Psychology must reach a clear understanding that with self-observation the objective relation of the experiences to be described is changed. This change has perhaps a greater significance than one is inclined to believe."[6] If Watt is right, we should be maintaining too much when, in self-observation, we set it down that we had just been attending here to his book and were continuing to do so. That held good no doubt prior to reflexion. Reflexion, however, changed the attentive "experience to be described," and indeed (according to Watt) in respect of the objective relation.

Every genuine scepticism, whatever its type and orientation may be, can be recognized by this fundamental absurdity, that in the arguments it uses it presupposes implicitly, as the conditions of the possibility of its validity, precisely that which it denies in its own theses. It is easy to recognize the presence of this feature in the arguments we are considering. He who merely says, I doubt the significance of reflexion for knowledge, maintains an absurdity. For as he asserts his doubt, he reflects, and to set this assertion forth as valid presupposes that reflexion *has* really and without a doubt (for the case in hand) the very cognitive value upon which doubt has been cast, that it does *not* alter the objective relation, that the un-

---

[6] *Loc. cit.*, p. 12.

reflective experience does *not* forfeit its essence through the transition into reflexion.

Further: In the arguments considered reflexion is continually referred to as a fact, and there is much talk as to what causes it or could not cause it; and at the same time very naturally "unknown," unreflective experiences are also referred to as facts, namely, as those out of which the reflective grow. Thus a *knowledge* of unreflective experiences including unreflective reflexions is presupposed throughout, whilst at the same time the possibility of such knowledge is put in question. That happens, in so far as doubt arises as to the possibility of making *any* statement *whatsoever* concerning the content of unreflective experience and the work of reflexion upon it: how far does reflexion alter the original experience, and does it not falsify it, so to speak, by converting it into something totally different from what it was?

But it is clear that if this doubt and the possibility which arises out of it were justified, there would not remain the slightest justification for the certainty that an unreflective experience or a reflexion exists or can exist at all. It is further clear that this certainty which, as we know, was the constant presupposition throughout can be known only through reflexion, and that it can be grounded as immediate knowledge only on reflective, dator intuition. So too as regards the assertion of the reality or possibility of the modifications which follow on reflexion. *Are* the like, however, given through intuition, they are given within an intuitional content; thus it is absurd to maintain that there is here nothing knowable, nothing respecting the content of the unreflected experience and the type of modifications which it undergoes.

This suffices clearly to expose the absurdity. Here, as everywhere, scepticism loses its force by harking back from verbal discussions to the essential intuition, the primordial dator intuition and the sovereign right which it possesses in itself. Everything depends on whether we really set this intuition in action, and are able to raise the matter in question into the light of genuine essential clearness: whether we can grasp expositions such as we have attempted in the previous paragraph in the same intuitive way as that in which they are carried out and presented.

The phenomena of reflexion are in fact a sphere of pure and perhaps of the clearest data. It is an *essential insight* always attainable because immediate; that, from the objectively given, as such, a reflective glance can be transferred to the object-giving consciousness and its subject; from the perceived, the corporeally "there" to the perceiving act; from the remembered, as it "hovers" before us as such, as "having been," to the remembering; from the statement as it comes from the given content to the stating activity, and so forth; whereby the perceiving comes to be given as a perceiving of just this perceived object, the momentary consciousness as the consciousness of just this momentary object. It is evident that essentially—not therefore on merely accidental grounds, merely "perhaps for us" and our contingent "psychological constitution"—it is only through reflexions of this kind that such a thing as consciousness or conscious content (in a real or intentional sense) can become known. Therefore God Himself is subject to this absolute and transparent necessity, just as surely as He is to the insight that $2 + 1 = 1 + 2$. Even He could win a knowledge of His consciousness and its content only through reflexion.[7]

This implies that reflexion cannot be entangled in any antinomian conflict with the Ideal of perfect knowledge. Every type of being, as we have already had to insist more than once, has ways of being given which are essentially *its own*, and therewith its own ways as regards methods of knowledge. It is strictly absurd in this connexion to treat essential peculiarities as defects, to the extent even of imputing them as contingent, empirical defects to "our human" way of knowing. Another question which must also be considered on lines of essential insight concerns the possible "range" of this or that type of knowledge, the question how we are to guard against statements which go beyond what is really given at the moment and transcend the eidetic grasp; and still another question is that of the methods proper to *empirical* thinking: how we humans, as psychologists may be, must proceed under the given psychological conditions so as to confer on our human knowledge as much dignity as the case admits of.

We must lay stress, moreover, on the point that our repeated recourse to insight (self-evidence or intuition) here as else-

[7] We are not here carrying over the conflict into the domain of theology: in epistemological reflexion the idea of God is a necessary limiting concept, or an indispensable pointer in the construction of certain limiting concepts, which even the philosophical atheist cannot dispense with.

where is no mere form of speaking, but, in the sense of the Introductory Section, signifies the regress to that which is ultimate in all knowledge, precisely as it does when we speak of insight in connexion with the most primitive logical and arithmetical axioms.[8] But he who has learnt to grasp with insight what is given in the sphere of consciousness will not be able to read without astonishment statements like the one already cited: "it is not possible to form any opinions concerning the way in which one comes to a knowledge of immediate experience." From such words one can only gather how strange to modern psychology essential analysis in its im-

----

[8] Whilst the work is going to press I read in a work of Th. Ziehen which has just appeared, entitled *Theory of Knowledge on a Psychophysiological and Physical Foundation,* a characteristic utterance concerning "that contemptible so-called intuition or self-evidence which has two chief properties: firstly, it changes from philosopher to philosopher and from one school of philosophers to another school of philosophers; and in the second place it shows a marked preference for coming in *precisely when the author is developing a very doubtful point of his theory; we are then to be protected from doubting by a piece of bluff.*" In this criticism, as the context shows, the attack is levelled at the doctrine of "general objects" or "essences," and at the theory of essential intuition as worked out in the *Logical Studies.* Ziehen then adds the following: "In order to distinguish these transempirical concepts from the common herd of ordinary concepts, a special generality, absolute exactness, and so forth, have often been ascribed to them. All this seems to me to be mere human presumption" (*id.,* p. 413). No less characteristic for this theory of knowledge is the utterance (p. 441) relating to the intuitive apprehension of the Ego (and held by its author to have a quite general bearing): "I can think of only one real testimony to a primary intuition of a kind such as this, the agreement of all individuals who think and feel in bearing witness to such intuitions." For the rest we would naturally not deny that the appeal to "intuition" has often meant talking nonsense. The question is only whether this nonsense in the case of an *alleged* intuition could be discovered in any other way than through *real* intuition. In the sphere of experience also the appeal to experience has involved much traffic in nonsense, and it would be hard if for that reason experience in general were to be set down as "bluff" and the "testimony" in its favour made to depend on the "agreement of all individuals who think and feel in bearing witness to such 'experience.'" Cf. on this point the second chapter of the first division of the present work.

manent aspect still is, although it gives the only possible method for fixing the concepts which must prove determinative in all immanent psychological description.[9, 10]

In the problems of reflexion here discussed, the inner connexion between phenomenology and psychology is brought home to us with special force. Every description of Essential Being which relates to types of experience provides an unconditionally valid norm for the possibilities of empirical existence. Naturally this also applies in particular to all the types of experience which even for psychological method are part of the mental life, as it holds good generally for all modes of inner experience. Thus phenomenology is the court of appeal for the fundamental questions of psychological methodology. The general conclusions which it has reached must be recognized and, as occasion requires, adopted by the psychologist as the condition for the possibility of all further developments of method in his field. What conflicts with it bears the stamp of *intrinsic psychological absurdity*, just as in the physical sphere every conflict with geometrical truths and the truths of the ontology of nature in general bears the stamp of *intrinsic absurdity in natural science*.

In accordance herewith we can trace an intrinsic absurdity of this kind in the hope expressed that the sceptical doubts concerning the possibility of self-observation may be overcome through *psychological induction* by the way of experimental psychology. Here again it is just as though one wished to overcome the corresponding scepticism in the domain of the knowl-

[9] Cf. my article in *Logos*, I, pp. 302–322.

[10] The two articles of A. Messer and J. Cohn (in the first volume of the *Jahrbücher der Philosophie*, edited by Frischeisen-Köhler), which have also come into my hands whilst this book is in the press, show once again how little even thorough and scholarly thinkers can succeed in freeing themselves from the grip of prevailing prejudices, and, in spite of all good will to the efforts of phenomenology, how little they are able to grasp the distinctive nature of phenomenology as a "doctrine of Essential Being." Both writers, and Messer in particular (as also in his earlier critical reflexions in the *Archiv. f. d. ges. Psychol.*, XXII), have misunderstood the meaning of my expositions; so much so that the doctrines which are there opposed as my own are *simply not mine at all*. I hope that the more detailed expositions of the present work will prevent the recurrence of such misunderstandings in the future.

edge of physical nature, the doubt whether in the end every external perception would not prove deceptive (since each, taken singly, could really deceive us) by means of experimental physics, which indeed presupposes at every step the authority of external perception.

Moreover, what is here stated in very general terms should become more convincing in the light of all that follows, more particularly through the clearing discussions concerning the scope of reflective essential insight. The relations here touched on between phenomenology (for between the eidetic psychology which here, for provisional reasons, is not yet separated off from it, and in any case is inwardly bound up with it) and psychology as an empirical science are to be discussed and clarified with all the deep problems they give rise to in the Second Book of this whole treatise. I am sure of this, that at a time not so very far distant it will have become a commonly accepted conviction that phenomenology (or eidetic psychology) is, methodologically, the basic science for empirical psychology, just as the material (*sachhaltig*) mathematical disciplines (e.g., geometry and kinematics) are basic for physics.

The old ontological doctrine, *that the knowledge of "possibilities" must precede that of actualities (Wirklichkeiten)* is, in my opinion, in so far as it is rightly understood and properly utilized, a really great truth.

## 80. The Relation of Experiences to the Pure Ego

Among the essential peculiarities of a general kind, distinctive of the transcendentally purified field of experience, the first place should be kept for the relation of that experience to the "pure" Ego. Every "*cogito*," every act in a specially marked sense, is characterized as act of the Ego, "proceeding from the Ego," "actually living" in it. We have already spoken on this point, and recall in a few sentences what we previously worked out.

When observing, *I* perceive something; similarly in recollection I am often "busied" with something; again, observing in a sense, *I follow* in imaginative fancy what goes on in the world of fancy. Or I meditate, draw inferences; I revoke a judgment, "refrain" if need be from judging at all. I approve or disapprove, I am glad or grieved, I wish, or I will and do; or again, I "refrain" from being glad, from wishing, willing, and action. In all such acts I am present, *actually present*. In reflexion I apprehend myself herein as the human being that I am.

But if I perform the phenomenological ἐποχή (*epokhe*— abstention), the whole world of the natural setting is suspended, and with it, "I, the man." The pure experience as act with its own proper essence then remains as residue. But I also see that the apprehension of the same as human experience, quite apart from the question of existence, introduces various features which do not need to be there, and that on the other side no disconnecting can remove the form of the *cogito* and cancel the "pure" subject of the act. The "being directed towards," "the being busied with," "adopting an attitude," "undergoing or suffering from," has this *of necessity* wrapped in its very essence, that it is just something "from the Ego," or in the reverse direction "to the Ego"; and this Ego is the *pure* Ego, and no reduction can get any grip on it.

We have hitherto spoken of experiences of the special "cogito" type. The remaining experiences which supply the general *milieu* for the actuality of the Ego certainly lack the marked relation to the Ego, of which we have just been speaking. And yet they too have their part in the pure Ego, and the latter in them. They "belong" to it as "its own," they are *its* background of consciousness, *its* field of freedom.

Yet notwithstanding these peculiar complications with all "its" experiences, the experiencing Ego is still nothing that might be taken *for itself* and made into an object of inquiry on its *own* account. Apart from its "ways of being related" or "ways of behaving," it is completely empty of essential components, it has no content that could be unravelled, it is in and for itself indescribable: pure Ego and nothing further.

There is therefore occasion for a variety of important descriptions, bearing on the special forms or modes of experience of the experiencing Ego, *as* actually enjoyed. In this connexion we continue to distinguish—despite the necessary interrelationship—the *experience itself* from the *pure Ego* of the experiencing process; and again: the *pure subjective phase of the way of experiencing* from the remaining, *Ego-diverted content of the experience*, so to speak. Thus there is a certain, extraordinarily important two-sidedness in the essential nature of the sphere of experience, concerning which we can also say that in experiences we must distinguish be-

tween a *subjectively and an objectively oriented aspect*: a form
of expression which should not indeed be misunderstood, as
though we taught that the "object" of knowledge might, in
this respect, be something analogous to the pure Ego. However, the form of expression will justify itself. And we hasten to
add that to this two-sidedness there corresponds, to a considerable extent at any rate, a division (though not any real separation) between two different sections of our inquiry, the one
bearing on pure subjectivity, the other on that which belongs
to the "constitution" of objectivity *as referred to* its subjective
source. We shall have much to say about the "intentional
reference" of experiences (and of the pure experiencing Ego)
to objects, and about many different factors of experience and
"intentional correlates" which are connected therewith. But in
comprehensive inquiries topics such as these can be studied
and described analytically or synthetically, without concerning
ourselves more deeply with the pure Ego and the ways in
which it plays its special part. We cannot indeed help touching
on it frequently in so far as it comes in as a necessary adjunct.

The meditations which we propose to follow up still further
in this Section of our work will bear, by preference, on the
objectively oriented aspect, as that which first presents itself
when we forsake the natural standpoint. The problems indicated in the introductory paragraphs of this Section already
refer to this aspect of objectivity.

## 81. Phenomenological Time and the Time-Consciousness

Phenomenological time as a general peculiarity of all experiences demands a separate discussion.

We must carefully note the difference between this *phenomenological time,* this unitary form of all experiences within
a *single* stream of experience (that of *one* pure Ego), and
"*objective*," i.e., "*cosmic*" time.

Through the phenomenological reduction consciousness has
forfeited not only its apperceptive "attachment" (in truth only
an image) to material reality and its relations in space, merely
secondary though these be, but also its setting in cosmical
time. The same time, which belongs essentially to experience
as such with the modes in which its intrinsic content is presented—and derived from these the modally determined now,
before and after, simultaneity, succession and so forth—is not
to be measured by any state of the sun, by any clock, by any
physical means, and generally cannot be measured at all.

Cosmical time stands to phenomenological time in a relation somewhat analogous to that in which the "extensity" [*spread*] that belongs to the immanent *essence* of a concrete sensory content (a visual "extensity," maybe, in the field of visual sensory data) stands to objective spatial "extension," to that, namely, of the appearing physical object, manifesting itself in visual "perspectives" through the medium of the sensory data in terms of which it appears. Just as it would be absurd to bring under the same generic essence a sensory phase such as colour or spread, and the phase of the thing proper which manifests itself perspectively through it, such as the colour and extension which belong to it as a thing, so is it also in respect of the phenomenologically and the cosmically temporal. In experience and its different phases, transcendent time can exhibit itself in the form of appearance; but in principle there is no sense either here or elsewhere in setting up between the exhibiting and the exhibited a figurative similarity which *qua* similarity would presuppose oneness of essence.

Moreover it should not be said, for instance, that the way in which cosmic time declares itself within the phenomenological is precisely the same as that in which other real essential phases of the world present themselves phenomenologically. The self-presentation of colours and other sensory qualities of the thing (in corresponding sensory data of the different fields of sense) is, to be sure, something essentially different, and different again the self-manifestation through perspectives of the spatial shapes of things in forms of outspreadedness within the sensory data. But in the cases here cited there is everywhere community of nature.

For the rest, as will be apparent in the light of the studies to be undertaken later, Time is the name for a completely *self-contained sphere of problems* and one of exceptional difficulty. It will be seen that in a certain sense our previous exposition has been silent, and necessarily so, concerning a whole dimension, so as to maintain free of confusion what first becomes transparent from the phenomenological standpoint alone, and quite apart from the new dimension constitutes a self-contained field of investigation. The transcendental "Absolute" which we have laid bare through the reductions is in truth not ultimate; it is something which in a certain profound and wholly unique sense constitutes itself, and has its primeval source in what is ultimately and truly absolute.

Fortunately we can leave the enigmas of the time-consciousness[11] in our preliminary analyses without imperilling their rigour. In the statements that follow we do no more than touch the fringe of the question.

The essential property which the term "temporality" expresses in relation to experiences generally indicates not only something that belongs in a general way to every single experience, but *a necessary form binding experiences with experiences*. Every real experience (we ratify this as self-evident on the ground of the clear intuition of an experiential reality) is necessarily one that endures; and with this duration it takes its place within an endless continuum of durations—a concretely *filled* continuum. It necessarily has a temporal purview concretely filled, and stretching away endlessly on all sides. And that at once tells us that it belongs to *one* endless *"stream of experience."* Every single experience can begin and end and therewith bring its duration to an end—for instance, an experience of joy. But the stream of experience cannot begin and end. Every experience, as temporal being, is an experience of its pure Ego. And to this the possibility (which, as we know, is no empty logical possibility) necessarily belongs, that the Ego may direct its pure personal glance to this experience, and grasp it as really being, or as enduring in phenomenological time.

But, again, it belongs to the *essence* of the situation that the Ego *is able* to direct its glance upon *the way in which* the temporal factor is being *given*, and to know self-evidently (as we all in fact do, living over in intuition what is written down for us) that no enduring experience is possible unless it is constituted within a continuous flow of modes of givenness as the unitary factor in the process, or the duration; further, that this mode of givenness *of* the temporal experience is itself in turn an experience, although of a new kind and dimension. The joy, for instance, which begins and ends, and during the interval endures, I can first gaze at as it is in its purity, following all its temporal phases. But I can also pay attention to its mode of declaring iself: to the modus of the actual "Now,"

[11] The labours of the author over this problem, which for long were unavailing, were, so far as their essential purpose was concerned, brought to a conclusion in the year 1905, and their results communicated in University lectures [since published as *Vorlesungen zur Phänomenologie des inneren Zeitbewusstseins*, 1928.—Ed.] at Göttingen.

and to this feature also that with this very "now," and in principle with every "now," a new and continuously new "now" links up in necessary continuity, and that in concert with this every actual now passes into a just vanished, the just vanished once again and continuously so into ever-new just vanishings of the just vanished, and so forth. And similarly for every "now" that has been newly linked on to its predecessor.

The actual *now* is necessarily something punctual and remains so, *a form that persists through continuous change of content*. It is the same with the continuity of the "just vanished"; it is a *continuity of forms* with contents ever new. And it also comes to this: the enduring experience of joy is "consciously" given in a consciousness-continuum of this constant *form:* an impressional phase as the limiting phase of a continuous series of retentions, which, however, are not on the same level but constitute *a continuous succession of intentional relationships*—a continuous chain of retentions of retentions. The form receives a continually fresh content; thus to each impression united with the experience of "now" a new impression, corresponding to an ever-new point of the duration, is continually "annexing itself"; the impression continuously transforms itself into retention, and this continuously into modified retention, and so forth.

To all this must be added continuous changes in an opposite direction: "after" corresponding to "before," a protentional continuum corresponding to the retentional.

## 82. Continuation. The Threefold Limit of Experience, as at Once the Limit of Reflexion upon Experience

But there is still more to be stated. *Every* present moment of experience, even if it be that of the initial phase of an experience freshly developing, has necessarily *a before as a limit*. But on grounds of principle this can be no empty previousness, a mere form without content, mere nonsense. It has necessarily the meaning of a past now which in this form contains a past something, a past *experience*. Every experience in its fresh beginning has necessarily been preceded in time by experiences, the past of experience is continually filled with content. But every present moment of experience has also, and necessarily, *an after as a limit*, and that also is no empty limit; every present moment of experience, be it even the terminal phase of the duration of an experience that is ceasing, passes off into a new "now," and that necessarily filled with content.

To this we can also add the following: necessarily attached to the now-consciousness is the consciousness of the just past, and this consciousness again is itself a now. *No experience can cease without a consciousness of the ceasing and the having ceased,* and that is a now filled with a new content. The stream of experience is an infinite unity, and the *form of the stream* is one that *necessarily envelops all the experiences of a pure Ego*—a form containing a variety of form-systems.

We defer the further elaboration of these insights and the indication of their vast metaphysical consequences to the further treatment held over for future publication.

The general peculiarity of experiences of which we have just been treating, considered as possible data for reflective (immanent) perception, is portion of a still more comprehensive peculiarity which finds expression in this *Law of Essential Being,* that every experience comes not only under the rubric of temporal *succession* is an essentially self-contained organization of experiences, but also under that of *simultaneity.* This means that every *present moment* of experience has about it a fringe of experiences, which also share the primordial now-form, and as such constitute the one *primordial fringe of the pure Ego,* its total primordial *now*-consciousness.

This fringe enters as a unity into the structure of the past modes as well. Every Before, as a modified Now, in regard to each focal experience to which it stands in the relation of a Before, is the centre of infinite extensions, including whatever belongs to the same modified Now, briefly its encircling stretch of "what has simultaneously been." The descriptions previously given should thus be completed by the bringing in of a new dimension, and not until we do this have we the *whole* phenomenological time-field of the pure Ego, which, from any one of "its" experiences as a centre, it can measure throughout according to the *three* dimensions of before, after, and at the same time; or in other words, the *whole, essentially unitary,* rigorously self-contained *stream* of temporal unities of experience.

*One* pure Ego, *one* Stream of experience filled with content along all three dimensions, and in such filling holding essentially together and progressing (*sich fordernder*) through its continuity of content: these are necessary correlates.

### 83. Apprehension of the Unitary Stream of Experience as "Idea"

With this *root-form of consciousness* the following stands in essential relation:

If the glance of the pure Ego, as the Ego reflects and perceptively understands, rests on some experience, there exists the *a priori* possibility of redirecting the glance to other experiences, *so far as* the bearing of this connexion extends. But in principle this *whole* connexion is *never* one that is or can be given through a single pure glance. Notwithstanding, even it is in a *certain*, though in an intrinsically different way intuitively graspable, namely, along the line of *"limitlessness in the progressive development"* of immanent intuitions, from the experience that has been fixated to new experiences within its fringe, and from the fixating of these to that of their experience-fringes, and so forth. When we speak of an *experience-fringe*, we have in mind not only the limits of phenomenological temporality along the lines already indicated, but differences that arise from *new forms* in the mode of presenting the data. Thus an experience that has become the object of a personally directed glance, and so has the modus of the *deliberately* looked at, has its own fringe of experiences that are not deliberately viewed; that which is grasped in a mode of "attention," and grasped with increasing clearness as occasion arises, has a fringe of background inattention showing relative differences of clearness and obscurity, as well as of emphasis and lack of relief. Thence spring eidetic possibilities: the bringing of what is not the object of a personally directed look within the focus of pure mental vision, raising the unemphatic into relief, and making the obscure clear and ever clearer.[12]

Advancing continuously from one apprehension to another, we apprehend in a certain way, I remarked, *the stream of experience as a unity also*. We do not apprehend it like a single experience, but after the fashion of an *Idea in the Kantian sense*. It is nothing set down and asserted at haphazard, but asbolutely and indubitably given, in a correspondingly wide sense of the word "given." This indubitability,

[12] Of the "limit" or "fringe" (*Horizont*) we can therefore speak here in much the same terms as we did in § 35 of a "zone" (*Hof*) and a "background" (*Hintergrund*).

although also grounded in intuition, has a quite different source from that which obtains for the Being of experiences, and is therefore given pure in immanent perception. It is precisely the distinctive feature of an ideation that mentally sees a Kantian "Idea," yet does not in so doing forfeit the transparency of its insight, that the adequate determination of its content, in this instance the stream of consciousness, is unattainable. At the same time we see that there belongs to the stream of experience, and its component factors as such, a series of distinguishable modes of presentation, the systematic study of which must furnish for the future a main task of general phenomenology.

We can also draw from our reflexions the eidetically valid and self-evident proposition, that *no concrete experience* can pass *as independent in the full sense of the term.* Each "stands in need of completion" in respect of some connected whole, which in form and in kind is not something we are free to choose, but are rather bound to accept.

For instance, if we consider any outer perception, shall we say this definite perception of a house taken in its concrete fullness, there then pertains to it as a necessary part of its determination the experience-context; but it is a particular, necessary, and yet *"non-essential"* part of its determination, being such, namely, that changes in it alter nothing in the experience's *own* essential content. *Thus the perception itself changes according as the determination of the context changes,* whereas the lowest specific difference of the genus "perception," its inner uniqueness, can be thought of as remaining identical with itself.

That two perceptions essentially identical in respect of this uniqueness should also be identical in respect of context-determination is in principle impossible, for they would then be individually *one* perception.

At all events, we can see this clearly in the case of two perceptions and of two experiences generally, which belong to *one* stream of experience. Every experience influences the (clear or obscure) setting of further experiences.

Closer inspection would further show that two *streams of experience* (spheres of consciousness for two pure Egos) *cannot be conceived* as having *an essential content that is identically the same;* moreover, as is evident from the foregoing, no *full-determinate* experience of the one could ever belong

to the other; only experiences of identically the same specification can be common to them both (although not common in
the sense of being individually identical), but never two experiences which in addition have absolutely the same "setting."

## 84. Intentionality as the Main Phenomenological Theme

We pass on now to a peculiarity distinctive of experiences,
which we may definitely refer to as the general theme of
"objectively" oriented phenomenology, namely, Intentionality.
It is to this extent an essential peculiarity of the sphere of
experience in general, since all experiences in one way or
another participate in intentionality, though we cannot in
one and the same sense say of *every* experience that it has
intentionality, as we can say for instance of every experience
which enters as object into the focus of possible reflexion—
be it even an abstract phase of experience—that it has a
temporal character. It is intentionality which characterizes
*consciousness* in the pregnant sense of the term, and justifies
us in describing the whole stream of experience as at once a
stream of consciousness and unity of *one* consciousness.

In the preliminary analyses of Essential Being in the Second Section of this work, analyses concerning consciousness
in general, we found it necessary (still before the entrance-
gate to phenomenology as we were, and specifically interested
in winning our way in through the method of reduction) to
work out in advance a series of definite sketches of the most
general kind, treating of intentionality in general, and serving
also to delineate the "act" of the "*cogitato*."[13] We made
use of these, and quite advisedly, at a further stage of our
inquiry, although the original analyses were not as yet carried
out under the express, authoritative guidance of phenomenological reduction. For they concerned the experiences' own
pure essence, and could therefore not be affected by the suspending of the apperceptive viewpoint and existential setting
of psychology. And since our present interest is to discuss
*Intentionality*, adopting the term as *an inclusive title for a
number of pervasive phenomenological structures*, and to outline the group of problems which concern the essential nature
of these structures (so far as this is possible in a general
introduction), let us run over what we have said before, re-

[13] Cf. *supra*, §§ 36–38.

casting it somewhat in sympathy with our present aims, which point in an essentially different direction.

We understood under Intentionality the unique peculiarity of experiences "to be the consciousness *of* something." It was in the explicit *cogito* that we first came across this wonderful property to which all metaphysical enigmas and riddles of the theoretical reason lead us eventually back: perceiving is the perceiving of something, maybe a thing; judging, the judging of a certain matter; valuation, the valuing of a value; wish, the wish for the content wished, and so on. Acting concerns action, doing concerns the deed, loving the beloved, joy the object of joy. In every wakeful *cogito* a "glancing" ray from the pure Ego is directed upon the "object" of the correlate of consciousness for the time being, the thing, the fact, and so forth, and enjoys the typically varied consciousness *of* it. But we learnt from phenomenological reflexion that this orientation of the Ego in presenting, thinking, valuing . . . this *wakeful* intercourse with the correlate-object, this directedness towards it (or indeed away from it, though with the glance upon it all the same), is not discoverable in every experience, whereas intentionality may always be concealed in it. Thus, for instance, it is clear that the objective background, from which the perceived object of the *cogitatio* emerges as the glance of the Ego singles it out, is an *objective* background in a really experienceable sense. That is, whilst we are even now turned towards the pure object in the modus *cogito*, various objects "appear," we are intuitively "aware of" them, they blend into the unity of a single intuition, that of a consciously grasped field of objects. This is a *potential field of perception* in the sense that a special perceiving (an awareness of the type *cogito*) can be directed towards everything that thus appears; but not in the sense that the variations of sensory perspective experienced as present, variations of the visual kind, for instance, spread out in one single visual field, are incapable of being objectively grasped at all until the glance of the Ego is turned towards them, when for the first time they shape themselves into intuitive appearances of objects.

We must further include here experiences that proceed from the background of actual consciousness, such as *"stirrings"* of pleasure, the early shapings of judgment, incipient wishes, and so forth, and from different depths of background-distance, or, as we can also say, of *farness from* or *nearness to the Ego,* since the pure Ego as it lives, wakeful, in the passing thought is the centre of reference. A liking, a wish, a judgment, and so forth, can in a specific sense be *"fulfilled,"* namely, by the Ego, which "takes an active part" in this fulfilling (or as in the "fulfilling" of sorrow actually "suffers"); but such modes of consciousness may already be *"astir,"* and emerge in the "background" without being "fulfilled" in this way. And yet in their own essential nature these nascent actualities (*Inaktualitäten*) are already a "consciousness of something." Accordingly we did not include in the essence of intentionality what belongs specifically to the *cogito,* the "glance-towards," or the Ego's turning-to (an attitude still to be understood and phenomenologically studied in manifold ways);[14] on the contrary, we have taken this *cogitatio* to be a special modality of the general function which we call Intentionality.

### Note on Terminology

In the *Logical Studies* this general function is referred to as "Act-character," and every concrete experience of this character as an "Act." The persistent misunderstandings to which this Act-concept has given rise have compelled me (here as in my lectures for a number of years back) to be more careful in regard to terminology, to delimit terms more closely, and no longer use the expressions "Act" and "intentional experience" as equivalent without proper reservations. The sequel will show that my original act-concept is completely indispensable, but that it is necessary to be constantly allowing for the modal difference between fulfilled and unfulfilled acts.

Where nothing is said to the contrary, and we are simply concerned with acts, the proper and, so to speak, focal acts, the fulfilled acts will be the ones exclusively intended.

Moreover, we may make this quite general remark, that in the beginnings of phenomenology all concepts or terms must in a certain sense remain fluid, always prepared to refine upon their previous meanings in sympathy with the progress made in the analysis of consciousness and the knowledge of new phenomenological stratifications, and to recognize differences in what at first to our best insight appeared an undifferentiated unity. All selected terms have tendencies of meaning

[14] Cf. *supra,* § 37.

due to the connexions in which they are used; they point in the direction of certain relations concerning which it subsequently transpires very often that they have their source in more than *one* essential stratum; with the accompanying conclusion that the terminology must be more effectively limited or otherwise modified. Thus it is not until a very highly developed stage of science has been reached that we can count on terminologies being definitely fixed. It is misleading and radically perverse to apply the formal and external standards of a logic of terminology to scientific work in the first stages of progressive effort, and in their first beginnings to exact from them terminologies of the kind first used to render stable the concluding results of great scientific developments. For the beginning every expression is good, and in particular every suitably chosen image which has the quality of directing our glance to a phenomenological result that can be clearly grasped. Clearness is quite compatible with a certain margin of indeterminacy. The further determining or clarifying is precisely the further task, as, on the other hand, the inner analysis which proceeds by comparisons or by varying the context: the splitting up into components or strata. Those who, not content with what is offered to them as intuitively manifest, demand "definitions" of the type provided by the "exact" sciences, or believe that with phenomenological concepts won from the rough analysis of a couple of illustrations and taken as firmly fixed they can think their scientific thought unhampered by intuition, and through such free-lancing further the cause of phenomenology, are still so truly beginners that they have not grasped the essential nature of phenomenology, nor the method of work which it intrinsically demands.

What we have said applies no less to the empirically directed psychological phenomenology in the sense of a description of psychological phenomena, which attaches itself to what is immanently essential.

The concept of intentionality, grasped in the indefinite breadth we have given it, is a concept which at the threshold of phenomenology is quite indispensable as a starting-point and basis. The general meaning which it indicates may, prior to closer study, be ever so vague; it may present itself in ever so great a number of essentially different formations; it may be ever so difficult to set out through clear and rigorous analysis what it strictly is that constitutes the pure essential nature of intentionality, which components of the concrete formations properly contain it, and to which of these it is inwardly foreign—at all events when we recognize experiences as intentional, and say of them that they are the consciousness of something, we are considering them from a definite and highly important point of view. In saying this, it remains for the rest a matter of indifference to us whether the matter at issue is concrete experiences or abstract strata of experience, for such also can show the peculiarity in question.

## 85. Sensile ὕλη, Intentional μορφή

We already intimated above (when we referred to the stream of experience as a unity of consciousness) that intentionality, apart from its puzzling forms and stages, resembled also a universal medium which in the last resort includes within itself all experiences, even those that are not characterized as intentional. At the level of discussion to which we have so far been limited, which stops short of descending into the obscure depths of the ultimate consciousness which constitutes the whole scheme of temporal experience, and accepts experiences rather as they present themselves in immanent reflexion as unitary temporal processes, we must, however, distinguish on grounds of principle:

1. All the experiences which in the *Logical Studies* were designated "primary contents"; [15]
2. The experience or phases of experience, which are the bearers of the specific quality of intentionality.

To the former belong, in the highest order of generality, unitary *"sensile"* experiences, *"sensory contents"* such as the data of colour, touch, sound, and the like, which we shall no longer confuse with the appearing phases of things, their colour-quality, their roughness, and so forth, which rather "exhibit" themselves experientially through their means. Similarly as regards sensile impressions of pleasure, pain, tickling, etc., and also the sensile phases of the sphere of "impulses." Such concrete data of experience are to be found as components in concrete experiences of a more comprehensive kind which as wholes are intentional, and indeed so that over those sensile phases lies as it were an "animating,"

---

[15] Vol. III, Sixth Study, § 58, p. 180. The concept of a primary content may, for the rest, be found already in my *Philosophie der Arithmetik*, 1891, pp. 72 ff.

*meaning-bestowing* stratum (or one with which the bestowal of meaning is essentially bound up), a stratum through whose agency, out of the *sensile-element, which contains in itself nothing intentional,* the concrete intentional experience takes form and shape.

Whether such sensile experiences in the stream of experience are of necessity everywhere the subjects of some kind of "animating synthesis" which informs them (including whatever features this in its turn demands and renders possible), or, as we also say, whether they ever take their part in *intentional functions,* does not here call for decision. On the other hand, let us also leave undecided in the first instance whether the characters that enter essentially into the setting up of intentionality can find concrete embodiment apart from any sensile foundation.

At all events, in the whole phenomenological domain (in the whole, that is, within the stage of constituted temporality, as must always be borne in mind), this remarkable duality and unity of *sensile* ὕλη (*hyle*—matter), and *intentional* μορφή (*morphe*—form, shape) plays a dominant part. In point of fact these concepts of matter and form thrust themselves right to the front when we bring before the mind clear intuitions of one kind or another or clearly shaped valuations, services, volitions, and so forth. Intentional experiences are there as unities through the bestowal of meaning (used here in a very wide sense). Sensory data offer themselves as material for intentional informings or bestowals of meaning at different levels, for such, that is, as are elementally plain and original, as we have yet to consider more closely. How well all this suits the case is shown from still another side by the theory of "correlates." And as regards the possibilities left open above, they might also be entitled *formless materials* and *immaterial forms.*

We add the following in the interest of terminology: The expression "primary content" no longer seems to us sufficiently significant. On the other hand, the expression "sensory experience" cannot be used to indicate this concept, since our customary reference to sensory perceptions, sensory intuitions generally, sensory delight, and the like, stand in the way, whereby not merely hyletic but also intentional experiences are described as sensory; clearly, too, the expressions "mere" or "pure" sensory experiences do not improve matters owing to the new ambiguities to which they are now exposed.

Moreover, the term "sensory" has in addition its own ambiguities, which cleave to it in the phenomenological reduction. Apart from the double meaning exemplified in the contrast between "sense-bestowing" and "sensory," an ambiguity which, perplexing as it occasionally is, can scarcely be avoided any longer, the following consideration must be noted: sensibility in a narrow sense indicates the phenomenological residuum of that which is mediated through the "senses" in normal outer perception. Subsequent to the reduction an essential affinity between the relevant "sensory" data of the external intuitions reveals itself, and there corresponds to it a unique generic essence, a fundamental concept of phenomenology. Moreover, in a further and essentially unitary sense, sensibility includes the sensory feelings and impulses also which have their own generic unity, and on the other hand an essential affinity of a general kind as well with those sensibilities in the narrower sense of the term, and all this apart from the common basis of meaning which the *functional* concept of ὕλη expresses in addition. Both together compelled the old transfer of the originally narrower meaning of sensibility to the spheres of sentiment and will, to the intentional experiences, namely, in which sensory data of the spheres here indicated play their part as functioning "materials." Thus, at all events, we need a new term which shall express the whole group through its unity of function and its contrast with the formative characters, and we choose for this purpose the expression *hyletic* or *material data,* also plainly and simply *materials (Stoffe).* Where it concerns us to awaken a memory for the old and, in their way, unavoidable expressions, we say *sensile (sensuelle),* or even *sensory (sinnliche) materials.*

What forms the materials into intentional experiences and brings in the specific element of intentionality is the same as that which gives its specific meaning to our use of the term "consciousness," in accordance with which consciousness points *eo ipso* to something of which it is the consciousness. Now since the terms "phases of consciousness," "awareness," and all similar constructions, and the term "intentional phases" likewise have become quite unusable through manifold equivocations, which will clearly reveal themselves in the following pages, we introduce the term *noetic phase,* or, more briefly put, *noesis.* These noeses constitute the specifications of *"Nous"* (mind, spirit) *in the widest sense* of the term, which in all the actual forms of life which belong to it brings us back to *cogitationes,* and then to intentional experiences generally, and therewith includes all that (and essentially only that) which is the *eidetic presupposition of the idea of a Norm.* At the same time it is not an unwelcome feature that the word "Nous" in one of its outstanding meanings recalls the word ["meaning" or] *"sense"* (*Sinn*), although the "bestowal of sense" which takes place in the noetic phases includes a variety of things, and only as its basis a "sense-bestowal" as adjunct to the pregnant concept of sense (*Sinn*).

There would also be good grounds for referring to this noetic side of experiences as the *psychical.* For through the reference to ψυχή (soul) and psychical, the scrutiny of the philosophical psychologists was directed with a certain show of preference to that which the term intentionality conveys, whereas the sensory phases were referred to the body and its sensory activities. This old tendency finds its most modern impress in Brentano's separation of the "psychical" from "physical phenomena." It is particularly important, since it blazed a fresh trail for the development of phenomenology— although Brentano himself remained a stranger to phenomenological ground, and although with his sharp distinction he failed to reach that for which he sought, namely, the separation of the empirical domains of psychology and the physical natural sciences. What concerns us here particularly in this matter is only the following: Brentano did not indeed find the concept of the material phase, and for this reason, that he took no account of the separation on grounds of principle of the "physical phenomena" as material phases (sensory data) from the "physical phenomena" as the objective phases that appear in the noetic apprehension of the former (the colour of a thing, the shape of a thing, and the like); but as against this he marked off on the other side the concept of the "psychical phenomenon" in one of his two clear-cut determinations, through the unique feature of Intentionality. Thereby he brought the "psychical" in that outstanding sense of the term which did not supersede the historical meaning of the word, but gave it a certain new accentuation within the field of view of our own time.

But as against the use of the word "psychical" as the equivalent of intentionality, there is this to urge, that it would be without any doubt unsuitable to indicate the psychical in this sense, and the psychical in the sense of the psychological (of that which is the distinctive object of psychology) in the same way. Moreover, in respect of this latter concept there is a disagreeable ambiguity which has its source in the familiar drift towards a "psychology without a soul." And there is further this closely connected point, that under the heading of the psychical, especially of the actually psychical in opposition to the corresponding "psychical dispositions," we think preferably of the experiences in the unity of the empirically given stream of experience. But it is now unavoidable to designate as also psychical, or as objects of psychology, the real bearers of this psychical quality, the animal natures or their "souls" and their psychically real properties. The "psychology without a soul" confuses, we would venture to think, the suspension of the soul-entity in the sense of this or that nebulous metaphysic of the soul with the suspension of the soul generally, that is, of the psychic reality given empirically as a fact, whose *subjective states* are the experiences. This reality is in no sense the mere stream of experience, bound to the body and empirically regulated in certain ways, for which rulings the dispositions-concepts are mere indicators. However that may be, the existing ambiguities, and above all the circumstance that the concepts of the psychical which at present prevail do not embody the specific mark of intentionality, render the word useless for our purposes.

We therefore hold to the word *noetic,* and say:

*The stream of phenomenological being has a twofold bed: a material and a noetic.*

Phenomenological reflexions and analyses which specially concern the material may be called *hyletically phenomenological,* as, on the other side, those that relate to noetic phases may be referred to as *noetically phenomenological.* The incomparably more important and fruitful analyses belong to the noetical side.

## 86. The Functional Problems

Yet the greatest problems of all are the *functional problems,* or those of the *"constituting of the objective field of consciousness."* They concern the way in which, for instance, in respect of Nature, noeses, animating the material, and weaving themselves into unitary manifolds, into continuous syntheses, so bring into being the consciousness of something, that in and through it the objective unity of the field of objects

(*Gegenständlichkeit*) may permit of being consistently "declared," "shown forth," and "rationally" determined.

*"Function" in this sense* (totally different from the mathematical) is something wholly unique, grounded in the pure *essence* of the noeses. Consciousness is just consciousness "of" something; it is its essential nature to conceal "meaning" within itself, the quintessence of "soul," so to speak, of "mind," of "reason." Consciousness is not a title-name for "psychical complexes," for fused "contents," for "bundles," or streams of "sensations." which, meaningless in themselves, could give forth no "meaning," however compactly massed they might be; but it is "consciousness" through and through, the source of all reason and unreason, all right and wrong, all reality and illusion, all value and disvalue, all deed and misdeed. Thus consciousness is *toto cælo* different from that which sensationalism takes it solely to be, from what in point of fact is in itself meaningless, and irrational material, though capable, to be sure, of rationalization. What this rationalization amounts to is a point which we shall soon learn better to understand.

The viewpoint of Function is the central viewpoint of phenomenology; the inquiries which radiate from it cover the whole phenomenological sphere pretty nearly, and in the last resort *all* phenomenological analyses enter its service in one form or another as integral portions or as lower grades. Instead of the single experiences being analysed and compared, described and classified, all treatment of detail is governed by the "teleological" view of its function in making "synthetic unity" possible. The treatment considers from the standpoint of the essence the various conscious groupings which in the experiences themselves, in their dispensings of meaning, in their noeses generally, are as it were *prefigured*, needing to be just drawn out from them; so, for instance, in the sphere of experience (*Erfahrung*) and empirical thinking, functional method turns to the many forms of conscious continua and of broken connexions of conscious experiences inwardly united through a common thread of meaning, through the unifying consciousness *of* one and the same objective, appearing now in this guise, now in that, presenting itself intuitively or determined by thought. It seeks to inquire how this self-same factor, how objective unities of every kind, immanent, but not real, are "known" or "supposed," how the identity of these suppositions is constituted by conscious formations of very different type yet of essentially prescribed structure, and how these formations should be described on strict methodical lines. And it seeks further to inquire how corresponding to the double heading "reason" and "unreason," the unity of the objective content of every objective region and category can and must in accordance with conscious insight be "brought out" or "broken up" respectively: shaped in the forms of reflective consciousness, "more closely" or "otherwise" determined, or else cast completely aside as "vain illusion." In connexion herewith come all the distinctions which bear the familiar yet enigmatic titles: "reality" and "illusion," "true" reality, "illusory reality," "true" values, "illusory" or disvalues, and so forth, here followed by the attempt to clear them up on phenomenological lines.

We must therefore study in the most general and comprehensive way how objective unities of every region and category "are consciously constituted." We must show systematically how all the connexions of our real and possible consciousness of them as essential possibilities are prescribed by their *essential* nature: the simple or secondary intuitions intentionally related to them, the thought-formations of lower and higher levels, the confused or the clear, the expressed or the not-expressed, the pre-scientific and the scientific, up to the loftiest formations of strict theoretical science. All fundamental types of possible consciousness, and the modifications, fusions, syntheses which essentially belong to them, must be made plain to sight and systematically studied in their eidetic generality and phenomenological purity; how through their *own* essence they prefigure all possibilities (and impossibilites) of being, how the existing object following essential laws that are absolutely fixed is the correlate of conscious connexions of a quite definite essential context, just as conversely the being of systems thus articulated is equivalent to the existing object, and this always with reference to all regions of Being and all grades of generality right down to the concreteness of Being itself.

From its pure eidetic standpoint which "suspends" the transcendent in every shape and form, phenomenology comes inevitably on its own ground of pure consciousness to this whole system of *problems which are transcendental in the specific sense,* and *for this reason* it merits the title of

*Transcendental Phenomenology*. On its own ground it must come to the point, not of treating experiences as so much dead material, as "systems of content," which simply are, but mean nothing, intend nothing, with their elements and ordered constructions, their classes and sub-classes; but rather of mastering its *own intrinsically peculiar group of problems* which present experiences as *intentional,* and that *purely through its eidetic essence* as "*consciousness-of.*"

Naturally *pure hyletics* finds its proper place in subordination to the phenomenology of the transcendental consciousness. Moreover, it has the character of a self-contained discipline, and as such has a value in itself; but on the other hand, and from the functional viewpoint, it wins significance from the fact that it furnishes a woof that can enter into the intentional tissue, material that can enter into intentional formations. Not only in point of difficulty, but also in regard to the relative rank of the problems to be considered, from the standpoint of the idea of an absolute knowledge, it stands clearly below noetic and functional phenomenology (two aspects, moreover, which in strictness should not be separated).

We proceed now to develop the subject more fully in the following chapters.

## Note

Stumpf, in his important Berlin Academy Essays,[16] uses the word "function" in the connexion "psychical function" in opposition to that which he calls "appearance." The distinction is intended as a psychological one, and as such fits in with the opposition we have set up (and applied in a psychological sense only) between "acts" and "primary contents." It should be noted that the terms in question bear a completely different meaning in our expositions from that which the distinguished scientist has given them. With superficial readers of the writings on both sides it has already frequently happened that they have confused Stumpf's concept of phenomenology (as doctrine of "appearances") with my own. Stumpf's phenomenology would correspond to what we set

[16] C. Stumpf, "Erscheinungen und psychische Funktionen" (pp. ff.) and "Zur Einteilung der Wissenschaften," both published in he *Abh. d. Kgl. Preuss. Akademie d. Wissensch.* for the year 906.

out above under the title hyletic, only that our exposition, from the standpoint of method, is essentially conditioned by the enveloping framework of transcendental phenomenology. On the other hand, the idea of hyletics *eo ipso* transfers itself from phenomenology on to the ground of an eidetic psychology, within the limits of which, as we take it, Stumpf's "phenomenology" would find its proper place.

# Chapter 9

## Noesis and Noema

### 87. Introductory Remarks

THE PECULIARITY of intentional experience is in its general form easily indicated; we all understand the expression "consciousness of something," especially in the illustrations which we make for ourselves. The harder is it to grasp the phenomenological peculiarities of the corresponding essence purely and correctly. That this heading marks off a vast field of toilsome discoveries, and eidetic discoveries at that, still seems to the majority of philosophers and psychologists (if we may judge from the literature on the subject) to be something strange even to-day. For no headway is made by simply seeing and saying that every presenting refers to a presented, every judgment to something judged, and so forth; nor indeed if in addition one points to Logic, Epistemology, and Ethics, with their numerous self-evidences, and *indicates* these as belonging to the essential nature of intentionality. That is also a very simple way of claiming that the phenomenological doctrine of the essence is something primitively old, a new name for the old Logic and such disciplines as may need to be ranked with it. For until we have grasped the transcendental standpoint in its uniqueness, and really appropriated the pure phenomenological ground, though we may indeed use the word phenomenology, we have not got the thing itself. Moreover, the mere shifting of the standpoint, the mere effecting of the phenomenological reduction, does not suffice to bring such a thing as phenomenology out of pure logic. For how far logical, and similarly pure ontological, pure ethical, or any other such *a priori* propositions which one may cite in this connexion, express what is really phenomenological, and to what phenomenological strata they may in any given context belong, this is in no sense obvious at first sight. On the contrary, there lie concealed here the most difficult problems of all, the meaning of which is naturally hidden from all those who have not as yet any inkling of the basic distinctions upon which all the others depend. As a matter of fact (if I may venture a judgment based on my own experience), it is a long and thorny way that leads from the insights of pure logic, from those of the theory of meaning, from ontological and noetical insights, and likewise from the current normative and psychological theory of knowledge, to the apprehension of immanent-psychological and then phenomenological data, and lastly to all the essential connexions which make the transcendental relations intelligible *a priori*. Similar considerations apply, wheresoever we fix our effort on the attempt to find a way through from objective insights to the phenomenological that essentially belong to them.

Thus "consciousness of something" is at one and the same time very obvious and highly obscure. The false tracks into which our first reflexions lead us, as we thread the maze, easily generate a scepticism which denies the inconvenient problem in all its bearings. Not a few shut themselves out altogether from the start because they cannot bring themselves to grasp intentional experience, the experience of perception, for instance, in company with its own proper essence as such. They do not succeed because they cannot replace the practice of living in perception, their attention turned towards the perceived object both in observation and in theoretical inquiry, by that of directing their glance upon the perceiving itself, or upon the *way* in which the perceived object with its distinguishing features is presented, and of taking that which presents itself in the immanent analysis of the essence just as it actually does present itself. If the right standpoint has been won and entrenched through practice, if above all there has been acquired the courage to follow up the clear essential data with an entire absence of all prejudice, and indifference to all current and borrowed theories, firm results follow forthwith, the same for all who adopt the same position. There follow as well-established possibilities the power of passing on to others what one has seen oneself, or testing the descriptions of others, sifting out intrusive phrases void of meaning they have slipped in unnoticed, and of exposing and eliminating errors which here too are possible, as they are in every sphere in which validity counts for something, by a further appeal to intuition. But now to the matters themselves!

## 88. Real (*Reelle*) and Intentional Factors of Experience. The Noema

If, as has been our custom in the present meditations generally, we look out for distinctions of a very general kind, such as can be grasped at once on the very threshold of phenomenology, so to speak, and are determinative for all further methodical advance, we at once stumble across what, in respect of intentionality, is a quite fundamental distinction, namely, that between the *proper components* of the intentional experiences, and their *intentional correlates*, or the components of them. In the preliminary eidetic inquiries of the Second Section of this work we have already touched on this distinction.[1] It helped us, in the transition from the natural standpoint to the phenomenological, to make clear the uniqueness of the phenomenological sphere. But that within this sphere itself, within the framework of the transcendental reduction, it should acquire a radical importance conditioning the entire problematics of phenomenology—this could not at that time be suspected. Thus on the one hand we have to distinguish the parts and phases which we find through a *real (reelle) analysis* of the experience in which we treat the experience as an object like any other, and question concerning its parts or the dependent phases which build it up on real (*reell*) lines. But on the other hand the intentional experience is the consciousness of something, and is so in the form its essence prescribes: as memory, for instance, or as judgment, or as will, and so forth: and so we can ask what can be said on essential lines concerning this "of something."

Every intentional experience, thanks to its noetic phase, is noetic, it is its essential nature to harbour in itself a "meaning" of some sort, it may be many meanings, and on the ground of this gift of meaning, and in harmony therewith, to develop further phases which through it become themselves "meaningful." Such noetic phases include, for instance, the directing of the glance of the pure Ego upon the object "intended" by it in virtue of its gift of meaning, upon that which "it has in its mind as something meant"; further, the apprehension of this object, the steady grasp of it whilst the

[1] Cf. § 41.

glance has shifted to other objects which have entered within the circle of "conjecture"; likewise the effects of bringing out, relating, apprehending synoptically, and taking up the various attitudes of belief, presumption, valuation, and so forth. All this may be discovered in the relevant experiences, however differently constituted they may be, and however variable in themselves. Now truly as this illustrative series of phases points to real (*reele*) components of the experiences, it also points, through the rubric "meaning," to components that are *not real*.

Corresponding at all points to the manifold data of the real (*reellen*) noetic content, there is a variety of data displayable in really pure (*wirklich reiner*) intuition, and in a correlative "*noematic content*," or briefly "*noema*"—terms which we shall henceforth be continually using.

Perception, for instance, has its noema, and at the base of this its perceptual meaning,[2] that is, the *perceived as such.* Similarly, the recollection, when it occurs, has as its own its *remembered as such* precisely as it is "meant" and "consciously known" in it; so again judging has as its own the *judged as such,* pleasure the pleasing as such, and so forth. We must everywhere take the noematic correlate, which (in a very extended meaning of the term) is here referred to as "meaning" (*Sinn*) precisely as it lies "immanent" in the experience of perception, of judgment, of liking, and so forth, i.e., *if we question in pure form this experience itself,* as we find it there presented to us.

We can make our meaning here fully clear through the help of an illustrative analysis (which we propose to carry out in the light of pure intuition).

Let us suppose that we are looking with pleasure in a garden at a blossoming apple-tree, at the fresh young green of the lawn, and so forth. The perception and the pleasure that accompanies it is obviously not that which at the same time is perceived and gives pleasure. From the natural standpoint the apple-tree is something that exists in the transcendent

---

[2] Cf. *Logical Studies,* Vol. II[1], the first study, § 14, p. 50, on "meaning that fulfils" (on this point see the Sixth Study, § 55, p. 169, on "the meaning of perception"); further, for what follows see the Fifth Study, § 20 f., on the "material" of an act; likewise the Sixth Study, §§ 25–29.

reality of space, and the perception as well as the pleasure a psychical state which we enjoy as real human beings. Between the one and the other real being (*Realen*), the real man or the real perception on the one hand, and the real apple-tree on the other, there subsist real relations. Now in such conditions of experience, and in certain cases it may be that the perception is a "mere hallucination," and that the perceived, this apple-tree that stands before us, does not exist in the "real" objective world. The objective relation which was previously thought of as really subsisting is now disturbed. Nothing remains but the perception; there is nothing *real* out there to which it relates.

Let us now pass over to the phenomenological standpoint. The transcendent world enters its "bracket"; in respect of its real being we use the disconnecting ἐποχή (*epokhe*—abstention). We now ask what there is to discover, on essential lines, in the nexus of noetic experiences of perception and pleasure-valuation. Together with the whole physical and psychical world the real subsistence of the objective relation between perception and perceived is suspended; and yet a relation between perception and perceived (as likewise between the pleasure and that which pleases) is obviously left over, a relation which in its essential nature comes before us in "pure immanence," purely, that is, on the ground of the phenomenologically reduced experience of perception and pleasure, as it fits into the transcendental stream of experience. This is the very situation we are now concerned with, the pure phenomenological situation. It may be that phenomenology has also something to say concerning hallucinations, illusions, and deceptive perceptions generally, and it has perhaps a great deal to say about them; but it is evident that here, in the part they play in the natural setting, they fall away before the phenomenological suspension. Here in regard to the perception, and also to any arbitrarily continued nexus of such perceptions (e.g., if we were to observe the blossoming tree *ambulando*), we have no such question to put as whether anything corresponds to it in "the" real world. This posited (*thetische*) reality, if our judgment is to be the measure of it, is simply not there for us. And yet everything remains, so to speak, as of old. Even the phenomenologically reduced perceptual experiences is a perception *of* "this apple-tree in bloom, in this garden, and so forth," and likewise the reduced pleasure, a pleasure in what is thus perceived. The tree has not forfeited the least shade of content from all the phases, qualities, characters *with which it appeared in this perception, and "in" this pleasure proved "beautiful," "charming," and the like.*

From our phenomenological standpoint we can and must put the question of essence: *What is the "perceived as such"? What essential phases does it harbour in itself in its capacity as noema?* We win the reply to our question as we wait, in pure surrender, on what is essentially *given.* We can then describe "that which appears as such" faithfully and in the light of perfect self-evidence. As just one other expression for this we have, "the describing of perception in its noematic aspect."

## 89. Noematic Statements and Statements Concerning Reality. The Noema in the Psychological Sphere

It is clear that all *these* descriptive statements, though very similar in sound to statements concerning reality, have undergone a *radical* modification of meaning; just as the described itself, though it figures as "the same exactly," is still something radically other than it was, in virtue, so to speak, of an inverting change of signature. "In" the reduced perception (in the phenomenologically pure experience) we find, as belonging to its essence indissolubly, the perceived as such, and under such titles as "material thing," "plant," "tree," "blossoming," and so forth. The *inverted commas* are clearly significant; they express that change of signature, the corresponding radical modification of the meaning of the words. The *tree plain and simple,* the thing in nature, is as different as it can be from this *perceived tree as such,* which as perceptual meaning belongs to the perception, and that inseparably. The tree plain and simple can burn away, resolve itself into its chemical elements, and so forth. But the meaning—the meaning of *this* perception, something that belongs necessarily to its essence —cannot burn away; it has no chemical elements, no forces, no real properties.

Whatever in purely immanent and reduced form is peculiar to the experience, and cannot be thought away from it, as it is in itself, and in its eidetic setting passes *eo ipso* into the Eidos, is separated from all Nature and physics, and not less from all psychology by veritable abysses; and even this image, being naturalistic, is not strong enough to indicate the difference.

The perceptual meaning belongs of course *also* to the phenomenologically unreduced perception (to the perception in its psychological sense). Thus we can here clearly see at once how the phenomenological reduction can fulfil for the psychologist the methodically useful function of fixing the noematic meaning in sharp distinction from the object pure and simple, and of recognizing it as belonging inseparably to the psychological essence of the intentional experience, which would then be apprehended as real.

On both sides, whether the standpoint be psychological or phenomenological, we must assiduously see to it that the "perceived" as meaning includes nothing (thus nothing should be ascribed to it on the ground of "indirect information") that does not "really appear" in that which in the given case is the perceptual manifestation of the appearing reality, and precisely in the mode, the way of presentation in which we are aware of it in the actual perception. *A unique kind of reflexion* may on every occasion detect this meaning, as it is immanent in perception, and it is only to that which is apprehended in it that the phenomenological judgment has to adjust itself and give faithful expression.

## 90. The "Noematic Meaning" and the Distinction between "Immanent" and "Real (*Wirklichen*) Objects"

Like perception, *every* intentional experience—and this is indeed the fundamental mark of all intentionality—has its "intentional object," i.e., its objective meaning. Or to repeat the same in other words: To have a meaning, or to have something "in mind," is the cardinal feature of all consciousness, that on account of which it is not only experience generally but meaningful, "noetic."

In the example we took and analysed, that which stood out as its "meaning" or "sense," does not of course exhaust the full noema; correspondingly the noetic side of intentional experience does not consist exclusively of the strict "sense-giving" phase to which "sense" or "meaning" specifically belongs as correlate. We shall presently show that the full noema consists in a nexus of noematic phases, and that the specific sense-phase supplies only a kind of necessary *nucleatic layer* in which further phases are essentially grounded, which for that reason, no doubt, though with an enlargement of the term's meaning, we should designate sense-phases.

But let us at first stand fast by the only clear conclusion we have reached. Intentional experience, so we showed, is undoubtedly so organized that, given a suitable viewpoint, a "sense" can be extracted from it. The situation which defines this meaning for us, the circumstance, namely, that the non-existence (or the being persuaded of the non-existence) of the presented or ideally constructed object in its plain and simple sense cannot steal the presented object as such from the relevant presentation (and so from the existing intentional experience generally), that a distinction must therefore be drawn between them, could not remain concealed. The difference, striking as it is, could not escape the impress of literary speech. As a matter of fact, the scholastic distinction between *"mental,"* *"intentional,"* or *"immanent"* object on the one hand, and *"real"* object on the other, points back to it. Meanwhile, the step from a first apprehension of a distinction affecting the nature of consciousness, to its right, phenomenologically pure fixation and correct valuation, is an immense step forward, and precisely this step, which for a consistent and fruitful phenomenology is the decisive one, was not taken. The decisive factor lies before all in the absolutely faithful description of that which really lies before one in phenomenological purity, and in keeping at a distance all interpretations that transcend the given. In this region appellations already announce interpretations, and often very false ones. Such betray themselves here through such expressions as "mental," "immanent" object, and are at any rate furthered through the expression "intentional" object.

A too easy suggestion lies ready to hand: In experience the intention is given with its intentional object, which as such belongs inseparably to it, thus lives *really* (*reell*) within it. What the experience intends, presents, etc., is and remains with it, whether the corresponding "real object" (*wirkliche Objekt*) exists in reality or not, or has been annihilated in the interval, and so forth.

But if we try in *this* way to separate the real object (in the case of outer perception the perceived thing of nature) from the intentional object, placing the latter as "immanent" to perception within experience as a real factor (*reell*), we are beset by the difficulty that now *two* realities must confront each other, whereas only *one* of these is present and possible. I perceive the thing, the object of nature, the tree there in the garden; that and nothing else is the real object of the perceiving "intention." A second immanent tree, or even an "inner image" of the real tree that stands out there before me, is nowise given, and to suppose such a thing by way of assumption leads only to absurdity. The copy as a real (*reelles*) element in psychologically-real perception would again be a reality (*ein Reales*) that *functioned* for another as image. But it could do this only through a representational form of consciousness in which for the first time something appeared—giving us a first intentionality—and this in its turn as an "image-object" functioned consciously for another such object, wherewith a second intentionality based on the first would be necessary. But it is no less evident that each one of these ways of being conscious already calls for the distinction between immanent and real object, and thus contains in itself the very problem that was to have been solved through the construction. Over and above this the construction in the case of perception is subject to the objection which we discussed in an earlier context;[3] to charge the perception of the physical with representative functions means substituting for it an image-consciousness which from the descriptive viewpoint is constituted in an essentially different way. Still the main point lies here, that in ascribing a representative function to perception, and consequently to every intentional experience, we unavoidably bring in an endless regress (as can be seen at once from our own criticism).

In the face of errors such as these, we must abide by what is given in pure experience, and place it within its frame of clearness just as it comes into our hands. The "real" object is then to be "bracketed." Let us consider what this means: starting as men in our natural setting, the real object is the thing out there. We see it, we face it, we have turned our eyes towards it and fixed them upon it, and as we find it there in space over against us, so we describe it and make our statements concerning it. In the matter of values we likewise

[3] Cf. *supra*, § 43.

take up an attitude; this that we see facing us in space pleases us or determines us to action; what there presents itself we lay hold of, work it up, and so forth. If we now carry out the phenomenological reduction, every transcendent setting, that above all which is bound up with perception, receives its suspending bracket, which envelops all the derivative acts, every perceptual judgment with the valuations grounded in it, and eventually the judgment of value, and so forth. What it comes to is this: we suffer all these perceptions, judgments, and so forth, but only on condition that they be regarded and described as the essentialities which they are in themselves; if anything in them or in relation to them is presented as self-evident, that we establish and fortify. But we allow no judgment that makes any use of the affirmation that posits a "real" thing or "transcendent" nature as a whole, or "co-operates" in setting up these positions. As *phenomenologists* we avoid all such affirmations. But if we "do not place ourselves on their ground," do not "co-operate with them," we do not for that reason cast them away. They are there still, and belong essentially to the phenomenon as a very part of it. Rather, we contemplate them ourselves; instead of working with them, we make them into objects; and we take the thesis of perception and its components also as constituent portions of the phenomenon.

So then we ask generally, keeping to the clear meaning of these suspensions, what is it "lies" self-evidently before us in the whole "reduced" phenomenon? Now in perception there lies also this, that it has its noematic meaning, its "perceived as such," "this tree blossoming out there in space"—understood as under the inverted commas—that in fact which belongs to the essence of the phenomenologically reduced perception—in short, its *correlate*. To speak in an image: The "bracketing" which perception has undergone prevents any judgment being passed on the perceived reality (i.e., any judgment that has its ground in the unmodified perception, and therefore accepts its thesis as its own). But it does not hinder any judgment to the effect that perception is the consciousness *of* a real world (provided the thesis thereof is not set in action), and it does not hinder any description of this perceptually appearing "real world as such" with the special modes in which we are consciously aware of this reality as appearing, e.g., simply as perceived, merely "one-sided," in this or that orientation, and so forth. We must now see to it with scrupulous minuteness that we do not put into the experience anything which is not really included in the essence, and that we "lay it in" precisely in the way in which it already "lies" in the essence itself.

## 91. Extension to the Farthest Reaches of Intentionality

What has hitherto been more fully discussed with reference to perception really holds good of *all types of intentional experience*. In memory, after reduction, we find the remembered as such; in expectation, the expected as such; in imaginative fancy, the fancied as such.

"In" each of these experiences there "dwells" a noematic meaning, and however closely self-related, indeed, so far as a central nucleus is concerned, essentially self-same, the latter remains in different experiences, it differs in kind none the less when the experiences differ in kind; the common ground here is at least differently featured, and necessarily so. The object considered may be in every case a blossoming tree, and in every case this tree may so appear that the faithful description of that which appears as such necessarily uses identical expressions. Yet the noematic correlates are for this very reason essentially different for perception, fancy, imaginative presentation, memory, and so forth. At one time that which appears is characterized as "corporeal reality," at another as fiction, then again as recollection brought before the mind, and so forth.

These are characters which we *find* as inseparable features *of* the perceived, fancied, remembered, etc., as such; *of the meaning of perception, the meaning of fancy, the meaning of memory*, and as *necessarily belonging to these in correlation with the respective types of noetic experiences*.

Thus, where our interest lies in describing the intentional correlatés faithfully and completely, we must never collect such data in a haphazard way, but group together characters that conform to certain essential laws, and fix their import with conceptual strictness.

We observe from this that within the *complete* noema (as we had in fact previously declared) we must separate out *as essentially different* certain *strata* which group themselves about a *central "nucleus,"* the sheer *"objective meaning,"* that which in our examples was something that could be everywhere described in purely identical objective terms, because in the specifically different though parallel experiences there could be an identical element. We see at the same time, if we again set aside the brackets suspending the theses, that running parallel with and corresponding to the different concepts of meaning, different concepts of *unmodified objectivities* must be distinguishable, of which the "object *simpliciter,"* namely, the identical element which is at one time perceived, a second time directly represented, and a third time exhibited in figured form in a picture, and so forth, indicates only *one* central concept. Meanwhile, as a mere preliminary, let this indication suffice.

We now glance round within the sphere of consciousness, taking a somewhat wider sweep, and, by turning to the main ways of being conscious, seek to get to know the noetic-noematic structures. As we follow up the real indications, we are at the same time winning direct assurance step by step of the *thoroughgoing* validity of the fundamental correlation between noesis and noema.

## 92. The Transformations of Attention in Regard both to Noesis and Noema

In our preliminary chapters we have already spoken more than once of a species of remarkable transformations of consciousness which cut across all other kinds of intentional occurrences, and constitute therefore a quite general structure of consciousness *sui generis*. We spoke metaphorically of a "mental glance" or "glancing ray" of the pure Ego, of its turnings towards and away. We brought the phenomena belonging to this context under a unity and into completely clear and distinct relief. Wherever the topic of "Attention" is concerned, they play the chief part without any phenomenological separation from other phenomena, and when mixed with these they are referred to as modes of attention. We on our side wish to retain the word attention, and in addition to speak of *attentional transformations,* but exclusively with reference to such as *we ourselves* have distinctly separated out, inclusive of the groups of interconnected phenomenal transformations to be more fully described in the sequel.

Our concern here is with a series of transformations possible *idealiter*, which already presuppose a noetic nucleus and certain characterizing phases of a different order which necessarily belong to it, transformations which do not of themselves work any change in the noematic effects which belong to this noesis, and yet exhibit modifications of the *whole* experience on its noetic as well as on its noematic side. The glancing ray of the pure Ego passes now through this, now through that noetic layer, or (as in the case, for instance, of memories) right through this or that intercalated stratum, sometimes directly, sometimes as reflected. Within the total given field of potential noeses or of noetic objects, we glance now at some whole, say the tree which is perceptually present, now at this or that part and phase of the same; then again at a thing standing close by, or at some complex organization and process. Suddenly we direct our glance towards some object of recollection which chances to occur to us. Our glance, instead of passing through the noeses of perception, which in a continuous and unitary way, though variously articulated, constitute for us the steadily appearing world of things, goes through a noesis of remembrance into a world of memory, moves about in the latter, wandering here and there, passes on to memories of other levels, or into worlds of fancy, and so forth.

For the sake of simplicity let us remain in *one* intentional stratum, that of the world of perception, which in simple certainty is just out there. Let us fix in idea and in respect of its noematic content some thing of which we are perceptively aware or some occurrence connected with it, just as we fix in its full immanent essence the whole concrete consciousness of the thing, or the occurrence in the corresponding section of phenomenological duration. Then the fixing also of the beam of attention in its own *appointed* circuit belongs to this idea. For the beam also is a phase of experience. It is then evident that modes of alteration of the fixed experience are possible which we indicate by the rubric "alterations in the distribution of attention and its modes." It is clear that the *noematic* factor of the experience here remains the same in so far as can now everywhere be said: Let the same objective reality be characterized always as corporeally existent, presenting itself in the same modes of appearance, the same orientations and manifesting characters. We may be made aware, moreover, of this or of that part of its content through the same modes of indeterminate intimation and unintuitional co-representation. We draw out certain parallel noematic elements and compare them, and the alteration we will suppose consists *merely* in this, that in one case of comparison this objective phase has the "preference," and in the other that; or that one and the same phase is at one time "primarily noted," at another noted only in a secondary way, or only "just noted" along with something else, if it is not indeed "completely unnoticed," although still continuing to appear. There are indeed different modes which belong specifically to attention as such. The group of *actuality-modes* separates itself off therewith from the mode of non-actuality; from that which we plainly call Inattention, the mode, so to speak, of the dead enjoyment of consciousness (*Bewussthabens*).

On the other hand it is clear that these modifications are not only those of the experience itself in its noetic aspect, but that they also cover its *noemata*, that, on the noematic side—without prejudice to the identical noematic nucleus—they exhibit a new class of characterizations. It is usual to compare attention with an illuminating light. What is attended to, in the specific sense, subsists in the more or less bright cone of light, but can also shelve off into the half-shadow and into the full darkness. Little as the image suffices to inculcate with the proper distinctness all modes calling for phenomenological fixing, it is still significant as pointing to changes in that which appears as such. This alteration of the lighting does not alter that which appears in and through the *meaning* it conveys, but brightness and darkness modify its mode of appearing; they are to be found in the directing of the glance to the noematic object and there described.

It is obvious, moreover, that the modifications in the noema are not of such a kind that they simply annex to something that remains the same throughout some merely external addition; on the contrary, our concern is with the necessary modes of the way in which the self-identical presents itself.

Looked at more closely, however, the situation at this point is not that the *whole* noematic content, characterized as occasion has determined in terms of the modus "attentional" (its *attentional kernel,* so to speak), must be upheld as a constant over against all arbitrary modifications of the attention. On the contrary, looking at the matter from the noetic side, we observe that certain noeses, whether of necessity or following fixed possibilities of their nature, are conditioned by modes of attention, and in particular through positive attention in the quite special sense of the term. All "enacted acts," the "actual positions assumed," e.g., that of "acting out" a decision which ends a doubt, that of setting aside, of the positing of a subject, and the consequent adjustment of the predicate, making a valuation and that "for the sake of another," the attitude in a choice, and so forth—all this presupposes positive attention to that to which I take up a position. but it leaves unaltered the fact that this function of the wandering glance, which alternately enlarges and restricts its mental span, signifies *a special dimension of correlative modifications noetic and noematic,* of which the systematic study on essential lines is one of the fundamental tasks of general phenomenology.

The attentional formations, in their modes of actuality, possess in a very special sense the *character of subjectivity,* and all the functions which are modalized through these modes, or presuppose them, as species their genera, win thereby this character also. The attending ray gives itself out as radiating from the Pure Ego and as terminating in the objective, being directed towards it or deviating from it. The shaft of attention is not separate from the Ego, but itself is and remains personal. The "object" is referred to, is the goal aimed at, set in relation to the Ego only (and by the Ego itself), but is not itself "subjective." An attitude which bears the personal ray in itself is thereby an act of the Ego itself; the Ego does or suffers, is free or conditioned. The Ego, so we also expressed, "lives" in such acts. This life does not signify the being of any "contents" of any kind in a stream of contents, but a variety of describable ways in which the pure Ego in certain intentional experiences, which have the general mode of the *cogito,* lives therein as the "free essence" which it is. The expression "as free essence" refers, however, to nothing more than such modes of life as the going freely out of oneself, or going back upon oneself, spontanteous doing, experiencing something from objects, suffering, and so forth. What goes on in the stream of experience outside the personal ray or *cogito* is characterized in an essentially different way; it lies outside the Ego's actuality, and yet, as has already been indicated in a previous context, it still belongs to the Ego in so far as it is the field of potentiality for the Ego's free acts.

So much towards the general characterization of the noetic-noematic positions, which must be treated with systematic thoroughness in the phenomenology of Attention.[4]

## 93. Transition to the Noetic-Noematic Structures of the Higher Sphere of Consciousness

In the series of discussions which immediately follow we wish to consider certain structures of the "higher" sphere of consciousness, in which *a number of noeses are built up, the one above the other, within the unity of a concrete experience,* and in sympathy wherewith the *noematic correlates* likewise are consolidated. For the law of the essence universally attested runs to this effect: *No noetic phase without a noematic phase that belongs specifically to it.*

Even in the case of the higher-level noeses—taking these in their concrete completeness—there figures on the noematic side a central nucleus which at first obtrudes itself prominently, the "meant (*vermeinte*) objectivity as such," the objectivity in inverted commas as the phenomenological reduction demands. There also this central noema must be understood in precisely that modified objective state in which it is in fact a noema, the consciously known as such. Subsequently it will be seen that here too this *new kind of objectivity*—for the objective taken in its modified form itself becomes again under the rubric "meaning," as, for instance, in our own scientific inquiries concerning it, an objective, although raised here to a unique dignity—has its ways of being given, its "characters," its mani-

---

[4] "Attention" is a main theme of modern psychology, and in no other direction does its dominant sensationalistic character come out more strikingly than in the handling of this theme, for not even the essential connexion between attention and intentionality —this fundamental fact that attention generally is nothing else than a fundamental kind of *intentional* modification—has ever, to my knowledge, been pointed out before. Since the appearance of the *Logical Studies* (cf. there the discussions under Vol. II, Second Study, § 22 f., pp. 160–166, and the Fifth Study, § 19, p. 405) there has indeed been an occasional reference, covering a few words, to a connexion between attention and "the consciousness of an object"; but apart from a few exceptions (I recall the writings of Th. Lipps and A. Pfänder), the reference has been made in a way which reveals a failure to understand that the question at issue concerns the radical and first *beginning* of the theory of attention, and that the further inquiry must be conducted within the framework of intentionality, and indeed not at once as an empirical, but *first of all* as an eidetic study.

fold modes, under which it is known in the complete noema of the noetic experience in question, or of some relevant branch of such experience. Here too, of course, all distinctions in the noema must find their corresponding parallel in the unmodified objectivity.

It is then further the business of closer phenomenological study to establish, in the case of the noemata of the changing specifications of a stable species (e.g., perception), what is essentially determined according to law through the species itself, and what through the differentiating specifications. But the determination is thoroughgoing; in the sphere of the essence there are no accidents; everything is connected through essential relations, and in particular through noesis and noema.

## 94. Noesis and Noema in the Sphere of the Judgment

From this sphere of derivative (*fundierter*) essences let us take as an instance the *predicative judgment*. The noema of the *judging process,* i.e., of the concrete experience of the judgment, is the "judged content of the judgment as such," but that is nothing other, at any rate so far as its chief nucleus is concerned, than what we ordinarily refer to simply as *the judgment.*

In order to grasp the full noema, we must seize it as we find it in reality (*wirklich*), in the full noematic concreteness in which we are aware of it in concrete judging. The judged content of the judgment it not to be confused with the matter judged about. When the judging process shapes itself on the basis of a perceiving or other plainly "positing" act of presenting, the noema of the presenting act becomes part of the judging act taken in its full concreteness (just as the presenting nocsis also becomes a constitutive part of the essence of the concrete noesis of the judgment), and within it takes on certain forms. The presented (as such) receives the form of the apophantic subject or object, and the like. For the sake of simplicity we neglect here for the moment the higher layer of verbal "expression." These "objects concerning which," in particular the objects we utilize for the subjects of our judgments, are the matters judged *about.* The whole that is formed out of them, *the whole somewhat* (*Was*) *as content of the judgment qua content,* and in addition taken exactly with the *concrete featuring,* and in the *form of presentation* in which we are "aware of" it in experience, constitutes the *full noematic correlate,* the *"meaning"* (in its *widest* sense) of the judgment as experienced. To put it more pregnantly, it is the "meaning as we have it through the way in which it is given to us," so far as this way of being given is traceable in it as a feature.

But the phenomenological reduction must not here be overlooked, demanding of us, if we wish to obtain the pure noema of our judgment as experienced, that we "bracket" the delivery of the judgment. If we do this, we find facing us in their phenomenological purity the full concrete essence of the judgment as experienced, or, as we now express it, *the noesis of the judgment, apprehended concretely as essence,* and the *noema of the judgment* which belongs to the noesis, and is necessarily one with it, i.e., the *"delivered judgment" as Eidos,* and here again in phenomenological purity.

The psychologizers everywhere will take offence at this; they are already disinclined to distinguish between judging as an empirical experience and judgment as "Idea," as essence. This distinction, so far as we are concerned, needs no further defence. But even one who accepts it is challenged. For he is required to recognize that this one distinction nowise suffices, and that there are many ideas we need to determine which in the essential nature of a judgment's intentionality fall on two different sides. It must above all be recognized that here, as with all intentional experiences, the two sides, noesis and noema, must be distinguished on principle.

We would note here, by way of criticism, that the concepts of *"intentional"* and *"epistemological" essence*[5] which were established in the *Logical Studies* are indeed correctly stated, but are still capable of a second interpretation so far as they can be understood in principle, as expressing not only noetic but also noematic essences, and that the noetic rendering as carried out there in a one-sided way is precisely not the one needed for the notion of the concept of the pure logical judgment (the concept which pure logic in the sense of pure mathesis demands, in contrast with the noetic concept of judgment in the noetics of normative logic). The distinction between the *passing of a judgment* and the *judgment as passed,* which has already established itself in ordinary speech, can point in the right direction, namely, that as *correlatively* related to the judgment as experienced we have *the* judgment *simpliciter* as noema.

[5] Cf. *Logical Studies,* Vol. II, Fifth Study, § 21, pp. 417 ff.

This then is what we should understand as the "judgment," or the *proposition* in the *pure logical sense,* only that pure logic is not interested in the noema in all its bearings, but only in so far as it is thought of as exclusively determined through a *narrower* essence; and in fixing this more closely the attempted distinction of the *Logical Studies* considered above has shown the way. If, taking our start from a definite judgment as we experience it, we seek for the full noema, we must, as above stated, take "the" judgment precisely as we are aware of it in this experience, whereas in the proceedings of formal logic the identity of "the" judgment has a far wider range. A self-evident judgment "S is P" and "the same" blind judgment are noematically different, but share an identical kernel of meaning which for the treatment of formal logic is alone determinative. The difference is similar to the one already touched on between the noema of a perception and that of a parallel presentation which has before it the same object with precisely the same determining content, characterized in the same way (as "certainly being," "doubtfully being," and the like). The kinds of act are different, and there still remains wide scope in other ways for phenomenological differences, but the noematic content is the same. And we add this further point that corresponding to the idea of the judgment as we have just characterized it, an idea which constitutes the fundamental concept of formal logic (that discipline of the *mathesis universalis* which relates to predicative meanings), there stands over against it as its correlative the noetical idea: "the judgment" in a second sense of that term, understood namely as judging in general, in eidetic generality determined purely by considerations of form. It is the fundamental concept of the formal noetical legitimacy-doctrine (*Rechtslehre*) of the judging process.[6]

[6] As concerns Bolzano's concept of the "judgment in itself," the "proposition in itself," we can see from the expositions of the *Wissenschaftslehre* that Bolzano never clearly realized the proper meaning of his pioneering conception. Bolzano never saw that we have here *two* intrinsically possible interpretations, both of which might be referred to as a "judgment in itself": the specific character of the judgment as we experience it (the *noetic* idea) and the *noematic* idea correlative to it. His descriptions and annotations are ambiguous. As an objectively biased mathematician, he had in view the noematic concept, although an occasional turn of phrase (cf. *id.,* I, p. 85, the quotation from Mehmel's *Denklehre*

All that we have just been saying holds also for other forms of noetic knowledge, and naturally, to take a special instance, for all such forms as are essentially related to judgments as predicative certainties, and with the corresponding suggestions, presumptions, doubts, and rejections. The agreement, moreover, can reach so far that in the noema we have a content of meaning everywhere the same, provided only with different "characterizations." *The same* "S is P" as *noematic nucleus* can be the "*content*" of a certainty, a suggested possibility, a presumption, etc. In the noema the "S is P" does not stand alone; in proportion as it is thought out as content it is something dependent; we are aware of it as occasion offers in changing characterizations which cannot dispense with the full noema; we are aware of it in the character of the "certain" or the "possible," of the "probable," the "null," etc., characters to which in their entirety the modifying inverted commas belong, and as correlates are specifically related to the noetic experiential phases of holding something as possible, as probable, as null and void, etc.

Herewith, as we see at once, two fundamental concepts of the "*content of a judgment*" differentiate, and similarly for the content of a supposition, the content of a question, and so forth. Logicians not infrequently so speak of the content of a judgment that (even without making the necessary distinction) either the noetic or the noematico-logical concept "judgment" —the two concepts we have previously characterized—is, as

---

cited with approval) appears to speak against this. He had it in view precisely as the arithmetician has number in view—his mind adjusted to numerical operations, but not to phenomenological problems concerning the relation between number and the consciousness of number. Phenomenology here, in the logical sphere as elsewhere, was something *completely foreign* to the great logician. That must be clear to anyone who has really studied Bolzano's *Wissenschaftslehre*, now, alas! so hard to obtain, and is moreover not inclined to confuse every working out of fundamental eidetic concepts—for phenomenology the naïve way of doing things—with one that is phenomenological. Were one to do this, then in the interests of consistency one would have to refer to every creative worker with mathematical concepts, a G. Cantor, shall we say, in respect of his brilliant conception of the groundwork of the group-theory, as a phenomenologist, and similarly also, in the last resort, the unknown creator of the groundwork of geometry in the grey days of yore.

the case may be, clearly indicated. Running parallel with these, and of course without ever clashing with them or with one another, we have the corresponding pairs of concepts in suppositions, questions, doubts, etc. But *here* we have a second meaning of the content of a judgment, as a "content" which the judgment can have identically *in common* with a presumption (or a presuming), with a question (or a questioning), and other act-noemata or act-noeses.

## 95. The Analogous Distinctions in the Spheres of Sentiment and Will

Analogous considerations apply then, as one may easily convince oneself, to the spheres of sentiment and will, to experiences of pleasure and displeasure, to valuation in every sense, to wish, decision, and practical action; these are all experiences which contain many and often varied intentional stratifications, noetic, and also, correlatively, noematic.

Moreover, the stratifications, speaking generally, are so ordered that the uppermost strata of the phenomenon as a whole can fall away without the residue ceasing to be a concrete complete intentional experience, and that conversely also a concrete experience can receive a new noetic stratum of an inclusive character; as when, for instance, "valuation" as a dependent phase stratifies itself over and above a concrete presentation, or conversely falls away again.

When a perceiving, fancying, judging, and the like lies in this way at the base of a stratum of valuation that completely covers it, we have, in *the stratified block as a whole,* called, after its highest stratum a concrete experience of valuation, *different noemata, different meanings.* The perceived as such belongs as meaning specifically to the perceiving, but enters into the meaning of the concrete valuing, providing this meaning with a basis. In correspondence herewith we must respectively distinguish the objects, things, qualities, the various matters which stand out in the valuing as having value, and the corresponding noemata of the presentations, judgments, and the like upon which the consciousness of value rests; and on the other hand the objects and the contents of value themselves, or the noematic modifications corresponding to these, and then generally the complete noemata (*Noemen*) which belong to the concrete consciousness of value.

Let us first note, by way of explanation, that in the interests of greater distinctness we are well advised (here and in other analogous cases) to introduce certain distinguishing relative terms, in order the better to keep separate worthful object and object of worth, worthful fact and fact of worth, worthful quality and quality of worth (which is itself once again equivocal). We speak of some mere "fact" as being worthful, having a worth-character, *worthfulness;* and in another direction of *concrete worth* itself, or *worthfulness in the object (Wertobjektität:* objectified value). We speak in similarly parallel terms of the *plain substantive meaning or position of affairs,* and of the *plain meaning or position in terms of worth* [or value], where the valuing involves a consciousness of the substantive meaning as a supporting foundation. Worthfulness in the object includes the object itself; it brings in *worthfulness* as a new objective stratum. The meaning, in terms of value holds in itself its own plain substantive meaning, the attribute of value, that of positivity likewise, and, over and above this, worthfulness.

We must further distinguish between worthfulness in the object plain and simple and *worthfulness in the object under the inverted commas,* which lies in the *noema.* Just as the perceived as such stands over against the preceiving in a sense which excludes any question concerning the genuineness of the perceived, so stands the valued as such in relation to the valuing, and again so that the Being of the Value (of the valued thing *and* its true being of value) remains unconsidered. For the apprehension of the noema all affirmations bearing on actuality must be suspended. And again, we must observe well that the *full* "meaning" of the valuing includes its What (*das Was daesselben*), together with the whole fullness of realization which marks our awareness of it in the experience of value under consideration; and that worthfulness in the object [objectified value], under the inverted commas, is not, without further question, the full noema.

The distinctions we have drawn may be carried through on similar lines in the *sphere of the Will.*

On the one side we have the *resolution* we make at any moment, with all the experiences which demand it as a basis, which indeed it includes within itself when taken in its concreteness. A variety of noetic phases belongs to it. Volitional affirmations presuppose affirmations in regard to values, positings of things, and the like. On the other hand, we find the *resolve* as a unique type of absorption into the object belonging specifically to the domain of will, and obviously grounded in other and similar noematic absorptions into the object. If then as phenomenologists we suspend all our real affirmations, the phenomenon of will, as a phenomenologically pure intentional experience, retains its *"willed as such,"* as *a noema proper to the will;* the "will's meaning" (*Willensmeinung*), and in the precise way in which it subsists as "meaning" in this will (on its full essentiality), and with whatever is willed "in all its ramifications."

We spoke just now of "meaning" (*Meinung*). This word thrusts itself upon us here at every point, as do also the words "sense" (*Sinn*) and "conceptual significance" (*Bedeutung*). To the function of meaning (*Meinen*), or intending (*Vermeinen*), corresponds then the *meaning as meant* (*Meinung*); to the *signifying* in conceptual thought (*Bedeuten*) corresponds the conceptual *signification* (*Bedeutung*). Meanwhile these terms all together are through associational transfer infected with so many ambiguities—and not least also with such as arise through gliding over into these correlative strata, which it should be the function of science to keep strictly and systematically apart—that one cannot be too careful in dealing with them. Our treatment of these topics is at present free to move on essential lines within the universe of "intentional experience" taken in its widest scope. But the use of the term "meaning" (*Meinen*), as above, is normally restricted within narrower areas, which function, however, at the same time as substrata of the phenomena of the wider field of inquiry. The word can therefore be used as a logical term (and the remark applies to its sister-expressions also) only within these narrower areas. For the generalities of our treatment our newly coined terms, and the illustrative analyses that accompany our introduction of them, will certainly serve us more effectively.

## 96. Transition to the Chapters that Follow. Concluding Remarks

We have bestowed such great care, though on general lines, on working out the difference between noesis and noema (where by noesis we understand the concrete completely intentional experience as modified through the stressing of its noetic components) because the grasp and mastery of it is of the greatest consequence for phenomenology, is indeed quite decisive for its proper grounding. At first sight it appears to be concerning itself with what is obvious: every consciousness is the consciousness of something, and the modes of consciousness are very different. But on nearer approach we realized the great difficulties. They concern the understanding of the mode of being of the noema, the way in which it should "lie" in experience, and become "consciously known" there. They concern quite particularly the clear-cut separation between the real (*reeller*) portions of one's whole experience which belong to the experiencing itself, and those which belong to the noema, and should be attributed to it as its own. Also the correct articulation in parallel structures of noesis and noema, which follows on the separation between them, gives trouble enough. Even if we have already happily completed certain main sections of the line of separation in question, taking presentations and judgments as our material, since it is here that the occasion for the cleavage first offers itself, and logic has already carried out in this field valuable, though not even remotely sufficient, preliminary work, it needs toil and self-discipline in respect of the parallel distinctions concerning "acts of the heart," not only to postulate and assert them, but really to bring them out clearly as they are actually given to us.

Involved as we are in meditations whose function it is to lead the thought upwards, it cannot be our task here to carry out portions of phenomenology in a systematic way. None the less our aims demand that we should penetrate more deeply into these matters than hitherto, and draft the beginnings of such inquiries. This is necessary in order to clarify the noetico-noematic structures, so far at least as to make their significance understood as regards the study of the problems and methods of phenomenology. A living picture of the fruitfulness of phenomenology, of the greatness of its problems, of its way of proceeding, can be won only when domain after domain has been actually tramped and the problem-vistas it possesses opened up for all to see. But each such domain will be really covered, and come home to our feeling as a firm ground for work only through carrying out phenomenological fencings and clearings, whereby also the meaning of the problems here to be solved can first be made intelligible. The analyses and indications of further problems which are still to follow should conform strictly to this conception, as indeed the previous one in part have already done. And though the novice may think that the material handled is complicated, we are really limiting ourselves to quite restricted fields of work. We show a natural preference indeed for what lies relatively close to the approaches into phenomenology, and for what is an unconditional preliminary to following up the main tracks that run through the domain systematically from end to end. It is *all* of it hard. It demands toilsome concentration on the data of the specifically phenomenological intuition of essential being. There is no "royal road" in phenomenology any more than in philosophy. There is only the *one* road, and its own essential nature must point it out.

---

In closing we would add the following remark. We have expounded phenomenology as a science *in its beginnings*. Only the future can teach us how many of the results of the analyses we have here attempted are destined to last. Much of what we have described must certainly, *sub specie æterni*, be otherwise described. But we should and must strive in each step we take to describe faithfully what we really see from our own point of view and after the most earnest consideration. Our procedure is that of a scientific traveller in an unknown part of the world who carefully describes what he finds on the trackless ways he takes—ways that will not always be the shortest. He should be full of the sure consciousness of bringing to expression what in relation to time and circumstance is the thing that *must* be said, which, because it faithfully expresses what has been seen, preserves its value always—even when further research calls for new descriptions with manifold improvements. In a similar temper we wish in what further lies before us to be loyal expounders of phenomenological formations, and for the rest to preserve the habit of inner freedom even in regard to our own descriptions.

# Chapter 10

## Theory of the Noetic-Noematic Structures: Elaboration of the Problems

## 97. The Hyletic and Noetic Phases as Real (*Reelle*). The Noematic as Non-real Phases of Experience

IN THE PREVIOUS CHAPTER, when introducing the distinction between noetic and noematic, we made use of the expression *real* (*reeller*) and *intentional analysis*. Let that be our point of connexion with what follows. A phenomenologically pure experience has its real (*reellen*) components. For simplicity's sake let us limit ourselves to noetic experiences of the lowest level, and therefore to those in which the intentionality is not complicated by a number of noetical layers superposed one on the other of the kind we noted in the case of acts of thought, feeling, and will.

By way of illustration let us take a sensory perception, the simple perception of a tree, which we get as soon as we glance out into the garden, when, in a unitary act of consciousness, we see this tree there, at one moment appearing to be motionless, then stirred by the wind, and presenting also modes of appearance which differ greatly in so far as during the course of our continued observation we shift our spatial position in regard to it, stepping to the window maybe, or changing the position of head or eyes, and at the same time perhaps relaxing the mechanism of accommodation or tightening it up. In this way the unity of *a single* perception can include in itself a great variety of modifications, which we, as observing from the natural standpoint, attribute now to the real object as *its* changes, now to a real (*realen*) and positive (*wirklichen*) relationship to our real (*realen*) psychophysical subjectivity, and lastly to this subjectivity itself. But we have now to describe what remains over as phenomenological residuum, when we effect the reduction to "pure immanence," and *what in that case should count as a real (reelles) integral part of the pure experience*, and what should not be so regarded. And we have then to be fully clear about this, that whilst the "perceived tree as such," or, alternately, the full noema which is not affected by the suspending of the reality (*Wirklichkeit*) of the tree itself and the whole real world, does indeed belong to the essence of the perceptual experience in itself, on the other hand this *noema*, with its "tree" in inverted commas, is *as little contained realiter* (*reell*) *in the perception as is the tree of the real natural order* (*Wirklichkeit*).

What do we really (*reell*) find in the perception as pure experience, included within it as the parts, pieces, and indivisible phases of a whole, are included in that same whole? We have already drawn attention to such genuine, real (*reellen*) constituents on a previous occasion under the titles of *material* and *noetic* constituents. Let us now contrast them with the noematic factors.

The colour of the tree-trunk, as we are aware of it under the conditions of pure perception, is precisely "the same" as that which before the phenomenological reduction we (as "natural" human beings, at any rate, prior to any admixture of physical knowledge) took to be that of the real (*wirklichen*) tree. Now *this* colour, as bracketed, belongs to the noema. But it does not belong to the perceptual experience as a real (*reelles*) integral part of it, although we also find in the experience "a colour-like something," namely, the "sensory colour," the hyletic phase of the concrete experience in which the noematic or "objective" colour "manifests itself *in varying perspectives*."

But one and the same noematic colour of which we are thus aware *as* self-same, in itself unchanged within the unity of a continuously changing perceptual consciousness, runs through its perspective variations in a continuous variety of sensory colours. We see a tree unchanged in colour—its own colour as a tree—whilst the positions of the eyes, the relative orientations, change in many respects, the glance wanders ceaselessly over the trunk and branches, whilst we step nearer at the same time, and thus in different ways excite the flow of perceptual experience. Let us now start sensory reflexion, reflexion upon the perspective variations: we apprehend these as self-evident data, and are also able, shifting the standpoint and the direction of attention, to place them with full evidential certainty in relation with the corresponding objective phases, recognize them as corresponding, and thereby also see without further difficulty that the perspective colour-variations, for instance, which belong to some fixed colour of a thing are related to that fixed colour as continuous "variety" is related to "unity."

We even win, on carrying out the phenomenological reduction, the general essential insight that the object "tree" in a perception *in general* can *only then* appear as *objectively* determined just as it appears in the perception, when the hyletic phases (or, should a continuous series of perceptions be in question, the continuous hyletic transformations) are just these and no others. Thus it follows that every alteration of the hyletic content of the perception, when it does not cancel the perceptual consciousness outright, must at least have the result that that which was appearing becomes objectively "another," either in itself or in the mode of orientation which marks the manner of its appearing, and so forth.

All considered, it is also quite beyond doubt that "unity" and "variety" here belong to *totally different dimensions*, and so indeed that *every hyletic* element has its place as a *real* (*reelles*) integral part in the concrete experience, whereas that which "exhibits" itself in its variety and "varies perspectively" has its place in the *noema*.

But, as we have previously put it, the material elements are "animated" through noetic phases, they undergo (whilst the Ego is turned not to them, but to the object) "formal shapings" (*Auffassungen*), "gifts of meaning," which we grasp, in reflexion, upon and with the material elements. Whence it immediately follows that not only the hyletic phases (the sensory colours, sounds, etc.), but also the animating apprehensions—or *taking both together*, the *appearing* of the colour, the sound, and every such quality of the object—belong to the "real" (*reellen*) constitution of the experience.

The following holds good generally: perception in itself is the perception of *its* object, and to every component which "objectively" directed description picks out in the object, there corresponds a real (*reelle*) component of the perception; but only so far, be it observed, as the description holds faithfully to the object *just as* it "stands before us" in *this* perception itself. Also we can indicate all these noetic components only by falling back on the noematic object and its phases, and referring, shall we say, to the consciousness, more clearly the perceptual consciousness *of* the trunk of a tree, or of the colour of the trunk, and so forth.

On the other hand, our deliberations showed that the real (*reelle*) experiential unity of hyletic and noetic factors is totally different from that of the factors of the noema "of which we are aware" within that same unity; and again, from the unity which unites all those real elements of experience with that which comes to consciousness in and through them as noema. The "*transcendentally constituted*" product, shaped "on the basis" of the material experiences, and "through" the noetic functions, is indeed something "given," and when we faithfully describe the experience and its noematic object of awareness in pure intuition, something *self-evidently* given; but it belongs to the experience in a completely different sense from that in which the real (*reellen*) and consequently proper constituents of the experience belong to it.

The reference to the phenomenological reduction, and similarly to the pure sphere of experience as "transcendental," depends precisely on our finding in this reduction an absolute sphere of materials and noetic forms, to whose interlacings, nicely articulated *in accord with an immanent essential necessity*, belongs this wonderful conscious possession of something definitely or definably given in such and such a way, standing over against consciousness itself as in principle other, irreal, transcendent; and it rests on the recognition that here is the ultimate source for the only conceivable solution of the deepest problems of knowledge affecting the essential nature, and the possibility of objectively valid knowledge of the transcendent. The "transcendental" reduction practises ἐποχή in respect of reality (*Wirklichkeit*); but to the residue thereby left over belong the noemata with the noematic unity which lies in them themselves, and with these the mode in which what is real (*Reales*) is specifically given in consciousness itself, and our consciousness becomes aware of it. The knowledge that it is here throughout a question of *eidetic*, and therefore unconditionally necessary connexions opens a big field of inquiry, that of the essential relations between the noetic and the noematic, between the experience and the correlate of consciousness. But this last-mentioned title for the essence includes the objectivity of consciousness, as such, and at the same time the noematic forms in which anything is intended or given. Within the sphere from which we have drawn our illustration there first grows up the general assurance that perception does not consist in just holding the object presently before one, but that it belongs (*a priori*) to the proper essence of the perception to have "its" object, and to have it as the unity of a *certain* noematic content (*Bestandes*), which for other perceptions of "the same" object is always something different again, though always essentially prescribed in advance; and that it precisely belongs to the essence of the present object when objectively determined in such and such a way, to be noematic in perceptions of the descriptive type in question, and to be this nowhere else, and so forth.

## 98. Mode of Being of the Noema. Doctrine of Forms for Noeses and for Noemata

To complete the discussion, much still remains to be added. It should be closely noted in the first place that every transition from a phenomenon to the reflexion which analyses it *realiter* (*reell*), or to the function of a quite different kind which analyses its noema, generates new phenomena, and that we should be falling into error if we confused the new phenomena which in a certain sense are transformations of the old with these old ones, and ascribed to the former what is respectively real or noematic in the latter. For instance, we have no intention of saying that the material contents, it might be the perspectively varying colour-contents, are present in the perceptual experience precisely as they are in the analysing experience. There, to consider the one point only, they were contained as real (*reelle*) phases, but they were not perceived therein, not objectively apprehended, as they are in the analysing experience, where they figure as the termini of noetic functions which were not previously present. Although these material contents are further burdened with the functions concerned in their presentation, yet these too have undergone an essential change (though indeed along another dimension). Of this we shall have more to say later. The distinction has obviously an essential bearing on phenomenolgical method.

Having made this remark, let us turn our attention to the following points which concern the special theme of our inquiry. In the first place every experience is so articulated as to leave open the intrinsic possibility of directing the glance upon it and its real (*reellen*) components, and likewise in the contrary direction upon the noema, e.g., the seen tree as such. Now what is given through this latter glance is indeed itself, logically speaking, an object, but one that is wholly *dependent*.

Its *esse* consists exclusively in its "*percipi*," except that the meaning of this statement is about as far removed as it can be from that of Berkeley, since here the *percipi* does not contain the *esse* as a real (*reelles*) constituent.

This is naturally carried over into the eidetic mode of treatment: the Eidos of the noema points to the Eidos of the noetic consciousness; both belong *eidetically* together. The intentional object as such is what it is as the intentional object of a consciousness that is *articulated* thus or thus, and is the consciousness of it.

But despite this dependence, the noema permits of being considered on its own account, of being compared with other noemata, of being studied in respect of its possible transformations, and so forth. We can draft on *general* lines a *pure doctrine of noematic forms* to which there would correspond as its *correlative* a general and not less pure *doctrine of the forms of concrete, noetical experiences*, with their *hyletic* and *specifically noetic* components.

These two doctrines of forms would not of course stand related to each other *in any sense as images in a mirror*, or as though they could pass over the one into the other through a mere change of signature, e.g., through simply substituting for every noema N the "consciousness of N." This indeed already follows from what we have developed above when discussing the interconnexion of unitary qualities in the *noema* of a thing, and its hyletic varieties of perspectival manifestation in the possible perceptions of things.

Now it might seem that the same must hold good in regard to the specifically *noetical* phases also. We could point in particular to those phases which contrive it so that a complex variety of hyletic data, of colour or touch, for instance, assumes the function of varied perspectival shading of one and the same objective thing. Indeed, we need only recall the fact that as regards the material elements themselves in their essential nature the relation to the objective unity is not unambiguously indicated, but rather that the same material nexus may experience a variety of discontinuous formative shapings, the one emerging within the other, and then springing beyond it, and that corresponding to these we are made aware of *different* objectivities. And does not this already make it clear that *in the animating synthesizings* (*Auffassungen*) *themselves* as phases of experience there lie *essential differences*, which differentiate themselves *pari passu* with the shifting appearances whose changes they follow, and in and through whose animation they constitute a "meaning," and differentiate it? We are tempted in consequence to draw this inference: A *parallelism* between noesis and noema does indeed exist, but is such that the formations must be described *on both sides*, and in their essential correspondence to one another. The noematic field is that of the unitary, the noetic that of the "constituting" variety factors (*Mannigfaltigkeiten*). The consciousness that "functionally" unites the varied elements, and at the same time constitutes unity, *never*, as a matter of fact, shows identity where in the noematic correlate we have an identity of the "object" presented. Where, for instance, different sections of an enduring act of perceiving through which the unity of a thing is being constituted show something identical, this one tree that remains unchanged within the meaning of this perceiving process—as we seek to orient ourselves this way and that, viewing it now from in front and now from behind, noting in respect of the visually apprehended qualities at any one spot that they are at first indistinct and vague, then distinct and determinate, and the like—there we become aware of the object subsisting in the noema as self-identical in the strict sense of the word, but in the different sections of its immanent duration our consciousness of it is something non-identical, its parts being merely conjoined, and one only in virtue of its continuity.

Now, whatever the amount of truth in all this, the inferences drawn are not quite correct, and in general the greatest caution is required in dealing with these difficult questions. The parallelisms that we find here—and there are *several* of them which are only too easily confused—are beset with great difficulties that still stand in great need of being cleared up. We must carefully keep in view the difference between concrete noetical experiences, the experiences with their hyletic phases, and the pure noeses, as mere systems of noetic phases. Again, we must keep distinct the full noema, and, as for instance in the case of perception, the "appearing object as such." Let us take this "object," and all its objective "predicates"—the noematic modifications of the predicates of the perceived thing, plainly posited as real in normal perception— then both it and these predicates are indeed unities as opposed to the multiplicities of conscious experiences (concrete noeses) with their constituting function. But they are also unities of *noematic* multiplicities. We recognize this so soon as we draw into the circle of our consideration the noematic characterizations of the noematic "object" (and its "predicates"), which hitherto we have badly neglected. Thus the colour that appears is certainly a unity over against *noetic* multiplicities, of those in particular which have a noetic quality of apprehension. But closer study shows that to all transformations of this character, if not in the "colour itself," which appears continuously, then in its changing "modes of presentation," for instance in its "orientation in regard to me," there correspond *noematic* parallels. Thus generally then do noetic "characterizations" mirror themselves in the noematic.

*How* that should be the case must be (and not only for the phase of perception here favoured for purposes of illustration) a theme of wide-embracing analyses. We shall analyse in turn the different types of consciousness with their varied noetic characters, and study them closely on the basis of the noetic-noematic parallels.

But we must stress this point in advance, that the *parallelism* between the *unity of the noematically "intended" object*, of the object we have in "mind" (*im "Sinne"*), and the *constituting formations of consciousness (ordo et connexio rerum— ordo et connexio idearum) should not be confused with the parallelism between noesis and noema*, understood in particular as a parallelism of noetic and corresponding noematic characters.

It is to this last-mentioned parallelism that the discussions which immediately follow refer.

## 99. The Noematic Nucleus and its Distinguishing Marks in the Sphere of Presentations and Representations

It is thus our task to widen considerably the circle of what has been put forward along the two parallel lines of noetic and noematic states respectively, so as to reach the full noema and the full noesis. What we have hitherto had preferably in view, not indeed without some presentiment of the great problems included therein, is only a central nucleus, and even then lacking a clearly defined edge.

We recall in the first place that "objective meaning," which we discovered on a former page[1] through the comparison of noemata of different *types* of presentations, of perceptions, memories, images, etc., as one to be described in objective

[1] Cf. *supra*, § 91.

terms only, and even in reciprocally identical terms in the favourably selected limiting case when an object, a tree, for instance, remains completely similar in quality and orientation, and is in every respect similarly apprehended whilst being pictured in the varying media of perception, memory, fancy, etc. In contrast with the selfsame "appearing tree as such," with the selfsame "objective" manner (*Wie*) of its appearing, there remain, as we pass from one kind of intuition or other form of presentation to another, the differences in the *mode of givenness*.

We are made aware of this identical element at one time in a "*primordial*" way, at another "*through memory*," then again "*imaginatively*," and so forth. But what are thereby indicated are *characters in the "appearing tree as such,"* discoverable when the glance is directed to the noematic correlate, and not to the experience and its real (*reellen*) states of being. It is *not* "*ways of being conscious*" in the sense of noetic phases that are rendered through these expressions, but *ways in which that of which we are aware itself and as such* presents itself. As features of the "ideal" (*Ideellen*), so to speak, they are themselves "ideal," and not real.

More accurate analysis shows us that the characters mentioned above by way of illustration do not belong to *a single* series.

On the one hand we have the plain *reproductive* modification, the plain representation, and this, remarkably enough, *figures in its own essential nature* as the *modification of something other than itself*. The representation refers us back to perception in its proper phenomenological essence: for instance, my recall of a past event implies, as we have already remarked, the "having perceived it"; thus in a certain way we become aware of the "corresponding" perception (perception of the same core of meaning) in memory, though it is not really contained in it. Memory in its own essential nature is in fact a "modification of" perception. *Correlatively* that which is characterized as past presents itself in itself as "having been present," as a modification therefore of the "present," which in its unmodified form is the "primordial," the "corporeally present" of perception.

On the other hand, the *imaginative* modification belongs to another series of modifications. It represents "in" the form of an "image." But the image can appear in a primordial form, e.g., the "painted" picture (not indeed the picture as a *thing*, of which we say, for instance, that it hangs on the wall)[2] which we grasp in and through perception. But the image can be also something that appears as reproduced, as when we have presentations of imagery in memory or free fancy.

We observe at the same time that the characters of this new series do not only refer us back to those of the first, but also presuppose certain complications: the latter with reference to the distinction between the "picture" and the "copy," a distinction which belongs noematically to the essential nature of consciousness. We also see from this that the noema here holds within itself a *pair* of characters which refer to each other, although they belong to different objects of presentation.

Finally, the *sign-furnishing presentations* with the analogous contrast of *sign* and *thing signified* offer a type of modifying noematic characters (to which there correspond, as everywhere, noetic parallels), which is closely related to the preceding, but none the less new; and here again presentative groups, and as correlates of their peculiar unity as sign-furnishing presentations, *pairs* of noematic characterizations that belong to each other, appear in noematic pairs of objects.

One also observes that just as the "image" in itself, in virtue of its meaning as image, presents itself as the modification *of* something, which apart from this modification would be there in its corporeal or represented selfhood, so it is precisely with the "sign," but likewise in its own way as the modification of something.

## 100. Levels in the Construction of Presentations in Noesis and Noema, in Accordance with Essential Laws

All the types of presentational modification of which we have so far treated are always capable of being reformed on new levels in such a way that the intentionalities in noesis and noema rest on one another *in descending levels*, or rather *dovetail into one another* in a peculiar way.

There are *simple forms of representation*, simple modifications of perceptions. But there are also *representations* at further stages, *at a second or third, or, on essential lines, at any desired level*. Memories "in" memories may serve as an example. Living in memory we bring before us into consciousness a connected experience. We can bring this explic-

[2] For further discussion of this distinction, cf. *infra*, § 111.

itly before us by first reflecting "in" memory (which on its side is a representative modification of a primordial act of reflecting), and then finding the connected experience characterized as "having been lived" under the form of memory. Among the experiences so characterized, whether we reflect upon them or no, memories themselves may now appear, characterized as "memories that have been lived," and we can glance through and past them on to remembered matter of the second level. And then within the connected experiences modified in this secondary way memories can once more appear, and so *idealiter in infinitum.*

A mere change of signature (the precise nature of which we will presently learn to understand) translates all these events into the type of *free fancy*; we have fancies in fancies, and so from one level to another the dovetailing can be indefinitely carried on.

On similar lines we may also have *mixtures*. Every representation essentially implies in its own procedure in respect of the stage just below it representative modifications of *percepts,* which through reflexion which functions so wonderfully in this process of representation are brought to the focus of conscious apprehension; within the unity of the phenomenon of representation we may find the production of memories, expectations. fancies, and so forth, *adjoining* those of perceptions, and the acts of representation involved in the whole process may themselves belong to any one of these types, and all this at different stages.

This also holds good of the complex types, presentation as *copy* and *presentation as sign*. Let us take an example which shows very complicated and yet lightly grasped constructions of perceptions out of perceptions of a higher level. A name on being mentioned reminds us of the Dresden Gallery and of our last visit there: we wander through the rooms, and stand before a picture of Teniers which represents a picture gallery. When we consider that pictures of the latter would in their turn portray pictures which on their part exhibited readable inscriptions and so forth, we can measure what interweaving of presentations, and what links of connexion between the discernible features in the series of pictures, can really be set up. But for the illustrating of *our insight into essences,* in particular of our insight into the ideal possibility of carrying on the dovetailing processes indefinitely, we do not need to consider such complicated cases as these.

## 101. Characteristics of Levels as Such. Different Types of "Reflexions"

In all such constructs of successive levels, which at every joint of their structure contain some modification of the processes of representation, and often as a repetition, it is clear that *noemata of corresponding stages in the construction* are progressively being constituted. In the consciousness that we have of a copying process, at the second stage, an "image" in itself is characterized as a second-level image, or as the image of an image. If we recall how yesterday we recalled a youthful experience, the noema "youthful experience" is in itself characterized as a remembrance of the second level. Hence this general conclusion:

To every noematic level there belongs a *level characteristic* serving as a kind of indicator, the possession of which stamps that which possesses it as belonging to that particular level, whether for the rest this individual be a primary object or lie along this or that line of reflective vision. For *to every level there inwardly belong certain possible reflexions*; for instance, in respect of things remembered at the second level of remembrance there pertain reflexions upon those perceptions of these same things which belong to the same level (and are thus represented on the second level).

Further, every noematic level is a "presentation" *"of"* the data of the levels that follow. But *"presentation"* does not here mean presentational experience, and the word "of" does not express the relation of consciousness to its object. It is, as it were, a *noematic intentionality over against the noetic*. The latter carries the former in itself as a correlate of consciousness, and its intentionality passes in a certain way through the noematic and beyond it.

This becomes clearer as we direct a noticing glance of the Ego upon the objective field of consciousness. The glance penetrates through the noemata of the series of levels, reaching the *object of the last level*, and there holding it steady whilst no longer penetrating through and beyond it. But the glance can wander also *from level to level*, and instead of simply passing through them all, is rather directed with fixating effect upon what is given each in turn, and that either in a *"straightforward"* or in a *reflecting line of vision*.

In the example cited above, the glance can remain at the level of the Dresden Gallery: we go back "in recollection" to Dresden, and walk through the gallery. Again, still immersed in recollection, we can get absorbed in the pictures, and now find ourselves in the picture-world. Then, in a picture-consciousness of the second level we turn to the painted picture of the gallery, and gaze at the pictures painted within it; or our reflexion, passing from level to level, is turned upon the noeses, and so forth.

This variety of the possible directions in which our glance can turn belongs essentially to the manifold of mutually related and reciprocally grounded intentionalities, and wherever we find analogous groundings—and in what follows we shall get to know many more of quite another kind— there arise analogous *possibilities of a change of reflexion*.

It need not be said how greatly these relationships stand in need of penetrating scientific study on essential lines.

## 102. Transition to New Dimensions in Characterization

It is clear that in respect of *all* the peculiar characterizations we have come across in the structurally diversified domain of modification through variations in the form of representation, we *must* distinguish, and on the grounds already alleged, between the noetic and the noematic. The noematic "objects"—the object as copy or the copied object, the object functioning as sign and the significate, *disregarding* their own proper characterizations "copy of," "copied," "sign for," "signified"—are unities of which we have evident awareness in experience, but which yet transcend experience. But if this is so, then characters which stand out *on* them as we consciously apprehend them, and, when we direct our glance upon them, are grasped as *their* unifying features, cannot possibly be regarded as real (*reelle*) *phases of experience*. How the two stand related to each other, that which is a real (*reeller*) constituent of experience, and that in it of which we are aware as non-real, may be a matter presenting the most difficult problems; none the less we must keep the two separate at every point, and just as much indeed in respect of the noematic nucleus, of the "intentional object as such" (taken in its "objective" mode of presentation), which functions as the passing bearer of the noematic "characters," as in respect also of the characters themselves.

But of characters such as these that cleave to the noematic nucleus, there are still other instances of quite different type, and of these the modes of attachment to the nucleus vary widely. They come under *radically different genera*, under radically different *dimensions of characterization*, so to speak. And we would point out from the outset that all characters still to be indicated in this connexion, or that have already been indicated (mere headings for necessary analytico-descriptive studies), *have a universal phenomenological range of application*. And though in our first treatment of them we show a preference for the intentional experiences that have the relatively simplest constitution, for such as can be grouped together under a definite and fundamental concept of *"presentation,"* and furnish the necessary basis for all other intentional experiences, the same *summa genera* and characteristic differences belong also to all these derived (*fundierten*) experiences, and consequently *to all intentional experiences generally*. The situation then is this, that at all times and of necessity we are aware of a noematic nucleus, a "noema of the object" that *must* be characterized somehow, and indeed by differences, alternative and mutually exclusive, selected from *each* genus.

## 103. Characters Distinctive of Being and of Belief

Looking around now for new characters, our attention is first drawn to the fact that interlinked with the groups of characters previously treated, we have characters which are clearly of a wholly different type, namely, the *characters of Being*. As noetic characters, correlatively related to modes of Being—as *"doxic"* or *"belief characters"*—we may cite as closely linked with intuitable presentations the perceptual belief present as a real (*reell*) factor in normal perception, and functioning therein as a "sense of reality," and, more closely still, perceptual assurance or its equivalent; to it corresponds in the appearing "object" as noematic correlate the ontical character *"real"* (*wirklich*). The same noetic or noematic character is shown in the "certainty" which may accompany all repeated representation, in *"sure"* recollection of every kind, whether in respect to what has been, to what now is, or to what will be in the future (as in anticipative expectation). Such are *"thetic"* acts, acts that *"posit"* Being. In making use of this expression, however, we must bear in mind that when it also points to an act, or to some special mental attitude, the reference must be ignored.

That which appears in the way of perception or recollection possessed in the region we have so far been considering the character of "real" (*wirklich*) Being *simpliciter*, of "certain" Being as we also say when contrasting it with other ontical characters. For this character can be modified, and even, in relation to one and the same phenomenon, transformed through actual modifying processes. The way of *"certain" belief* can pass over into that of *suggestion* or *presumption*, or into that of *question* and *doubt;* and, according to the line taken, that which appears (characterized in respect of that first order of characterizations which takes in the "primordial," the "reproductive," and the like) will adopt the *ontical modalities* of the *"possible,"* the *"probable,"* the *"questionable,"* and the *"doubtful"* respectively.

For instance, a perceived object stands out there at first as a plain matter of course, a certainty. Suddenly we are doubtful whether we have not been made the victims of a mere "illusion," whether what we see or hear, etc., is not "mere seeming." Or else that which appears preserves its ontical certainty, but we are uncertain with regard to some one or other of its sets of qualities. The thing "suggests" a man. Then a contrary suggestion sets in: it might be a moving tree, which in the gloom of the wood resembles a man in motion. But the "weight" of the one "possibility" is now considerably reinforced, and we decide in its favour perhaps, definitely presuming that "it was surely a tree."

Similarly the modalities of Being change, and this far more frequently, in the course of recollection, and so indeed as in great measure to set themselves up or exchange their signatures purely within the limits of intuition or of obscure presentation, without any type of "thinking" in the specific sense of the term, or "concept" and predicative judgment playing any part in the matter at all.

We see at the same time that the phenomena in this context summon us to various elucidatory studies, that characters of diverse types emerge (e.g., the *"decided,"* the *"weights"* of possibilities, and the like), and that in particular, also, the question concerning the essential bases of occasional characters, and concerning the whole structure of noemata and noeses, as organized in conformity with essential laws, calls for deeper investigation.

It suffices us here as elsewhere to have set out the *problems in their proper connexions.*

## 104. Doxic Modalities as Modifications

With respect to the series of belief-modalities with which we are now specially concerned, we have still to point out that in it once again the outstanding, *specifically intentional meaning of the world "modification"* comes to its own, the meaning we have elucidated in our previous analysis of the series of noetic and noematic characters. In the series we are now concerned with the certainty of belief clearly plays the part of the unmodified, or, as we should say here, the *"unmodalized" root-form of the way of belief*. Corresponding to this as its correlative, the *ontical character pure and simple* (the noematic being "certain" or "real") functions as the *root-form of all modalities of Being*. In point of fact, all ontical characters which spring from it, the *specific* so-to-be-called modalities of Being, contain in the very meaning they bear a back-reference to the root-form. The "possible" states *in itself* just as much as "being possible"; the "probable," "doubtful," "questionable," so much as "being probable," "being doubtful and questionable." The intentionality of the noeses is reflected in these noematic relations, and we again feel driven to speak directly of a *"noematic intentionality" as "parallel" to the noetic* properly so called.

These considerations may then be applied to the full *"positions,"* i. e., to the unities which functionally unite a meaning-nucleus with an ontical character.[3]

For the rest it is convenient to apply the term modality of Being to the whole series of these ontical characters, so as also to include under it the unmodified "Being," whenever it needs to be treated *as a member of this series*; much as the arithmetician also includes the unit "one" under the name "number." In a similar sense we generalize the verbal meaning of doxic modalities, whereunder often, with a conscious sense of ambiguity, we shall bring together the parallel meaning of the noetic and the noematic.

We must pay heed further to the ambiguities of the word "certain," when we refer to unmodalized Being as "being

---

[3] For further treatment of the concept of "Satz," or "proposition" in the unusually extended meaning [of "position"] which we give to it, see the first chapter of the Fourth Section of this work (pp. 331 ff.).

certain"; and not only in this respect that it sometimes means the noetic and sometimes the noematic "being certain." It also serves, for instance (and the usage is very confusing) to express the correlate of affirmation, the "yes" as counterpart to "no" and "not."[4] This usage must be strictly excluded. The meanings of words are constantly shifting within the limits of immediate logical equivalence. But our business is to set out the equivalences everywhere, and to prune off sharply whatever reference to phenomena of an essentially different nature may lurk behind the equivalent concepts.

The certitude of belief is belief in its plain and simple form, belief in the pregnant sense of the term. As a matter of fact, as our analyses have shown, it holds a highly remarkable and unique position among the variety of acts which are all included under the title "Belief"—or, often under the title, here very misleading though used by many, "Judgment." A proper expression is needed which takes this unique position into account, and effaces every reminder of the popular tendency to place certitude on a level with the other modes of belief. We introduce the term *primary belief* (*Urglaube*) or *Protodoxa* (*Urdoxa*) as suitably expressing the intentional back-reference of all "modalities of belief" which we have previously affirmed. We note further that we shall be using this latter expression (or, alternatively, "doxic modality") for *all* intentional modifications which are grounded in the essential nature of the protodoxa, including those to be set forth *afresh* in the analyses that follow.

The radically false doctrine, according to which a genus "Belief" (or "Judgment") simply splits up into certainty, supposal, and so forth, as though the relation could be expressed by spinning out a series of co-ordinate species (at whatever point the series might break off), just, as in the case of the genus "sensory quality," colour, sound, and so forth are co-ordinate species, scarcely calls for criticism, so far as we are concerned. Moreover, here as elsewhere we

---

[4] [TRANSLATOR'S NOTE.—This strictly applies only to the German meaning of the word *gewiss*, which stands for "certainly" as well as for "certain." But our use of the term "certainly" to indicate affirmation will help the reader to grasp the author's meaning at this point.]

must refrain from following up the consequences of our phenomenological conclusion.

## 105. The Modality of Belief, as Belief; the Modality of Being, as Being

When with regard to the highly remarkable developments we have just been setting forth we speak of an intentionality through which the secondary modes refer back to the proto-doxa, the meaning of this form of speech requires that it be possible for our mental glance to vary its incidence in a way which is indeed essentially characteristic of intentionalities of higher level. This possibility, moreover, is actually realized. *On the one hand,* living within the probability-consciousness, in an atmosphere of presumption, we can look towards what is probable; but *on the other hand* towards the probability itself and as such, that is towards the noematic object *in* the character which the presumption-noesis has given it. But the "object" with its own meaning, together with this probability-character, is *from the second viewpoint given as being* (*seiend*): consciousness in relation to this will accordingly be that of plain belief in the unmodified sense of the term. Just in the same way we can live ourselves into a possibility-consciousness (in "suggestion"), or into a questioning and doubt-ful attitude, the glance directed to *what* we are aware of as possible, questionable, doubtful. But we can also look upon the possibilities, upon the questionable and doubtful situations as such, and eventually, rendering the insight explicit, grasp the state of being possible or questionable or doubtful as a constitutive character of the object meant, and in this sense predicable of it; it is then given as *being* in the unmodified sense of the term.

We are thus able to state in a general way this highly re-markable peculiarity of the essential nature of things, that *every experience in relation to all the noetic phases which through its noeses shape themselves about the "intentional object as such" functions as a belief-consciousness in the sense of the Protodoxa*; or as we can also say:

Not only does every addition of new or modification of old noetic characters constitute new noematic characters, but therewith *eo ipso new ontical objects* constitute themselves for consciousness; to the noematic characters there correspond predicable characters inherent in the object meant, and indeed as real (*wirkliche*), and not mere noematically modified predicables.

These statements will gain in clearness when we have become more familiar with new noematic spheres of study.

## 106. Affirmation and Negation together with Their Noematic Correlates

As still a further modification that harks back to the proto-doxa, and indeed one that in virtue of its essential intentional back-reference to every variety of belief-modality may very well be reckoned as of a higher grade, is *rejection*, with its analogue *acceptance;* or, more specifically expressed, *negation* and *affirmation*. Every negation is the negation of something, and this Something points us back to this or that modality of belief. Thus noetically negation is the "modification" of some "position," the latter term signifying not an affirmation, but a "setting down" (*Setzung*) in the extended sense of some form of belief-modality.

Its new *noematic* form of service is the "*cancelling*" of the corresponding positing character, its specific correlate is the cancellation character we designate as "*not.*" The cancelling mark of negation strikes out something posited, or, to speak more concretely, a "*posited meaning*" (*Satz*), and indeed through the cancelling of its specific *positional character*, i.e., its ontical modality. Thereby this character and the posited statement itself appear as a "*modification*" *of something else*. Or to state the same thing differently: through the transformation of the plain consciousness of Being into the corresponding consciousness of negation, the plain character "being" (*seiend*) turns in the noema into that of "*not being.*"

In an analogous way, out of the "possible," the "probable," the "questionable," we get the "impossible," the "improbable," the "unquestionable." And therewith the whole noema is modified, the whole "*posited meaning*" taken in its concrete noematic fullness.

Just as, to speak in an image, negation cancels, so does affirmation "*underline*"; it "*confirms*" *a position by* "*accepting*" it, instead of "removing" it as negation does. That also provides a series of noematic modifications that run parallel with the modifications in the way of cancellation; but this cannot be followed up here any further.

Hitherto we have ignored what is peculiar in the "attitude"

of the pure Ego, which in and through rejection, more specifically that of the negating type, "*directs*" itself *against* the matter rejected, the being that is to be cancelled, as in affirmation it *inclines* towards that which is affirmed, and directs itself *towards* it. This descriptive side also of the whole matter should not be overlooked, and calls, on its own account, for analytic study.

And so again we must do justice likewise to the circumstance that following the dovetailing of intentionalities in one another, different directions of the mental glance may be taken as occasion suggests. We can live within the negating consciousness, in other words, we "carry out" the negation; the glance of the Ego is then directed to that which undergoes cancellation. But we can also direct the glance in a comprehensive way upon the cancelled as such, upon that which is *provided with the cancelling mark*; the latter then stands forth *as a new "object*," and indeed *in the plain original doxic mode "being*" (*seiend*). The new standpoint does not generate the new ontical object; we are already aware of what we reject in its cancelled character even in the "carrying out" of our rejection; but it is only at the new standpoint that the character becomes a *determination that can be predicated* of the noematic kernel of meaning. Similiar remarks apply of course to affirmation also.

Thus in this direction as well there lie problems calling for a phenomenological analysis of essence.[5]

## 107. Reiterated Modifications

What we have already done in the way of starting such analyses enables us to take at once the following further step in the direction of increasing insight.

Since what is negated and affirmed (*Negat und Affirmat*) is always an object that *is*, it can, like everything we are conscious of as a mode of Being, be affirmed or denied. There follows then, *in consequence* of the very constitution of Being, which at every step renews its own nature, an *ideally infinite chain of reiterated modifications*. Thus the first step

---

[5] It would be instructive, on the basis of the elucidations of the essential nature of doxic distinctions attempted in the present chapter, to think over the penetrating work of A. Reinach, *Zur Theorie des negativen Urteils* (Münchner Philos. Abhandlungen, 1911), and to bring its forms of inquiry under our own angle of vision.

in this direction gives us the "not-notbeing," the "not-impossible," "not-unquestionable," "not-improbably-being," and so forth.

The same holds good, as can be immediately seen on looking back, of all the modifications of Being which have been referred to on previous pages. We can bring consciously before ourselves once again that something is possible, probable, questionable, and so forth, in the mode of possibility, probability, questionability, and to the noetic formations there correspond the noematic ontical formations. It is possible that it is possible, that it is probable, questionable; it is probable that it is possible, that it is probable, and similarly for all such complications. Then again, to the formations of the higher levels there correspond affirmed and negated positions, which once more can be modified, and in this way again, speaking ideally, we wander off into infinity. We are far from being concerned here with mere verbal repetitions. As witness, we need only bring to mind the Theory of Probability and its applications, wherein possibilities and probabilities are continually being considered, denied, doubted, presumed, questioned, established, and so forth.

But we must always remember, when speaking of modifications in this connexion, that the reference may be, on the one hand, to a possible transformation of the phenomena, thus to a possible actual operation; and on the other hand to the much more interesting essential property of the noeses or noemata, of harking back, in virtue of their own essential nature, and without any accompanying regard as to their genesis to something other, something unmodified. But whether we take the one viewpoint or the other, we stand in either case on pure phenomenological ground. For when we speak here of transformation and genesis, our sole concern is with essential happenings of a phenomenological character, and our words have not the least reference to empirical experiences as natural facts.

## 108. Noematical Characters are not Determined through "Reflexion"

It is necessary in regard to each new group of noeses and noemata which we have brought to clear consciousness that we should assure ourselves afresh of the fundamental bit of knowledge which runs so counter to the habits of thought of the psychologizers, that the distinction between noesis and noema must be real and correctly drawn, in fact exactly as faithful description requires. If one has already become familiar with the pure immanent description of the essence (a point which so many fail to reach who otherwise think highly of description), and has come to the understanding that consciousness must always have ascribed to it an intentional object that belongs to it, and is capable of being described on immanental lines, there is still a great temptation to apprehend noematic characters, and especially the one we have just been considering, *as mere "determinations of reflexion."* We understand, as we recall the current and narrow conception of reflexion, what this means, to wit: determinations which accrue to the intentional objects through the latter being referred *to those ways of being conscious* in which they figure precisely as the objects of consciousness.

Thus the negated, the affirmed, and the like, are to be reached in this way, that the object of the "judgment" in reflexion is characterized as negated when the reflexion bears on the negating, as affirmed when it bears on the affirming, as probable when it bears on the presuming, and so everywhere. But this view is a mere subjective construction,[6] which already proclaims its perversity through the fact that if these predicates were really no more than relating predicates of reflexion, they could be *given* only in the actual reflecting upon the act-aspect and in relation to it. But they are evidently *not* given through such reflexion. We grasp what concerns the correlate as such through the glance being turned directly on the correlate itself. We grasp the negated, the affirmed, the possible, the questionable, and so forth, as directly qualifying the appearing object as such. In no wise do we here glance back upon the act. Conversely the noetic predicates which emerge through such reflexion are far from having the same meaning as the noematic predicates in question. Connected with this is the fact that even from the standpoint of *truth* "not-being" is clearly only equivalent to and not identical with "being validly negated"; similarly "being possible" is not identical with "being held possible in a valid way," and the like.

If we still needed further witness, natural speech, unembarrassed by any psychological prejudices, would here supply it. Looking into the stereoscope we say that the pyramid that

[6] Cf. *Logical Studies,* Vol. III, Sixth Study, § 44, pp. 139 ff.

here appears is "nothing," is mere "illusion." That which appears, as such, is the obvious subject of predication, and we ascribe to this noema of a Thing (which is in no sense a Thing) whatever character we discover in it, even the nothingness. Only we must have the courage here, as everywhere in phenomenology, to accept in the phenomenon what really presents itself to mental insight, and in the form in which it so presents itself, and instead of twisting its meaning to describe it *honestly*. All theories must adjust themselves to these descriptions.

## 109. The Neutrality-Modification

Among the modifications which relate to the sphere of Belief, we have still to indicate one of the highest importance which occupies a position all by itself, and should therefore in no way be placed on a line with those so far discussed. The unique way in which it stands related to the various attitudes of Belief, and the circumstance that it is only as we touch the deeper strata of inquiry that its own distinctive character is opened up—as having no specific connexion with the sphere of belief, rather as a highly important modification of consciousness *of a general kind*—justifies us in giving it here a more detailed treatment. We shall also have the opportunity thereby of bringing under discussion a genuine modification of Belief which we have yet to consider, with which the new modification in question may very easily be confused, namely, that of Assumption.

We are dealing now with a modification which in a certain sense completely removes and renders powerless every doxic modality to which it is related, but in a totally different way from that of negation, which, in addition, as we saw, shows in the negated a positive effect, a non-being which is itself once more being. It cancels nothing, it "performs" nothing, it is the conscious counterpart of all performance: its *neutralization*. It lies enclosed in every "withholding of performance," "setting out of action," "bracketing," "leaving postponed," and so "having postponed," "thinking oneself into" the performance, or "merely thinking" what is performed without "helping to bring it about."

Since this modification has never been scientifically set out, and has therefore not been fixed terminologically (when the topic has been touched on it has always been confused with other modifications), and since there is no unequivocal name for it even in ordinary speech, we can only reach it by enveloping tactics and by a gradual process of elimination. For all the expressions we have just collected to serve as a preliminary indication of what it means contain some surplus of meaning. An arbitrary doing of some kind is everywhere included in the meaning indicated, whereas there should be no hint of this in the meaning we are seeking to fix. We therefore set it aside. The result of this doing has certainly a distinctive content, which, apart from the fact that it "springs from" the doing (which would of course *also* be a phenomenological datum), can be considered in itself, in detachment from all such arbitrariness as something both possible and actual within the sphere of experience. Let us then exclude all volitional elements from the "leaving postponed," and also avoid interpreting it in the sense of what is doubtful or hypothetical, and there remains a certain having "postponed" something, or, better still, a "having let it stand," where we have not in mind anything that has been "really" let stand. The positing characteristic has become powerless. The belief is no longer seriously a belief, the presumption not seriously a presumption, the denying not seriously a denying. It is *"neutralized"* belief, presumption, denial, and the like, and their correlates repeat those of the unmodified experiences though in a radically modified way: the simply being, the being possible, probable, questionable, likewise the non-being, and all that has been previously negated or affirmed—this is all consciously there, but not in the "real" way, only as "merely thought," as "mere idea." Everything has the modifying "suspensory bracket," closely related to that of which we have previously spoken so much, which is also so important for preparing the way into phenomenology. The positings pure and simple, the positings that have not been neutralized, have as correlated results "positions" (*Sätze*), which are collectively characterized as "states of being" ("*Seiendes*"). Possibility, probability, questionability, non-being, and yea-being—all *that* is itself something "which is," characterized as such in the correlate, and "intended" (*vermeint*) as that in consciousness. But the neutralized positings are essentially distinguished by this mark, that *their correlates* contain *nothing that can be posited, nothing that can be really predicated*; in no respect does the neutral consciousness play towards that of which it is aware the part of a "belief."

## 110. Neutralized Consciousness and the Critical Authority of the Reason. The Nature of Assuming

It is clear that we have here a really unique peculiarity of Consciousness. The proof is that the non-neutralized noeses, the noeses *properly so-called*, are *essentially* subject to the *critical authority of the reason*, whereas *in the case of the neutralized noeses, the question concerning reason and unreason has no meaning*.

Likewise, correlatively, for the *noemata*. Every noema characterized as in state of being (as certain), or as possible, presumable, questionable, null, and so forth, can be so characterized either "validly" or "invalidly"; it can "veritably" be, possibly be, it can be nothing at all, and so forth. *Mere supposal* "*posits*," on the contrary, *nothing*; it is *not an affirmatory consciousness*. The "mere thought" of realities, possibilities, and so forth, "*makes no pretensions*" in regard to reality, it is neither to be recognized as correct nor rejected as incorrect.

All mere supposal (*Sich-denken*) can indeed be translated into an *assumption* or *supposition* (*Ansetzen*), and this new modification (just as in the case of supposal) is subject unconditionally to the thinker's arbitrary preference. But "suppositing" (*Ansetzen*) is again akin to positing (*Setzen*), the *supposition* again a kind of "*position*" (*Satz*), only that it is a quite unique modification of the position of belief, which contrasts with the main series discussed above, following a sideline of its own. It can enter as a member (as a supposition in the form of the "antecedent" or consequent of a hypothetical proposition) into the unity of positions (*Setzungen*), which permit of rational judgments being passed upon them, and so itself come under the rules of rational valuation. We cannot say of a mere uncertain thought that it is correct or incorrect, but we can say this of the supposition that enters into a hypothetical judgment. It is a fundamental error to confuse the one and the other, and to overlook the equivocation which lies in our reference to a mere supposal or a mere thought.

In addition we have the similarly misleading equivocation which lies in the word "to think," when it is referred now to the quite special sphere of the thought that discriminates, apprehends, and expresses logical thought in a specific sense of the term, and now to the positional as such, which, as we here had it directly in view, does not call for any discriminating nor for any apprehending in the way of predication.

We find all the happenings here considered in the sphere of mere sensory intuitions (with their transitions into obscure presentations) to which we have in the first instance assigned a preferential position.

## 111. Neutrality-Modification and Fancy

But yet another dangerous ambiguity of the expression "mere supposal" comes in for consideration. We must protect ourselves here against a very closely besetting confusion, namely, that between *neutrality-modification* and *fancy*. The confusing element here, and one not lightly to be disentangled, lies herein that fancy is itself in fact a neutrality-modification, that in spite of its being of so special a type its significance is universal and applicable to *all* experiences, and that it also plays its part in most of the formations of supposal, and must then be distinguished from the general neutrality-modification with its manifold formations that conform to all the types of the positing function.

More closely stated, *the process of fancy in general is the neutrality-modification of the "positing" act of representation*, and therefore of remembering in the widest conceivable sense of the term.

We must notice here that in ordinary speech *representation*[7] (Reproduction) and *fancy* cut across each other. We employ the expressions in such a way that, in conformity with our own analyses, we leave the general word "representation" with its meaning undetermined in respect of the question whether the "positing" act it expresses is a proper or a neutralized one. Representations generally divide them into the two groups: *memories* of every kind and *their neutrality modifications*. However, as will be further apparent,[8] this

_____

[7] [TRANSLATOR'S NOTE.—The German word here used is *Vergegenwärtigung,* "bringing to present consciousness," or "representation." If it is to be equivalent to "Reproduction," as the author intimates, "reproduction" cannot be identified with its customary meaning of "bringing *back* to present consciousness," but must be given the more general meaning of "bringing to present consciousness."]

[8] Cf. the reference to Essence and counter-essence (§. 114).

division cannot be accepted as a genuine classification.

On the other hand, every experience generally (every really living one, so to speak) is an experience "which is present." It belongs to its very essence that it should be able to reflect on that same essence in which it is necessarily characterized as *that which* certainly and presently *is*. In accordance with this there corresponds to every experience, as to every individual Being of which we are primordially aware, a series of ideally possible memory-modifications. To *experiencing*, as the *primordial consciousness of experience,* there correspond as possible parallels memories of the same experience, and therefore also *fancies* as its neutrality-modifications. So it is for every experience, however the direction of the glance of the pure Ego may be ordered. The following may serve by way of elucidation:

Whenever we may have represented objects of one kind or another—let us at once suppose that it is a mere world of fancy, and that we have our attention turned towards it—it then follows as pertaining to the essence of the fancy-active consciousness that not only the fancy-world itself, but also, at the same time, the perceiving activity which has "given" it, is modified into the form of fancy. We turn our attention to this world and to the "perceiving within the fancy" (i.e., to the neutrality-modification of the memory), yet only then when, as we previously put it, we "reflect within the fancy." But it is of fundamental importance not to confuse *this* modification, which ideally can at any time be carried out, and would transfer every experience, even the fancy-making experience itself, into the *mere fancy* which exactly corresponds to it, or, what *amounts to the same thing*, into the *neutralized recollection,* with that neutrality-modification which we can set over against every *"positing"* experience. In this respect memory is a quite special form of positing experience. As other forms we have normal perception, the perceptive or reproductive consciousness of possibility, probability and questionability, the consciousness of doubt, of negation, affirmation, supposition, and so forth.

We can satisfy ourselves with the help of an illustration that the *neutrality-modification of the normal perception* which posits its object with unmodified certainty is *the neutral consciousness of the picture-object,* which we find as a component in our ordinary observation of a depicted situation perceptively presented. Let us try to make this clear, and let us suppose that we are observing Dürer's engraving, "The Knight, Death, and the Devil."

We distinguish here in the first place the normal perception of which the correlate is the "*engraved print*" as a *thing*, this print in the portfolio.

We distinguish in the second place the perceptive consciousness within which in the black lines of the picture there appear to us the small colourless figures, "knight on horseback," "death," and "devil." In æsthetic observation we do not consider these as the objects (*Objekten*); we have our attention fixed on what is portrayed "*in the picture*," more precisely, on the "*depicted*" realities, the knight of flesh and blood, and so forth.

That which makes the depicting possible and mediates it, namely, the consciousness of the "picture" (of the small grey figurettes in which through the derived noeses something other, through similarity, "presents itself as depicted"), is now an example for the neutrality-modification of the perception. This *depicting picture-object* stands before us *neither as being nor as non-being*, nor in any *other positional modality*; or rather, we are aware of it as having its being, though only a quasi-being, in the neutrality-modification of Being.

But it is just the same with the *object depicted*, if we take up a *purely æsthetic* attitude, and view the same again as "mere picture," without imparting to it the stamp of Being or non-Being, of possible Being or probable Being, and the like. But, as can clearly be seen, that does not mean any privation, but a modification, that of *neutralization*. Only we should not represent it as a transforming operation carried out on a previous position. Occasionally indeed it can be this. None the less it need not be it.

## 112. Repeatability of the Fancy-Modification at Successive Levels; Non-repeatability of the Neutrality-Modification

The radical difference between fancy in the sense of a neutralizing presentation, and a neutralizing modification generally reveals itself—if we may emphasize, and somewhat sharply, this additional decisive point of difference—in the fact that the *fancy-modification* as a presentation is *repeatable* (*iterierbar*) (there are fancies of any specifiable level, fancies "in" fancies), whereas the *repetition* (*Wiederholung*) *of the neutralizing "operation" is essentially excluded.*

Our assertion that it is possible to repeat in this way reproductive (as also copy-making) modifications would seem to have met with pretty general opposition. That attitude will not be changed until practice in general phenomenological analysis is more widespread than is the case at present. So long as one treats experiences as "contents" or as mental "elements," which in spite of all the fashionable attacks against atomizing and hypostatizing psychology are still looked upon as a kind of minute matter, so long as the belief accordingly prevails that it is possible to fix the difference between "contents of sensation" and the corresponding "contents of fancy" only through material characters of "intensity," "fullness," and the like, no improvement is to be looked for.

One must first learn to see that we are concerned here with a difference in the *consciousness*, that the fancy-image therefore is not a mere faded datum of sense, but in its own way a fancy *of* the corresponding sense-datum; further, that this "of" cannot find its way in through any thinning, however drastic, of the intensity, or the content, etc., of the sense-datum in question.

He who is versed in the art of reflecting on consciousness (and has previously learnt in a general way to see the data of intentionality) will without further difficulty *see* the levels of consciousness which lie before us in the fancy that is in a fancy or the memory in a memory or a fancy. He will then also see what lies in the essential construction of these successive formations, namely, that *every fancy at a higher level* can pass freely over into a *direct fancy* of that which in the former case is fancied only indirectly, whereas this free possibility does *not* obtain in the transition from *fancy* to the *corresponding perception*. Here as a challenge to spontaneity there opens up a chasm which the pure Ego can cross only in the essentially new form of realizing action and creation (wherein also the power to hallucinate at will must be taken into account).[9]

[9] In respect of the points from the doctrine of neutrality-modifications which have so far been dealt with, the *Logical Studies* have in the main, especially in what concerns the relation to fancy, already won their way to a correct grasp of the subject. Cf. (*loc. cit.*) the Fifth Study, and particularly in § 39, the contrast there drawn between "qualitative" and "imaginative modification," in which the former has the meaning of the neutrality-modification which we have *here* referred to. Since Meinong's book, *Über*

## 113. Actual and Potential Positings

Our reflexions on neutrality-modification and positing necessitate further important developments. We have used the expression "positing" consciousness in a wide sense which requires to be differentiated.

Let us separate *actual* from *potential positing,* and as the general title, which we are still unable to do without, adopt that of *"positional consciousness."*

The difference between the actuality and the potentiality of the *positing process* stands in close relation to the actuality-differences of attention and inattention, of which we have previously spoken,[10] but in no way coincides with them. By taking the neutrality-modification into account, the general distinction between the actuality and non-actuality of the directness of the Ego in attention becomes infected with a double meaning, or, alternatively, there slips into the concept of the expression "actuality" a double meaning, the essential nature of which we must make clear.

The neutrality-modification came before us in marked contrast with *real* belief, presumption, and the like, with the peculiarly modified consciousness of a "mere thinking oneself into" a belief, presumption, and so forth; or, to speak in terms of the correlative, in contrast with having "really" (*wirklich*) before "oneself," or having "really posited" that which is, that which probably is, and so forth, and *not* having really posited it in the mode of a mere "standing undecided." But from the outset we also pointed out the essentially

---

*Annahmen* (1902), has dealt in detail with questions which are closely related to those discussed in the present chapter, I am bound to explain why I could connect the discussion only with my old writings and not with his book. In my opinion this book, which here as elsewhere reveals such extensive coincidences with the parallel sections of the *Logical* Studies—in respect of content and theoretical ideas alike—has not made any real advance on my own attempts, whether in respect of substance or method. Many elements in my thought, upon which, now as before, I believe I should lay stress, are not considered there, and this applies particularly to the points treated above. The confusions which these last discussions of ours have served to lay bare precisely constitute the central core of Meinong's view of assumptions.

[10] Cf. §§ 35, 37, 92.

different attitude of a non-neutral and a neutral consciousness respectively with respect to the potentiality of the positing function. Out of every "real" (*wirklichen*) consciousness we can draw forth various positings potentially included in it, and these are then *real* (*wirkliche*) positings; in whatever is really meant, in a thetic sense, there real predicables lie concealed. But a neutral consciousness "contains" in itself no "real" (*wirkliche*) predicables of any kind. The unfolding of its content through the focal actualities of attention, through a turning to the different predicates of the object we are aware of, gives as result nothing but neutral acts or modified predicates. This different type of potentiality, according as the consciousness is neutral or non-neutral, this remarkable fact that the general potentiality of the directed glancings of attention thus bifurcates, now calls for deeper inquiry.

The reflexions of the last paragraph but one left us with this result, that every real experience as a present state of being—or, as we can also say, as the temporal unity constituted in the phenomenological time-consciousness—bears its ontical character with it in a certain way, *just like something that has been perceived.* To every actual present state of experience there corresponds in idea (*ideel*) a neutrality-modification, namely, a possible present state of fancy-experience which exactly corresponds to it in content. Every such experience in the form of fancy is characterized not as being really present, but as being "as though" (*gleichsam*) it were present. It is in fact exactly as though one were comparing the noematic data of some perception or other with those of an active state of fancy (fanciful contemplation) which corresponds to it precisely in idea (*ideel*). Every perceived item is characterized as "really present Being"; every parallel item in the form of fancy is characterized as the same in content, but as "mere fancy," "as though it were" present Being. Thus:

*The original time-consciousness itself functions as a perceptual consciousness,* and has its counterpart in a corresponding fancy-consciousness.

This all-enveloping time-consciousness, however, is *not* of course *a continuous immanent perception* in the *pregnant* sense, i.e., in the sense of an *actual positing* perceiving, which is itself an experience in our sense, lying in immanent time, having present duration, constituted in the time-consciousness. In other words, it is not of course a continuous inner reflecting, in which experiences *posited* in the specific sense were to be *grasped as existing* (*seiend*) and actually objectified.

Among experiences there are some that stand out, called immanent reflexions, more specifically immanent perceptions, which as directed upon their objects apprehend Being actually and posit it. Beside these, among the same experiences, there are perceptions that point to a transcendent object, that similarly posit Being, the so-called external perceptions. "*Perception*" in the normal sense of the word does not only indicate generally that this or that thing *appears* to the Ego in *embodied presence*, but that the Ego is *aware* of the appearing thing, grasps it as really being there, and posits it. This actuality of the act of positing it as being there is, in accordance with previous findings, neutralized in the perceptive consciousness of an image. With the glance turned towards the "image" (not towards that of which it is the copy), we do not apprehend anything real (*Wirkliches*) as object, but an image, a fiction. The "apprehension" has the actuality of the directing activity, but is not "real" (*wirkliche*) apprehension, but mere apprehension in the modified form of the "*as if*" ("*gleichsam*"); the positing is not actual positing, but modified into the "as if."

Through withdrawal of the mental glance from the fiction, the attentional actuality of the neutralized position passes over into potentiality; the image still appears, but is not "observed"; in the mode of the "as if" it is not apprehended. In the essential nature of this situation and its potentiality there lie possibilities for actual directings of the mental glance, which, however, never give rise here to actualities in the way of *positing*.

The conditions are similar when we compare "actual" (not-neutral, really positing) *recollections* with those in which that which is remembered, through a diverting of the glance perhaps, still appears indeed, but is no longer actually posited. The potentiality of the *positing* of that which "still" appears here means that through the actuality of attention there spring forth not only apprehending *cogitationes* in general, but such as in all strictness "really" (*wirklich*) apprehend and actually posit. In the neutrality-modifications of memories, i.e., in mere *fancies*, we have once again the attentional potentialities of which the transformation into actualities gives "acts" (*cogitationes*) indeed, but wholly neutralized acts, doxic positings after the mode of the "as if." We are aware of the fancied object not as "really" present, past or future; it only "hovers," as that which possesses no posited actuality. No mere directing of the glance can set this neutrality aside, just as little as in other cases it can generate positional actuality.

Every perception—let the observation still serve us for further illustration—has its perceptual background. The specifically apprehended thing has its *environment*, which appears perceptively with it, lacking all special placing in the sphere of that which is out there, yet adjusted to the nature of the environed thing. It too is an environment "that really is," and it is a feature of our awareness of it that it is intrinsically *possible* for actual glances that functionally posit Being to direct themselves towards it. It is in a certain measure a *unity of potential positings*. So it is with memory in respect of its background of recollection, or also with perception, or, it may be, memory in respect of its fringe of retentions and protentions, of recollections that hark back and recollections that anticipate, which, in greater or less abundance, and changing off and on their grade of clearness, press forward, but do not pass into actual thetic form. In all these cases the actualization of the "potential positings" necessarily leads through corresponding directings of the mental glance (attentional actuality) to further and yet further actual positings, and this belongs to the essence of these situations. But if we pass over to the parallel neutrality-modifications, everything translates itself into the modification of the "as if," even the "potentiality" itself. The image-object or fancy-object has also (and necessarily) attentional backgrounds. Again, the word "background" is a title for potential directions of interest and "apprehensions." But the fixing of the interest in the direction of reality does not lead on principle to positings, but always only to positings of the modified kind.

Similar considerations—and the point is one that still specially interests us—apply to the modal variations of the specific theses of belief (the doxic primary theses), to the presumptions, suggestions, questions, and so forth, and similarly to denials and affirmations. The correlates in them of which we are conscious, the possibility, probability, nullity, and the like, *can* undergo doxic positing, and at the same time specific "objectivation"; but whilst we "live" "in" the presuming, questioning, rejecting, affirming, and the like, we carry out no doxic primary theses, though we do indeed carry out other "theses" in the sense of a necessary generalization of the concept, namely, *presumption-theses*, *questionability-theses*, *denial-theses*, and so forth. But we *can* always pass the corresponding doxic judgments: the *ideal possibility* of *bringing to actuality the potential theses* involved in them has its ground in the *essential nature* of the phenomenological situation.[11] This actualization, again, when it deals from the outset with actual theses, always leads to actual theses as potentially involved in the initial theses. If we translate the initial theses into the speech of neutrality, potentiality is translated into the same speech. If in mere fancy we presume, ask questions, and the like, all our previous conclusions still hold good, but with a changed signature. All the doxic theses and modalities of Being derived from the original act or the act-noema, and through the possible shiftings of the focus of attention, are now neutralized.

## 114. Further Concerning Neutrality-Modification and the Potentiality of the Theses

The difference between non-neutral and neutral consciousness, if we are to follow the analyses we have made, concerns conscious experiences not merely in the attentional modus of the *cogito*, but also in that of attentional sub-focal actuality. It then makes itself felt in the twofold demeanour of these "backgrounds" of consciousness on the occasion of their attentional transformation into "foregrounds," or, to speak more strictly, on their transformation into attentional actualities wherewith the original experience passes over into a doxic *cogito*, indeed into a protodoxa. Naturally this is possible under all circumstances, for it belongs to the essential nature of every intentional experience that it can "glance towards" its noeses as well as its noemata, the noematically constituted objectivities and their predicates, positing and apprehending them after the way of the protodoxa.

The situation, as we may also put it, is this: that *the neutrality-modification* is *not* a *specific* modification attached to the *actual* theses, the only ones that are truly theses, but concerns *a fundamentally essential peculiarity of all consciousness generally*, which finds expression in a certain attitude towards actual protodoxic positionality or non-posi-

[11] Cf. *supra*, § 105.

tionality. Whence the necessity of exhibiting it in the actual primary positings or in the modification they undergo.

More closely described our topic is as follows:

*Consciousness generally,* of whatever kind and form it may be, *is traversed by a radical cleavage.* In the first place there belongs, as we know, to every consciousness in which the pure Ego does not from the outset live as "bringing it about," which therefore has not from the outset the form of the "*cogito,*" the essentially possible modification which transfers it into this form. Now there are *two* fundamental possibilities connected with *the way in which consciousness is brought about* within the modus *cogito,* or otherwise expressed:

*To every cogito there belongs a counterpart that exactly corresponds with it,* and is such that *its noema possesses* in the parallel *cogito* its *exactly corresponding counter-noema.*

The relation of the parallel "acts" consists in this, that one of the two is a "*real (wirklicher) act,*" the *cogito* a "real," "*really positing,*" *cogito,* whereas the other is the "*shadow*" of an act, an act *improperly so-called,* a *cogito* that does not "really" posit. The one really effects something; the other is the mere reflexion of an effect.

Corresponding to this we have the radical difference of the *correlates:* on the one side the constituted noematic effect which has the character of the unmodified, real effect, on the other the "*mere thought*" of the exactly corresponding effect. The real and the modified correspond *idealiter* with absolute precision, and *yet* have *not the same essential nature.* For the modification is transferred to the essence; to the *primordial essence* there corresponds its *counter-essence* as a "shadow" of the same essence.

In the metaphorical speech concerning shadows, reflexion, and image, there should of course be no suggestion of mere illusion or deceitful intention, for thereby real acts or positional correlates would be given. Nor need the warning be renewed against the other tendency so ready to hand, to confuse the modification here in question with the fancy-modification which likewise creates for every experience—as the present phase of experience in the inner consciousness of time —a counterpart, its own fancy-image.

The radical separation of intentional experiences into two classes; which are to one another as reality to the ineffectual mirroring of the noematic function, proclaims its meaning to us here (as we leave the doxic domain) in the following *fundamental propositions*:

Every *cogito* is in itself either a primary form of doxic positing or not. But by virtue of a system of laws, which again belong to the essential nature of consciousness in its basic generality, every *cogito* can be transferred to a primary positing of a doxic type. But only in complex ways, and in particular as follows: every *"thetic character"* in the broadest sense of the term, which constitutes itself as correlate of a noetic "thesis" (used here in a correspondingly broad sense) in the noema of the *cogito* to which it belongs, undergoes transformation into an ontic character, and therewith takes on the form of a *modality of Being with the very widest range* of meaning. In this way the character of "probable," which is the noematic correlate of presumption, and indeed specifically of the "act-character" of the "thesis" of presumption as such, changes into probable *Being;* likewise the noematic character of the "questionable," this specific correlate of the thesis of questionability, changes into the form of questionable *Being;* the correlate of negation into the form of *non-being;* all of these mere forms which have, so to speak, taken on the stamp of the actual primary doxic thesis. But this reaches farther still. We shall be finding ground for extending the thetic concept to cover all act-spheres, and therefore also for speaking, for instance, of pleasure-theses, wish-theses, will-theses, with their noematic correlatives, "pleasing," "wished for," "as it practically should be," and the like. These correlates also, through the transfer, possible *a priori*, of the act in question into a primary doxic thesis, assume the form of modalities of Being with an extremely extended range of meaning; thus "pleasing," "wished for," "as it should be," and so forth, become predicable, for in the actual positing of the root-belief we are conscious of these as *being* pleasing, wished for, and so forth.[12] But, in these examples, we are to understand the transfer as implying that it preserves the noema of the original experience in its whole essential quality, with this sole exception, that the mode of presentation of data will have changed with the transfer in some law-conforming way. This point, however, will need to be further developed.[13]

[12] Cf. *supra*, the sentences towards the close of § 105.
[13] Cf. *infra*, § 117, first paragraph.

The two cases are radically distinguished in this respect, that the protodoxa, as the case may be, is either a real, so to speak a really believed belief, or else its nerveless counterpart, mere "supposal" (of Being *simpliciter,* possible Being, and so forth).

What results, through processes of inward change from that doxic transformation of the original experience, whether developments of its noematic constituents into *real* primary doxic positings, or an unfolding into protodoxic *neutralities* exclusively, that is predetermined with absolute rigour through the *essential nature* of the intentional experience in question. Thus from the outset a firm conceptual system of *potential ontical positings* is traced in the very essence of *every* conscious experience, and indeed, following the prefigured articulation of the consciousness in question, a field of possible real positings or of possible neutral "shadow-positings."

And again: *consciousness in general* is so articulated as to be of a twofold type: original and shadow, *positional* and *neutral* consciousness. The distinguishing feature of the one is that its doxic potentiality leads to real positing doxic acts, and of the other that it gives rise only to the shadow-pictures of such acts only to neutrality modifications of the same; in other words, that it contains in its noematic constitution nothing that can be doxically grasped, or, which amounts to the same thing, no "real" (*wirkliches*) noema, but only its counter-image. Moreover, neutral experiences are restricted just to *one* form of doxic positionality: that which belongs to them as data of the immanent time-consciousness, determining them as the modified consciousness of a modified noema.

The expressions "*positional*" and "*neutral*" should from now on serve our terminological needs. Every experience, whether it has the form of the *cogito,* whether it is or is not in any special sense act, comes under this opposition. Thus *positionality* does not imply the presence of a real position or the performing act through which it is established; it expresses only a certain potential capacity for carrying out actual acts of doxic positing. Yet let us include under the concept of positional experience the case in which an experience is from the outset a position already established, a suggestion which is less likely to give offence as to each completed positing there belongs a plurality of potential positings.

The difference between *positionality* and *neutrality* expresses, as has been already shown, no property peculiar to belief-positings only, no mere kind of belief-modification such as presuming, questioning, and the like, or, in other directions, assuming, denying, affirming, thus not the intentional variations of a primary modus of belief in the pregnant sense of the term. It is in fact, as we had stated in advance, a *distinction in the nature of consciousness of a universal kind,* but one which in the course of our analysis appears, and on good grounds, to be connected with the distinction already specially indicated in the narrow sphere of the doxic *cogito* between positional (i.e., actual, real) belief and its neutral counterpart (the mere "supposal"). Indeed, there has been revealed highly remarkable and deep-lying interconnexions of an essential nature between the act-characters of belief and all other kinds of act-characters, and therefore all types of consciousness generally.

## 115. Applications. The Extended Concept of Act. Act-Fulfilments and Impulses to Act

It is important to take into account again some observations already made.[14] The *cogito* in general is explicit intentionality. The concept of intentional experience generally already presupposes the opposition between potentiality and actuality, and that in its quite general meaning, in so far as it is only in the transition to the explicit *cogito* and in *reflexion* on experience that has not been made explicit and on its noetic-noematic constituents, that we are able to know that it conceals within itself intentionalities, or noemata which are peculiar to it. Consider, for instance, the consciousness of the unobserved but subsequently observable background in perception, memory, and so forth. The explicit intentional experience is a "completed" "I think." But the same "I think" can also pass over into an "unfulfilled" condition through changes in the process of attention. The experience of a fulfilled perception, a fulfilled judgment, feeling or volition, does not disappear when the attention turns "exclusively" to something new, and the Ego consequently "lives" exclusively in a new *cogito*. The earlier *cogito* "rings off," sinks into "obscurity," but it still continues to experience a

---

14 Cf. *supra,* § 84.

modified form of Being. Similarly *cogitationes* in the background of experience press their way up, sometimes following the path of recollection or neutrally modified, sometimes unmodified. For instance, a belief, a real belief, "stirs" within us; we already believe "before we know it." Under certain conditions likewise movements of pleasure or displeasure, desires, even resolves, are already lively before we "live" "in" them, before we carry out the *cogito* proper, before the Ego "gets busy" judging, pleasing, desiring, willing.

Thus the *cogito* indicates in fact (and from the start it is as such that we have introduced the concept) the act *proper* of perceiving, judging, pleasing, and so forth. But on the other hand the whole structure of experience in the cases described, with all its theses and noematic characters, remains the same, though it lacks this developed actuality. Let us then separate more clearly *fulfilled acts* from *acts that are not fulfilled*; the latter are either acts "that have missed fulfilment or *impulses to act (Aktregungen)*. We could also quite well use the last word quite generally for acts that are not fulfilled. Such impulsive stirrings are lived with all their intentionalities, but the Ego does not live in them as *"a fulfilling subject."* Thereby the concept of Act is extended in a definite and wholly indispensable sense. The fulfilled acts, or, as in a certain respect it is better to call them (in respect of the fact, namely, that we are here dealing with processes), *the acts in process of fulfilment,* compose what *in the broadest sense* we term *"attitudes" (Stellungnahmen)*, whilst the reference to attitudes in the pregnant sense of the term points back to consolidated (*fundierte*) acts in ways to be discussed more fully at a later stage: for instance, to attitudes of hate, or of the hater to the hatred, which, on its side, has already been constituted for consciousness within noeses of a lower level as a person or thing which is out there; attitude, affirmative or negative, to the claim to have Being, and the like, would likewise belong here.

It is now clear that acts in the broader sense, just as in the case of the specific *cogitationes*, carry with them the differences between neutrality and positionality, which already prior to the transformation into *cogitationes* are noematically and thetically effective, only that we first perceive these effects through acts in the narrower sense, through *cogitationes*. The positings, which may be positings in the modus of the "as if," are already really present in them together with the noeses as a whole to which these positings belong: the ideal condition being presupposed that they do not, sympathetically with the transformation, enrich their intention and otherwise get altered. In any case we can exclude these changes (and also especially the intentional enrichments and reshapings which pass into the flow of experience after the transformation).

Throughout our whole series of discussions under the title "Neutrality" the doxic positings had a privileged place. Neutrality was indicated under the rubric potentiality. Everything rested on this, *that every thetic act-character generally* (every act-"intention," e.g., the intention in pleasure-giving valuation and will, the specific character of the positing act in pleasing and in willing) *conceals in its essential being a character of the genus "doxic thesis," which "coincides with"* it in certain ways. According as the act-intention concerned is not neutralized or is neutralized, so is it with the doxic thesis included in it, here thought of as the *primary* [*or proto-*] *thesis.*

This preference given to the doxic primary thesis will be less marked in the analyses that follow. It will be clear that the conformity to law in the realm of essences which we have brought out in our inquiries demands closer determination so far as firstly and in general the *doxic modalities* (in the specific sense which also includes assumptions) must replace or represent the doxic primary theses as the "doxic theses" included in all theses. But within this general preference for doxic modalities the doxic primary thesis, the certainty that marks belief, has the quite special advantage that these modalities themselves must be transformed into theses of belief, so that once again all neutrality has its indicator in the doxic potentiality, and in the quite special meaning which it bears in relation to the primary thesis. The manner in which the doxic in general "covers" all the varieties of the thetic will in this connexion receive its closer determination.[15]

Now the propositions which have been set down provisionally in their widest generality (lacking though they may be in certain respects), and made really clear only in special

[15] Cf. further below, § 117.

act-spheres, need for their foundation a broader basis. So far we have not discussed at all deeply the parallelism of noesis and noema in all the intentional domains. This main theme of the present section of the book brings its own motive to bear in urging the extension of the analysis. In carrying out this extension what we have set out in general concerning the neutrality-modification will at the same time be confirmed and completed.

## 116. Transition to New Analyses. The Secondary Noeses and Their Noematic Correlates

So far we have been studying a series of general features in the structure of noeses and noemata within a large and yet very limited framework. Our studies, to be sure, have been on a very modest scale, and have not gone farther than was required for bringing these features into relief, and for realizing our leading aim, that, namely, of providing a general yet significant idea of the groups of problems which the universal twin-theme Noesis and Noema brings with it. Our studies, despite the manifold complications they draw into their analyses, were concerned only with a mere underflow of the stream of experience, to which belong those intentionalities which are still of a relatively simple structure. If we except the anticipatory reflexions in which we last indulged, we selected by preference sensory intuitions, in particular those of appearing realities, as also the sensory *presentations* which are derived from these intuitions through dimming their brightness, yet are of course united with them through community of kind. The common genus is indicated by the term "presentation," though we also considered all the phenomena which essentially belonged to these presentations, such as the reflective intuitions and presentations generally of which the objects are no longer sensory things.[16] The universal range within which our results are valid—suggested indeed by the very way in which we have ordered the in-

[16] The firm delimitation on essential lines of the most general *concept of presentation*, taking as a starting-point the spheres already indicated, is naturally an important problem for systematic phenomenological research. In regard to all such questions I would refer to the prospective publications from whose store of theoretical material the positions so briefly indicated in the present Studies have been drawn.

quiry, leaving the feeling that whatever might bind us to the lower domain had subsidiary significance—thrusts itself upon us as soon as we extend the limits of our research. We then see that all the differences between a central core of meaning (a notion which certainly requires further analysis) and the thetic characters which group themselves about it recur, and so likewise do all modifications which—like those of representation, attention, neutralization—invade the central meaning along their own lines, whilst leaving it none the less its "identical" character.

We can now proceed along *two different* directions, leading on both sides to intentionalities which are grounded in presentations: either in the direction of the noetic *syntheses,* or in that which leads us up to novel through *secondary types of "positings."*

If we follow this latter direction, we come across (as the first and simplest possible, free, that is, from syntheses either at the lower or higher levels) the *affective, appetitive, volitional noeses* which are based on "presentations," perceptions, memories, symbols, and so forth, and clearly display in their structure the evidences of a stratified formation. In dealing with acts in their entirety, we now give priority everywhere to the positional forms (not thereby excluding the neutral substrata), since what is to be said of them also holds good in a sufficiently modified form of the corresponding neutralizations. For example, an æsthetic pleasure is grounded in a neutrality-consciousness of perceptive or reproductive content (*Gehalt*), a joy or sorrow in a (non-neutralized) belief or a modality of belief, a voluntary desire or aversion likewise, but related to something valued as pleasant, beautiful and the like—and so forth.

What interests us here, before we enter at all into the divisions of this structure, is that with the new noetic phases *new noematic phases,* on the correlative side, also appear. On the one side appear new characters, *analogous to the modes of belief,* but *themselves* possessing at the same time, in their new content, the capacity for being doxologically posited; on the other side *new varieties of "formative synthesis"* unite with the correspondingly new varieties of phase; there is constituted a *new meaning which is based upon that of the underlying noesis,* and at the same time envelops it. The new meaning introduces a totally *new dimension of meaning*: with it there is constituted no new determining marks of the mere *"material"* (*Sachen*), but *values of the materials*—qualities of value, or concrete objectified values: beauty and ugliness, goodness and badness; or the object for use, the work of art, the machine, the book, the action, the deed, and so forth.

Moreover, every full experience of the higher level also shows in its full correlate a structure similar to that which we perceived (*erschaut*) at the lowest level of noeses. *In the noema of the higher level the valued as such is as it were a meaning-nucleus girt about with new thetic characters.* The "valuable," the "pleasing," "joyous," etc., are similar in function to the "possible," "probable"; or again, as the case may be, to the "not at all," or the "yes indeed," although it would be perverse to give it a place in this series.

Further, the consciousness in respect of this new character is once again a *positional* consciousness: the "valuable" can be doxically posited as being valuable. The "state of being" (*seiend*) which belongs to the "valuable" as *its* characterization can be thought of also as *modalized,* as can every "state of being" or "certainty"; the consciousness is then a consciousness of *possible value;* the "matter" (*Sache*) only suggests itself as valuable; or again, we are aware of it as *probably valuable,* or as *not-valuable* (here the meaning does not go so far as "valueless," as bad, ugly, and the like; what is expressed in the not-valuable is simply the cancelling of the "valuable"). All such modifications affect the consciousness of value, the valuing noeses, not in a mere external way, but inwardly, and the same remark applies to the noemata also (cf. below, § 117).

We find again a variety of deep-reaching changes in the form of the modifications of attention, according as, in keeping with the multiplicity of essential possibilities, the attentive glance *traverses* the different intentional strata to the "matter" alluded to and its phases beyond—a coherent system of modifications with which we are already acquainted as the lower level—but then also on to the values, the established distinctions of the higher level through the apprehensions which constitute them; and again to the noemata as such, to their characters, or, in the other act of reflexion, to the noeses—and all this in the different specific modes of attention, marginal observation, non-observation, and the like.

The attempt to unravel these complicated structures sharply

and clearly, and to clarify them adequately, necessitates exceedingly difficult inquiries. We must ask, for instance, how "formative syntheses of value" are related to those of fact, how the new noematic characterizations (good, beautiful, and so forth) stand to the modalities of belief, how they group themselves systematically in series and divisions, and many similar questions.

## 117. The Secondary Theses and Conclusion of the Doctrine of the Modifications of the Neutralizing Process. The General Concept of "Theses"

We have still to consider the relation of the new noetic and noematic strata of consciousness to the neutralizing process. We connected this modification with doxic positionality. This, as we can easily convince ourselves, plays, in point of fact, that part in the strata now specially before us which we ascribed to it in advance in the most extended act-sphere, and have specially discussed in that of the modalities of judgment. In the consciousness of presumption, the "presumable," the "probable" lies included positionally; and so also the "pleasant" in the consciousness of pleasure, the "joyous" in the consciousness of joy, and so forth. It lies therein, i.e., it is available for doxic positing, and therefore it is predicable. Accordingly every feeling-consciousness (*Gemütsbewusstsein*) with its new kind of secondary feeling-noeses comes under the concept of positional consciousness, as we had recast this concept, in relation to doxic positionalities, and lastly to positional certainties.

But on closer view we shall have to say that in relating the neutrality-modification to the doxic positionality, important as are the insights upon which the relating rests, we have in a certain sense taken a roundabout way.

Let us first be clear on this point, that acts of pleasure (whether "performed" or not), likewise acts of feeling (*Gemüt*), and will of every kind, are "acts," "intentional experiences," and that thereto belongs in its place (*jeweils*) the "intentio," the "attitude." Otherwise expressed, they are in a very wide but essentially unitary sense *"positings,"* only not of the doxic kind. We casually remarked above, and quite correctly, that act-characters generally are "Theses"— theses in an extended sense of the term, and only in a special sense belief-theses or modalities of the same. The essential analogy of the specific pleasure-noeses with the belief-positings is manifest, likewise that of the wish and will noeses, and so forth. In valuing also, in wishing and in willing, something is "posited," quite apart from the doxic positionality which "lies" in them. That indeed is the source also of all the parallel relatings of the different types of consciousness and of all classifications of the same; strictly, the modes of positing (*Setzungsarten*) were the things classified.

It belongs to the essence of every intentional experience, what ever else may be found in its concrete make-up, to possess at least one "positing characteristic," one "thesis," as a rule several bound together in a dependency-scheme; in this plurality one is then necessarily the *archon*, so to speak, uniting all others in itself and dominating them throughout.

The highest generic unity which unites all these specific "act-characters," these "positing" characters, does not exclude essential and generic differences. Thus the affective positings are related to the doxic as positings, but do not by any means belong so intimately together as do all the modalities of belief.

With the generic community, in essence, of all positional characters, that of its noematic positional correlates (of the "thetic characters in the noematic sense"), and if we take the latter with its broader noematic foundations, the essential community of all "positions" (*Sätze*) is *eo ipso* given. But therein in the last resort are grounded those analogies which have at all times been felt to hold between general logic, general theory of value, and ethics, which, when pursued into their farthest depths, lead to the constituting of general *formal* disciplines on lines parallel to the above, formal logic, formal axiology, and the formal theory of practice.[17]

Thus we are led back to the *generalized* heading, "*Thesis*," to which we now refer the following proposition:

*Every consciousness is either actually or potentially "thetic."* The earlier adopted concept, that of "*actual positing*," and with it that of *positionality*, undergoes thereby a corresponding extension. As a consequence, our doctrine concerning the neutralizing process and its relation to positionality is transferred to the concept of the "thesis" in its ex-

[17] For further consideration of this point, cf. *infra*, Part Four, Chapter 13.

tended form. Thus the general modification which we call the neutralizing belongs to the thetic consciousness generally, whether it be fully carried out or not, and indeed *directly* in the following way: On the one hand we have characterized the positional theses by this feature, that they are either actual theses or may be translated into such; that they accordingly have noemata that can be posited as "real," can be actually posited in the extended sense. In opposition to these we have the "as if" theses, the theses improperly so-called, the ineffectual mirrorings, incapable of carrying on any actual thetic functions in respect of their noemata even when neutralized. The difference between neutrality and positionality runs parallel to that between noetic and noematic; and in the form in which it is here understood it concerns all sorts of thetic characters directly, without taking the way round through the "positions," in the narrow and alone current meaning of the word "primary doxic positings," yet through which alone it can authenticate itself.

But this means that the priority assigned to these special doxic positings has its deep positive basis. In the light of our analyses it is precisely the doxic modalities, and in particular the primary doxic thesis, that of the certainty of belief, which have the unique advantage of covering through their positional potentiality the whole sphere of consciousness. Every thesis of whatever genus can, in conformity with essential laws, and through the doxic characterizations which belong inalienbly to its essential nature, be transformed into an actual doxic positing. A positional act posits, but whatever be the "quality" of its positings it posits doxically; whatever is posited through it in other modes is posited also as being, only not as actually being. And yet actuality can, in essence, be produced by way of an "operation" that remains possible in principle. Every "statement" (*Satz*), every statement of a wish, for instance, can therefore be transformed into a doxic statement, and it is then in a certain way both in one: at once a doxic statement and the statement of a wish.

In this connexion the scheme of essential order, as we have already pointed out, is at first this, that the *prerogative of the doxic pertains properly and in its universal bearing to doxic modalities also*. For every affective experience, every valuation, wish, and will is characterized *in itself* either as being certain or as being suggested, or as a presumptive or doubtful valuing, wishing or willing.[18] Value, for instance, when our standpoint is not that of the doxic modalities of position, is precisely not actually posited in its doxic character. We become aware of value in valuing, of the pleasant in pleasure, of the joyous in rejoicing, but sometimes so that in valuing we are not quite "sure," or that the matter only suggests itself as valuable, as perhaps valuable, whilst we still refrain from taking sides in the valuations we pass upon it. When we live ourselves into such modifications of the valuing consciousness, we do not need to take the doxic point of view. But we can do so if we become absorbed in the suggestion thesis, and then pass over into the corresponding thesis of belief, which, taken predicatively, assumes the form: "the matter should be worth while"; or, if we turn to the noetic side and to the valuing Ego, "it suggests itself to me as valuable (perhaps valuable)." Similarly for other modalities.

*All thetic characters harbour doxic modalities of this kind,* and when the modus is that of certainty, doxic primary theses which, on lines of noematic meaning, *coincide with* the thetic characters. But since this also holds for the doxic variations, doxic *primary theses* are also present in every act (but no longer, as before, noematically coincident).

We can therefore also say: *Every act, as also every act-correlate, harbours explicitly or implicitly a "logical" factor.* It can always be made logically explicit, by means, namely, of the essential generality of the action whereby the noetic stratum of the "act of expression" attaches itself to all that is noetic (or that of the expression itself to all that is noematic). Whereby it is evident that with the transition to the neutrality-modification the expressing act itself and what it expresses are as such neutralized.

It results from all this *that all acts generally—even the acts of feeling and will—are "objectifying" acts, original factors in the "constituting" of objects,* the necessary sources of different regions of being and of the ontologies that belong therewith. For example: the valuing consciousness constitutes over against the mere world of positivity the typically new "axiological" objectivity, a "being" of a new region, so far at any rate as actual doxic theses in virtue of the intrinsic nature of the valuing consciousness generally are indicated in ad-

[18] Cf. *supra,* § 116.

vance as ideal possibilities which give prominence to objectivities with a new type of content—values—as "intended" in the valuing consciousness. In acts of feeling they are affectively intended; they come, through actualizing the doxic content (*Gehalt*) of these acts, to forms of being meant that are first doxic and then expressly logical.

Every act-consciousness which is not doxically carried out is, as non-doxic, a *potentially* objectifying function; *only the doxic cogito actually exercises an objectifying function.*

Here lies the deepest of the sources for shedding light on the *universality of the logical,* in the last resort that of the predicative judgment (to which we must add the stratum of meaningful expression which we have not yet subjected to closer study), and from that standpoint we can also understand the ultimate ground for the universality of the supremacy of logic itself. Proceeding further, we grasp the possibility, indeed the necessity, of formal and material noetic discipline, or, alternatively, of noematic and ontological disciplines essentially related to the intentionality of feeling and will. We shall take up this theme later, as we must first fill up certain gaps in our inquiry.[19]

## 118. Syntheses of Consciousness. Syntactic Forms

If we now look along the second of the two directions indicated above,[20] on the forms of *synthetic* consciousness, there appear within our horizon various ways of constructing experiences through an intentional connexion, which, as essential possibilities, belong partly to all intentional experiences generally, partly to the peculiar features of special types of these experiences. One consciousness is bound up with another, not only in a merely general way, but so as to constitute *one* consciousness, of which the correlate is *one* noema, and this on its own side is grounded in the noemata of the noeses that are linked together.

We have not had in view here the *unity of the immanent time-consciousness,* although we must not forget it, seeing that it is the all-enveloping unity of all the experiences of a stream of experience, and indeed a unity of *consciousness* that binds consciousness with consciousness. Any single

[19] For further consideration of this point, cf. *infra,* the concluding chapter of Part Four.
[20] Cf. § 116.

experience we may select shapes itself within a continuous "original" time-consciousness as a unity stretched out in phenomenological time. Adopting a suitable reflective standpoint, we are able to note the mode of conscious presentation of the stretches of experience which belong to the different sections of experienced duration, and subsequently to state that the whole consciousness which constitutes this unity of duration is continously compounded out of sections in which the sections of the duration as we experience them are constituted; and that the noeses, therefore, do not only unite together, but constitute *one* noesis with *one* noema (that of the filled duration of experience). which is grounded in the noemata of the united noeses. And what holds good for a single experience, holds good also for the whole stream of experience. Foreign to each other as experiences may essentially be, they constitute themselves collectively into *one* time-stream, as members of the *one* phenomenological time.

Meanwhile we have expressly excluded this primary synthesis of the original time-consciousness (which is not to be conceived as an active and discrete synthesis) with the forms of inquiry which belong to it. The syntheses we wish now to speak of are not those to be found within this time-*consciousness,* but within the limits of *time itself, of* concretely filled phenomenological time; or, what comes to the same thing, the syntheses of the experiences plain and simple, taken as we have so far always taken them as unities having duration, as perishing processes in the stream of experience, which is itself no other than the filled phenomenological time. On the other hand, we are not proposing to discuss—most important though they certainly are—the *continuous syntheses,* such, for instance, as essentially belong to every consciousness that constitutes the thinghood of things in space. We shall have ample opportunity later of getting to know these syntheses more closely. We turn our interest rather to the *articulated syntheses,* to the distinctive ways in which discrete, discontinuous acts are bound together in an articulated unity, in the unity of a synthetic act of a higher order. We do not refer to a continuous synthesis as an "act of higher order";[21] the unity (noetic, as also noematic and objective) belongs rather to the same grade as that which is unified. It is, moreover, easy to see that much matter of a general bearing to be developed in the following pages applies to continu-

[21] Cf. the *Philosophie d. Arithmetik,* p. 80 *et passim.*

ous syntheses in the same way as it does to articulated, or *polythetic*, syntheses.

As examples of synthetic acts of a higher grade, we may cite in the sphere of the will the *will that refers beyond* "for the sake of another"; and likewise in that of *acts of feeling*, the *pleasure that refers beyond*, the rejoicing "*with regard to*," or, as we can likewise say, "for another's sake." And so with all similar act-events in connexion with the different types of act. Manifestly all *acts that indicate a preference* also belong here.

We propose to subject to closer consideration another and in a certain sense universal group of syntheses. It includes *collective* (taking together), *disjunctive* (concerning the "this or that"), *explicative, relating* syntheses, and generally the whole series of syntheses which determine the formal ontological forms in conformity with the pure forms of the synthetic objectivities constituted within them, and on the other hand, with respect to the structure of the noematic creations, are reflected back in the apophantic *meaning-forms of formal logic* (the logic of propositions noematically oriented throughout).

The relation to *formal* ontology and logic already indicates that we are there concerned with an essentially closed group of syntheses, possessing in respect of the kinds of experience to be united, which on their side also should be noetic unities of any degree of complexity, a range of possible application that is illimitably universal.

## 119. Transformation of Polythetic into Monothetic Acts

With regard to *all* kinds of articulated syntheses of polythetic acts, we must first observe the following:

Every synthetically unitary consciousness, however many special theses and syntheses it may involve, possesses the total object which belongs to it as a synthetically unitary consciousness. We call it a total object in contrast with the objects which belong intentionally to the lower or higher grade members of the synthesis, so far as they all contribute to it on the principle of consolidated grounding (*Fundierung*), and find their place within it. Every noesis, with its own distinctive form of self-limitation, though it be a dependent stratum, contributes its quota to the constitution of the total object; just as, for instance, the valuing phase, which is dependent, as it is necessarily grounded in a consciousness of the positive material concerned, constitutes the objective value-stratum, that of the "quality of value."

Among new strata such as the above must also be reckoned the specifically synthetic strata among the syntheses of consciousness previously indicated as the most universal, i.e., all the forms which specifically spring from the synthetic consciousness as such, the forms of union, and the synthetic forms which attach to the component members themselves (in so far as they are included in the synthesis).

Within the synthetic consciousness, we said, there is constituted a synthetic total object. But it is "objective" in a quite different sense from that in which the constituted object of a plain thesis is so. The synthetic consciousness or the pure Ego "within" it has *many rays* turned upon its object; the plain thetic consciousness has only *one* such ray. Synthetic collecting is a "plural" consciousness; it is just one and one and one taken together. Likewise within a primitive relating consciousness the relation is constituted as a twofold positing . And similarly everywhere.

Every such many-rayed (polythetic) constitution of synthetic objectives—which are essentially such that *"originally"* we can be aware of them *only* synthetically—possesses the essential law-conforming possibility of *transforming the many-rayed object of awareness into one that is simply one-rayed, of "rendering objective"* in the specific sense and in a *monothetic* act what is synthetically constituted in the many-rayed object.

Thus the synthetically constituted collection is objective in a special sense; it becomes the object of a plain doxic thesis through the back reference of a plain thesis to the primitively constituted collection referred to above, through a peculiar noetic attachment of a thesis to the synthesis. In other words, *the plural consciousness can be essentially translated into a singular consciousness,* which withdraws the plurality from it as *one* object, a something single; the plurality on its side can now be united with other pluralities and previous objects placed in relation to them, and so forth.

The situation is clearly the same for the *disjunctive consciousness,* built up as it is on a pattern wholly analogous to that of the collective consciousness, and for its ontic or noematic correlates as the case may be. Likewise out of the *relating* consciousness the originally and synthetically constituted *relation* can be taken in the form of a plain thesis attached thereto and made into an object in the special sense, and as such compared with other relations, and generally employed as a subject of predicates.

But we must further make it completely self-evident that the simply objectified and the synthetically unitary are really the same, and that the thesis or extracted relation which comes after does not add anything of its own to the synthetic consciousness, but just takes what the latter gives. What is manifestly also self-evident is the essentially different mode of presentation.

In Logic this conformity with law proclaims itself through the *Law of "Denominative equivalence,"* according to which there corresponds to every proposition and to every distinguishable formal part of it a denominative expression: to the statement itself, let us say "S is P," corresponds the *denominative that-clause*; for instance, in the subject-place of new propositions we have "being P" corresponding to the "is P"; *similarity* corresponding to the relational form "similar," *plurality* to the plural form, and so forth.[22]

The concepts which have sprung out of the "denominative reductions," conceived as exclusively determined through the pure forms, make up *formal-categorical modifications of the idea of objectivity generally,* and supply the fundamental conceptual material of formal ontology, and included therein all formal mathematical disciplines. This statement is of crucial importance for understanding the relation of formal logic as apophantic logic to formal ontology in its universal form.

## 120. Positionality and Neutrality in the Sphere of the Syntheses

All strict syntheses, and we had such continually before us, are built up on simple theses, the word being understood in that general sense which we have fixed above as embracing all "intentions," all "act-characters"; and *they themselves* are theses, theses of a higher level.[23] All our conclusions concerning actuality, focal and marginal, concerning neutrality and

---

[22] Cf. the first attempts in this direction in the *Logical Studies*, Vol. II, Fifth Study, § 34 to § 36; further, Vol. III, § 49 of the Sixth Study; and generally for the doctrine of synthesis consult Part Two of this Study.

[23] Moreover, the concept of synthesis has an ambiguity which

positionality can be transferred accordingly—and no long words are needed to show this—to the syntheses.

On the other hand a closer inquiry would here be needed to determine the various relations in which the positionality and neutrality of the basic theses stand to that of the theses grounded upon them.

It is clear generally, and not only for the specially grounded acts we call Syntheses, that one cannot say off-hand that a positional thesis of a higher grade presupposes only positional theses at the lower grades. So too an actual essential insight is a positional and not a neutralized act, grounded in some illustrative intuiting consciousness which on its side can very well be a neutral, a fancy consciousness. The conditions are similar for an æsthetic pleasure in respect of the object of pleasure being manifested, and for a positional representative consciousness in respect of the representing "image."

If we turn now to consider the group of syntheses that interests us, we recognize at once that *in it every synthesis is dependent, so far as its positional character is concerned, on that of the grounding noeses*; more exactly, that it is positional (and can be so only) when all the sub-theses are positional, and neutral when they are not this.

The collective function, for instance, is either really collective or collective in the mode of the "as if"; it is really, or else in neutralized form, thetic. In the one case all the acts related to the single members of the collection are real theses, and not so in the other case. Similar conditions obtain in regard to all the other syntheses of the class reflected in the logical syntactics. Pure neutrality can never function for positional theses; it must at least undergo the transformation into "suppositions," into hypothetical antecedent or consequent clauses, into hypothetically supposited denominatives, as "the Pseudo-Dionysius," for instance, and other similar expressions.

## 121. The Doxic Syntactics in the Spheres of Feeling and Will

If we now ask how the syntheses of this group find expression in the syntactic forms of stated meaning, which the

---

is scarcely hurtful in that it sometimes designates the full synthetic phenomenon, and sometimes the mere synthetical "Act-character," the most fundamental thesis of the phenomenon.

logical theory of positional forms systematically develops, the reply is ready to hand. There are in fact, so the answer runs, *doxic syntheses,* or, as we can also say, in recollection of the logicogrammatical syntactical forms which take their impress, *doxic syntactics.* As belonging to the specific essence of doxic acts, we may cite the syntactic "and" together with the syntactic "and" together with the plural forms, and the syntactic "or" and the positing, as a relating act, of a predicate on the basis of a subject-positing, and so forth. No one doubts that "belief" and "judgment" in the logical sense belong closely to each other (even if one does not propose to identify them), and that syntheses of belief (*Glaubenssynthesen*) find their "expression" in the forms of stated meaning. Correct as this is, one can clearly perceive that this way of putting it does not bring out the whole truth. These syntheses "and," "or," "if," or "because," and "thus," in brief the syntheses which at first present themselves as doxic, are by no means *merely* doxic.

It is a fundamental fact[24] that such syntheses also belong to the strict essential nature of the non-doxic theses, and in the following sense:

There is undoubtedly such a thing as collective joy, collective pleasure, collective will, and so forth. Or, as I am accustomed to express it, there is besides the doxic "and" (the logical), also an axiological and practical "and." The same is true of the word "or," and all the syntheses therewith connected. For example: the mother who glances lovingly at her little flock embraces each child singly and all together in *one* act of love. The unity of a collective act of love is not a love and a collective presentation to that end, though the latter may be attached to love as its necessary foundation. Loving is itself collective; it is as many-rayed as the presentation, and perhaps the plural judging which "underlies" it. We should speak in precisely the same direct way of a plural loving as of a plural presenting or judging. The syntactical forms enter into the essential being of acts of feeling, namely, into the thetic layer specifically peculiar to them. This cannot here be developed for all syntheses; we must be content with the indication offered by the example just given.

But let us recall the essential and intimate affinity between

[24] The author stumbled upon this thought (more than ten years back) during the attempt to realize the idea of a formal axiology and formal theory of practice as an analogue to formal logic.

doxic theses and theses generally, which we inquired into above. In every thesis generally, in accord with that which when functioning as a love-intention, for instance, it noematically effects, there lies concealed a doxic thesis running parallel to it. Manifestly the parallelism between the syntactical forms which belong to the sphere of the doxic thesis and those that belong to all other theses (the parallelism between the doxic "and," "or," and so forth, and the value-possessing and purposive) is a special case of the same essential and intimate affinity. For the synthetic acts of feeling—synthetic, namely, in respect of the syntactical forms here discussed—constitute *synthetic objectives of feeling,* which come through corresponding acts to explicit objectification. The beloved group of children as *object of affection* is a collective object, which means, applying what we have considered above to the matter of the correlative, not only a positive collective object and a love *directed to it,* but *a collective object of love.* Just as noetically a ray of love proceeding from the Ego splits up into a bundle of rays, each of which is directed towards a single object, so too there are distributed over the collective object of affection as such as many *noematic characters of love* as there are objects collected at the time, and there are as many positional characters which combine synthetically into the noematic unity of a positional character.

We see that all these syntactical forms are parallel forms, i.e., that they belong as much to the acts of feeling (*Gemüt*) themselves, with their specific components of feeling and syntheses of feelings, as to the doxic positionalities which run parallel to them and share the same essential nature, and may be extracted from them through suitable glancings towards the upper and lower levels at the moment. Naturally this can be transferred, *mutatis mutandis,* from the noetical to the noematical sphere. The exiological "and" essentially conceals in itself a doxic, and every axiological syntactical form of the group here considered a logical factor; just as every plain noematic correlate contains within itself a "that which is," or some other modality of Being, and as its substratum the form of "something" and the forms which otherwise belong to it. And at all times it is a matter of essentially possible special directings of the mental glance and of thetic or synthetic-doxic modes of procedure included herewith to shape out of an act of feeling in which we live, so to speak, wrapped in the feeling, and thus without actualizing the doxic potentialities, a new act in which what was at first only a potential objectivity of feeling is transformed into one that is actual, doxic, and, it may be, expressly explicit. Moreover, it is possible, and in everyday life very usual, to look, for instance, towards several intuitional objects, positing them doxically, and to fulfil at the same time a synthetic act of feeling, a unitary act of collective pleasure, perhaps, or a unifying selective act of feeling, of a pleasure that favours or a displeasure that rejects; whilst we do not go so far as to give a doxic turn to the whole phenomenon. We do so, however, when we make a statement, for instance, concerning our pleasure in the many, or in one out of the many; concerning the preferability of the one as compared with the other, and the like.

There is no need to insist on the importance of carefully carrying out analyses such as the above for increasing our knowledge of the essential nature of axiological and practical objectivities, meanings and modes of consciousness, and therefore also of the problems of the "origin" of the ethical, æsthetical, and essentially allied concept and judgments (*Erkenntnisse*).

Since it is not our proper task here to solve phenomenological problems, but to set in scientific relief the main problems of phenomenology, and to indicate in advance the lines of study that bear on these problems, we must be content to have developed thus far the matters here treated.

## 122. Modes of Carrying Out Articulated Syntheses.

### The "Thema"

To the realm of theses and syntheses there belongs an important group of general modifications, and the brief indications of its nature we propose to give can best be added at once and at this precise point.

A synthesis can be *carried out* step by step; it becomes, it arises through *original production*. This primordiality of becoming in the stream of consciousness is a quite peculiar one. The thesis or synthesis becomes, in so far as the pure Ego actually advances step by step; itself lives in the step and "steps on" with it. Its *free spontaneity and activity* consists in positing, positing on the strength of this or that, positing as an antecedent or a consequent, and so forth; it does not live within the theses as a passive indweller; the theses radiate from it as from a primary source of generation. Every thesis begins with a *point of insertion*, with a point at which *the positing has its origin*; so it is with the first thesis and with each further one in the synthetic nexus. This "inserting" even belongs to the thesis as such, as a remarkable modus of original actuality. It somewhat resembles the *fiat*, the point of insertion of will and action.

But we should not confuse the general and the particular. The spontaneous resolve, the purposive, accomplishing action is *one* act beside other acts; its syntheses are special syntheses among others. But *each* act of whatever kind can start off in this *spontaneity modus of a so-to-speak creative beginning*, in which the pure Ego steps on the scene as subject of the spontaneity.

This mode of insertion passes over immediately and in accordance with an essential necessity into another mode. For instance, the *apprehending* and *taking possession of* involved in perceiving turns again and without a break into "*having in one's grasp.*"

Still another new modal alteration supervenes when the thesis was a mere step towards a synthesis, when the pure Ego takes a new step, and now in the pervading unity of the synthetic consciousness "*still maintains*" in its grasp what it had just grasped: apprehending the new thematic object, or primary thema, but still keeping the member previously apprehended as belonging to the same total thema. For example, when collecting things together I do not allow the object just perceptively apprehended to slip away whilst I turn my apprehending glance to the new object. In the process of proving something, I go step by step over the thoughts that serve as premises; a synthetic step once taken, I do not abandon it; I do not lose hold of what I have won, but the modus of actuality has been essentially altered through the effective introduction of the new thema of primary actuality.

Moreover, we have *also* to deal, though in no sense *merely*, with obscurations. The differences which we have just sought to describe present rather, in contrast with the differences of clearness and obscurity, a completely new dimension, although the two kinds of difference interlace so closely.

We further observe that these new differences, no less than the differences in clearness and all other intentional differences, come under the law of the correlation of noesis and noema. Thus once again there correspond to the noetic actuality-modifications of the kind here in question, the noematic. That is, the mode of presentation of the "intended (*Vermeinten*) as such" is altered in and through the shiftings of the thesis, or the steps of the synthesis, and these changes can be shown to affect the noematic content at the time being also, and can be brought into relief as one of its strata.

If the actuality-modus (in noematic parlance the mode of presentation)—disregarding for a moment the changes that are continually in flux—is necessarily transformed and in accordance with certain *discrete types*, there persists none the less throughout the transformations an essential common element. Noematically something is preserved in the form of an identical *meaning*; on the noetic side the correlate of this meaning, and further the whole form of articulation according to theses and syntheses.

But a new modification of the essence now take place. The pure Ego can *withdraw* itself wholly from the theses; it *releases* the thetic correlates *from its "hold"*; it *"turns to another thema."* What had just been its thema (theoretic, axiological, and so forth), with all its articulations more or less obscured, has not disappeared from consciousness; it is still consciously apprehended, but no longer held in thematic grasp.

This holds good for single theses as well, and also for the links in a synthesis. I am at present meditating; a whistle from the street distracts me momentarily from my thema (in this case a thought-thema). A moment in which I am turned towards the sound, forthwith a return to the old thema! The apprehension of the sound is not blotted out, we are still conscious of the whistle in a modified way, but we no longer hold it in our mental grasp. It does not belong to the thema, not even to a parallel thema. We notice that this possibility of simultaneous *themata* and thematic syntheses *which may cut across and "disturb" each other* points to still further possible modifications, and we note how the title-heading. *"Thema,"* related to all the basic types of acts and act-syntheses, is itself an important theme for phenomenological analysis.

## 123. Vagueness and Distinctness as Modes in the Fulfilling of Synthetic Acts

Let us now consider further modalities of the act of fulfilment which lie, so to speak, in the direction opposite to the favoured modus of actuality as it springs from its primary source. A thought, simple or decked out with various thetic characters, can emerge as a "*vague*" thought. It then appears like a simple presentation without any articulation that is actual and thetic. Perhaps we recall a proof, a theory, a conversation—it "occurs to us." And yet at first we are not turned towards it; it emerges in the "background." Then a personal glance is turned single-ray-wise upon it, apprehending the relevant noematic objectivity in an inarticulate grasp. A new process can now set in; the vague reminiscence passes into one that is *distinct* and clear; step by step we recall the course of the proof, we "re"-produce the theses of the proof and the syntheses, we "re"-capitulate the stages of yesterday's conversation, and the like. Of course all such reproduction in the way of reminiscence, of reproducing "earlier" originary productions, is something non-essential. It may be that we have begun to unfold a *new* theoretical idea for carrying through a complicated theory, at first in a vague though unitary way, then in definite steps freely taken, and have transformed it into synthetic actualities. All that is here indicated can of course be applied in a similar way to all kinds of acts.

This important difference between *vagueness* and *distinctness* plays an important part in the phenomenology of "expressions" still to be discussed, explicit presentations, judgments, acts of feeling, and so forth. We have only to think of the way in which we are accustomed to grasp the synthetic constructions, still very complex, which make up the "intellectual content" of our reading at any time, and consider what, in our understanding of the matter read, and in respect of this so-called intellectual foundation of the expressions, comes to really primordial actualization.

## 124. The Noetic-Noematic Stratum of the "Logos." Meaning and Meaning Something

Acts of expression, act-strata in the specific "logical" sense, are interwoven with all the acts hitherto considered, and in their case no less than in the others the parallelism of noesis and noema must be clearly brought out. The prevalent and unavoidable ambiguity of our ways of speaking, which is caused by this parallelism and is everywhere operative where the concomitant circumstances are mentioned, operates also of course when we talk of expression and meaning.

Ambiguity is dangerous only so long as it is not known to be such, or the parallel structures have not been kept apart. But if that has been done, we have only to be careful that we are quite certain on the occasion in question as to which of the structures our words must be related.

Let us start from the familiar distinction between the sensory, the so to speak bodily aspect of expression, and its non-sensory "mental" aspect. There is no need for us to enter more closely into the discussion of the first aspect, nor upon the way of uniting the two aspects, though we clearly have title-headings here indicated for phenomenological problems that are not unimportant.

We restrict our glance exclusively to "meaning" (*Bedeutung*), and "meaning something" (*Bedeuten*). Originally these words relate only to the sphere of speech, that of "expression." But it is almost inevitable, and at the same time an important step for knowledge, to extend the meaning of these words, and to modify them suitably so that they may be applied in a certain way to the whole noetico-noematic sphere, to all acts, therefore, whether these are interwoven with expression acts or not.[25] With this in view we ourselves, when referring to any intentional experiences, have spoken all along of "Sinn" (sense), a word which is generally used as an equivalent for "Bedeutung" (meaning). We propose in the interests of distinctness to favour the word *Bedeutung* (meaning at the conceptual level) when referring to the old concept, and more particularly in the complex speech-form "*logical*" or "*expressing*" meaning. We use the word *Sinn* (Sense or Meaning *simpliciter*) in future, as before, in its more embracing breadth of application.

Let us suppose, to take an example, that there is a perceived object out there, an object with a definite meaning, and monothetically posited in determinate fullness. We discriminate, making the given meaning more explicit, and relate the discriminated parts or phases within a unity, following some such scheme as "This is white." But our attitude here is the primitive one we are wont to take up as a rule and off-hand in a first plain perceptual grasp of

[25] Cf. in this connexion the *Philosophie der Arithmetik*, p. 28 f., where the distinction is already drawn between the "psychological description of a phenomenon" and the "statement of its meaning," and mention is made of a "logical content" as opposed to the psychological.

a thing. The process makes no call whatsoever on "expression," neither on expression in the sense of verbal sound nor on the like as verbal meaning, and here the latter can also be present independently of the verbal sound (as in the case when this sound is "forgotten"). But if we have "*thought*" or *stated* "This is white," a new stratum is there with the rest, and unites with the "meant as such" in its pure perceptive form. On these lines everything remembered or fancied can, as such, have its meaning made more explicit and expressible. Whatever is "meant as such," every meaning (*Meinung*) in the noematic sense (and indeed as noematic nucleus) of any act whatsoever *can be expressed conceptually* (*durch* "*Bedeutungen*"). Thus we posit quite generally the following:

Logical meaning (*Bedeutung*) *is an expression.*

The verbal sound can be referred to as expression only because the meaning which belongs to it expresses; it is in it that the expressing originally lies. "Expression" is a remarkable form, which permits of being adapted to every "meaning" (to the noematic "nucleus"), and raises it to the realm of the "Logos," of the *conceptual,* and therewith of the "*general.*"

Moreover, the terms just used are understood in a quite definite sense, which must not be confused with other meanings which the terms admit of. Speaking generally, the terms in question point to a large field of phenomenological analyses, which are fundamental for clarifying the essential nature of logical thinking and its correlates. From the noetic standpoint the rubric "expressing" should indicate a special act-stratum to which all other acts must adjust themselves in their own way, and with which they must blend remarkably in such wise that every noematic act-meaning, and consequently the relation to objectivity which lies in it, stamps itself "conceptually" in the noematic phase of the expressing. A peculiar intentional instrument lies before us which essentially possesses the outstanding characteristic of reflecting back as from a mirror every other intentionality according to its form and content, of copying it whilst colouring it in its own way, and thereby of working into it its own form of "conceptuality." Yet these figures of speech which here thrust themselves upon us, those of mirroring and copying, must be adopted with caution, as the imaginativeness which colours their application might easily lead one astray.

Problems of exceptional difficulty beset the phenomena which find their place under the headings "mean" (*Bedeuten*) and "meaning" (*Bedeutung*).[26] Since every science, viewed from the side of its theoretical content, of all that constitutes its "doctrine" (theorem, proof, theory), is objectified in a specific "logical" medium, the medium of expression, it follows that for philosophers and psychologists who are guided by general logical interests the problems of expression and meaning lie nearest of all, and are also the first, generally speaking, which, so soon as one seeks seriously to reach their foundations, compel towards phenomenological inquiry into the essential nature of things.[27] Thence one is led to the queries how to interpret the "expressing" of "what is expressed," how expressed experiences stand in relation to those that are not expressed, and what changes the latter undergo when expression supervenes; one is then led to the question of their "intentionality," of their "immanent meaning," of their "content" and quality (i.e., the act-character of the thesis), of the distinction of this meaning and these phases of the essence which lie in the pre-expressive from the the meaning of the expressing phenomenon itself and its own phases, and so forth. One gathers still in various ways from the writings of the day how little justice is apt to be done to the great problems here indicated in their full and deeplying significance.

The stratum of expression—and this constitutes its peculiarity—apart from the fact that it lends expression to all other intentionalities, is not productive. Or if one prefers: *its productivity, its noematic service, exhausts itself in expressing, and in the form of the conceptual which first comes with the expressing.*

Moreover, the expressing stratum, from the side of its thetic character, is completely one in essence with that which finds expression, and in the covering process absorbs its

[26] As can be gathered from the second volume of the *Logical Studies,* in which they figure as a main theme.

[27] In point of fact, this was the way along which the *Logical Studies* endeavoured to penetrate into Phenomenology. A second way, starting from the opposite side, from the side, namely, of experience and the data of sense which the author has also followed since the beginning of the 'nineties, did not find full expression in that work.

essence so completely that we call the expressive presenting just presenting; and expressive belief, presumption, doubt, in themselves and as a whole, belief, presumption, doubt; similarly we call expressive wish or will just wish or will. It is, moreover, an illuminating fact that the difference between positionality and neutrality is characteristic of the expressive also, and we have already considered it above. *The expressing stratum cannot have a thesis, positional or neutral, that is otherwise qualified than the stratum that suffers expression,* and when the two cover each other we find not two theses to be kept separate, but *one thesis only.*

The attempt to clarify here the relevant structures meets with considerable difficulties. Already the recognition that after abstracting from the stratum of sensory verbal sound, there lies before us in reality still another layer which we here presuppose, thus in every case—even in that of a thinking that is ever so vague, empty, and merely verbal—a stratum of meaning that expresses, and a substratum of expressed meaning—is not one that is easy to make, nor again is the understanding of the essential connexions of these stratifications easy. For we should not hold too hard by the metaphor of stratification; expression is not of the nature of an overlaid varnish or covering garment; it is a mental (*geistige*) formation, which exercises new intentional influences (*Funktionen*) on the intentional substratum and experiences from the latter correlative intentional influences. What this new image in its turn amounts to must be studied in relation to the phenomena themselves and all their essential modifications. Of special importance is the understanding of the different kinds of "generality" which there emerge; on the one hand, that which belongs to every expression and phase of expression, even to the dependent "is," "not," "and," "if," and so forth; on the other hand, the generality of "general names" like "man" as contrasted with proper names like "Bruno"; or again, such as belong to an essence in itself syntactically formless as compared with the different generalities of meaning which have just been touched on.

## 125. The Completing Modalities in the Sphere of Logical Expression and the Method of Clarification

In order to clear up the difficulties here indicated, special regard must be had to the differences of actuality-modus treated above.[28] to the modalities of the completing of the act which concern all theses and syntheses, including therefore the expressive. But this in a *twofold way*. On the one hand they concern the stratum of meaning, the specifically logical stratum itself, on the other hand the basic substrata.

In the course of reading we can draw out every meaning fully and freely articulate it, and can connect meanings synthetically together in the way already indicated. Through this *completion of the acts of meaning in the mode of self-production* we win complete *distinctness of "logical" understanding*.

This distinctness can pass over into vagueness in all the modes above described; the sentence just read sinks into obscurity, loses its living articulation, ceases to be our "thema," "still within our grasp."

But we must separate such distinctness and vagueness from that which affects the expressed substrata. A distinct understanding of word and sentence (or a distinct articulated fulfilling of the act of stating) is compatible with the *vagueness of the foundations*. This vagueness does not bespeak want of clearness merely, although it *also* does this. The substratum can be a confused unity (and mostly is this), a unity that does not carry its articulation actually in itself, but owes the same to its merely adjusting itself to the stratum of logical expression which is really articulate and carried out in primal actuality.

This has a highly important methodological significance. We call attention to the point that our previous discussions concerning the *method of clarification*[29] with regard to the statement, which is the vital element of science, need supplementing in certain essential respects. What is needed in order to reach from vague thinking to strict, fully explicit knowledge, to the distinct and at the same time clear fulfilling of acts of thought, is now easily indicated. In the first place all *"logical" acts* (those of meaning something), so far as they were still in the modus "vagueness," must be transferred to the mode of primordial spontaneous actuality; we have to set up a state of complete *logical distinctness*. But an analogous proceeding must be carried out in the basal *substratum;* we must transform all that is lifeless into vitality,

[28] Cf. *supra,* § 122.
[29] Cf. § 67.

all vagueness into distinctness, all unintuitability also into intuitability. Only when we carry out this work in the substratum—provided that in so doing incompatibilities do not emerge rendering all further work superfluous—does the method previously described come into action, whereby we have to take into account the fact that the concept of intuition, of clear consciousness, is transferred from monothetic to synthetic acts.

For the rest, as a deeper analysis shows, everything turns on the *kind of self-evidence* which the occasion requires and on the stratum concerned. All self-evidencing insights which bear on relations of a *purely logical character*, on the essential connexions of noematic *meanings*—those therefore which we obtain from the basic laws of formal logic—require that the meanings be given, that, in other words, statements be given which express the forms prescribed by the relevant law of meaning. The dependence of the meanings brings it about that the exemplification of the essential logical constructs which mediate the law's self-evidence have lower layers connected with them, those in fact which are brought to logical expression: but *these lower layers do not need to be brought to clearness when it is pure logical insight that is involved*. With corresponding modifications this holds good for all the "analytical" forms of applied logical knowledge.

## 126. Completeness and Generality of Expression

We must further lay stress on the difference between *complete* and *incomplete expression*.[30] The unity of the expressing and the expressed in the phenomenon is indeed that of a certain congruence, but the upper layer need not extend its expressing function over the entire lower layer. Expression is complete when *the stamp of conceptual meaning has been fixed upon all the synthetic forms and significations of the lower layer;* incomplete when this is only partially effected: as when, in regard to a complex process, the arrival of the carriage, perhaps, bringing guests that have been long expected; we call out: the carriage! the guests! This difference of completeness will naturally cut across that of relative clearness and distinctness.

An incompleteness of a totally different kind from the one

[30] Cf. *Logical Studies,* Vol. II, Fourth Study, §§ 6 ff.

just discussed is that which belongs to the essential nature of the expression as such, namely, to its *generality*. "I would like," expresses the wish in a general form; the form of command, the command; "might very well be" the presumption, or the likely as such, and so forth. Every closer determination in the unity of the expression is itself again expressed in general form. It lies in the meaning of the generality which belongs to the essential nature of the expressing function that it would not ever be possible for all the specifications of the expressed to be reflected in the expression. The stratum of the meaning function is not, and in principle is not, a sort of duplication of the lower stratum. Many directions of variability in the latter do not appear at all in the meaning whose function it is to express; they and their correlates do not "express themselves" at all; so it is with the modifications of relative clearness and distinctness, the attention modifications, and so forth. But in that also to which the specific meaning of the speech-form of expression points there are essential differences, as in respect of the way in which the synthetic forms and the synthetic materials find expression.

We must also refer here to the "dependence" of all formal meanings and all "syncategorematic" meanings generally. The isolated "and," "if," the isolated genitive "of the heavens," can be understood and yet dependent, in need of completion. The question here is what this standing in need of completion betokens, and what it amounts to in respect of the two strata and with regard to the possibilities of incompleteness in the function that means this, that, or the other.[31]

## 127. Expression of Judgments and Expression of the Noemata of Feeling

We must be clear about all these points if one of the oldest and hardest problems of the sphere of meaning is to be solved, a problem which hitherto, precisely because it lacked the requisite phenomenological insight, has remained without solution: the problem, namely, as to *how statement as the expression of judgment is related to the expressions of other acts*. We have expressive predications in which a "thus it

[31] Cf. *loc. cit.*, § 5.

is!" comes to expression. We have expressive presumptions, questions, doubts, expressive wishes, commands, and so forth. Linguistically we have here forms of sentence whose structure is in part distinctive, while yet they are of ambiguous interpretation by the side of sentences that embody statements we have sentences embodying questions, presumptions, wishes, commands, and so forth. The original debate bore on the issue whether, disregarding the grammatical wording and its historical forms, we had here to do with coordinate types of meaning, or whether the case was not rather this, that all these sentences, so far as their meaning is concerned, are not in truth sentences that state. If the latter, then all act-constructions, such, for instance, as those of the sphere of feeling, which in themselves are not acts of judgment, can achieve "expression" only in a roundabout way through the mediation of an act of judging which is grounded in them.

The whole policy, however, of making the problem bear on *acts*, on noeses, is sufficient, and the persistent overlooking of the noemata, upon which precisely in reflexions on meaning such as these the mental glance is directed, is prejudicial to the understanding of the matters involved. In order simply to reach a point where the problems can be correctly set, it is altogether necessary that we should take into account the different structures we have indicated: we need the general knowledge of the correlation between noetic and nomatic as pervading all intentional relations and all thetic and synthetic strata; likewise the separation of the stratum of logical meaning from the substratum to be expressed through it; further, the insight into the directions essentially possible here as elsewhere in the sphere of intentionality, both those taken in reflexion and those in which modifications take place; but more particularly we need the insight into the ways in which out of every consciousness *substantitive meanings* of a noetic and noematic kind are to be disengaged. The *root-problem* to which we are referred back in the long run must, as the whole connected series of our last problem-analyses shows, be formulated thus:

*Is the medium for the expressing of meaning, this unique medium of the Logos, specifically doxic? Does it not, in the process whereby the expressing of meaning is adjusted to the meaning expressed, coincide with the doxic element latent itself in all positionality?*

This would not of course exclude the possibility of there being various ways of ex····ing such experiences, those of feeling, for instance. A single one of these would be the direct plain expression of the experience (or of its noema, in the case of the correlative meaning of the term "expression") through the immediate adjustment of an articulated expression to the articulated experience of feeling whereby doxic and doxic tally together. Thus it would have been the *doxic* form dwelling in respect of all its component aspects within the experience of feeling that made possible the adjustability of the expression, as an exclusively doxothetic experience, to the experience of feeling, which, as such, and in respect of all its members, is multithetic, but thereunder necessarily doxothetic also.

To speak more accu....ly, this *direct* expression, if it would be true and complete, should be applied only to the *doxic non-modalized* experiences. If I am not certain as to what I wish, it is then not correct when I say in direct adaptation: May S be P. For all expressing, according to the basic interpretation we have given of it, is a doxic act in the pregnant sense, i.e., a believing certitude.[32] Thus it can express only certainties (e.g., certainties of wish or will). The expression in cases such as the above can be rendered only indirectly in some such form as: "Perhaps may S be P." In so far as modalities make their appearance, we must, if we would secure as fit an expression as possible, have recourse to the doxic theses with modified thetic content, which, so to speak, lie concealed in them.

Letting this interpretation pass as correct, we must still supplement it by the following considerations:

There exist at all times *a number of alternative indirect expressions* involving "roundabout phrases." It is part of the essential nature of every objectivity as such, through whatever acts it may have been constituted, whether plain and simple, or manifold and synthetically grounded, to admit of various possible ways of developing it relationally; thus

---

[32] One may *not* say that an expressing act *expresses* a doxic act, if by the expressing act one understands, as we do here at every point, the act of meaning itself. If, however, the phrase "expressing act" relates to the verbal sound, one could very well speak after the manner in question, but the sense would then be completely altered.

to every act, an act of wishing, for instance, there may be annexed different acts relating to it, to its noematic objectivity, to its noema as a whole: linkings of subject-theses, predicate-theses added to these, wherein, maybe, that which in the original act was intended as a wish is developed in the form of a judgment and expressed in a corresponding way. The expression is then *directly* adjusted *not to the original phenomenon,* but to the *predicative* form *derived* from it.

Moreover, we must not fail to observe that *explicative* or *analytic* synthesis (judgment *prior* to its expression as conceptual meaning), on the other hand statement or *judgment in the ordinary sense,* and lastly *doxa* (belief) are matters that must be kept well apart. The commonly called "theory of judgment" is viciously ambiguous. It is one thing to clear up the essential nature of the idea of doxa, another to clarify the essence of statement or that of the related developments.[33]

---

[33] This whole subsection should be compared with the concluding chapter of the Sixth Study, *Logical Studies,* Vol. III. It will be seen that during the intervening period the author has not stayed where he was, but that in spite of much that is disputable and immature the analyses of the earlier book move in the direction of progress marked out by the present volume. They have been attacked in various ways, yet without any real understanding of the new motives of thought and new ways of formulating problems which were there attempted.

# PART FOUR

# REASON AND REALITY
## (WIRKLICHKEIT)

# Chapter 11

## Noematic Meaning and Relation to the Object

### 128. Introduction

THE PHENOMENOLOGICAL EXCURSIONS of the last chapter have led us into pretty well all intentional domains. Adopting a far-reaching viewpoint, we have followed the line of cleavage between real (*reeller*) and intentional, noetic and noematic analysis. Thus guided, we have everywhere come across structures that ramified afresh incessantly at every point. We can no longer close our eyes to the evidence that this cleavage points in fact to a fundamental structural distinction that runs right through all intentional structures, and must therefore constitute a leading motive governing the development of phenomenological method, and must determine the course of all researches that bear on the problems of intentionality.

It is also clear that with this cleavage *eo ipso* a separation has emerged between two radically opposed and yet essentially interrelated regions of Being. We have previously stressed the point that Consciousness in general must count as an independent region of Being. But we then recognize that the description on essential lines of the nature of consciousness leads us back to the corresponding description of the object consciously known, that the correlate of consciousness is inseparable from consciousness and yet not really (*reell*) contained in it. Thus the noematic separated itself off as an *objectivity* that belongs to consciousness and is yet *unique*. In this connexion we note the following: Whilst objects *simpliciter* (taken in the unmodified sense) stand under radically different *summa genera*, all meanings of objects and all noemata taken in their completeness, however they may otherwise differ, belong intrinsically to a single supreme genus. But then it is also true that the essences, noema and noesis, are mutually inseparable: every lowest difference on the noematic side points eidetically back to lowest differences of the noetic. This naturally applies to all formulations of genus and species.

The knowledge of the essential two-sidedness of intentionality in the form of noesis and noema brings this consequence with it, that a systematic phenomenology should not direct its effort one-sidedly towards a real (*reelle*) analysis of experiences, and more specifically of the intentional kind. But the temptation to do this is at first very great, because the historical and natural movement from psychology to phenomenology brings it about that as a matter of course we take the immanent study of pure experiences, the study of their own proper essence, to be a study of their real components.[1] On both sides in truth there open up vast domains of eidetic inquiry, and these are constantly related to each other, yet as it turns out keep separate for a long stretch. In great measure, that which has been taken for noetic act-analysis has been obtained when the mental glance was directed towards the "meant as such," and it was really noematic structures which were there described.

In the discussions that immediately follow we propose to direct our attention to the general structure of the noema, and from a point of view which has hitherto been repeatedly referred to by name, but was yet not the leading one for the purpose of noematic analysis: the *phenomenological problem of the relation of consciousness to an objectivity* has, above all, its noematical aspect. The noema in itself has an objective relation, through its own proper "meaning." If then we ask how the "meaning" of consciousness transmits itself to the "object," its own object, and in manifold acts of very varied noematic content can yet remain "the same," and how we perceived this in the meaning itself, new structures present themselves of which the exceptional importance is at once obvious. For moving forward in this direction and, on the other hand, reflecting on the parallel noeses, we eventually strike the question what the "claim" of consciousness to be really "related to" an objective, to have an objective "reference," properly comes to, how objective relations which are "valid" and "invalid" are to be made clear phe-

---

[1] This is still the standpoint of the *Logical Studies*. The nature of the facts themselves may to a considerable extent compel us to carry out noematical analyses, but these are still considered rather as indicators pointing to the parallel noetic structures: the essential parallelism of the two structures had not yet been clearly grasped.

nomenologically in the light of the distinction between noesis and noema; and thus we find confronting us the great *problems of the Reason* which it will be our aim in this division of our treatise to clarify on trancendental lines and to formulate as *phenomenological* problems.

## 129. "Content" and "Object"; the Content as "Meaning"

In the previous analyses a universal noematic structure played a constant part indicated by the separating off of a certain *noematic "nucleus"* from the changing *"characters"* that belong to it, whereby the noema in its fullest specification appears drawn into the stream of modifications of various kinds. This nucleus has not yet received adequate scientific recognition. It stood out intuitively as a unity, and sufficiently clearly to enable us to concern ourselves with it in a general way. It is now the proper time to consider it more closely and to set it at the centre of phenomenological analysis. As soon as this is done there emerge distinctions of universal importance that run through all kinds of act, and lead the way to great masses of material for research.

We start from the ordinary equivocal phrase: the content of consciousness. Under content we understand the "meaning" of which we say that in it or through it consciousness refers to an objective as its "own." As the superscription and final end of our discussion, so to speak, we take the following proposition:

Every noema has a *"content,"* namely, its "meaning," and is related through it to "its" *object*.

In more recent times one often hears it proclaimed as a great step in advance that now at last the basic distinction between act, content, and object has been achieved. The three words in this setting have almost become catchwords, especially since the publication of Twardowski's fine treatise.[2] Meanwhile, though the author's merit in having discussed in a penetrating way certain current confusions, and exposed their latent fallacies, is undoubtedly a great one, it must still be said that in regard to the clearing up of the essential concepts involved he has not taken (and we do not impute any blame to him on this account) any considerable step beyond what was well known

[2] K. Twardowski, *Concerning the Theory of the Content and Object of Presentations,* Vienna, 1894.

(despite their carelessness and confusion) to the philosophers of former generations. Prior indeed to a systematic phenomenology of consciousness no radical progress was possible. With concepts that are left phenomenologically obscure, such as "act," "content," and "object," of "presentations," we can make no headway. What is it that may not call itself act and content of a presentation, and indeed presentation itself? And what can be so called should itself be scientifically understood.

In this respect a first and, as it would appear to me, a necessary step was tentatively taken through the phenomenological emphasis given to the terms "material" and "quality," and through the idea of "intentional essence" as distinguished from "epistemological essence." The onesidedness of the noetic orientation, within which these distinctions were first drawn and intended, is easily overcome by a proper regard to the noematic parallels. We can interpret the concepts noematically thus: "quality" (judgment-quality, wish-quality, and so forth) is nothing other than what we have hitherto treated as "positing" character, "thetic" character in the widest sense. The expression which has its origin in contemporary psychology (that of Brentano) appears to me now little suitable; every particular thesis has its quality, but should not itself be called a quality. The "material" which within limits coincides with the "what" that the positing characteristic takes from the "quality" manifestly corresponds to the "noematic nucleus."

The task now before us is to develop these initial positions consistently, to cast light upon them from a deeper source, to dissect the involved concepts more accurately, and to carry them out correctly through all the domains of noesis-noema. Every really successful step taken in this direction must be of exceeding importance for phenomenology. We are not concerned here with specialist side-issues, but with essential phases which enter into the central structure of every intentional experience.

In order to get into closer touch with our material, we add the following reflexion:

Intentional experience, one is wont to say, has *"objective reference"*; but one also says, it is *"consciousness of something,"* consciousness, for instance, of an apple-tree in blossom here in this garden. We shall not find it necessary at first, in regard to such examples, to keep the two phases apart. If we recall our previous analyses, we find the full noesis related to the full noema as to its full intentional some-what. But it is then clear that this relation cannot be the same as is intended in the phrase concerning the reference of consciousness to its intentional objective; for to every noetic, in particular to every thetic-noetic phase, there corresponds a phase in the noema; and in the latter, set apart over against the nexus of thetic characters, is the noematic nucleus characterized through these. Let us further recall the "directed glance," which under certain circumstances traverses the noeses (passing through the actual *cogito*), transforming the specifically thetic phases into rays of the positing actuality of the Ego, and let us accurately note how this Ego with its rays is now "directed upon" the ob-jective as apprehending what is, or as presuming or wishing, and so forth, how its glance penetrates the noematic nucleus; we will then be observant that the phrase concerning the re-lation (more specifically the "direction") of consciousness to its objective points towards a *most inward* phase of the noema. It is not the nucleus itself just indicated, but some-thing which, so to speak, constitutes the necessary midpoint of the nucleus and functions as "bearer" of the noematic peculiarities which specially belong to it, of the noematically modified properties, namely, of the "meant as such."

As we go more closely into this, we become aware that in fact the distinction between "content" and "object" must be drawn not only in the case of "consciousness," of the inten-tional experience, but also in that of the *noema taken in itself*. Thus the noema also refers to an object and possesses a "content," "by means of" which it refers to the object, the object being the same as that of the noesis; so the "paral-lelism" is once again thoroughly verified.

## 130. Delimitation of the Essence "Noematic Meaning"

Let us approach these remarkable structures still more closely. We simplify our reflexion by leaving the attentional modifications unconsidered, further by restricting ourselves, following the grading of the strata involved, now in one partial thesis, now in another, whilst the remaining theses continue operative indeed, but in a secondary way. We shall subse-quently make it clear and without further difficulty that through simplifications of this kind our analyses lose nothing in universal validity. We are dealing precisely with an essence which remains unaffected by such modifications.

Let us then place ourselves with a living *cogito*. In accordance with its essential nature it is in a quite special sense "directed" upon an objective. In other words, there belongs to its noema an "objectivity"—in inverted commas—with a certain noematic constitution unfolded in a definitely limited description, which, as *the description of the "meant objective just as it is meant," avoids all subjective expressions*. Formal-ontological expressions are there utilized, such as "object," "constitution," "positive content"; material ontological expressions such as "thing," "figure," "cause"; determinations of content such as "rough," "hard," "coloured"— they all have their inverted commas, thus bearing a noematically modified meaning. On the other hand, for the description of this intended objective as such all such expressions as "perceptively," "recollectively," "clearly and intuitionally," "intellectually," "given," are *excluded*—they belong to another order (Dimension) of descriptions, not to the objective we are aware *of*, but to the *way in which we are aware* of it. On the other hand, in the case of an appearing thing as object, it would fall again within the limits of the description in question to say: "in front" its colour, shape, and so forth are of such and such a *well-defined* kind, "behind" it has "a" colour, but one that is *"not more closely defined,"* and generally in this and that respect it remains "undetermined" whether it is thus or so.

This holds not only for natural objects, but quite generally —for objectified values (*Wertobjektitäten*) for instance. The description of these applies to the "matter" intended and, in addition, to the predicates of "value," as when "in the sense" of that form of our meaning which consists in valuing we say of the tree as it appears that it is covered with "gloriously" scented blossom. Even the predicates of value have then their inverted commas; they are the predicates not of a value *simpliciter*, but of a value-noema.

Herewith, clearly, a fully *dependable content* is marked off *in every noema*. Every consciousness has its "what" (*Was*), and means "its" objective; it is evident that in the case of every such consciousness we must be able as a matter of principle to carry out a noematic description of this same objective "exactly as it is meant"; through development and conceptual apprehension of our data we acquire a definite system of *predicates* either formal or material, determined in positive form or left "indeterminate" (intendedly "empty"),[3] and these predicates in their *modified conceptual sense* determine the *"content"* of the object-nucleus of the noema in question.

## 131. The "Object," the "Determinable X in the Noematic Sense"

But the predicates are predicates of *"something,"* and this "something" belongs together with the predicates, and clearly inseparably, to the nucleus in question: it is the central point of unification which we referred to above. It is the nodal point of connexion for the predicates, their "bearer," but in no wise their unity in the sense in which any system or connexion of predicates might be called a unity. It must be distinguished from these, although it should not be set alongside them and should not be separated from them, as inversely they themselves are *its* predicates: inconceivable without it and yet distinguishable from it. We say that in the continuous or synthetic process of consciousness we are persistently aware of the intentional object, but that in this experience the object is ever "presenting itself differently"; it may be *"the same,"* only given with other predicates, with another determining content; "it" may display itself only in different aspects whereby the predicates left indeterminate have become more closely determined; or "the" object may have remained unchanged throughout this stretch of givenness, but now "it," the selfsame, changes, and through this change becomes more beautiful or forfeits some of its utility-value, and so forth. If this is always understood as the *noematic description* of what is meant at the time, as such, and if this description, as is always possible, is drawn on the level of pure adequacy, then the self-same intentional "object" separates itself off self-evidently from the shifting and changing "predicates." There detaches itself as the *central noematic phase*: the *"object,"* the "objective unity" (*Objekt*), the *"self-same,"* the "determinable subject of its possible predicates"—*the pure X in abstraction from all predicates*—and it disconnects itself *from* these predicates, or more accurately from the predicate-noemata.

---

[3] This emptiness of indeterminacy should not be confused with intuitional emptiness, the emptiness of the obscure presentation.

To the *one* object we attach a variety of modes of consciousness, acts or act-noemata. Manifestly this is nothing accidental; no one of these is thinkable unless various intentional experiences are also thinkable, bound together in continuous or in properly synthetic (polythetic) unity, in which "it," the object, is consciously grasped as self-same and yet in a noematically different way: the characteristic nucleus shifting, and the "object," the pure subject of predicates remaining self-same. It is clear that we can already regard every partial interval in the immanent duration of an act as an "act," and the total act as a certain accordant (*einstimmige*) unity of the continuously interlinked acts. We can then say: sundry act-noemata have everywhere here *a variety of nuclei,* yet so that, despite this fact, they *close up together in an identical unity,* a unity in which the "something," the determinable which lies concealed in every nucleus, is consciously grasped as self-identical.

But *separated* acts, as, for instance, two perceptions or a perception and a memory, can likewise close together in a "harmonious" unity, and by means of the unique nature of this closing together, which is clearly not foreign to the essential being of the acts thus linked together, the Something of the initially *separated nuclei,* which at one time may be determined thus or thus and at another otherwise determined, is now consciously grasped as the same Something, or as in common accord the same "object."

Thus in every noema there lies as point of unification a pure objective something such as the above, and we see at the same time how in respect of the noema two generically different concepts of object are to be distinguished: this pure point of unification, this *noematic "object simpliciter,"* and the "*object as modally determined*" (*Gegenstand in Wie seiner Bestimmtheiten*), including the occasional indeterminacies which "remain open," and in this model way contributory to the total meaning. Moreover, this "modal form" is to be understood as that precisely which the act at the time prescribes, and as such therefore it really belongs to its noema. The "*meaning*" (*Sinn*), of which we have frequently spoken, *is this noematic "object in its modal setting"* ("*Gegenstand im Wie*") with whatever the *description as featured above* was able to detect as self-evident in it and to express in conceptual form.

Let it be noted that we were careful to adopt the term

"meaning" (*Sinn*) just now and not "nucleus" (*Kern*). For it will turn out that with a view to getting the real, concrete complete nucleus of the noema we must take into account one further direction in which differences must be drawn, a direction which has not left any impress on the characterized description which has defined "meaning" (*Sinn*) for us. But keeping here, in the first instance, purely to that which our description grasps, "meaning" figures as a basic portion of the noema. It changes, speaking generally, from noema to noema, but under certain circumstances remains absolutely unchanged, and may even be characterized as "self-identical," in so far as the "object modally determined" admits of being described both (*beiderseits*) as identically the same and as absolutely unchanged. It cannot be lacking in any noema, nor can its necessary centre, the point of unification, the pure determinable X. No "meaning" apart from this empty "something," nor again without "determining content." It is evident, moreover, that such qualifications are not first inserted in the subsequent analysis and description, but that as condition of the possibility of a description that carries its own evidence with it, and prior to that description, they lie really (*wirklick*) in the correlate of consciousness.

Through the bearer of meaning which (as an empty X) belongs to meaning, and the *possibility*, grounded in the essential nature of meaning, and the *possibility*, grounded in the essential nature of meaning, *of harmonious combination into unities of meaning of any desired grade*, not only has every meaning (*Sinn*) its "object," but different meanings refer to *the same* object, just in so far as they can be organized into unities of meaning, in which the *determinable X's of the united meanings coincide* (*sur Deckung kommen*) *with one another and with the X of the total meaning of the unity of meaning under consideration*.

Our discussion passes from the monothetic acts to the *synthetic*, or, to be more distinct, to the polythetic. Every member of a thetically articulated consciousness has the prescribed noematic structure; each has its X with its "determining content"; but in addition the noema of the synthetic total act, with reference to the "leading" (*"archontische"*)[4] thesis, has the synthetic X and its determining content. The glancing ray of the pure Ego, parting into a

[4] Cf. § 117.

plurality of rays, rests in the act of fulfilment upon the X that is coming to synthetic unity. Under the transformation of the denominative function the total synthetic phenomenon is modified, and in such a way that a ray of actuality rests on the supreme synthetic X.

## 132. The Nucleus as Meaning in the Mode of its Full Realization

Meaning (*Sinn*) as we have determined it is *not a concrete essence* in the constitution of the noema as a whole, but a kind of abstract *form* that dwells in it. If we hold the meaning firm, the "meaning meant" (*"Vermeinte"*) that is, with the precise determining content wherewith it is meant, there emerges clearly a *second* concept of the "object in its modal setting"—*as determined, namely, through the modes in which it is given*. If, moreover, we disregard attentional modifications, and all differences like that of the modes of fulfilling, we are led to consider—and always still in the favoured sphere of positionality—the saturation-differences in clearness which, epistemologically, are so determinative. That of which we are obscurely conscious, as such, and that of which we are clearly conscious are in respect of their noematic concreteness (*Konkretion*) very different, as much so as are the experiences as a whole. But there is nothing to hinder the determining content whereby the obscurely grasped object is indicated from being absolutely identical with that of the clearly grasped object. The descriptions would coincide, and a synthetic consciousness of unity could so envelop the twofold consciousness that it might really be one and the same object that was indicated. We shall accordingly reckon the concrete fullness of the neomatic constituent in question as the *full nucleus, the meaning in the mode of its full realization.*

## 133. The Noematic Meaning as Posited. Thetically and Synthetically Posited Meanings (Positions). Posited Meanings in the Domain of Presentations

A careful application of these distinctions within all act-domains would now seem to be called for, together with a supplementing back-reference to the *thetic phases* which bear a special relation to the meaning as noematic. In the *Logical Studies* (under the title Quality) they were included from the outset within the concept of meaning (of the "essence in the mode of meaning"), and within this unity the two components "ideal content" (meaning (*Sinn*) as we now interpret it) and Quality were accordingly distinguished.[5] Yet it seems more suitable to define the term Meaning (*Sinn*) merely as that "ideal content" (*Materie*), and then to indicate the unit of meaning and thetic character as *posited meaning* (*Satz*). We have then *single-membered posited meanings* (as with perceptions and other thetic intuitions) and many-membered *synthetic posited meanings*, such as predicative doxic posited meanings (judgments), posited meanings in the form of presumptions with predicatively articulated material, and so forth. Single and many-membered alike are further *the posited meanings expressing pleasure, wish, command, and so forth*. The concept of proposition (*Satz*) is certainly extended thereby in an exceptional way that may alienate sympathy, yet it remains within the limits of an important unity of essence. We must constantly bear in mind that for us the concepts meaning (*Sinn*) and posited meaning (or position) (*Satz*) contain nothing of the nature of expression and conceptual meaning, but on the other hand include all explicit propositions and all propositional meanings.

According to our analyses these concepts indicate an abstract stratum belonging to the full tissue of all noemata. To grasp this stratum in its all-enveloping generality, and thus to realize that it is represented in *all act-spheres,* has a wide bearing on our way of knowledge. Even in the plain and simple *intuitions* the concepts meaning (*Sinn*) and posited meaning (*Satz*) which belong inseparably to the concept of object (*Gegenstand*) have their necessary application, and the special concepts *intuitional meaning* (*Anschauungssinn*) and *posited intuitional meaning* (*Anschauungssatz*) must of necessity be coined. So, for instance, in the domain of outer perception, after abstracting from the character of perceivedness, as something present in this noema prior to all developing and conceptual thought, we must extract by force of

---

[5] *Loc. cit.,* Vol. II, Fifth Study, §§ 20 and 21, pp. 411–425. For the rest, cf. Vol. III, the Sixth Study, § 25, pp. 86–90. The neutral having-"postponed" is, of course, not now reckoned by us, as it was then, as a "quality" (thesis) beside other qualities, but as a modification which "mirrors" all qualities, and therefore all acts generally.

vision from out the "perceived object as such" the meaning of object, the *thing-significance* (*Dingsinn*) *of this perception* which changes from perception to perception (even in respect of "the same" thing). If we take this meaning in its *full sense,* in its intuitional *fullness,* there results a definite and very important concept of *appearance.* To these meanings correspond posited meanings generally: intuition-meanings, presentation-meanings, perceptual meanings, and so forth. In a phenomenology of external intuitions which, as such, has to do not with objects *simpliciter,* in the unmodified sense, but with noemata as correlates of the noeses, concepts such as the ones here set out stand in the centre of scientific inquiry.

If now we return in the first place to the general thema, we have before us the still further task of distinguishing systematically the fundamental types of meaning, the plain and the synthetic (i.e., pertaining to synthetic acts) meanings of the first and higher grades. Following in part the basic divisions of determinations of content, and partly the basic forms of synthetic formations which play a similar part in the case of all domains of meanings, and thus taking everything into account which *a priori,* both as to its form and its content, is determinative for the general structure of meanings, common to all spheres of consciousness or peculiar to generically limited spheres, we ascend to the *Idea of a systematic and universal doctrine of the forms of meanings.* If in addition we bring under consideration the systematic distinction of the positing characters, we have also carried out at the same time a *systematic treatment of types* (*Typik*) *of positions* (*Sätze*).

## 134. The Apophantic Formal Doctrine

A main task here is to sketch out a systematic "analytic" *formal doctrine of "logical" meanings, or posited predicative meanings, of* "judgments" in the sense of formal logic, which takes into account only the forms of the *analytic* or *predicative synthesis,* leaving undetermined the significant terms which enter into these forms. Although this task is a special one, it has still a universal bearing in this way that the total predicative synthesis indicates the class of all possible meaning-types of possible operations; the operations of analysis (*Explikation*) and of the linking of the elements in relational patterns are everywhere equally applicable: as in the relation of the determining quality to its subject, of the part to the whole, of the related to its subject of reference, and so forth. Interwoven with these are the operations of conjunction, disjunction, and hypothetical connexion. All this prior to any statement and prior also to the expressive or "conceptual" mode of apprehenson which emerges for the first time with the statement-form, and clings to all forms and contents (*Materien*) as significant expression.

This formal doctrine, which we have already touched on, in idea, several times, which according to our indications constitutes the intrinsically necessary substratum for scientific *mathesis universalis*, loses its isolation through the results of our present inquiries, finding its home within the general ideally conceived formal doctrine of meanings generally, and its last place of origin in noematic phenomenology.

Let us approach the whole matter more closely.

The analytic-syntactical operations, we said, are possible operations for all possible meanings and positions, whatever determining content the noematic meaning in question (which is indeed no other than the "meant" (*vermeinte*) object as such, and in the mode in which its content is presented at the time) may include "undeveloped" in itself. But it can always be developed, and any one of the operations which is essentially connected with the developmental "analysis" will permit of being carried out. The synthetic forms which grow up in this way (in accord with the grammatical "syntactics," we called them also the syntactical) are quite well defined, belong to a well-established system of forms, can be isolated through abstraction and grasped conceptually and through the medium of expression. Thus, for instance, we can treat that which is perceived as such in plain perceptive thesis, analytically, and after such fashion as is revealed in the expressions: "This is black; it is an inkstand; this inkstand is not white; if white, it is not black," and the like. Each new step brings us a new meaning; in the place of the original single-membered meaning we have a synthetic meaning posited, which, according to the law of the expressibility of all posited protodoxic meanings, may be brought to expression or to predicative statement. Within the articulated meanings that are posited each member has its syntactical form originating in the analytic synthesis.

Let us suppose that the positings which belong to these forms of meaning are *doxic primary positings*: there grow up thus different forms of judgments in the logical sense (*apophantic propositions*). The aim before us, that of determining all these forms *a priori*, of controlling with systematic thoroughness the infinitely manifold formal constructions, yet all delimited in conformity with law, points us to the Idea of a *formal doctrine of apophantic propositions, or syntactics*.

The positings, and in particular the synthetic positing as a whole, can also be *doxic modalities*. We presume, let us suppose, and develop the supposition in the modus "presumably" aware of, or something is questionable, and we develop the questionable in a consciousness which reflects the state of being questionable, and so forth. If we bring the noematic correlates of these modalities to expression ("S might well be P," "Is S P?" and the like), and if we do the same also for the plain predicative judgment itself, as we also express affirmation and denial (e.g., "S is not P," "But S is P," "S is certainly, really P"), *the concept of form is then extended*, and so also the idea of the formal doctrine of propositions. The form is now multiply determined, partly through the strict syntactical forms, partly through the doxic modalities. A total thesis, moreover, always remains belonging to the total meaning posited, and a doxic thesis is included in it. At the same time every such posited meaning and the conceptual "expression" which directly fits it can, through a development of meaning and predication which transforms the modal characteristic into a predicate, be transformed into a stated meaning, with a judgment which judges concerning the modality of a content of this and that form (e.g., "It is certain, it is possible, it is probable that S is P").

As with the modalities of judgment, so similarly with secondary *theses*, with the meanings and positions of the *spheres of feeling (Gemüts) and of will*, with the syntheses that specifically belong to them and the corresponding modes of expression. The goal of the new formal doctrines of posited meanings, and specifically of these meanings in the form of syntheses, is then easily indicated.

Moreover, we see *that in a suitably extended formal doctrine of doxic positions*—when in just the same way as with the modalities of Being we also transfer the modalities of shall and should (if the analogical phrase be allowed) to the content (*Materie*) of the judgment—*the formal doctrine of all positions* is once again deflected. What this transfer means it needs no long exposition to say, but at the most calls for exemplifying instances. Instead of saying "May S be P," we say "May it be that S be P," it is as wished (not is wished); in the place of "S shall be P," we say "That S be P, that shall be," it is as willed, and so forth.

The task of Phenomenology, as itself sees it, lies not in the systematic elaboration of these formal doctrines, wherein, as may be learnt from the apophantic form, we can deduce from primitive axiomatic basic formations the systematic possibilities of all further formations; its field is the analysis of the *a priori* shown forth in *immediate* intuition, the fixing of immediately transparent essences and essential connexions and their descriptive cognition in the systematic union of all strata in pure transcendental consciousness. What the theorizing logician isolates in the formal theory of meaning, and by reason of the one-sided direction of this interest treats as something apart without taking any understanding heed of the noematic and noetic systems in which it is phenomenologically interwoven,—that the phenomenologist takes in the full range of its relationships. His great task is to follow up the phenomenological interlacings of essences *in all directions*. Every plain axiomatic exhibition of a basic logical concept becomes a new heading for phenomenological inquiries. That which has already been plainly set out in widest logical generality as "posited meanings" (as in judgment), as categorical or hypothetical proposition, as attributive determination, nominalized adjective or relative, and the like, gives rise, so soon as it is once again embedded in the corresponding noematic connexions between essences, whence the glance of the theorist drew it forth, to difficult and far-reaching problems of pure phenomenology.

## 135. Object and Consciousness. Transition to the Phenomenology of Reason

As every intentional experience has a noema and therein a meaning through which it is related to the object, so, inversely, everything that we call by the name of *Object*, that of which we speak, what we see before us as reality, hold to be possible or probable, think of in however vague a way, is in so far already object of consciousness; and this means that whatever the world and reality may be or be called must be represented within the limits of real and possible consciousness by corresponding meanings and positions, filled more or less with intuitional content. When therefore phenomenology performs its "suspending" operations, when as transcendental it brackets all actual positing of realities (*Realitäten*) and carries out the other bracketings, as we have previously described them, we can now understand in the light of a deeper reason the meaning and the legitimacy of the earlier thesis: that whatever is phenomenologically disconnected remains still, with a certain change of signature, within the framework of phenomenology.[6] The real (*realen*) and ideal positivities (*Wirklichkeiten*), which come under the suspending clause, are represented in the phenomenological sphere by the whole nexus of corresponding meanings and positions (*Sinnen und Sätzen*).

Thus, for example, every real natural thing is represented by all the meanings and significant positions with their fluctuating filling, through which, as so and so determined and further to be determined, it figures as the correlate of possible intentional experiences; represented thus by the variations "of the full nucleus," or, what amounts here to the same thing, by the system of all possible "subjective modes of appearing," in which it can be noematically constituted as self-identical. But this constituting relates in the first instance to an essentially possible individual consciousness, then also to a possible community-consciousness, i.e., to an essentially possible plurality of personal centres of consciousness and streams of consciousness enjoying mutual intercourse, and for whom *one* thing as the self-same objective real entity must be given and identified intersubjectively. It must not be forgotten that all our discussions, including therefore the ones now before us, are to be understood in the sense of the phenomenological reductions and in eidetic generality.

On the other hand, to every thing, and eventually to the whole world of things, with the one space and the one time, there correspond the systems of possible noetic events, of the possible experiences of particular individuals and community-units that relate to these events, experiences which, as parallel to the noematic manifolds previously treated, contain in their own essence this peculiar feature of being related to this world of things through their import and posited meaning. In them accordingly there appear the relevant manifolds of hyletic data, with the appropriate "apprehensions," thetic act-characters, and so forth, which in their connected unity

6 Cf. § 76.

make up what we call the *empirical consciousness* of this thinghood. Over against the thing in its unity stands an infinite ideal manifold of noetic experiences of a quite determinate essential content, over which, despite the endlessness, a proper oversight can still be kept, all the experiences agreeing in this that they are a consciousness of "the same" object. This unanimity is evidenced in the sphere of consciousness itself through experiences which on their side again belong with the rest to the group which we have here delimited.

For the limitation to the empirical consciousness was intended only by way of illustration, as was also the restriction to "things" of the "world." Everything, however far we stretch the framework, and on whatever level of generality and particularity we may also be moving—even down to the lowest concreta—is essentially prefigured. As the sphere of experience is determined in accordance with its essential and transcendental structure as rigorously conforming to law, so is every possible construction on essential lines according to noesis and noema fixedly determined, just as every possible figure that can be constructed in space is somehow determined through the essential nature of space, according to unconditionally valid dispensations of law and order. What on both sides is here called possibility (eidetic existence) is thus absolutely necessary possibility, an absolutely firm joint in the absolutely firm structure of an eidetic system. The goal of inquiry is to know this system scientifically, i.e., to stamp it into theoretical form and to control it systematically through concepts and formulations of laws which spring from pure essential intuition. All the fundamental distinctions drawn by formal ontology and the theory of categories attached to it— the doctrine concerning the division of the regions of Being and their ontical categories, as also concerning the constitution of the material ontologies that fit them—are, as we shall understand in detail as we press farther forward, the main headings of phenomenological studies. And to these, there necessarily correspond noetic-noematic systems of essences which must permit of being systematically described and determined according to possibilities and necessities.

If we consider more closely what the essential connexions between object and consciousness as characterzied in the above treatment mean and must mean, we become conscious of an ambiguity, and on following it up we notice that we are facing a crucial turning-point in our inquiries. We assign to an object a variety of "posited meanings," or alternatively of experiences possessing a certain noematic content, and in such a way indeed that through it syntheses of *a priori* identification are possible, whereby the object can and must remain the same. The X in the different acts or act-noemata furnished with a differing "determining content" is necessarily known as the same. But *is it really the same?* And *is the object itself real?* Could it not be unreal whilst the various agreeing and even intuitionally saturated posited meanings—whatever their essential content might be—fulfilled their function according to the measures of consciousness?

We are not interested in the fact-world of consciousness and the fulfilling of its functions, but in the essential problems which might here need formulating. Consciousness, or the conscious subject itself, *passes judgments* about reality, asks questions about it, thinks it probable or doubts it, resolves the doubt and thereby passes "*verdicts of the reason.*" Must not the essence of this judicial right and correlatively the essence of "reality"—related to all kinds of objects, and following all the categories, formal and regional—permit of being clearly understood within the system of essential connexions of the transcendental consciousness, thus in a purely phenomenological way?

There was then an ambiguity in what we said about the noetic-noematic "constitution" of objectivities, e.g., thing-objectivities. In any case, we were then thinking especially of "real" objects, of things of the "real world," or at least of "a" real world in general. But what then does this "real" mean for objects which are indeed given to consciousness, yet only through meanings and positions? What does it mean for the posited meanings themselves, for the differentiating of the essences of these noemata, or of the parallel noeses? What means it for the particular modes of its construction according to form and fullness? How does this structure specify itself in sympathy with the special regions of objects? The question then is, how in the spirit of phenomenological science we are to describe, noetically and noematically, all the connexions of consciousness which render necessary a plain object (and this in common speech always means a *real* object) precisely in its character as real. But in the *extended* sense of the term an object—"whether it is real or not"—is "constituted" within certain connexions of consciousness which bear in themselves a transparent unity so far as they carry with them essentially the consciousness of an identical X.

In fact, our treatment does not concern realities (*Wirklichkeiten*) merely, in whatever pregnant sense the term be used. Questions concerning reality are to be found in *all* forms of knowledge as such, even in our own, the phenomenological, which relates to the possible constitution of objects: they all have their correlates in "objects" which are meant to possess "real Being." When is the noematically "meant" identity of the X "real identity"—so it may everywhere be asked—instead of being "merely" meant, and what does this "merely meant" (*vermeint*) mean?

Thus we must devote a new series of reflective studies to the problems of reality (*Wirklichkeit*) and to the correlative problems of the rational consciousness which lays out this reality within itself.

# Chapter 12

# Phenomenology of the Reason

WHEN WE SPEAK of objects *simpliciter,* we mean as a rule real objects that truly are and belong to this or that category of Being. Whatever we assert then concerning objects— provided we speak reasonably—we must submit, whether as meant or spoken, to *"logical grounding," "proof"* (*Ausweisen*) in that of statement, *"that which truly or really (wirklich) is"* and *"that which is rationally demonstrable"* (*Ausweisbar*) *are intrinsically correlated*; and so for all doxic modalities ontical or positional. Of course the possibility of a rational demonstration (*Ausweisung*) which stand here in question is not to be understood as empirical but as "ideal, as an essential possibility.

## 136. The First Basic Form of the Rational Consciousness: the Primordial Dator "Vision"

If we now ask what is meant by a rational setting forth (*Ausweisung*), i.e., wherein the *rational consciousness* consists, we find at once the intuitive representing of examples and the beginnings of essential analysis carried out upon them the source of several distinctions:

We have *in the first place* the distinction between positional experiences in which what is set down acquires *primordial givenness*, and those in which it does *not* acquire such givenness; between *"perceiving," "seeing" acts, that is* —*understood in a broad sense*—and *non-"perceiving"* acts.

Thus a recollective consciousness, for example that of a landscape, is not given in a primordial sense; the landscape is not perceived as though we were really seeing it. In stating this we have not wished to say that the recollective consciousness has no independent right of its own, but just that this is not one of "seeing." Phenomenology presents an analogue of this opposition for *all types of positional* experiences. We can, for instance, predicate in a "blind" way that $2 + 1 = 1 + 2$; we can, however, carry out the same judgment with insight. The positive fact (*Sachverhalt*), the synthetic objectivity which corresponds to the synthesis of judgment, is then primordially given, grasped in a primordial way. It is this no longer *after* the living fulfilment of the insight, for the latter passes off at once into the obscurity of a retentional modification. The latter may indeed have a rational advantage over any other dim or confused consciousness of the same noematic meaning, over an "unthinking" reproduction, for instance, of something once previously learnt and perhaps with insight; but it is no longer a consciousness primordially given.

These distinctions do not concern the pure meaning and position, for this is the same for both members of every such pair of examples, and may also be consciously and intuitively grasped as identical every time. The distinction concerns *the way in which the mere meaning or position*, which as a mere abstractum requires a plus in the way of supplementing phases in the full development (*Konkretion*) of the noema of consciousness, is or is not filled out.

Fullness of meaning is not the only requisite; we are also concerned with the mode (*Wie*) of the filling out. One mode of experiencing the meaning is the "*intuitive*," whereby we are made aware of the "meant object as such" through direct mental vision, and as a particularly outstanding case we have that wherein the mode of direct vision is the primordial *object-giving* mode. The meaning in the perception of the landscape is perceptively filled out, and we become aware of the perceived object with its colours, forms, and so forth (so far as they "fall within perception") in the mode of the "embodied." We find similar distinctions in all act-spheres. The situation has again its two aspects in the parallelistic sense, a noetic and a noematic. In the noematic setting we find the character of embodiment (as the primordial state of being filled out) blent with pure meaning, and *the meaning stamped with this character now functions as the foundation of the noematic character of positionality*, or, which here means the same thing, the ontical character. The parallel holds good of the noetic setting also.

*A specific character of rationality pertains, however, to that of positionality as its own*, as a *distinction* which is *then and only then essential* to it when it is a positing grounded not merely in meaning generally but in a filled out, primordial dator meaning.

Here and in every kind of rational consciousness the phrase "belonging to" receives the meaning of "being its own." For instance: To the corporeal appearing of a thing there *belongs* in all cases positionality. It is not only one with this appearing in a general way (as a mere general fact, shall we say, which is here unquestioned); it is one with it in a unique sense, it is *"motivated"* by it, and still again not merely in a general way but *"rationally motivated."* And this means that the positing has its *original ground of legitimacy* in the primordial givenness. In other forms of givenness the ground of legitimacy need not exactly be wanting; what is, however, lacking is the prerogative of the *original* ground which plays its outstanding part in the relative appreciation of the grounds of legitimacy.

The positing of the essence or essential relationships "primordially" given in our *vision of Essential Being* likewise "belongs" to its positing "material," to the "meaning" in its mode of givenness. It is reasonable and, as believing certitude, originally motivated positing; it has the specific character of *"that which understands"* (*der "einsehenden"*). If the positing is a *"blind"* one, if the meanings of the words are determined on the basis of a dim act-background of which we are only confusedly aware, the rational character of the insight is necessarily lacking; with such mode of givenness (if we are still to use this word here) of the significant fact (*Sachverhaltes*), or, alternatively, with such noematic accompaniment of the nucleus of meaning, the character of reason is *essentially incompatible*. On the other hand, this does not exclude a secondary rational character, as the example of the imperfect reproduction of essential cognitions shows.

Insight, *self-evidence* generally, is thus an entirely distinctive occurrence; at its "centre" it is the *unity of a rational positing with that which essentially motivates it*, the whole situation here indicated being intelligible in terms of the noema as well as of the noesis. The reference to motivation fits excellently the relation between the (noetic) positing (*Setzen*) and the noematic meaning posited (*Satz*) *in its mode of intuitional saturation* (*Erfülltheit*). The expression *"self-evident posited meaning"* in its noematic rendering is immediately intelligible.

The twofold meaning of the word self-evidence in its application now to noetic characters, or full acts (e.g., self-evidence of judging), now to noematic positions (e.g., self-evident logical judgment, self-evident stated meaning), is a case of the general and necessary ambiguities of the expressions related to the phases of correlation between noesis and noema. The phenomenological indication of the source they spring from renders them harmless, and even permits us to recognize their indispensability.

We have yet to note that the expression *"fulfilment"* (*Erfüllung*) has still another ambiguity which lies in a quite other direction: at one time it is *"fulfilment of intention,"* as a character which the actual thesis takes on through the special mode of meaning; at another it is precisely the peculiarity of this mode itself or the peculiar property of the meaning in question, to conceal "rich resources" which motivate in accordance with reason.

## 137. Self-Evidence and Insight. "Primordial" and "Pure" Assertoric and Apodeictic Self-Evidence

The pairs of examples made use of above illustrate at the same time a *second* and a *third* essential difference. That which we ordinarily call self-evidence and *insight* (or *seeing into*) is a positional doxic and also *adequate* dator consciousness which "excludes Otherness"; the thesis is motivated in a quite exceptional way through the adequacy of the given material, and is in the highest sense an act of the reason. The arithmetical example illustrates that for us. In the example of the landscape we have indeed a seeing, but not the experience-of-self-evidence (*Evidenz*) in the ordinary pregnant meaning of the word, a "seeing into." When the contrasted examples are looked into more closely, we are struck by a *double difference*: in the one example we are treating of the *essence*, in the other of the *individual*; in the second place the primordial givenness in the eidetic example is *adequate*; in the example from the sphere of experience it is *inadequate*. Both differences which intercross under certain circumstances will prove of importance in respect to the type of insight (*Evidenz*) involved.

So far as the first difference is concerned, we may state on phenomenological grounds that the so to speak *"assertoric" seeing of an individual*, for instance, the "awareness" of a thing or of some individual state of things, is in its rational character essentially distinguished from an *"apodeictic" seeing, from the in-seeing of an essence or an essential relationship*; but also likewise from the modification of this in-seeing, which may take place through a mixing of the two, namely, in the case of the application of an insight to something assertorically seen, and generally in the *knowledge of the necessity of* a posited particular being so-and-so.

Evidential Vision (*Evidenz*) and Insight, in the ordinary meaningful (*prägnanter*) sense, are taken as meaning the same thing, namely, apodeictic in-seeing. We propose in our terminology to separate the two words. We are in real need of a more general word which shall include in its meaning assertoric seeing and apodeictic in-seeing. We should consider it as a phenomenological finding of great importance that they both really belong to *one* generic essence, and that, understood in a still more general way, *Rational Consciousness in general designates a summum genus of thetic modalities*, in which the "seeing," used in its very widest sense, and as bearing on primordial givenness, constitutes a well-defined class. In giving a name to the summum genus one has the option either of extending the meaning of the word "seeing" (as we did just now, but going very much farther) or of widening the meaning of the words "in-seeing" and "evidential vision" (*Evidenz*). It might be most suitable to choose the word: *evidential vision* to stand for the most general concept; the expression *primordial evidental vision* would then be available for representing every rational thesis characterized by a relation of motivation in respect of the primordiality of what is primordially given. We should then have to decide further between the *assertoric* and *apodeictic forms of evidential vision*, and to leave to the word *insight* the special task of designating this *apodeictic character*. Proceeding still farther, we would set up as opposites *pure* insight and *impure* insight (the latter including the cognition of the necessity of an element of fact, the Being of which does not need to be self-evident), and likewise, and in a quite general way, we would draw a contrast between *pure and impure evidential vision*.

Further differences arise as our inquiry deepens, differences concerning the bases of motivation and affecting the character of the evidential vision; for example, the difference between *purely formal* ("analytic," "logical") and *material* (synthetic-*a priori*) evidential vision. But at this point we should not go beyond the briefest indications.

## 138. Adequate and Inadequate Self-Evidence

Let us now turn back to the second of the two differences indicated above, which is closely connected with that between adequate and inadequate givenness, and gives us occasion at the same time to describe an outstanding type of "impure" evidential vision. The positing act (*Setzung*) grounded in the corporeal appearance of the *Thing* is indeed rational, but the appearance is never more than a one-sided "imperfect" appearance; not only are we conscious in corporeal form of the very object that is in process of appearing, but of the thing itself *simpliciter*, the whole in its collective though only one-sidedly intuitional and in addition variously undetermined meaning. But of course that which "verily" appears must not be separated from the Thing as though it were itself a separate thing; its correlate of meaning constitutes a *dependent* part within the full meaning of the Thing, a part which can have unity of meaning and independence only within a whole which *necessarily* conceals in itself components of emptiness and of indeterminacy.

In principle a thing in the real world, a Being in this sense, can within the finite limits of appearance appear only " *inadequately*." Essentially connected therewith is the fact that *not rational positing which rests on an appearance that presents itself so inadequately* can be "*definitive*," "invincible"; that no such positing in its particularity is equivalent to the downright assertion that "the Thing is real," but only to the assertion "It is real" on the supposition that the advance of experience does not bring in its train "stronger rational motives" which exhibit the original positing as one that must be "cancelled" in the further connexion. Moreover, the positing is rationally motivated only through the appearance (the imperfectly fulfilled perceptual meaning) in and for itself, considered in its particularized detail.

The phenomenology of the Reason in the sphere of the types of Being which can on principle be only inadequately given (the sphere of *transcendents* in the sense of realities (*Realitäten*) has therefore to study the different occurrences within this sphere which have been indicated *a priori* and in advance. It has to make clear how the inadequate consciousness of givenness, the partial appearing, is related to one and the same determinable X, whilst continuously advancing towards ever-fresh appearances which are continuously passing over into one another, and also to indicate the essential possibilities which here present themselves; how, on the one hand, a sequence of experiences is possible here and constantly motivated on rational lines through the rational placements [*positings*] that are continuously at one's disposal, namely, the course of experience in which the empty places of the appearances that have preceded get filled again, the indeterminacies more closely determined, moving forward all the time towards *a thoroughgoing harmonious filling out, with the steadily increasing rational power that goes with this.* On the other hand, we have to make clear the opposite possibilities, the *cases of the fusions or polythetic syntheses where there is disagreement or determination otherwise* of that X which we are constantly aware of as one and the same—otherwise, that is, than in harmony with the original bestowal of meaning. We have to show, moreover, how positional components of the earlier course of perception suffer *cancellation* together with their meaning; how under certain circumstances the whole perception *explodes*, so to speak, and breaks up into "*conflicting apprehensions of the Thing*," into *suppositions* concerning the thing; how the theses of these suppositions annul one another, and in such annulling are modified in a peculiar way; or how the one thesis, remaining unmodified, "conditions" the cancelling of the "contrary thesis"; and other contingencies of the same kind.

As further and closer objects of study we may note the peculiar modifications which the original positings of the Reason suffer owing to the fact that in the course of harmonious filling out they undergo a *positive phenomenological enhancement* with respect to their motivating "*power*," that they increase steadily in "*weight*," that they thus constantly and essentially possess weight, but one that differs *gradually*. The other possibilities also call for analysis, in respect of such points as how the weight of positings suffers from "*counter-motives*," how in *doubt* they mutually "*balance*" *one another*, how one placement in rivalry with another of "greater" weight is "*outweighed*," "*abandoned*," and so forth.

In addition, of course, the circumstances which are essentially determinative of the changes in the positional characters in the sense in which they belong to the *positional content* should be subjected to a comprehensive analysis on essential lines (e.g., the circumstances accompanying the "conflict" or the "rivalry" of appearances). For here, as everywhere, in the phenomenological sphere, there are no contingencies, no mere matter-of-fact connexions (*Faktizitäten*); all is essentially and definitely motivated.

In a similar way the *inquiry into the essential nature of all kinds of rational acts in their immediacy* should be carried through in connexion with a general phenomenology of the noetic and noematic given material.

*To every region and category* of would-be objects corresponds phenomenologically not only a *basic kind of meaning or position*, but also a *basic kind of primordial dator-consciousness* of such meaning, and, pertaining to it, a *basic type of primordial self-evidence*, essentially motivated through a primitive givenness that conforms to the basic divisions just referred to.

Every such self-evidence, the word being understood in the extended sense we have given to it, is either *adequate*, incapable in principle of being either "strengthened" or "weakened," thus *without the graded differences of a weight*; or it is *inadequate*, and therewith *capable of increase and decrease*. Whether in any given context the former or the latter kind of self-evidence is possible depends on its generic type; it is thus prefashioned, *a priori*, and to demand the perfection which self-evidence possesses in one content (e.g., that of essential relations) in other contexts which essentially exclude it is simply absurd.

We have still this remark to make, that we were obliged to transfer the original meaning of the concepts "adequate" and "inadequate," which relates to the mode of presentation, to the essential peculiarities of the rational positings themselves, grounded on them. We were enabled to do so by the very fact of their connexion. It is one of those unavoidable equivocations due to transference, which lose their power to harm so soon as one recognizes them as equivocal, and has clearly and consciously distinguished the derived from the original.

## 139. Interweavings of All the Varieties of Reason. Theoretic, Axiological, and Practical Truth

An act of positing, whatever its quality may be, has, in harmony with what we have stated hitherto, its justification, in and through the very positing of its meaning, provided only that it is rational; the rational character is itself the character of rightness. This character "belongs" to it essentially, and not contingently as a mere fact under the accidental conditions of an empirically positing Ego. Correlatively meaning as posited can also be said to have its own rightness: it stands within the rational consciousness equipped with the noematic character of rightness, which essentially belongs moreover to the posited meaning in its capacity as the noematic thesis so qualified together with this content of meaning. Or to state it more accurately, there "belongs" to it a fullness made up in this way, which on its own side furnishes the ground for the rational character of the thesis.

The posited meaning here has its justification (*Recht*) in itself. But it may also be that "*just something may be said on behalf of a position*"; without being "itself" rational, it can still have a share of reason. We recall—to keep within the doxic sphere—the peculiar connexion of the doxic modalities with the protodoxa:[1] they all point back to it. If, on the other hand, we consider the rational characters which belong to these modalities, the thought at once obtrudes itself upon us that they all, differ as they may in regard to content and the conditions of motivation, point back, so to speak, to one primary rational character which belongs to the domain of primary belief, to the case of primordial and in the last resort perfect self-evidence. It will be observed that between these two kinds of back-reference there are deep-lying essential connexions.

Just to indicate the following: A presumption can be characterized as rational in itself, if we follow that in it which harks back to the corresponding primary belief; and if we adopt this in the form of a "supposing," "something then speaks for this." It is not the belief itself *simpliciter* that is characterized as rational, although it has a share in reason. We see that further rational distinctions of a theoretical kind need to be drawn and studied here. Essential connexions between the *different* qualities, connexions of a *reciprocal* kind, with the rational characters which are peculiar to them, detach themselves here, and *in the end all the lines of connexion converge back upon the primary belief* and *its primary reason*, upon the "*Truth*."

*Truth* is manifestly the correlate of the perfect rational character of the protodoxa, the believing certainty. The expressions: "A protodoxic posited meaning, a stated meaning, for instance, is true," and "The character of perfect rationality attaches to the corresponding belief and judgment," are equivalent correlates. We are not referring here, of course, to any fact of experience or to any individual judger, although it is eidetically taken for granted that truth can be actually given only where there is an actual consciousness of the self-evident, and this applies therefore also to the truth of this "being taken for granted" itself, that of the previously indicated equivalence, and so forth. If the protodoxic self-evidence, that of believing certainty, is lacking, then, we say, with respect to its content of meaning "S is P," a doxic modality may be self-

---

[1] Cf. § 104.

evident, the presumption, for instance, that "S should be P." This modal self-evidence is manifestly equivalent to and necessarily connected with a protodoxic self-evidence of altered meaning, namely, with the self-evident position, or the truth, "that S is P is presumable (probable)"; on the other hand also with the truth, "there is something to be said for the assertion that S is P"; and again: "there is something to be said for the assertion that SP is true," and so forth. All this points to essential connexions which need phenomenological inquiries reaching down to fundamentals.

Self-evidence, however, is in no sense a mere title for rational developments of this kind in the sphere of belief (and indeed in that of the predicative judgment only), but holds *for all thetic spheres*, and particularly also for the important rational connexions that run *between* them.

It therefore concerns the highly difficult and far-reaching problems of the reason in the sphere of the theses of feeling (*Gemüts*) and will,[2] as also their interlacings with the "theoretical," i.e., doxic reason. The "theoretical" or *"doxological truth,"* or *self-evidence*, has its parallels in the *"axiological and practical truth or self-evidence,"* whereby the "truths" of this last heading come to be expressed and known[3] in the form of doxological truths, namely, in the specifically logical or apophantic. It does not need to be said that for dealing with these problems fundamentally we need studies of the kind we have already attempted to initiate: studies that concern the essential relations connecting the doxic theses with all other kinds of placement, those of feeling (*Germütes*) and will, and those again that lead all doxic modalities back to the protodoxa. Even thereby also we may bring ourselves to understand from ultimate grounds why the assurance of belief and, correspondingly, the truth plays so dominant a part in all affairs of the reason; a part which, for the rest, is such as to make us take for granted that in respect of a solution the problems of Reason in the doxic sphere must have precedence of the problems of the axiological and practical Reason.

---

[2] A first impulse in this direction was given through Brentano's brilliant work, *On the Origin of Social Knowledge* (1889), a work to which I am most gratefully indebted.

[3] Knowledge is chiefly a name for logical truth, as characterized from the standpoint of the subject, and as correlate of its self-evidencing judging; but is also a name for every kind of self-evidencing judging itself, and, lastly, for every doxic act of reason.

## 140. Confirmation. Warranty (*Berechtigung*) apart from Self-Evidence. Equivalence of the Positional and Neutral Insights

Further study is demanded in respect of the problems offered by the *connexions of "congruence"* (*Deckung*) which (to name only an outstanding case) must be set up on essential lines *between acts of the same meaning or position, but of different rational value*. For instance, a self-evident and a non-self-evident act may be congruent in such a way that in the transition from the latter to the former the self-evident act takes on the character of proving something to be, the non-self-evident act that of *itself* proving to be. The positing with insight that characterizes the one functions as "confirmatory" of the insight-lacking positing of the other. The "posited meaning" is "verified" or "confirmed," the imperfect mode of givenness is transformed into the perfect. The particular form this process takes or can take is prescribed by the essential nature of the relevant types of positing, or of the posited meanings in question in their perfected fulfilment. For every class of posited meanings the forms of verification that are intrinsically possible must be clearly laid down on phenomenological lines.

If the positing is not irrational, motivated possibilities may be drawn from its essence to show that and how it can be translated into an actual rational positing that verifies it. It can be seen that it is not every imperfect self-evidence that here prescribes a course of fulfilment which terminates in a *corresponding* primordial self-evidence, of the same sort and meaning; on the contrary, a verification of this primordial kind, so to speak, is intrinsically excluded by certain kinds of self-evidence. This is true, for instance, of the recall of a recollection (*Rückerinnerung*) and in a certain way of all recollecting generally, and likewise essentially of empathy to which, in the second volume of this book, we shall ascribe a basic kind of self-evidence (and into whose nature we shall there inquire more closely). In any case, very important phenomenological themes are therewith indicated.

We must further note that the motivated possibility of which we spoke above is to be sharply distinguished from empty possibility:[4] it is definitely motivated through that

---

[4] This is one of the most essential ambiguities of the term "possibility," though there are still others (the *formal-logical* possibility, mathematico-formal freedom from contradiction). It is

which the posited meaning with such filling as is given to it includes within itself. It is an empty possibility that this writing-desk here on its underside, which is at present invisible to me, rests on ten legs instead of on four legs, as is really the case. This four-ness, on the contrary, is a motivated possibility in respect of the definite perception which I am just enjoying. For every perception generally it is a motivated consideration that the "conditions" of perception *can* change in certain ways, that "in consequence" the perception *can* pass over correspondingly into a perceptive series of a definite type prescribed by the very meaning of my perception, and tending to fulfil the perception and confirm its posited meaning.

For the rest, in respect of the "empty" or "mere" possibility of proof, there are two further cases to distinguish: either *the possibility coincides with the reality*, in such wise, namely, that seeing-into the possibility brings with it *eo ipso* the primordial rational consciousness and consciousness of givenness; or that is not the case. The latter holds in the example we have just made use of. *Real experience*, and not merely running through "possible" perceptions after bringing them into consciousness, supplies a real *proof of positings which claim reality (Reales)*, such as the existential positings of natural processes. On the other hand, in the case of every *positing of an essence* or an essential position, the *intuitional realization of its completed filling out is equivalent to the filling out itself*, just as *a priori* the intuitional realization, even the mere fanciful representation of an essential connexion and insight into the same, are "equivalent," i.e., the one passes into the other through a mere alteration of the standpoint, and the possibility of this reciprocal transition is not accidental but essentially necessary.

## 141. Immediate and Mediate Rational Positing. Mediate Self-Evidence

Confessedly all mediate grounding leads back to the immediate. The *primary source of all rightness (Rechtes)*, in

---

of intrinsic importance that the possibility which plays its part in the theory of probabilities, and consequently that the consciousness of possibility (the attitude of suggestion) of which we spoke in connexion with the theory of doxic modalities as a parallel to the presumption-consciousness, has *motivated* possibilities as its correlates. A probability never builds itself up out of unmotivated possibilities, only motivated possibilities have weight, and so forth.

respect of all domains of objects and the positing acts related to them, lies in immediate and more narrowly specified *primordial self-evidence*, or in the primordial givenness which motivates it. But one can draw further from this source indirectly in different ways: the rational value of a positing act which in itself has no self-evidence can be derived from it, or, if it is immediate, strengthened and confirmed.

Let us consider the latter case, and with the aid of an example indicate the difficult problems which concern the *relation of the non-self-evident immediate rational positing acts to primordial self-evidence* (in our sense of the term, as bearing, that is, on the primordial nature of givenness).

In a *certain* way indeed every clear *recollection* possesses an original and immediate right; considered in and for itself, it "weighs" something, whether little or much, it has a "weight." But it has only a relative and imperfect right. In respect of that which it reproduces, let us say a past event, there lies in it a relation to the actual present. It posits the past and necessarily posits with it the relevant field of view, though in a dim, vague, undetermined way; brought to clearness and thetic distinctness the latter would have to permit of being developed in a context of recollections thetically carried out, and to terminate *in actual perceptions, in the actual* "hic et nunc." The same holds for every sort of remembering in our *very broad* use of the term in which it is related to all the modes of time.

In positions such as these, essential insights unmistakably declare themselves. They point to the essential connexions with the exhibition of which the meaning and the kind of verification of which every recollection is capable and "stands in need of" would be presented more clearly. With every advance from one recollection to another in the clarifying connexions of memory, which terminate in the perceptual present, the memory gets strengthened. The strengthening is to a certain extent reciprocal, the memory-weightings are functionally inter-dependent, each recollection in its context of memories has a power which increases with the extension of that context, and is greater than it would have been in a more restricted connexion or alone by itself. But if the development reaches through to the *present moment, something of the light of perception and its self-evidence shines back along the whole series of recollections.*

One could even say: *the rationality and legitimacy (Rechtscharakter) of memory springs up in secret* through the *power of perception*, which in all confusion and obscurity is still operative even when the latter "lacks its full consummation."

But in any case such verification is *needed* to bring out clearly *what* it strictly is that bears the mediated reflexion of perceptual authority (*Wahrnehmungsrechtes*). Memory has its *own kind of inadequacy* in that it can blend what is "really remembered" with what is not remembered, or again in the fact that different recollections can take place and yet pass as the unity of one memory; whereas through the receding of the horizon of memory which takes place in actual recall, the series of recollections which then open out divide so that the one single memory-picture "explodes," and scatters in a plurality of mutually incompatible memory-intuitions, whereby there would be occurrences to describe similar to those which (in a manner that clearly permits of being extensively generalized) we have had occasion to point out in respect of perceptions.[5]

All this may serve to indicate by way of illustration large and important groups of problems dealing with the "*confirming*" *and* "*verifying*" *of immediate rational positings* (as also to illustrate the division of rational positing acts into pure and impure, unmixed and mixed); but above all we may grasp here *one* sense in which it is valid to say that all mediate rational positings, and, in further sequence, all rational cognition that is predicative and conceptual, throw us back upon *self-evidence*. We are to understand, of course, that only the primordial self-evidence is an "original" source of authority (*Rechtsquelle*), and the rational positings of memory, for instance, and so of all reproductive acts including that of empathy are not original and are in certain ways "derived."

We may however, draw from the source of the primordially given in shapes and forms of a quite different mould.

One such form has already been indicated by the way: the weakening of rational values in the continuous transition from living self-evidence. But let us now indicate an essentially different group of cases where a posited meaning is *mediately* related, within a *synthetic connexion self-evident* at every link of it, to grounds that are immediately self-evident. Therewith emerges a new and general type of rational positions, of a different rational character, phenomenologically, from immediate self-evidence. So here also we have a kind of

[5] Cf. *supra*, § 138.

derived *"mediate self-evidence"*—the kind for which as a rule the expression "mediate self-evidence" is exclusively reserved. This derived self-evidential character is such in its essential nature that it can emerge only with the last link of a system of positions which, starting with those that are immediately self-evident, takes different forms as its course proceeds, every step in advance being supported on grounds of self-evidence; whereby these self-evidences are partly immediate, partly already derived; partly transparent, partly not; primordial, or non-primordial. Therewith a new field of the phenomenological theory of reason is indicated. Our task here is to study, from the side both of the noesis and the noema, the general and the special "events" of the essential order of *reason in mediate supportings, provings* of every kind and form, and in all thetic spheres whatsoever; to refer to their phenomenological origins the different "principles" of such proof, which are of essentially different kind, for instance, according as it treats of objectivities that are presented as immanent or transcendent, adequate or inadequate; and to make these "principles" "intelligible " through this ultimate reference, not omitting to take into account all the phenomenological strata involved.

## 142. Being and the Thesis of Reason

With the general understanding of the essence of the reason —and this is the goal of the group of inquiries indicated—of the reason stretched to its widest to cover *all varieties of the positing act,* including the axiological and the practical, the general elucidation of the essential correlations which unite the *idea of true* (*wahrhaft*) *Being* with the ideas of truth, reason and consciousness must *eo ipso* be secured.

In this direction we very soon reach a general insight, namely, that not merely "object that truly is" and "to be rationally posited," but also "truly being," and an object to be posited in an original and perfect thesis of the Reason in an incomplete and merely "partial" form. The meaning which underlies it as its material would not in any prescribed direction lying within one's mental reach leave any "open" possibilities for the determinable X: no determinability which was not already an established determination, no meaning that was not fully determined and its defining limits set. Since the thesis of the reason should be an original one, it must have its rational ground in the *primordial givenness* of that which is in a full sense determined: The X is not only meant in its full determinacy, but therein primordially given. The import of the indicated equivalence is then as follows:

To every object "that truly is" there intrinsically corresponds (in the a priori of the unconditioned generality of the essence) the idea of a possible consciousness in which the object itself can be grasped in a primordial and also perfectly adequate way. Conversely, when this possibility is guaranteed, the object is eo ipso "that which truly is."

This too is here specially significant, namely, that we find definitely prescribed in the essential nature of every category of formative synthesis (which is the correlate of every category of the object) the possible shapes, perfect or imperfect, which it can concretely take. Again, it is prescribed on essential lines for every imperfect synthesis of this kind how it may perfect itself, how its meaning may be completed, intuitionally filled, and how the intuition is to be further enriched.

Every category of the object (every region and every category in our own more restricted and pregnant sense of the term) is a general essence which must itself be brought on grounds of principle to adequate givenness. In its adequate givenness it prescribes a transparent (einsichtige) general rule for every special object of which we become aware in the variety of concrete experiences (these experiences would here be naturally taken not as individual particularities (Singularitäten) but as essences, as concreta of the lowest class). It prescribes the rule that determines how an object subordinate to it is to be brought in respect of its meaning and mode of presentation to full determinacy, to adequate primordial givenness; through which discrete or continuously developing connexions of consciousness, and through which concrete exhibitions out of the essential nature of these connexions, are effected. We shall understand how much these short sentences contain when we study these problems more closely in the concluding chapters (starting from § 149). At this point a brief illustrative indication may suffice: The invisible determinations of a thing—this we know with apodeictic certainty—are, like all thing-determinations, necessarily spatial; this gives a law-conforming rule for the possible spatial modes of completion in respect of the invisible sides of the appearing thing, a rule which, in its full development, we call pure geometry. As further determinations of a Thing we have the temporal and the material determinations. To these, in their turn, new rules apply for possible (not therefore freely disposable) completions of meaning, and in further sequence for possible thetic intuitions or appearances. The essential content these may possess, the standards to which their matter conforms, and the criteria for determining the characters which their forms of apprehension, noematic or noetic, may legitimately possess, this too is all prescribed *a priori.*

## 143. The Adequate Presentation of a Thing as an Idea in the Kantian Sense

Yet before we grapple with these problems, a postscript is needed to remove the illusory sense of contradiction with our previous exposition (§ 138). There we remarked that on principle we could only have inadequately appearing (therefore also only inadequately perceivable) objects. But we must not overlook the modifying qualification we made: inadequately perceivable, we said, *within the finite limits of appearance.* There are objects—and all transcendent objects, all *"realities"* (*Realitäten*) which are included under the rubric Nature or World are here included—which cannot be given with complete determinacy and with similarly complete intuitability in any limited finite consciousness.

But *as "Idea"* (in the Kantian sense), *the complete givenness is nevertheless prescribed*—as a connexion of endless processes of continuous appearing, absolutely fixed in its essential type, or, as the field for these processes, a *continuum of appearances* determined *a priori,* possessing different but determinate dimensions, governed by an established dispensation of essential order.

This continuum is more closely defined as infinite in all directions, consisting in all its phases of appearances of the same determinable X, so ordered as a connected system and so determined as to its essential content that any one of its *lines* when carried continuously forward gives a harmonious system of appearances (which is itself to be designated as a unity of mobile appearance), wherein the given X, ever one and the same, is with unbroken consistency "more closely" and never "otherwise" determined.

If now a self-contained unity of the course covered, a finite act therefore that is mobile only within the limits of its finitude, is in virtue of the pervasive infinity of the continuum unthinkable (it would give an absurd finity infinity), the idea of this continuum and the idea of the completed givenness thereby prefigured lies, none the less, *transparent* before us— open to insight as only an "Idea" can be, designating through its essential nature a *type of insight that is all its own.*

The idea of an infinity essentially motivated is not itself an infinity; the insight that this infinity is intrinsically incapable of being given does not exclude but rather demands the transparent givenness of the Idea of this infinity.

## 144. Reality and Primordial Dator Consciousness: Concluding Determinations

Thus it remains as a result that the Eidos True-Being is correlatively equivalent to the Eidos Adequately given-Being and Being that can be posited as self-evident; and this, moreover, in the sense either of finite givenness or of givenness in the form of an Idea. In the one case Being is "immanent" Being, Being as a completed experience or noematic correlate of experience; in the other case it is transcendent Being. i.e., Being whose "transcendence" rests precisely in the infinitude of the noematic correlate which it demands as ontical "material."

Where the dator intuition is *adequate* and *immanent,* the sense (*Sinn*) primordially filled out, though not indeed the sense *simpliciter,* coalesces with the object. The object is just that which is grasped and posited in adequate intuition as a primordial Self, transparent in virtue of its primordiality, and absolutely transparent in virtue of the completeness of the meaning and its complete primordial filling-out (*Erfüllung*).

Where the dator intuition is of a *transcending* character, the objective factor cannot come to be adequately given; what can alone be given here is the *Idea* of such a factor, or of its meaning and "epistemological essence," and therewith an *a priori* rule for the well-ordered infinities of inadequate experiences.

On the ground of experiences that have at times been enjoyed and of this rule (or varied system of rules which covers their case) we cannot indeed unambiguously infer how the further course of experience must proceed. On the contrary there remain open countless possibilities which, however, are prefigured according to type through the very richly organized *a priori* ordering. The system of geometrical rules determines with absolute precision all the possible forms of

motion which might supplement the bit of observed movement here and now before us, but it does not indicate a single
real course for the motion of the object that is really moving.
How the empirical thought which is grounded in experience
comes here to the rescue; how anything of the nature of the
scientific determination of thing-like particulars as empirically posited units (*Einheiten*) which yet include an infinite
number of possible determinations, all varied in meaning, is
at all possible; how, within the topic (*Thesis*) of Nature we
can reach the goal of unambiguous determination, in accordance with the *Idea* of the natural object or event, etc. (which
as the Idea of an individual particular is fully determinate):
this all belongs to a new stratum of inquiry. It belongs
to the phenomenology of the reason in its specific experiencing, more particularly to the physical, psychological, and,
in general, natural scientific reason, which refers the ontological and noetic rules which belong to the science of experience as such back to its phenomenological sources. But
that means that it seeks out and eidetically investigates the
phenomenological strata, noetic and noematic, in which the
content of these rules is embedded.

## 145. Critical Consideration of the Phenomenology of Self-Evidence

It is clear from the foregoing treatment that the *phenomenology of the Reason, noetics in a pregnant sense of the
term*, which proposes to subject to intuitive research not indeed consciousness generally, but the rational consciousness,
throughout presupposes general phenomenology. That—in the
realm of positionality[6]—*thetic consciousness of every kind
(Gattung)* stands *under certain norms* is itself a phenomenological fact; the norms are no other than essential laws
which relate to certain noetic-noematic connexions to be
regorously analysed and described in respect of their kind
and form. Naturally we have everywhere to reckon with
*"unreason"* also, as the negative counterpart of reason, just
as the phenomenology of self-evidence includes in itself that

---

[6] All thetic occurrences when transferred to the sphere of fancy
and neutrality are left "mirrored" and "powerless"; so it is also
with all occurrences of the Reason. We do not confirm, but only
quasi-confirm, neutral theses; they are not self-evident, but "as
if" (*gleichsam*) self-evident, and so forth.

of its counterpart, *absurdity*.[7] The *general doctrine of the essence of self-evidence* with its analyses bearing on essential distinctions of the most general kind constitutes a relatively small although fundamental portion of the phenomenology of Reason. Therein we confirm—and the considerations we have just advanced may already suffice to make the point quite clear—what was briefly maintained at the beginning of this book[8] as against perverse interpretations of the meaning of self-evidence.

Self-evidence, in fact, is not any sort of conscious indicator affixed to a judgment (and ordinarily it is only in relation to judgment that one speaks of self-evidence) and calling to us like a mystical voice from a better world: Here is the Truth! as though such a voice had anything to say to free spirits like ourselves and had not to make good its title to authority. We do not need any longer to get even with sceptical considerations, nor to consider misgivings of the old type which cannot be overcome through any theory of self-evidence that makes it a matter of indicators and feelings: the doubt, namely, whether a malicious demon (of Cartesian invention) or a fateful alteration of the actual course of the world might not bring it about that every false judgment were provided with this indicator, this feeling of intellectual necessity or transcendent obligation, and the like. If we get down to the relevant phenomena themselves and study them in the framework of a phenomenological reduction, we recognize with complete clearness that we are here dealing with a quite special mode of positing (and with nothing so little therefore as with a content affixed somehow to the act, with an appendage of any sort whatsoever), a mode of positing which belongs to eidetically determined essences constitutive of the noema (e.g., the modus of insight into essential being which in a primordial way gives an original transparency to the make-up of the noema). One recognizes further that once again essential laws govern the relation of those positional acts which do not possess this special constitution to such as do possess it; that there is such a thing, for instance, as con-

---

[7] Cf. *Logical Studies*, Vol. III, Sixth Study, § 39, pp. 121 ff., esp. p. 126. In general the whole of the Sixth Study supplies phenomenological prolegomena for dealing with the problems of the Reason discussed in the present chapter.

[8] Cf. *supra*, Chapter II, especially § 21.

sciousness of the *"fulfilment of the intention,"* of authorizing and strengthening with special reference to the thetic characters, just as there are also the corresponding *opposed characters* of the *depriving of all authority and power*. We further recognize that the logical principles require a profound phenomenological elucidation, and that the principle of contradiction, for instance, takes us back to the essential connexions of possible confirmation and possible invalidation (or, alternatively, rational cancellation).[9] Speaking generally, we obtain the insight that we have here and at every point to do, not with contingent facts but with eidetic eventualities which stand in their eidetic connexions, and therefore that what obtains in the Eidos functions as an absolutely unassailable standard for the fact. In this phenomenological chapter we also get clear on this point, that not every positional experience (e.g., an experience of judgment of any kind) can become self-evident in the same way, and more specifically not every such experience can become immediately self-evident; further, that all modes of rational positing, all types of immediate or mediate self-evidence, are rooted in phenomenological connexions within which the radically different object-regions separate out from one another on noetic-noematic lines.

It particularly concerns us to study systematically the continuous identity-unisons and the synthetic identifications in all domains according to their phenomenological constitution. If one has first become acquainted—and this is the first step and a necessary one—with the inner construction of inten-

---

[9] Cf. *Logical Studies,* Vol. III, Sixth Study, § 34, pp. 111 ff. It is to be regretted that W. Wundt passes here an altogether different judgment, as he does indeed upon phenomenology as a whole. The inquiry, which does not transcend in the least the sphere of pure intuitional data, he interprets as "Scholasticism." The distinction between the act that bestows and the act that fulfils meaning he designates (*Kleine Schriften,* Vol. I, p. 613) as our "chosen formal schema," and the net result of our analyses he declares to be the "most naïve verbal repetition": "self-evidence is self-evidence, abstraction is abstraction." He introduces the concluding words of his criticism with the words which I will take the liberty of quoting: "Husserl's founding of a new logic which has a theoretical rather than a practical turn ends in the case of each of his conceptual analyses, so far as these possess a positive content, with the assurance really that A = A and is nothing other than this" (*ibid.,* pp. 613–614).

tional experiences in regard to all general structural forms, with the parallelism of these structures, the stratifications in the noema, such as meaning, the subject-bearer of meaning, thetic characters, concrete fullness, it behoves us in all synthetic unifications to make fully clear how there take place therein not merely acts of binding generally, but a binding into the unity of *one* act. In particular, clarity and analytic insight come to us in respect of many such questions as: how identifying unifications are possible, how here and there the determinable X acquires a determinate and valid value, and how this affects the determinations of meaning and their vacancies, i.e., their phases of indeterminacy; and in respect also of such matters as intuitive fullness (*Füllen*), and forms of confirmation, of proof and of progressive knowledge as it passes from lower to higher levels of consciousness.

These studies in rationality, however, and all that go along with them, are carried out from the "transcendental," the phenomenological standpoint. No judgment there carried out is a judgment on a natural basis, presupposing as background the thesis of natural reality, not even where the study in question is the phenomenology of the consciousness of reality, of the knowledge of nature, of the realization of natural values and insight into their bearings. We seek out everywhere the formations of the noeses and the noemata, we sketch out a systematic and eidetic morphology, and set out everywhere the essential necessities and possibilities; the latter as necessary possibilities, i.e., unifying forms of compatibility prescribed by the essential natures of things and girt about with essential laws. "Object" as we everywhere understand it is a title for essential connexions of consciousness; it first comes forward as noematic X, the subject-bearer of different essential types of meanings and positions. It appears further as the title for certain connexions of the reason, eidetically considered, in which the contained X that unifies in terms of meaning receives its rational placing.

As similar titles for determinate, eidetically circumscribed groups to be fixed through inquiries into essences, and uniting "teleologically" connected formations of consciousness, we have such expressions as "possible," "probable," "doubtful" object. The connexions are ever changing afresh, and in their otherness must be precisely described: thus, for instance, it is easy to see that the *possibility* of the X being determined in such and such a way is not merely proved through the primordial givenness of this X with its provision of meaning (*Sinnesbestande*), through the reference therefore to a real element, but that also mere suggestions consolidated through reproduction can strengthen each other mutually by coming harmoniously together; and that likewise *doubtfulness* comes to light in the phenomena of conflict between the modalized intuitions of a certain descriptive specification, and so forth. Connected therewith are the inquiries of a theoretically rational type which relate to the distinction between positivities (*Sachen*) values, and practical objectives, and seek out the constitutive conscious constructions for the same. Thus phenomenology really envelops the whole natural world, and with this the ideal worlds it shuts off: it includes them as "world-meaning" through the conformities to essential law and order which connect objective meaning and noema generally with the self-contained systems of the noeses, and especially through the rationally ordered essential connexions, whose correlate is "real object," which therefore on its own side acts on occasion as an indicator of fully determined systems of conscious formations teleologically unified.

# Chapter 13

## Grades of Generality in the Ordering of the Problems of the Theoretic Reason

OUR MEDITATIONS upon the forms of inquiry proper to a phenomenology of the reason have so far been proceeding on a plane of generality which did not permit the essential ramifications of the problems raised and their connexions with the formal and regional ontologies to stand out at all clearly. In this respect we must try to be more specific, only so will the full meaning of the phenomenological eidetics of the reason and the whole wealth of its problems be revealed to us.

## 146. The Most General Problems

Let us get back to the sources of all forms of rational inquiry and follow them in their ramifyings as systematically as possible.

The title of the problem which in its scope covers phenomenology in its entirety is Intentionality. This indeed expresses the fundamental property of consciousness; all phenomenological problems, including the hyletic, find their ordered place within it. Thus phenomenology starts off with problems of intentionality, but at first quite generally and without drawing into its own circle of consideration the question of the real (or true) Being of what we are conscious of when we are conscious. We leave unconsidered the fact that positional consciousness with its thetic characters can, in the most general sense of the term, be designated as "sense-positing" (*Vermeinen*), and finds its necessary place as such under the rational oppositions of validity and invalidity. We were able to approach these problems only in the last chapters, with reference to the main structures of consciousness which we had learnt to understand in the interval. And since our concern was with eidetic beginnings, we carried out the analyses with the greatest possible generality, as indeed the nature of the case demanded. In all eidetic spheres the systematic procedure is from higher to lower generality, though analysis, when on the trail, may attach itself to particulars. We spoke of reason and the rational thesis generally, of primordial and derived, of adequate and inadequate self-evidence, of essential insight and individual self-evidence, and the like. The descriptions we outlined already presupposed an extensive phenomenological basis, a whole series of difficult distinctions which we had worked out for ourselves in the chapters treating of the most general structures of consciousness. Without the concepts meaning, posited meaning, meaning posited and fulfilled (epistemological essence in the language of the *Logical Studies*), it is quite impossible to reach the radical formulation of any problem of the theoretical reason. These concepts presuppose others again and the cleavages of essence that correspond to them: the differences of positionality and neutrality, those of the thetic characters and their contents of meaning (*Materien*), the separating out of the peculiar modifications of essence which do not come under the Eidos "posited meaning," as, for instance, the attentional modifications, and so forth. At the same time, that we may not underrate the scope of the analyses required in the most general stratum of theoretical reason of which we are here speaking, we stress the fact that the essential descriptions of the last chapter should count only as mere beginnings. As everywhere else, so also here, we were only carrying out our methodic intention to prepare so much firm ground for every intrinsically new stratum that might be pictured as a field of phenomenological inquiries as to make these latter secure, formulate the initial and fundamental problems that relate to these, and cast free glances towards the encircling line of problems in the far distance.

## 147. Ramifications of the Problem, Formal Logic, Axiology, and Praxis

The general phenomenology of the reason differentiates as we take into account further structural differences which have a determining influence upon rational characteristics: differences depending on the fundamental type of thesis in question, on the differences between basic (*schlichter*) and derived theses, and the differences which cross with these of unilateral (*eingliedrige*) theses and syntheses. The main groups of problems of the reason (problems of self-evidence) relate to the main types of theses, and the positing material (*Setzungsmaterien*) which these essentially demand. At the head, of course, come the protodoxa, the doxic modalities with the ontical modalities that correspond to them.

In pursuing such ends of the theoretical reason we come necessarily to the *problems on which depends the proper understanding of Formal Logic as a form of the theoretical reason*, and of the parallel disciplines which I have called *Formal Axiology and Praxis*.

I would refer back in the first place to the earlier discussions concerning the purely formal doctrine of positions (*Sätze*), and in particular of *synthetic* positions, relating to the predicative doxic synthesis, as also the synthetic forms that belong to the doxic modalities, and further to the acts of feeling (*Gemüt*) and will (the forms of preference, for instance, those of valuing and willing "in the interests of another," the forms of the axiological "and" and "or"). In these formal doctrines we are concerned with the pure form of synthetic (*Sätze*) in their noematic aspect, without bringing into question their rational validity or invalidity. Thus they do not yet belong to the stratum of the doctrine of rationality.

But as soon as we throw out these questions, and propound them indeed for positions generally so far as they are conceived as exclusively determined through pure forms, we are in the sphere of Formal Logic and of the parallel formal disciplines mentioned above, which are essentially built up upon the corresponding formal doctrines as their underlying strata. *In the synthetic forms*—which as such manifestly presuppose much that concerns the theses or positions of the relevant positional *category*, whilst leaving it specifically indeterminate —*there lie a priori conditions of possible validity which come to expression in the essential laws of the disciplines in question.*

More specifically there lie in the pure forms of the *predicative* (analytic) synthesis *a priori* conditions of the possibility of *doxic rational certainty*, or in noematic terms, of *possible truth*. In thus setting it out objectively, we obtain Formal Logic in the narrowest sense of the word; *formal Apophansis* (the formal Logic of "judgments") which thus has its basis in the formal theory of these "judgments."

Similar remarks apply to the syntheses belonging to the spheres of feeling (*Gemüt*) and will, and to their noematic correlates, to their types of synthetic "positions" therefore, whereof the systematic formal doctrine must again furnish the basis for the construction of the doctrines of formal validity. In the pure synthetic *forms* of these spheres (as, for instance, in the connexions of ends and means) there are in reality concealed the *conditions of the possibility of axiological and practical "truth."* Thereby, through the "objectivation," which takes place also in acts of feeling (*Gemüt*), for instance, all axiological and practical *rationality* is converted, in the way we have learnt to understand, into doxic rationality, and noematically into *truth*, objectively into *reality*; we speak of true or real ends, means, grounds of preference, and so forth.

Special phenomenological inquiries of an extremely important kind are concerned with each of these connexions. Already the fashion in which the formal disciplines just cited are characterized is phenomenological, and presupposes many of the results of our analyses. The worker in *pure logic*, "dogmatically" treated, grasps through abstraction the apophantic forms ("proposition in general" or "judgment," categorical, hypothetical, conjunctive, disjunctive, and so forth), and establishes for them axioms of formal truth. He knows nothing of analytic synthesis, of essential relations, noetic and noematic, of the incorporation within the essence-systems of pure consciousness of the essences he has extracted and conceptually determined; in his inquiries he studies apart what can be fully understood only in this fullness of essential connexion. It is phenomenology which, by reverting to the sources of intuition in transcendentally purified consciousness, makes it clear to us what is precisely involved in the fact that we sometimes speak of formal conditions of truth, sometimes of those of knowledge. It enlightens us in a general way concerning *essence* and *essential relations* in respect of the concepts knowledge, self-evidence, truth, being (object, positive content, and so forth); it teaches us to understand the structure of the judging process and of the judgment, the way in which the structure of the noema determines knowledge, how the "posited meaning" thereby plays its special part, and again the varying possibility of its cognitive "fullness." It shows which modes of filling out are essential conditions for the rational character of self-evidence, which types of self-evidence are in question on any occasion, and so forth. In particular it enables us to understand that the *a priori truths of Logic* concern essential connexions between the *possibility of the intuitive filling* out of the posited meaning (whereby the corresponding positive content attains synthetic intuition) and of the *pure synthetic form* of the posited meaning (the pure logical form), and that that possibility is at the same time the condition of possible validity (*Geltung*).

It also shows that on closer scrutiny a twofold distinction must here be made, corresponding to the correlation of noesis and noema. In the formal Apophansis (in the syllogism, for instance) our discourse is of judgments as noematic propositions and their "formal truth." The standpoint is noematic throughout. On the other hand, in *formal apophantic noetics,* the standpoint is noetic, and our talk is of rationality, correctness of the judging-process; *standards* of correctness are laid down (*ausgesprochen*), and these with relation to the forms of the propositions. For instance, we cannot maintain that a contradiction is true; he who judges in accordance with the forms of premises of the valid inferential moods "must" draw the conclusions proper to the corresponding forms, and so forth. These parallels are at once intelligible when considered in a phenomenological connexion. The events which concern the act of judging, the noesis and likewise the essentially corresponding events in the noema, of the Apophansis are studied precisely in their necessary interconnexion and within the full tissue of consciousness.

The same considerations hold, of course, for the remaining formal disciplines in respect of the parallelism of noetic and noematic orderings.

## 148. Problems of the Theoretical Reason as Bearing on Formal Ontology

Shifting our orientation, we pass from these disciplines to the corresponding *Ontologies*. Phenomenologically, the connexion is already given through the general adjustments of mental vision that are seen to be possible, and can be carried out within each act; whereby the constituents thus made visible are reciprocally interconnected through a network of essential laws. The primary point of view looks towards the objective; noematic reflection leads to the noematic, noetic reflection to the noetic contents. By abstraction from these contents the disciplines that here concern us extract pure forms: formal Apophantic extracting noematic, and the parallel noetic, noetic forms. And just as these forms are bound mutually together through essential laws, so are they both united with ontic forms, which can be grasped through glancing back to the ontic constituents (*Bestände*).

Every formal-logical law may be transformed into an equivalent formal-ontological law. The judgment, instead of being passed upon judgments, will now bear upon substantive meanings (facts), and again upon objects instead of upon elements of judgments (e.g., denominative meanings), and upon characteristic marks instead of upon predicative meanings, and so forth. We no longer talk of the truth and validity of propositions, but of the constituents of the substantive meanings (facts), of the Being of objects, and so forth.

Of course, the phenomenological import (*Gehalt*) of this transition is to be made clear through referring it back to that of the standard concepts.

Formal Ontology, moreover, extends far beyond the sphere of such mere transformations of the formal apophantic truths. Important disciplines grow out of it through those "denominative reductions" of which we have previously spoken. In the plural judgment the plural figures as a plural thesis. Through the denominative transition it becomes the object, group; and thus the fundamental concept of the *Theory of Groups* grows up. In this theory judgments are passed *upon* groups as upon objects possessing their own peculiar types of properties, relations, and so forth. The same holds for the concepts relation, number, etc., as the basic concepts of *mathematical disciplines*. As with the merely formal doctrines of the proposition, so here we must repeat our statement that it is not the task of phenomenology to develop these disciplines and to carry on mathematics, syllogistic exercises, and the like. It is only in the axioms and their conceptual content that phenomenology finds a proper subject-matter for its analyses.

What we have said applies automatically to *Formal Axiology and Praxis*, as well as to the *formal ontologies* to be set alongside these as theoretical desiderata, and *treating of values* (in a very broad sense of that term), of goods—in short, of all the ontic spheres which are correlates of the effective and volitional consciousness.

The reader will notice *that the concept of "formal ontology" has broadened its meaning in the course of these discussions*.[1] Values, the objectivities of practice, are properly classed under the formal heading "object" or "something in general." From the standpoint of universal analytic Ontology they are thus materially determined objects, the "formal" ontologies of

[1] Cf. § 119, p. 309 f.

values, and the material disciplines of practical objectivities that belong to them. On the other hand, the analogies which have their ground in the parallelism of the thetic genera (belief or its modality, valuing, willing), and the syntheses and syntactical formations specifically co-ordinate with them, have their force, and indeed a power so effective that Kant directly designates[2] the relation of the willing of the end to that of the means as "analytic," thereby indeed confusing analogy with identity. The analytic proper which belongs to the predicative synthesis of the doxa should not be confused with its formal analogue which is related to the syntheses of theses of feeling and will. Profound and important problems of the phenomenology of the reason are involved in the thorough clearing-up of these analogies and parallels.

## 149. Problems of the Theoretical Reason as Bearing on the Regional Ontologies. The Problem of the Phenomenological Constituting Function

After we have discussed the problems of the theoretical reason which the formal disciplines set us, we have to effect the transition to the *material,* and in the first instance to the *regional ontologies.*

Every objective region consciously constitutes itself. An object determined through the regional genus has, as such, so far as it is real, its modes of being perceptible, clearly or obscurely presentable, conceivable, provable, prescribed *a priori.* Thus we come back again, in respect of the grounds of rationality, to the meanings, significant positings, and cognitive essences; not to the mere forms, however, but rather, since we have in mind the material generality of the regional and categorical essence, to significant positings, whose determining content is taken in its *regional* determinacy. *Every region here offers the clue for a distinctive self-contained group of inquiries.*

Let us take as guiding clue the region "material thing." If we correctly understand what this guidance means, we therewith grasp at the same time a general problem which determines the development of a great and relatively self-

[2] Cf. *Grundlegung zur Metaphysik der Sitten* (A. 417): "He who wills the end wills also the necessary means in his power indispensable to achieving it. This *proposition, so far as the willing is concerned, is analytic.*"

contained phenomenological discipline: *the problem of the general "constitution" of the objectivities of the region "Thing" in the transcendental consciousness*, or, expressed more briefly, "of the phenomenological constitution of the Thing in general." In sympathy therewith we also learn to know the method of inquiry proper to this leading problem. The very same is then applicable to *every* region and every discipline that relates to its phenomenological constitution.

What we are concerned with is as follows: The Idea of the Thing—we restrict ourselves to this particular region—when we now speak of it, is represented in consciousness by the conceptual thought "Thing," possessing a certain noematic structure (*Bestand*). To each noema there essentially corresponds an ideal self-contained group of possible noemata which have their unity herein, that they are capable of a synthetic unification through the covering relation. If the noema, as in this case, is concordant (*einstimmiges*), we find in the group intuitional and in particular primordial dator noemata also, wherein all the specifically different (*andersartigen*) members of the group find fulfilment in the identifying congruence (*Deckung*) drawing from them, in the case of positionality, confirmation, fullness of rational power.

Thus we start from the verbal and perhaps wholly obscure presentation of a Thing, exactly as presented to us. We freely produce intuitional representations of the same "Thing"-in-general and make clear to ourselves the vague meaning of the word. Since we are concerned here with a "general presentation," we must proceed with the help of illustrations. We produce at random fancy intuitions of things, free intuitions, shall we say of winged steeds, white ravens, golden mountains, and the like; these would in any case be things, and presentations of them serve therefore for purposes of illustration just as well as presentations of things of real experience. Through such material we apprehend in idea and with intuitive clearness the essence "Thing" as the subject of noematic determinations closely limited along general lines.

We must observe (recalling what has already been established in an earlier context)[3] that the essence "thing" is indeed in this way primordially given, but that this givenness cannot on principle be adequate. We can bring the noema or thing-meaning to the point of adequate presentation; but the various thing-meanings, even when taken in their fullness, do not con-

[3] Cf. § 143.

tain the regional essence "thing" as a primordially intuitable constituent immanent in them, just as little indeed as the various meanings relating to one and the same individual thing contain the individual essence of this thing. In other words, whether it is the essence of an individual thing that concerns us or the regional essence of Thing in general, in no case does a single intuition of a thing or a finite closed continuum or collection of thing-intuitions suffice to obtain in *adequate* form the desired essence in the total fullness of its essential determinations. An *inadequate* insight into the essence is, however, always obtainable; and it always has this great advantage over an empty apprehension of the essence, such as can be set up by way of illustration on the basis of an obscure presentation, that it has the essence primordially given.

This holds good for all grades of essential generality, from the essence of the individual up to the given Thing.

But it is an essential insight of a general kind that *every imperfect givenness* (every inadequate object-giving noema) contains *within itself a rule for the ideal possibility of its perfecting.* It belongs to the essence of the appearance in centaur form which I have before me now—an appearance which gives the essence of the centaur in a merely one-sided way— that I seek out the different aspects of the thing, and in free fancy can determine and render intuitable what is at first undetermined and left open. In regard to the development of this process of phantasy, as it becomes ever more perfectly intuitional and more clearly determinative, we are in large measure *free* agents; we can indeed at our own free pleasure endow the fancied centaur intuitionally with more closely determining properties and changes of property; but *we are not completely free* if our advance is to take the form of a *consistent* (*einstimmigen*) course of intuition in which the determinable subject remains the same and *can* always remain harmoniously determinable. We are, for instance, bound by a law-conforming *space* as a frame which the idea of a possible thing in general strictly prescribes for us. However arbitrarily we may vary the form of what we fancy, one spatial shape will inevitably pass over into another.

But what does this reference to rule or law phenomenologically mean? What is implied in the fact that the inadequately given *region "Thing" prescribes rules for the course of possible intuitions*—and therefore manifestly for the course of possible perceptions?

The answer is as follows: To the essence of a thing-noema there belong, as can be seen with absolute clearness, ideal possibilities of *"limitlessness in the development"*[4] *of intuitions of the same order* (*einstimmiger*), and indeed in prescribed directions of a determinate type (hence with parallel limitlessness also in the continuous juxtapositions of corresponding noeses). We here recall the earlier discussions concerning the acquisition of the "Idea" of Thing in general, and the insight accompanying it, discussions which remain valid for every lower stage of generality down to the lowest concretum (*Konkretion*) of the individually determined thing. Its transcendence expresses itself in those limitlessnesses in the development of intuitions. Again and ever again intuitions may pass over into intuitional continua, and continua already given be extended. No thing-perception is terminal and conclusive; space always remains for new perceptions which would determine the indeterminacies more closely and fill in the perceptual gaps. With every such advance the determining content of the thing-noema constantly attached to the self-same thing X is enriched. It is an essential insight that *every* perception and perceptual manifold is capable of being extended; the process is thus endless; accordingly no intuitive apprehension of the essence of the Thing can be so complete that a further perception could not bring it something noematically new.

On the other hand, we apprehend as self-evident and adequate the "Idea" of a Thing. We grasp it in the *free* process of running through the possibilities, in the consciousness of the limitlessness of the development of intuitions of the same order. We thus grasp at first the Idea of the Thing empty of all intuitional content, and of this individual thing as something which is given "just so far" as the agreeing intuition "reaches," but remains at the same time determinable *"in infinitum."* The "and so forth" is an absolutely indispensable phase in the thing-noema, and we have a clear insight of its necessity.

On the ground of the consciousness of this limitlessness as presented in the form of illustration, we apprehend further the "Idea" of the definite directions of infinite development, and that indeed in the case of all the intuitional channels along which our perception runs. Again we apprehend *the regional "Idea" of the Thing in general* as that of the self-same some-

[4] Cf. Kant's *Critique of Pure Reason,* the 5th Space-argument (A. 25).

thing which maintains itself in and through the properly *jointed*, determinate infinities of each regional channel, and proclaims itself in the definitely articulated infinite series of noemata that belong to them.

It follows then that like the Thing itself every *quality* that belongs to the thing's essential content (*Gehalt*), and above all every *constitutive "form"* is an Idea, and this holds good of all grades from the generality of the region to the lowest particularity. In closer detail:

The Thing in its ideal essence presents itself as *res temporalis*, in the *necessary "form" of Time*. Intuitive "ideation" (which here as vision of the "Idea" very specially merits its name) teaches us to know the Thing as necessarily enduring, as in principle endlessly extensible in respect of its duration. We grasp in *"pure intuition"* (for this ideation is the phenomenologically clarified concept of Kant's pure intuition) the "Idea" of temporality and of all the essential phases included in it.

The Thing according to its Idea is further *res extensa*; it is, for instance, capable in respect of its spatial relations of infinitely various changes of shape, and, where the configuration or change of configuration remains identically constant, of infinitely various changes of position; it is "movable" *in infinitum*. We grasp the *"Idea" of space* and the Ideas which it includes.

Finally, the Thing is *res materialis*, it is *substantial* unity, and as such the unity of *causal connexions*, endlessly varied in their possible structures. With these specifically real properties also we strike upon Ideas. *All* components of the Thing-Idea are themselves Ideas, *each implying the "and so forth"* of "endless" possibilities.

That which we here develop is not "theory," not "metaphysic." It concerns essential necessities, indissolubly involved in the thing-noema, and, correlatively in the thing-giving consciousness, demanding throughout to be apprehended with clear insight and systematically studied.

## 150. Continuation. The Thing-region as Transcendental Clue

Now that we have got some understanding of the most general possible kind of the infinities which the intuition of a thing as such (in respect both of noesis and noema) conceals within itself—or as we can also say: the Idea of the Thing and the dimensions of the infinite which the Idea implicitly contains—we shall also soon be able to understand the extent to which the *Thing-region* may serve *as a guiding clue* in phenomenological inquiries.

As we intuit an individual thing, and continue intuiting its movements, its approachings and recedings, its turnings round and about, its changes of form and quality, the causal relations in which it stands, we *run through* certain continua of the intuiting process correlated with each other in this way or in that and uniting in one unity of consciousness; our glance is thereby directed towards the identical element, the X of the meaning (positional or neutralized), the self-same one that changes *itself,* turns round, and so forth. So it is also, when in *free* intuition we follow up the infinite series of possible modifications along the different main directions, in the consciousness of limitlessness in the development of this process of intuition. And likewise, again, when we pass over to the standpoint of ideation and make clear maybe the regional Idea of the Thing: proceeding therein like the geometer in the freedom and purity of his geometrical intuition.

But all this gives us no knowledge of the processes of intuition itself and the essences and essential infinities which belong to *it,* or of its constitutive material or noetic phases, of its noematic constituents, of the strata that on the one side as on the other are distinguishable and eidetically apprehensible. We do not *see* what we are actually experiencing (or are unreflectively aware of in the modification of fancy). We therefore need the change of standpoint, the different "reflexions"—hyletic, noetic, noematic— (in their togetherness rightly called reflexions since they are deviations from the original "straight" direction of the glance towards the X). It is these reflexions which now open to us a vast and inwardly coherent field of inquiry, or a stupendous group of problems coming under the Idea of regional Thing.

The question then arises:

*How are we to describe systematically the noeses and noemata which belong to the unity of the intuitionally presenting Thing-consciousness.*

If we restrict our attention to the noematic sphere, the question runs thus:

What expressive form do the manifold positing intuitions, the *"positing intuitional meanings,"* take in which a "real" thing presents itself and exhibits (*ausweist*) its *reality* intuitionally in original experience?

Or again, abstracting from the doxic thesis, how do the mere *appearances*—noematically understood—express themselves which, in themselves and from the pure eidetic standpoint, "bring to its appearing" one and the same thing, the fully determined thing at the time-being, which belongs as a *necessary* correlate to this manifold of intuition and appearance? Phenomenology is never content, on principle, with vague talk or obscure generalities, but systematically demands a definite clarification, analysis and description shedding light on the essential connexions and penetrating to the remotest specifications attainable: it demands thoroughgoing *work*.

The *regional Idea* of the Thing, its self-identical X with the determining content of meaning, posited as being this or thus, *prescribes rules for the manifolds of appearances*. It comes to this: they are not manifolds in general, coming together by accident, as indeed already follows from this that in themselves and on purely essential lines they relate to the Thing, the determinate Thing. The regional Idea prescribes series of appearances that are fully determinate, definitely ordered, progressing *in infinitum,* and, taken in their ideal totality, precisely limited and fixed, a definite inner organization of their modes of development, which, for purposes of inquiry, hang essentially together with the partial Ideas which are designated in a general way as the components of the regional Idea of Thing. As a part of this organization, it transpires, for instance, that the unity of a mere *res extensa* is conceivable apart from the unity which regulates the Idea of the *res materialis,* although no *res materialis* is conceivable which is not also *res extensa.* The fact stands out (as always in eidetic-phenomenological intuition) that every appearance of a thing necessarily conceals in itself a stratum which we call the *Thing-schema:* referring thereby to the spatial form filled out simply with "sensory" qualities—lacking every determination of "substantiality" and "causality" (in inverted commas, to be understood as noematically modified). Already the associated Idea of a *mere res extensa* may stand as title for a wealth of phenomenological problems.

What in our innocence of phenomenological niceties we take for mere facts: that a spatial thing always appears to "us humans" in a certain "orientation," oriented, for instance, in the visual field of view as above and below, right and left, near and far; that we can see a thing only at a certain "depth" or "distance;" that all the changing distances at which it can be seen are related to a centre of all depth-orientations "localized" by us in the head, invisible though familiar to us as an ideal limiting point—all these alleged facts (*Faktizitäten*) contingencies of spatial perception which are foreign to the "true," "objective" space, reveal themselves down to the most trivial empirical subdivisions (*Besonderungen*) as essential necessities. Thus we see that not only for us human beings, but also for God—as the ideal representative of absolute knowledge—whatever has the character of a spatial thing, is intuitable only through appearances, wherein it is given, and indeed must be given, as changing "perspectively" in varied yet determined ways, and thereby presented in changing "orientations."

We must now seek not only to establish this as a general thesis, but to follow it up into all its particular formations. The problem of the *"origin of the presentation of space,"* the deepest phenomenological meaning whereof has never yet been grasped, reduces itself to the phenomenological analysis of the *essential* nature of all the noematic (and noetic) phenomena, wherein space exhibits itself intuitionally and as the unity of appearances, and of the descriptive modes of such exhibiting "constitutes" the spatial.

The *problem of the constituting function* clearly betokens nothing further than that the regulated series of appearances which *necessarily* hold together within the unity of a single appearing object are open to intuition, and can be theoretically apprehended—and this in spite of their infinities (which in and through its determinate "and so forth" can be unequivocally controlled)—that they can be analysed and described in their own *eidetic* peculiarity, and that the *law-conforming function of the correlation between the determinate appearing object as unity and the determinately infinite multiplicities of appearances* can be fully seen into and so disrobed of all its mysteries.

This holds good for the unity which lies in the *res extensa* (*and* also the *res temporalis*), and not less for the higher, the grounded unities which the expression *"material,"* i.e., *substantial-causal thing,* indicates. All these unities constitute themselves on the level of empirical intuition in "manifolds," and the two-sided essential connexions must everywhere through all its strata be completely illuminated, in respect of meaning, fullness of meaning, of thetic functions, and so forth. Finally, there must grow out of this the perfect insight into *what the Idea of the real Thing represents in the phenomeno-logically pure consciousness*, how it is the absolutely necessary correlate of a structurally investigated and essentially de-scribed noetic -noematic connexion.

## 151. Strata of the Transcendental Constitution of the Thing. Supplementary Considerations

These inquiries are essentially determined by the different *formations and strata in the constituting of the Thing within the limits of the primordial empirical consciousness*. Each formation and each stratum in it has this character, that it *constitutes a unity of its own*, which on its side is a *necessary connecting-link* in the full constituting of the Thing.

If we take perchance the formation of the plain perceptual constituting of the Thing, whereof the correlate is the sensory thing set out with sensory qualities, we relate ourselves to a single stream of consciousness, to the possible perceptions of a single perceiving personal subject. We find here various strata of unification, the *schemata of sensation* (*sensuellen*), the *"visual things"* of higher and lower order, which must be completely set out within this order and studied with reference to their noetic-noematic constitution, singly and in their inter-connexions. The *uppermost* stratum of this formation is that of the *substantial-causal Thing*, a reality already in the specific sense of the term, but remaining always constitutively bound to one empirical subject and its ideal perceptual manifolds.

The *formation next above this* is then the *intersubjective identical thing*, a constitutive unity of higher order. Its con-stitution is related to an indefinite plurality of subjects that stand in a relation of "mutual understanding." The intersub-jective world is the correlate of the intersubjective experience, mediated, that is, through *"empathy."* We are therefore re-ferred to the various unities of sensory things (*Sinnendingein-heiten*) already constituted individually by the many subjects, and thus in further sequence to the corresponding perceptual manifolds belonging to the different personal subjects and streams of consciousness; but before all to the new factor of empathy and to the question how it plays a constitutive part in "objective" experience and gives unity to those separated manifolds.

Moreover, all inquiries must be conducted with the completeness and the comprehensiveness demanded by the nature of the case. Thus above, in conformity with the aims of an Introduction, we held before our mind a mere preliminary situation, a basic system of constitutive appearance-manifolds, namely, that in which one and the same thing shows continuously a single aspect (*einstimmig erscheint*). The perceptions in their limitless unfolding along all the systematic lines of development approximate to the purity of the covering relation; the theses are being continually confirmed. Here we have closer determination only, never determination otherwise. No thing-determination that has come to be posited as the outcome of a previous course of experience (within this ideally closed system) undergoes "cancellation" and "substitution" through other determinations of that same category of quality which is formally prescribed through the regional essence. Nothing disturbs the agreement, and there are no compensating events that obliterate a disturbance, to say nothing of that "exploding" of the agreement in which the posited thing is entirely cancelled. But these counter-cases must be no less taken into our phenomenological reckoning, since they also play or might play their part in connexion with the possible constitution of an empirical reality. The way of fact-knowledge, as of ideally possible knowledge, leads through errors, and this already at the lowest stage of knowledge, that of the intuitive grasp of reality. Thus the courses of perception, in which partial breaches of agreement occur, and the agreement can be maintained only through "corrections," must be systematically described in respect of all its essential constituents, noetic and noematic: the changes in the mode of apprehension, the peculiar thetic occurrences, the transvaluings and disvaluings of the previously apprehended as "illusion" or "deception"; the transition into conflict" still unresolved along certain lines, and so forth. Over against the continuous synthesis of agreement, the syntheses of conflict, of misinterpretation and differing definition, and whatever they may else be called, must come into their rights, for a phenomenology of "true reality" the *phenomenology of "vain illusion"* is wholly indispensable.

## 152. Transfer of the Problem of the Transcendental Constituting Function to Other Regions

It will be easily seen that what has been said by way of illustration in regard to the constitution of the material

*Thing*—and indeed in respect of the constituting process within the system of the manifolds of experience which lie *prior to* all "thinking"—must apply as regards both problem and method to *all object-regions*. In the place of sensory perceptions" we would then naturally have the types of primordial dator acts essentially attached to the regions in question, and these acts must be previously set out and investigated through phenomenological analysis.

Very difficult problems adhere to the *interlacing of the different regions*. They condition the interlacings in the constituting formations of consciousness. The *Thing* is not anything isolated over against the experiencing subject, as will have already become apparent from the indications given above concerning the intersubjective constitution of the "objective" world of things. But this experiencing subject itself is constituted in experience as something real, as *man or beast*, just as the *intersubjective communities* are constituted as animal communities.

These communities, although essentially grounded in psychical realities, which, on their side, are grounded in the physical, reveal themselves as a new type of *objectivities of higher order*. It can be seen quite generally that there are many kinds of objectivities which defy all psychologistic and all naturalistic misinterpretations. Such are all types of *objects bearing a value*, all *practical* objects, all concrete cultural organizations which as hard realities determine our actual life, *the State, for instance, the Church, custom, the law*, and so forth. All these objective entities (*Objektitäten*) must be described in the way in which they come to be presented according to their fundamental types and in their proper order of formation, and *the problems of phenomenological shaping* (*Konstitution*) set and solved in their case.

The shaping of these entities leads back quite naturally to that psychical subjects and of things or their analogues in space: they are grounded indeed in such realities. Material reality as the lowest formation remains in the last resort the foundation of all other realities and therefore undoubtedly *the phenomenology of material nature holds a pre-eminent position*. But looked at without prejudice and referred back phenomenologically to its sources, the grounded unities, though grounded, are *new in type*; the new factor, moreover, which is therewith constituted, can never, as we learn indeed from essential intuition, be reduced to the mere sum of other realities. Thus in fact *every peculiar type of such realities* brings with it *its own constitutive phenomenology*, and therewith a *new concrete doctrine of the reason.* In principle our task remains everywhere the same: we have to bring to knowledge the complete system of conscious formations, covering all levels and strata, which constitute the primordial givenness of all such objective entities, and therewith make intelligible the equivalent, in terms of consciousness, of the relevant type of "reality." Everything also which we should say in truth so as to exclude the many understandings into which we so easily fall concerning the correlation of Being and Consciousness (as, for instance, that all reality "resolves itself into psychic factors") can be stated only on the ground of the essential connexions of the constitutive groups, as apprehended from the phenomenological standpoint and in the light of intuition.

## 153. The Full Extension of the Transcendental Problem. The Inquiries Classified

A discussion on so general a level as has hitherto been alone possible cannot awake any adequate idea of the tremendous extent of the investigations which we have so far as possible recognized and demanded. To this end, for the main types of realities at least, a set of detailed studies would be needed; we should need to proceed as we did in respect of the forms of inquiry needed for investigating the general structure of consciousness. Meanwhile in the sequel to this work the discussion which the thought of the present day finds so absorbing over the controversial questions concerning the mutual relation of the great groups of sciences bearing the titles natural science, psychology, and science of mind, and especially concerning their relation to phenomenology, will at the same time provide the opportunity for bringing the problems of phenomenological shaping more closely and more distinctly before us. Here, however, so much will already have become clear, that these controversies deal with really serious problems, and that regions of inquiry open out which treat of *all genuine matters of principle in all the material sciences.* The "matter of principle" is indeed nothing else than that which centres round the regional ideas in the shape of basic concepts and fundamental forms of knowledge, and finds, indeed must find, its systematic unfolding in corresponding regional ontologies.

What we have said can be transferred from the material to the *formal* sphere and to the *ontological disciplines* appropriate to *it,* therefore to all principles and generally to all sciences that rest on principles, if we suitably widen the Idea of phenomenological shaping. It is true that thereby the limit of constitutive research so widens out that it is eventually capable of including the whole of Phenomenology.

This will indeed force itself upon our notice as we add the following supplementary considerations:

First and foremost, the problems regarding the constituting of the object are related to the manifolds of a possible *primordial dator*-consciousness—in the case of Things, for instance, to the totality of possible *experiences*, perceptions of one and the same thing. Connected with this is the supplementary consideration of the reproductive positional type of consciousnes and the inquiry into their constitutive rational function, or, which amounts to the same thing, their function for plain intuiting cognition; similarly the consideration of the obscurely presenting (but plain) consciousness and the problems of reason and reality which relate to it. In short, we keep in the first instance within the *mere sphere of "presentation."*

But united with these are the corresponding inquiries, related to the functions of the *higher* sphere, the so-called *sphere of the "understanding" or the "reason,"* in the narrower sense of the term, with its analytic, relating and otherwise "logical" (also then axiological and practical) syntheses, with their "conceptual" operations, their statement-meanings, their new and mediate forms of grounding. Thus objectivities which were at first given (or thought of in Idea as given) in *monothetic acts,* in mere experiences, let us say, can be made subject to the play of *synthetic operations,* and through synthetic objectivities constitute increasingly higher formations which in the unity of the total thesis contain a plurality of theses, and in the unity of their total content (*Materie*) contain a plurality of mutually detachable (*abgliedernde*) contents (*Materien*). We can collect, "construct" collections (groups) of differing order of formation (groups of groups), we can set in relief "parts" out of the "whole," place properties and predicates over against their subjects, set objects "in relation to" objects, "make" the one at our pleasure into the centre of reference (*Referenten*), the other into the object referred to, and so forth. We can carry out such syntheses "really" and "properly," i.e., under the conditions of *synthetic primordiality;* the synthetic objectivity has then, in respect of its synthetic form, the character of the primordially given (for instance, of the really given collection, subsumption, relation, and so forth), and it has the full character of primordiality, if the theses have it, if the thetic act-characters are primordially motivated as rational. We can also make use of free fancies, set in relation the primordially given and the quasi-given, or carry out the syntheses throughout in the modified form, transform what we are thus conscious of into a "supposition" (*Ansatz*), "construct" hypotheses, "draw consequences" therefrom, or carry out comparisons and distinctions, subject once again the likenesses or differences thereby given to synthetic operations, uniting with all this ideations, essential positings or suppositings, and so on *in infinitum.*

Moreover, Acts of a lower or higher grade of objectivation, partly intuitional, partly unintuitional, it may be wholly confused, lie at the basis of the operations. In the case of obscurity or confusion we can make it our business to clear up the synthetic "constructions," to open up the question of their possibility, their fulfilment (*Einlösung*) through "synthetic intuition"; or again, that of their "reality," that of their redeemableness (*Einlösbarkeit*) through explicit and primordial dator synthetic acts, it may be by way of mediate "inferences" or "proofs." Phenomenologically all these types of syntheses in correlation with the synthetic objectivities "constituted" within them should be subjected to an inquiry with the object of shedding light on the different modes of presentation and their significance for the "real Being" of such objectivities, or for their *true* possible being or their *real* probable being, and similarly in reference to all questions of rationality and of truth or reality. *Here also then* we have *"problems of phenomenological shaping"* (*Konstitutionsprobleme*).

Now the logical syntheses are indeed grounded on the lowest theses with their plain and simple ideal bearings or meanings, but in such a way that the essential conformities of the synthetic level with law and order, and especially with the laws of reason—in a very wide but definitely circumscribed "formal" sphere—are independent of the special ideal bearings (*Materien*) of the members of the synthesis. On this depends precisely the possibility of a *general* and *formal Logic* which abstracts from the "content" of logical knowledge and thinks it in indeterminate freely variable generality (as "something or other"). *Inquiries also relating to the constituting process divide accordingly* into those which connect with the *formal* basic concepts, and take *these* alone as "guiding clues" to the problems of rationality, or of reality and truth; and on the other hand into those previously portrayed, which connect with the *regional* basic concepts, and in the first instance with the concept of *Region itself*, and indeed with the question *how* an individual member of such a region comes to be given. With the *regional categories* and the studies indicated by these, the *special determination which the form of synthesis* undergoes *in virtue of the regional content* comes to its own, and so too does the influence which the *special binding connexions* (such as find expression in regional axioms) *exert upon the regional reality*.

What is here detailed obviously applies to all the spheres of act and object, *also to the objectivities for the constituting whereof acts of feeling (Gemütsakte) with their specific theses and contents a priori have to come in,* and in a way which, again, in respect to the clearing up both of the form and the particularity of the content it is the great, scarcely suspected, let alone adopted, task of the corresponding constitutive phenomenology to initiate.

Therewith the inner relation also of the constitutive phenomenologies to the *a priori ontologies*, and eventually to *all* eidetic disciplines (excepting indeed phenomenology itself), is made evident. The *sequences in the development of the doctrines of essential being, both formal and material,* prescribe in a certain way the *corresponding sequences of the constitutive phenomenologies,* determine their orders of generality, and, in the basic concepts and principles, both ontologically and materially eidetic, give them the *"guiding clues."* For example, basic concepts of the ontology of nature, such as Time, Space, Matter, and their proximate derivatives, are indicators of strata of the constituting consciousness of material thinghood (*Dinglichkeit*), just as the corresponding principles are indicators of the essential connexions in and between the strata. The phenomenological clearing up of the pure logical doctrine makes it then intelligible that and why all *mediated* propositions also of the pure doctrines of Time, of geometry, and so of all ontological disciplines, are indicators of essential conformities to law and order on the part of the transcendental consciousness and its constituting manifolds.

But it must be expressly noted that in these connexions between constitutive phenomenologies and the corresponding formal and material ontologies there is *no hint of a grounding of the former on the latter. Phenomenology does not judge ontologically* when it recognizes an ontological concept or proposition as the indicator of constitutive and essential connexions, when it sees in it a clue to intuitive revelations (*Aufweisungen*) which carry their authority and their validity purely in themselves. This general conclusion will receive on a later occasion further confirmation in a more thoroughgoing treatment which, in virtue of the importance of this whole matter (*Sachlage*), is emphatically called for.

A comprehensive solution of the problems of phenomenological shaping which shall take equally into consideration the noetic and the noematic strata of consciousness would be manifestly equivalent to a complete phenomenology of the reason in respect of all its formal and material formations, whether non-normal (negatively rational) or normal (positively rational). But we are further compelled to admit that a phenomenology of the reason so complete as this would coincide with phenomenology in general, and that in systematically carrying out all the disciplines of consciousness which are demanded under the collective title "constitution of the object" all and sundry descriptions of consciousness would need to be included.

**Analytical Index**

# Analytical Index

(Modelled on the corresponding Index in the original German, as compiled by Dr. LUDWIG LANDGREBE of Freiburg-im-Breisgau, 1928, on the basis of Dr. Gerda Walther's *Ausführliches Sachregister*, 1923.)

[TR. NOTE.—The references in this Index are to the Subsections, *not*, as in the original, to the pages. The letters *a, b, c* refer to the first, second, and final third of the subsections respectively. *Ab* refers to the area where *a* and *b* connect; *bc* to the connecting area between *b* and *c*. Where there is no mention either of *a, b,* or *c*, the reference is to the section as a whole. Dr. Landgrebe's headings and references have been faithfully followed in the order given, except where the requirements of the English version necessitated some omission, addition, or deviation. Explanatory comments appear where needed within square brackets. Every reference in Dr. Landgrebe's Index has been tested, and the slips, very few, thereby avoided, though there may of course be fresh ones in the English version, for which Dr. Landgrebe is not responsible. The more important references—as so judged by Dr. Landgrebe—have their section number, in the English as in the German version, cast in heavier type.]

## A

*Absolute,* logical A. (primordial object) 15 *b*; A. of immediate perception 44 *b*, 46 *a*, 49 *c*; A. of the divine Being 58 *c*; transcendental A. not the final one 81 *b*.

*Abstraction,* A. and Ideation 22 *b*; A. and phenomenological reduction 51 *a, b*.

*Abstractum, abstract,* A. as dependent essence 15 *b*; a. and concrete 15 *c*; a. and concrete genera and sciences 72 *a*.

*Absurdity;* (i) *Absurdität.* Phenomenology of A. 145 *a*.
(ii) *Widersinn.* Concept of A. 52 *a* (ftn.).

*Act* (Akt)—(v. also "Experience ii" and "cogito")—*Primordial A.* (v. "Primordiality")—*thetic, positional, etc. A.* (v. "Thesis," etc.), *A.-character* (v. also "thetic character" under "Thesis").

A. as focal (wakeful) consciousness 35 *c*; the concept of A. in the *Logical Studies* 36 *a*, 84 *c*; A. and glancing towards 37 *a*; immanently and transcendently directed A. 38 *b*; A. and Pure Ego 80; fulfilled A. (attitudes) and unfulfilled (that have missed fulfilment or else *Impulses to act*) 84 *b*, 115 *b*; A. proper identified with fulfilled A. 84 *c*; the fulfilling of an A. (wakeful attitude) presupposes attention 92 *b*; every A.-

character a thesis in wider sense 114 *b*, 117 *a*; *A.-shadow* 114 *a*; A. proper as explicit intentionality 115 *a*; only through A. in the narrower sense are the effects of conscious activity perceivable 115 *b*; the essential community of all A.-characters 117 *a*; every A. harbours a logical element; all A. objectifying acts 117 *c*; A. of higher order as polythetic 118 *b*; transformation of polythetic into monothetic A. 119; modalities of A.-fulfilment 122; expressibility of all A. 124 *a*; perceiving and non-perceiving A. 136 *a*.

*Secondary or grounded (fundierte) A.*—[complex A., A. based or founded on others. The "fundierende" A. is the primary A. that "underlies" the secondary, the latter being "consolidated" through it and with it.] (V. also "Synthesis,") —Twofold intentionality of secondary A. 37 *c*; noesis and noema of secondary A. 93 *a*, 116, 117, 118 *b, c*; transferability of all non-doxic into doxic A. 121 *c*.

*Actuality. Focal A* (Aktualität). *Marginal or Nascent A.* (Inaktualität); wakeful or focal (aktuell), dormant or marginal (inaktuell) (v. also "Glance" and *cogito*).

F.A. fundamental form of the wakeful life 28 *a*; wakeful and dormant A. as explicit and implicit (potential) consciousness 35; F.A. and apprehension 37; F. (wakeful, developed) A. and background 84 *b, c*; modes of F.A. as modes of attention and the mode of M.A. 92; ambiguity of F.A. as positionality and as directedness generally (positional and neutral) 113; F.A. spontaneously producible 117 *b*; F.A. and the hold of the Ego 112; modes of F.A. and modes of clearness 122 *b* and 123.

[Where, as in § 113, "aktuelle" is opposed to "potentielle" and the "potential" is not "marginally" or "nascently actual," indeed not actual at all, it is translated as "actual" *simpliciter*. The assumption is that in English "actual" stands for what is immediately present here and now, and is opposed to what is past, future, or absent, and, above all, to what is merely possible or potential. Marginal consciousness is a form of actuality, potential consciousness is not.]

Cf. M.A. (Inaktualität) with "Neutrality" and "Background." Vide also "Non-actuality" and "Potentiality."

*Adequacy*, A. of experience 44 *c*; A. of self-evidence 137 *a*, 141 *c*–144; A. of perception 83, 149 *b*.

*Æsthetic*, characterization of the *a.* standpoint 111 *c*, 120; "Origin" of the concepts and forms of knowledge that pertain to A. 121 *c*.

*Affirmation*, A. as the confirming of a position 106 *b*; what is affirmed is always an object that *is*; reiterated A. 107; what is affirmed is not determined through reflection 108; synthetic A. 115 *b*.

*Analysis:* (i) *"Analyse"*—Intro-Analysis (v. "Perception-immanent"); hyletic, constitutive, etc., A. (v. "υλη," "Constituting function," etc.; real (reelle) A. as noetic, intentional as noematic 88, 97, cf. 128.

    (ii) *"Analysis."* v. "Explicative synthesis."

*Analytic, a.* = pure logical 10 *b*; a. synthesis and judgment 127 *c*, 134 *a*; a. and synthetic self-evidence 137 *c*; the A. proper and its analogues 148 *c*.

*And*—(Und), doxic, axiological and practical "a." 121; generality of "a." 124 *c*; "and so forth" as indispensable phase in the noema of "Thing" 149 *c*, 150 *c*.

*Animalia,* A. as realities in the world 39 *b*, 152 *a*; A. and pure consciousness 53; A. as theme of psychology 85 *c*.

*Anticipation* (Vorerinnerung) = Expectation (Vide).

*Apodeicticity,* A. and essential necessity 6 *b*; apodeictic self-evidence 137.

*Apophansis* (v. "Proposition" under "Position"), 10 *c*, 147 *b*.

*Apophantics,* A. and formal Ontology 119 *c*, 134 *b*; concept and method of formal A. 134; formal A. and *a priori* conditions of validity 147 *b*; apophantic noetics and phenomenology 147 *c*.

*Appearance*—(Erscheinung), A. and physical ("true") Thing 40 *b*, 52; multiplicity of A. and unity of the Thing 41 *b*, 42 *b*, *c* (v. also "Noesis" and "Noema"); multiplicity of A. and noematic unity 97 *b*; identical manner of appearing and change in the mode of presentation 99 *a*; multiplicity of A. regulated through the Idea of Region 150 *b*.—Normal way of appearing 44 *b*; A. in the rôle of that which appears, as such, and of absolute experience 52 *c*; that which appears, as such, identified with the noema 88 *c*; that which appears, as such, modified through attentional transformations 92 *b*; —Stumpf's view of A. as "primary content" 86 *c* Note; A. as the full sense of perception 133 *b*; A. as rational motive in the positing of the transcendent, conflict and rivalry of A. 138 *a*, 151 *b*, *c*. Consult also "Conflict," "Rivalry," "Illusion."

*Apperception,* A. and the linking-on of consciousness with the body 53 *a*, *b*; transcendence-instituting A. and the phenomenological standpoint 53 *c*, 81 *a*.

*Appetitive, a.* impulses based on "presentations" 116 *b*.

*Application* (Anwendung), A. of eidetic truths 6 *b*, 137 *b*; A. of regional categories 16 *b*, 142 *c*.

*Apprehension* (Erfassung), A. of the essence (v. "Essential Insight"); A. as sheer act of the Ego 28 *a*; A. as focal actuality 35 *c*, 67 *c*; apprehending (heeding) turning towards are not one and the same function in secondary (grounded) acts 37; advantage of perfectly clear A. 69 *a*; real and neutralized A. 113 *b*; A. and "having in one's grasp" 122 *a*.

*A priori. a.* insights, cognitions, sciences, etc. (v. "Essential Insight," "Essences, Science of," etc.); a. categories 16.

thing 42 *a*, 45 *c* (v. also "Thing"); the totality of B. and the totality of realities (Realitäten) not one and the same 55 *a*; transcendent and transcendental B. 76 *a*, 86 *c*; (v. also "Transcendence"). The B. of every region constituted in consciousness 86 *c*; immanent B. as finite givenness, transcendent B. given as Idea 144 *a*, *b*.

Characters and modalities of B. as noematic characters 102 *c*, 103; the character of B. *simpliciter,* as the original form of all modalities of B. 104 *a*; the modality of B. as itself B. 105; reiterated modalities of B. 107; characters of B. are not determinations of reflexion 108; non-being not identical with "being validly negated" 108 *bc*; modality of B. in the broadest sense 114 *b*; in the logical sphere that which truly or really *is* and that which is demonstrable are correlates 136, Preface; that which truly is as Idea and a thesis of the Reason are correlates 142.

*Being in itself* (An Sich Sein), an object that has B. is, in principle, a correlate of consciousness 47 *c*; colour "in itself" as given in complete clearness 68 *a*, *b*.

*Belief* = Doxa (Vide).

*Belonging to* (Zugehörigkeit), as rational motivation 136 *b*, 139 *a*.

*Blind* (blind),—b. judging and judgment with insight 94 *b*, 136 *a*.

*Body* (Leib),—B. and soul within a real (realer) unity, B. and the general thesis of the world 39 *b*; B. connects consciousness with the real world 53 *a*; pure consciousness and the annulling of the B. 54 *a*.

*Bracketing.* V. "Reduction."

## C

*Cancellation, Cancelling* (Durchstreichung)—v. also "Negation" —106, 138 *d*, 151 *b*.

*Category,*—categorical intuition (v. "Intuition"); C. and region 10, concept of logical C.; meaning-C. and formal objective C. 10 *c*; C. as concepts (conceptual meanings) and as essences 10 *c*; syntactical and substractive C. 11; concept of the syntactical C. 14; formal ontological C. as eidetic singularities 13 *a*.—Concept of regional C. 16 *b*; the doctrine of C. must start from pure consciousness as the original C. 76 *a*; correspondence of each C. of objects with a basic type of primordial self-evidence 138 *c*, 145 *b*; C. of Apprehension and correlate of the object-C. 142 *b*; regional C., regional content (Materie) and synthetic forms 153 *bc*.

*Causality,* C. as relation of dependence between realities 49 *c*; physical C. made manifest in the appearing Thing 52 *b*, *c*; C. and the constituting of a Thing 149 *c*, 150 *c*.

*Ceasing* (Aufhören),—consciousness of the C. of an experience 82 *a*.

*Certain, Certainty,*—v. "Protodoxa"; equivocal meaning of C. 104 *b*.

*Clarification.* V. "Clearness."

*Classification,*—C. of the sciences as separating of the regions 17 *c*, 153 *a;* C. of the types of consciousness as a C. of the modes of positing 117 *a*.

*Clearness* (Clarity), differences in C. and perspective variation 44 *c;* grades of C. from absolute nearness to obscurity 67 *b;* normal clarification as intensive 68; modes of C. and modes of actuality 122 *b;* C. of expression and C. of the underlying layers (substrata): the two constituents of the method of clarification 125 *b;* C. and completeness of expression 126; C. and primordiality 136 *a;* C. of immanent perception 83 *a;* C. of recollection 141 *a;* C. of synthetic constructions (Gibilde) 153 *b*.

   *Method of Clarification* 67, **125** *b, c;* 149 *a*.

*Clue* (v. "Guiding Clue").

*Cogito* (v. also "Act" and "Experience (ii)"),—C. in the broadest sense includes all experiences 28 *a*, 34 *b;* C. in the narrower sense as wakeful actuality-consciousness 35 *b;* a glancing-towards in every C. 37 *a;* C. and the pure Ego 35 *c*, **57,** 80; C. that "really posits" and C. improperly so-called (neutral C.) 114 *a;* every C. can be transformed into a primary positing, real or neutral 114 *b;* C. as explicit intentionality (act properly so-called) **115** *a;* doxic C. as actually exercising an objectifying function 117 *c;* direction of the C. to the object 129 *c*.

*Coincidence* (Deckung), coinciding, covering, coming together, congruence—identifying C. (v. also "Identification-synthesis"), C. of thetic characters with the primary doxa 115 *b, c;* 117 *c;* C. of expression and expressed 124 *c;* C. of different meanings 131 *c;* Congruence as between acts of different rational value 140 *a;* C. of possibility and reality 140 *c*.

*Collective function* (Kolligieren),—collective synthesis: a taking together 118 *c;* C. as plural consciousness 119 *b;* C. either real or fictional 120 *c;* Collective joy, pleasure, will, love— the unity of a collective act of love "singly and all together" 121 *b;* pre-conceptual C. ("conjunction") 134 *a*.

*Colour,* C. and perspective C.-variation 41 *b.* (v. also "Perspective Variation"); noematic or objective C. and sensory C. 97 *a, b*.

*Command.* Generality of the form of C. (Befehlsform) 126 *b*.

*Completeness* (Vollständigkeit), expression is complete when the stamp of conceptual meaning has been fixed upon all the synthetic forms and significations of the lower layer 126 *a*.

*Concept* (Begriff) C. and essence 10 *c*, 22 *c;* equivocal use of C. 22 *c*, 61 *b;* C. as spontaneous product 23 *a;* exact C. (ideal C.) and morphological (descriptive) C. 73 *c;* conceptuality and expression 124 *b;* C. as representing the Idea in consciousness 149 *a*.

*Concrete Existence, positing of* (Daseinssetzung),—cf. also "Stand-

ence) between C. and reality **42** *a*, **44** *a*, *b*; **46**; pure C. as the field of Phenomenology **50**; absolute C. and C. in its *psychological* aspect **33** *b*, **53**, **76** *b*, **88** *b*, *c*; absolute C. as sense-giving **55** *a*; C. as transcendental Being **76** *a*; C. as source of Ontologies **117** *c*.

*Constituting* (*function*)—*phenomenological* shaping—C. of a thing, v. "Perception, transcendent," and "Thing"; C. of the "stream of experience," v. "Experience, Stream of," and "Time-Consciousness."

C. as a dispensing of meaning in pure consciousness **55**, separation of the constitutive and the noetical problems **80** *c*; C. as central viewpoint of phenomenology **86** *a*; transcendental C. through noetic functions and on the basis of material experiences **97** *c*; original C. as an objectifying function (v. "Object") **117** *c*; ambiguity of the concept of a C. function **135** *c*; general problem of the C. function and its guiding clues **149, 150, 152.**—C. of all transcendences in pure consciousness **50** *b*; C. of the empirical in pure consciousness **54**; original C. of total objectivities in synthetical consciousness **119** *a*; individual and intersubjective C. **135** *a*; problems of phenomenological shaping as problems of the Reason **153** *b*; problems of phenomenological shaping presented by formal and material regions respectively **153** *b, c.*

*Content*—(i): *Inhalt.*

C. as essence of experience **34** *c*; "primary" C. and intentional experiences **85** *a*, **86** *c*; C. of the judgment as noematic nucleus, ambiguity of this concept of C. **94** *c*; C. as meaning (Sinn) **129** (v. also "Meaning"); conceptually apprehended C. **130** *c.*

(ii): *Materie* (Ideal C.).

I.C. as noematic meaning **88** *b.* Note, **129** *b*, **133** *a*; positional C. **138** *c.*

*Contingency* (Zufälligkeit), C. of individual Being, C. and essence, **2**; C. of the world of things **46** *b*, **49** *a.*

*Continuum.* C. of the stream of experience (Vide), the perceptual C. (Vide).

*Copying* (Abbildung), *depicting*—v. "Image" (Bild).

*Corporeality* (v. also "Thing"), C. and extension (v. "Extension"), connexion of consciousness with C. (v. "Body").

*Correlate*, C. as noema **90** *c* (v. also "Noema"), correlation of intuition and object (v. "Intuition"), C. of perception (v. "Perception"), and so forth.

*Counter-essence* **114** *a.*

*Counter-noema* **114** *a.*

*Counter-thesis* **138** *b.*

*Criticism* and Phenomenology **62, 63** *c.*

# D

*Dator* = Object-giving (gebend), lit. "giving" *simpliciter.* [The expression is borrowed from Bernard Bosanquet's translation of a passage of Husserl's *Ideen* in his *Contemporary Philosophy*, pp. 139–143. Cf. p. 140.—Tr.]

*Demonstrable* (ausweisbar). V. "Proof."

*Denominative reduction* (Nominalisierung) 148 *b*. Law of Denominative Equivalence 119 *c*.

*Dependence* (Unselbständigkeit), concept of D. 15 *a*.

*Depicting.* V. "Copying."

*Derivatives* (Ableitungen), syntactic 11.

*Description* (Beschreibung and Deskription). D. and exact determination 73 *b*, *c*; noematic D. 130.

*Difference* (Differenz),—lowest specific D. = eidetic singularity (Vide), 12 *a*; mutually exclusive (disjunct) and overlapping lowest D. 15 *c*; the lowest D. and the region 72 *a*; lowest noematic and lowest noetic D. 128 *b*.

*Directedness towards* (Gerichtetsein auf, Richtung auf). V. "Glance," "Cogito," and "Turning to or towards."

*Disciplines* as dependent branches of regional ontologies 72 *a*, *b*. V. "Theory."

*Disconnexion* (Switching off) as Reduction (v. "Reduction").

*Disjunctive. d.* Consciousness 118 *c*, 119 *b*, 121 *a*.

*Distance.* "Near" and "Far" in relation to givenness, 67.

*Distinctness* (Deutlichkeit)—v. also "Clearness." D. and vagueness as modes of the fulfilling of synthetic acts 123; logical D. and D. of the substratum 125 *a*; D. and completeness of expression cut across each other 126.

*Dogmatic, d.* standpoint and Science 26, 62.

*Doubt* (Zweifel),—Cartesian attempt to doubt as an instrument of method 31; D., disconnexion (suspension) and assumption 31; D. as a character of Belief and its noematic correlate 103 *b*, 107 *a*, *b*; D. as state of balanced motivation 138 *b*.

*Doxa* (= Belief), doxic; doxic positing (Setzung) and doxically posited meaning (Satz = position).—V. also "Position" or "Posited meaning," "Thesis"; doxic characters (belief-characters) as noetic 103 *a*; D. implied in every kind of consciousness 105, 114 *b*, 115 *b*, *c*; 117 *c*, 121 *c*; belief-characters not determined through reflexion 108; real belief and the neutrality-modification 113 *a*; the doxic *cogito* as actually exercising an objectifying function 117 *c*; doxic syntheses and their parallels (v. also "Synthesis") 121; the doxic form alone expressible 127 *b*; D. (Belief), judgment and explicative synthesis 127 *c*; formal doctrine of doxically posited meanings 134 *c*, 147; predicative synthesis of the D. and it analogies 148 *c*.

*Protodoxa* (Urdoxa): The certitude of belief as primary belief (protodoxa) 104; doxic primary theses involved only in the positional functioning of consciousness 113 *c*; real and neutral P. 114 *c*; positional potentiality of the P. covering the whole sphere of consciousness 115 *b*, 117 *b*.

(v. "Logic"); formalization and generalization 13; pure logical F. not independent 15 *a*; intentional F. and sensile data; formless materials and immaterial F. 85 *a*, 97 *a* (v. also "Noesis"); synthetic F. 118 *b*, *c*; 153 *c* (cf. also "Syntheses"); syntactic F. 121, 134; F. of the conceptual as product of expression 124 *c*; extended concept of F. 134 *b*, *c*; formal (analytic) self-evidence 137 *c*.

    *Formal Theory:* F.T. of the noemata and F.T. of the noesis 98 *a*, *b*; F.T. of meanings generally and apophantic F.T. 133 *c*, and 134; F.T. of positions (Sätze) does not yet belong to the doctrine of rationality 147 *a*.

*Formative Synthesis,* formal shaping (Auffassung),—F.S. as an animating function identified with Noessi (v. "Noesis") 85 *a*, 97 *b*; direction of F.S. not unambiguous indicated (prefigured) in the material basis (Stoffen) 98 *b*; F.S. in the case of secondary acts 116 *b*; categories of F.S. and categories of the Object are correlates 138 *c* (general), 142 *b*.

*Forth-showing.* V. "Proof."

*Fringe.* V. "Horizon."

*Fullness* (Fülle),—saturation, full realization—v. also "Filling-out" and "Clearness"—, F. of the noematic nucleus 132, 133 *c*.

*Function,* attentional, v. "Attention"; intentional F., v. "Intentionality," and so forth; functional system of real (realen) causality 51 *c*, Note; F. as the central viewpoint of phenomenology 86; Stumpf's concept of psychical F. 86 Note; functional problems (cf. also "Constituting" 86 *a*, 97 *c*, 153 *a*.

# G

*Generalization.* G. and formalization 13.

*Generality.* Essential G. (v. "Essence"); unconditioned G. as essential G. 5 *a*; apprehension of essential G. 69; 137; G. and necessity 6; G. of natural laws and essential G. 6 *c*; pure G. and empirical extension 13 *c*; raised through expression to the level of G. 124 *b*; types of G. among expressions 124 *c*; G. and completeness of expression 126.

*Generally* (Ueberhaupt)—Judgments in the mode "generally" or "in general," and judgments about essences 5 *a*.

*General Thesis.* V. "Thesis."

*Genus* (Gattung),—G. as logical category 10 *c*; highest G. and eidetic singularity 12 *a*; G. and empty form 13 *a*; concrete and abstract G. 15 *c*, 72 *a*.

*Geometry,*—G. as illustrating regional eidetics 9 *c*; domain of G. as a definite manifold 72 *b*, *c*; character of geometrical concepts 74; G. gives rules for the possibilities of the appearing of things 142 *c*.

*Givenness,*—transcendent G. (v. "Thing" and "Perception, transcendent"), absolute G. (v. "Consciousness, transcendental"); primordial G. 1 *a* (v. also "Primordiality"); primordial G.

V. "Apprehension" and "Attention."—["Being towards" not to be identified with "discriminating mindfulness," 35 c; H. as related to apprehending, noting, attending 37 a; H. and mentally scrutinizing differentiated 37 c.]

*Heterogeneity* as essential difference 15 c.

*Horizon* (Horizont). H. (depth or fringe) and field of perception 27 a, b; temporal H. of the world 27 c; H. (encircling sphere) and background (Vide 28 c); indeterminacy of the H. (outlying zone, marginal field) as determinability 44 a, 47 c; unfolding of the H. (marginal zone) of the given 63 b, 69 b; "Before," "after," and "at the same time" as limits or fringes (H.) in every experience 82; H. (fringe) of experiences not deliberately viewed 83 a.

*Hyletic.* V. "νλη."

*Hypothesis* = Assumption (Annahme). Vide "Assumption."

# I

*I* (Ich). V. "Ego."

*Idea* (Idee), I. in the Kantian sense distinguished from Essence (Introduction c); blindness to Ideas 22 ab; I. in the Kantian sense as exact essence (Ideal limits) 74; adequate determination of the content of the Kantian Idea is unattainable 83, 149 c.

*Idealism,* phenomenological.[1] The world as intrinsic correlate of absolute consciousness 47, 51 a, 76 a; absolute Being of consciousness, intentional Being of the world 49; all real unities are unities of meaning presupposing, a consciousness that supplies the meaning, no subjective Idealism 55; every transcendent unity constituted in consciousness (concept of phenomenology as constitutive, transcendental phenomenology 86; the non-existence of the object meant does not rob consciousness of its meaning 88 c; an Object possible only as the unity of a certain noematic content 97 c; every object an object of consciousness; all reality in pure consciousness represented by the corresponding multiplicity of meanings and positions 135; all "reality" constituted in consciousness 135 c; "that which truly or really is" and "that which is rationally demonstrable" are correlates 136 (Preface); the Eidos "true-being" and the Eidos "can be set down as self-evident" (be adequately given) are correlates 144 a, 108; "object": a title for essential connexions of consciousness 145 c.

---

[1] [This expression itself is not used in the *Ideen,* although all its theses, taken in a correspondingly broad sense of the term, might also be described as "idealistic." The references here given should serve to bring out the distinctive character of phenomenological "Idealism."]

dator I. as course of genuine science 19 *c*; every primordial dator I. as a source of authority for knowledge 24, 79 *c*; I, as dator consciousness in the pregnant sense 67 *c*;—Individual I. and essential Insight 3; illustrative I. and apprehension of the essence 62 *c*, 149 *a*, *b*;—Adequate and inadequate I. 3 *a*; only immanent I. adequately dator, in I. that transcends, only the Idea is given 144;—Correlation between I. and object in the broadest sense 3 *b*; I. and experience 20 *a*; impure I. as intermediate grade of clarification 68 *c*; intuitional emptiness and emptiness of indeterminacy 130 *c*; intuitional meaning *simpliciter* and posited intuitional meaning 133 *b*; Kant's pure I. as Ideation 149 *c*.

Categorical I., c.I. as primordial dator consciousness 21 *a*; transference of the concept of I. to synthetic acts 125 *c*; synthetic primordiality 153 *b*.

(B): *"Intuition."* I as primordial dator I., v. "Primordiality"; every I. a ground of authority for knowledge 24 *a*, 79 *c*; I. and non-ambiguity of concept 66 *c*; sceptical objections against I. (Ziehen) 79 Note (2); I. and mediate knowledge 73 *a*, 75 *c*.

*Intuitional Saturation.* V. "Filling out" (Erfüllung).

*Inverted Commas* as a sign for phenomenological reduction (v. "Reduction").

*Irreal, Irreality.* [Pure consciousness is irreal, and therefore phenomenology which studies Pure consciousness, studies what is irreal. (See Introduction.) The term "irreal" is borrowed direct from the Author, who uses it to include the noematic as well as the noetic and hyletic aspects of pure consciousness. In this broad sense it is the "non-real" inverted commas, and as a rule has been translated "non-real." The noetic and hyletic phases, in contrast with the noematic, are "reell" as well as irreal. (See under the heading "Reell.") The noematic is the irreal in its ideal aspect. Or we may say that the "reele" phases of pure consciousness, the noetic and hyletic, are subjectively irreal, whilst the noematic are objectively as well as ideally irreal. Moreover, it is with the irreal as pure essence that phenomenology is alone concerned.—TR. Note.]

## J

*Joy* as intentional experience 84 *a*.

*Judgment, Judging.*—J. about essences and about instances of these essences (universal) 5; apodeictic J. 6 *a*; J. prescribes through its meaning the kind of grounding that is called for 19 *b*; refraining from J. 31 *c*; J. concerning the Real and concerning the appearing as such 89, 90 *c*; J. in the ordinary sense as "the judged content of the judgment as such" (noema of the judging process), judged content and matter judged about 94 *a*; noesis and noema of J. 88 *b*, 94; J. as proposi-

M. and expression 117 c, 124 b, 127 c, Note; M.-forms of Formal Logic and synthesis 118 c; logical M. (= Expression) and M. generally (Sinn) 124 a; distinctness of M. 125 a; stratum of M. no mere duplication of the lower stratum 126 b; dependent M. 126 c; whether the medium for the expressing of M. is specifically doxic 127 b.

III. *Meaning as functional act* (Meinen),—v. also "Intentionality,"—normal use of the term M. 95 c; every meaning as meant (Meinung: the meant as such) expressible in conceptual form 124 ab; the meant (Vermeintes) as such as noematic nucleus (Vide) 129 c, 130; the meant as such as object in modal setting 132 a, 134 a (v. also "Object ii"); the real object and the object as merely meant 135 b, c; meaning (sense-positing function = Vermeinen) as positional consciousness in general 146 a.

IV. *Substantive Meaning* (Sachverhalt). See under this heading.

*Mental Sciences* (Geisteswissenschaften),—M.S. as sciences of the world 1 c; M.S. also subject to phenomenological Reduction 56 c, 76 a, b.

*Method,*—M. of Clarification (Vide), M. of phenomenology (Vide Phenomenology), etc. Question as to the right M. of nature-Knowledge 26; M. is a norm which springs from the primary regional divisions of a domain and from its general structural arrangements 76 c.

*Mixture* of representations at varying stages 100 b, c.

*Modality,* M. of belief (doxic). V. "Doxa."

*Mode, manner, "how"* (Wie),—object or meaning "in the modal aspect" (im Wie) of its determinations,—v. "Object (ii)" and "Meaning (i)"; objective manner of appearing and differences in the mode of givenness 99 a.

*Modes* (*Modi*), M. of mindfulness, v. "Attention"; M. of givenness, v. "Givenness"; M. of turning to (or towards), v. "Turning to or towards," etc.

*Modification* (Abwandlung, Modifikation),—M. of Belief, v. "Doxa"; reproductive M., v. "Reproduction"; symbolic M., v. "Image"; neutrality-M., v. "Neutrality."

M. and Impressions 78 b; primary and reflective M. of experiences 78 c; specifically intentional meaning of the word "M." 104 a; reiterated M. of Being, each M. pointing back to what is unmodified 107; "qualitative" and "imaginative" M. of the *Logischen Untersuchungen* 112 c ftn.

μορφη—(cf. also "Formative Syntheses" and "Noesis"). Intentional μορφη distinguished from sensile ύλη 85 a.

*Morphology,*—morphological essence 74 b; phenomenology as eidetic M. 145 c.

*Motivation,*—System of M. (v. "Experience, proof of"); motivated possibility (v. "Possibility").—Concept of M. 47 *c*, ftn.; rational motivating 136 *b*; M. and self-evidence 136 *c*; power of M., counter-motive and outfill 138 *b*; M. and the character of "unreason" 139 *a*, *b*.

*Multiplicity, Variety*—(Mannigfaltigkeit).—Attentional M., v. "Attention"; M. of consciousness, M. of appearance, v. "Appearance." M. as formal ontological essence 61 *c*; concept of a definite or mathematical manifold 72 *c*; noetic variety and noematic unity 97 *b*, 98 *b*, 150 *c* (v. also "Noesis" and "Noema"); noematic M. and identity of object 98 *c*, 141 *a*, *b*.

[Frequently "Mannigfaltigkeit" seems best translated by "manifold." Cf. 72 *c*, 150 *b*.]

## N

*Natural Experience* (Erfahrung). V. "Experience (i)."

*Natural Sciences,*—N.S. as sciences of the world 1 *c*; the Idea of a completely rationalized empirical science of Nature 9 *b*; principle of the N.S. 24 *c*; knowledge of the essence indispensable for the N.S. 25; N.S. and Scepticism 26; Nature-research and transcendental study of consciousness 51 *a*; unity of all N.S. 51 *b*, 72 *b*; N.S. subject to phenomenological Reduction 56, 60 *b*, *c*; descriptive N.S. 74.

*Nature,*—Givenness and Proof (Forth-showing) of N. (v. "Experience, proof of," and "Perception of Things"). Natural standpoint (v. "Standpoint").—Generality of the laws of N. 6 *bc*; reality of N. not reality in general 19 *a*; vexed question of the possibility of a knowledge of external N. 46 *a*; All N. as All Reality (v. "Reality" and "World"), but not the All of Being 55 *a*; N. as correlate of consciousness 51 *c*, 55; unity of N. 51 *c*, 72 *a*; character of physical N. 52 *b*, *c*; teleology of N. and God 58 *a*; physical N. as concrete, definite multiplicity 73 *a*, *b*; material N. underlies all other realities, pre-eminent position of the phenomenology of material N. 152 *c*.

*Necessity,*—Essential N. (v. "Essential Being"); N. and matter-of-factness 2; N. and universality 6; analytic N. 16 *ab*.

*Necessity of Thought,*—"Feeling" of the N. 21, 145 *a*.

*Negation,*—N. the noetic modification of a positing act, noematic cancelling 106; everything negated is an ontical Object, reiterated (continued) N. 107; the negated not determined by reflexion 108 *b*; non-Being equivalent to Being validly negated 108 *bc*.

*Neutrality,*—N. and Assuming 31 *c*, 110 *b*, 120; neutralization as general modification of all thetic consciousness generally 109, 117 *b*; N. and positionality as a distinction in consciousness of universal range, neutralized consciousness is not subject to any questions concerning reason and unreason 109 *c*, 110 *a*; N.-modification and fancy 111; neutralization not repeatable 112; neutral consciousness also includes in itself no potential positings 113; N.-modification a fundamentally essential peculiarity of all consciousness generally, not attached (separately) to the actual theses 114 *a*; N. as shadow-consciousness 114 *ab*; neutral experiences can be posited doxically as data of immanent time-consciousness 114 *c*; N. and the grounding (consolidating) of positional syntheses 120.

*Noema* (pl. Noemata), *noematic*,—n. nucleus (v. "Nucleus"); n. meaning (v. "Meaning"); cf. also "Counternoema."

*Concept of N. and General References:* concept of N. 88 *b*; full N. and meaning as nucleatic layer 90 *a*, 91 *bc*, 98 *c*; the Theses also belong to the N. 90 *c*; changes in the N. through modifications of the attention as changes in the appearing object as such 92 *c*; N. of the judging function (v. also "Judgment") 94; N. in the spheres of feeling and will 95; Noemata of the higher level, to each level there belongs a level-characteristic 100, 101; neutralized N. and non-neutralized N. 109 *c*; N. and Counternoema 114 *a*; N. of secondary (grounded) acts 116 *b*; collective N. 121 *b*; N. and position (Satz: posited meaning) 133.

*Noema, Noesis, and Object:* thoroughgoing correlation of N. and Noesis 80 *c*, 91, 93 *a*, 97 *c*, 98 *b*, 102 *a*, 104 *a*, *b*; 138 *a*, *b*; perspectival variation of sensory data and n. unity 97 *bc*; noetic multiplicity and n. unity 98 *b*; n. multiplicity and the self-same Object 97 *c*, 98 *c*, 131 *b*, *c*; 135 *a*; noetic and n. intentionality 101; and N. has objective reference in virtue of its meaning ("content") 128 *c*, and 129 *a;* relation of N. to noesis not the same as the relation of consciousness to the object, 129 *c*.

*Mode of Being and Apprehension of the N.:* n. statements and statements concerning reality, 89; apprehension of the N. presupposes disconnexion from positings 95 *b*; N. not a real (reelles) constituent of experience 97 *a*; N. as dependent object, its esse = percipi 98 *a*; n. characters not determined through reflexion 108; generic sameness of all Noemata 128 *a*.

*Noesis, noetic. Concept of Noesis and general References:* N. as formative synthesis in its animating function shapes material elements into intentional experiences 85 *b*, 97 *b*; N. as a dispensing of meaning 86 *a*, 88 *a*; n. constituents as real (reelle) phase of experiences (v. "Reality (reell)") and intentionality 97 *a*; constituting of the N. in inner time-consciousness" (v. "Experience, Stream of," and "Time Consciousness") 118 *a*.—Attentional modifications of the N. 92; N. conditioned by the modes of attention 92 *c*.—N. of the higher levels 93; N. of the act of judging (v. "Judgment") 94; N. in the sphere of feeling and will 95; concrete noetic experiences and the purely noetic 98 *c*; characters of the N. as new ontical objects 105 *c*; N. neutralized and non-neutralized (v. also "Neutrality") 109 *c*; affective, appetitive, and volitional N. grounded in presentations 116 *b*; analogy between

ing and in its relation to a subject (v. "Intentionality") 37; objectively oriented aspect of experiences (v. "Noema") 80 *bc*; meaning of the distinction between "immanent" and "real" O. 90.

*Objectifying function, Objectification* (O.). The objectifying turn of thought—its function 37 *b*; secondary O. and Thing 44 *b*; O. as the original object-constituting function, objectifying all acts, the non-doxic potentially, the doxic Cogito actually 117 *c*; O. of synthetic objects 121 *b*.

*Objectivity* (Objektivität), O. of the world and Intersubjectivity 28, 29, 48 (v. "Intersubjectivity"); "meant O. as such" = noematic nucleus (v. "Nucleus" and "Noema"); O. of the noema 93.—Worthfulness in the object (Wertobjektität), or objectified value, as concrete worth 95 *b*; Resolve as volitional "absorption into the object" (Objektität) 95 *c*. (Vide also "Value.")

(ii) *Object* (*Gegenstand*)—O., Objectivity (Gegenständlichkeit),—O. that has Being in itself (v. "Being in itself"); eidetic O. (v. "Essential Being"); constituting of the O. (v. "Constituting function").

*Different concepts of O:* concept of O. in sense of formal logic 3 *b*; O. and original objectivity 10 *a*; the Individual as original O. 15 *b*; concept of syntactical objectivity 11 *a*; independent and dependent O. 15 *a*; indispensability of the general concept of O. 22 *a*; O. "concerning which" (O. as subject of predication) as the matter judged about 94 *a*, 5 *a*.

*Apprenhension of O.:* correlation of O. and intuition in broadest sense 3 *b*; to every region of O. there corresponds a basic type of primordial self-evidence 138 *c*; to every O. that truly is there corresponds the Idea of a possible dator consciousness, primordial and adequate 142 *b*; category of apprehension the correlate of the category of O. 142 *b*.

*Object and Noema* (v. "Noema" and "Meaning"): O. as known (bewusster), and experience 35 *b*; O. *simpliciter* and objective meaning 91 *c*; O. always the unity of a noematic content 97 *c*; objective unity not unambiguously prefigured in the material 98 *b*; O. as the unity of noematic multiplicities 98 *c*; all meanings of O. come under a highest genus 128 *a*; relation to the O. through the meaning 128 *c*, 129; description of the O. thought of, as such, as a description of the noematic meaning 130 *ab*; O. as the identical determinable X (Vide "X") as central noematic phase 131 *a*; O. as determined through the modes in which it is given as second concept of the modal O. 132; the sense (Sinn) primordially filled out and the O. coalesce in immanent intuition 144 *a*.

*Real O:* the existing (seiender) O. intrinsically the correlate of pure consciousness 86 *bc*, cf. 88 *a* and 135; meaning of the distinction between "immanent" and "real" O. 90; real O. and O. "merely" meant (vermeinter) 135 *b*, *c*; O.

## P

18 *b*; all types of intuition equally valid as sources of authority for knowledge ("Positivism") 20 *c*; the principle of all principles 24; the attempt to doubt and the suspending of the general thesis 31; concept of phenom. εποχη contrasted with that of positivism 32; pure consciousness as field of phenomenology 50 *c*; extent of the phenom. Reduction (for more detailed references, v. "Reduction") §§ 56–60; the significance of method of the doctrine of a phenom. Reduction 61; phenom. and extra-phenom. science of fact 62, Note; the self-suspending of the phenomenologist 64; the back-reference of phenomenology to its own self 65; possibility of fixing unambiguous terms on the basis of phenom. intuition 66; distinctive character of phenom. terms 84 *c* (Note on "Terminology").—Method of apprehending the essence; conditions of clearness, apprehension of the essence on the basis of perception and fancy 69, 70 (v. "Essential Insight"); problem of the possibility of a descriptive Eidetic 71, 73; purely descriptive procedure of Phenomenology 59 *c*, 75; exclusion of deductive theorizings 75 *c*.—Phenom. Reduction as a bracketing process; everything transcendent as correlate of consciousness: the theme of the inquiry 76 *a*, 135 *a*; the transcendental reduction leaves all noemata as residue 97 *c*, 145 *c*; phenomenology not restricted to the real (reelle) analysis of experiences 128 *b*.—Phenomenology proceeds entirely through acts of reflexion 77 *a*, 78 *a*, 78 *bc*, 80 *a* (v. "Reflexion"); whether phenomenology is itself affected by the sceptical doubts bearing on empirical psychology 79; intentionality as the first and main theme of phenomenology 84, 146 *a*; distinction between hyletic and noetic phenom. inquiries 85 *c*; function (constituting act) the central viewpoint of phenomenology 86 *a*; intentionality in its psychological and its phenom. aspects 90 *b*; concrete description of the suspending of ontic theses 90 *c*; the two constituents of the method of clarification 125 *b*; every region offers guiding clues for phenom. inquiry 149 *a*, 150.

*Phenomenology,*—phenomenological reduction, v "Reduction"; phenom. Idealism, v. "Idealism."

*Concept of P.:* P. as essential science of Non-realities (lit. "Irrealities"—"Irrealitäten"). Introduction *b*; P. and positivism 20 *c*; P. as descriptive theory of the essence of transcendental pure consciousness 50 *b*, 59 *c*, 60 *b*; 71 *a*, 75; phenom. science of fact 62, Note; P. as "first" philosophy 63 *c*; P. as concrete eidetic science, 73 *a;* P. and scepticism 79; general theme of P. Intentionality 84, 146 *a*; central viewpoint of P. Function 86 *a*; constitutive P. as transcendental 86 *c*, 153 *a;* Stumpf's P. as hyletics 86 *c*, Note.

*Scope of P.* (v. also "Reduction" and "phenom. Md."): bracketed matter included within the field of phenom. inquiry 76 *a*, 135 *a*; P. envelops the whole world as world-meaning 145 *c*.—P. and formal doctrine of posited meanings 134 *c*; general P. and P. of the Reason 145 *a*; pre-eminent position of the P. of material nature 152.

*P. and Psychology:* relation of P. and psychology, Introduction *a*; psychological and phenom. concept of consciousness 33; phenom. and psychological standpoints 53 *c*; every phenom. position can be reinterpreted in terms of eidetic psychology 76 *bc*; the question of phenom. method separated from that of psychological method 79 *a*; P. as court of appeal for the fundamental questions of psychological methodology 79 *c*; psychological and phenom. reflexion 80 *a*; function of phenom. Reduction for psychologists 84 *c*, 89 *b*, *c*; psychological Theory of Knowledge and P. 87 *b*; intentionality in its psychological and phenom. aspects 90 *b*, *c*; historical movement from psychology to P. 128 *b*.

*P. and the Sciences:* P. and Mathesis universalis 59; P. and material Ontology 60; P. independent of all sciences 60 *c*; P. and criticism of the dogmatic sciences 62; phenom. and extra-phenom. science of fact 62, Note; P. as belonging to a class of eidetic sciences other than the mathematical 75 *c*; P. and formal logic 147 *b*; P. and formal Ontology 148; sequences in the development of constitutive P. and corresponding sequences in the ontological sciences 153 *c*.

*Phenomenon,*—P. as appearance, Introduction *a*; P. of psychology (real) and of phenomenology (non-real, irreal), Introduction *b*; meaning of Brentano's separation of psychical and physical P. 85 *bc*; reduced P. as noematic meaning 90 *c*.

*Philosophy* and Phenomenology 62 *b*, 63 *c*.

*Physical*—, p. Thing and perceived Thing 40; meaning of p. determinations 52 *b*, *c*.

*Picture.* V. "Image."

*Pleasure* (Gefallen),—the grounding of P. 95 *a*, 116 *b*; noema of P. 88 *b*, *c*; P. as positing function 117 *a*; the P. that refers beyond as illustrating a synthetic act of a higher grade 118 *c*; collective P. 121 *a*.

*Plural* (*plural*),—p. consciousness 119 *ab*, 121 *a*, *b*; P. denominated as the basic concept of the Theory of groups, 148 *b*.

*Plurality* (Vielheit) as correlate of the plural consciousness 119 *b*.

*Plurality* (Mehrheit), as "the state of being more or many" occurs in 119 *c*, in connexion with denominative transformations of the predicate.

*Polythetic,* 118 *b*, 119.

*Positing,* positing act, placement (Setzung) = Thesis (v. "Thesis," "Position," "Positionality"); positional character (v. "thetic character"), rational positing (v. "Reason"); actual, potential P. (v. "Actuality")—and so forth.

P. of the essence not dependent on the P. of facts 4 *c*; P. of facts in applying eidetic truths 6 *b*; P. in valuing, wishing, and willing 95 *b*, *c*; 117 *a*; actual and potential, real and neu-

the rationality of S.F. 9 *b*; phenom. and extra-phenom. S.F. 62 *c*. Note; the dividing of S.F. runs parallel to that of the Sciences of Essential Being 72 *ab*.

*Secondary* (fundierte) Acts. V. "Act, secondary or grounded."

*Seeing* (Sehen),—S. in the broadest sense as primordial dator consciousness 19 *c*, 136 *a*, and preamble; (v. also "Primordiality"); assertoric and apodeictic S. (Insight) 137. Seeing and reflexion: we do not *see* what we are actually experiencing 150 *a*, cf. 45 *c*.

*Self-evidence* (Evidenz), *Evidential Vision*,—S.E. and Intellectual Transparency (Einsichtigkeit) 20 *c*, Criticism of the doctrine of feelings of S.E. 21, 145 *a*; S.E. in the apprehension of the essence (v. "Apprehension") and clearness of the subsumed particulars 69 *c*; pure logical S.E. not dependent on the clearness of the lower layers 125 *c*; S.E. as the unity of a rational positing with that which essentially motivates it 136 *c*; twofold sense of S.E. (noetic and noematic) 136 *c*; S.E. as rational consciousness generally, assertoric and apodeictic S.E. (Insight—pure and impure, formal and material, 137; adequate S.E. without the graded differences of a weight, inadequate and capable of increase and decrease 138 *c*; the character of primary rationality attaching to primordial and complete S.E. 139 *ab*; theoretical, axiological, and practical S.E. 139 *c*; verifications through appeal to the primordial not possible for every type of S.E. 140 *ab*; primordial S.E. as the primary source of all right, primordial and mediate S.E. 141; quasi-S.E. in the sphere of neutrality 145 *a*. Note.

*Self-givenness.* V. "Givenness."

*Self-observation* (v. also "Reflexion"),—the difficulties of S.O. 79.

*Sensation* (*Empfindung*),—Sensory datum as a real (reelles) phase of experience, non-intentional 36 *c*; sensory data as perspective variations 41 *c*, 97 *b*; outspreadedness of sensory data 81 *a*; sensory contents and intentional form 85 *a*; sensory data as "physical phenomena" 85 *c*; sensory colour as a real (reelles) phase of experience 97 *a*; difference between sensory datum and fancy-image not a difference of intensity 112 *b*.

"Sensory" = "sensile." V. "sensile."

*Sensationalism* (Sensualismus) and the theory of Attention 92 *c*. Note.

*Sensibility* (Sinnlichkeit), concept of S. 85 *b*.

*Sensile* (sensuell), s. data (v. "sensory data" under "sensation," υλη and "material" (stoff)), s. experiences 85 *a*, *b*.

"Sensile" (sensuell) and "sensory" (sinnlich) practically synonymous 85 *b*.

*Sensory Thing* (Sinnending). V. also "Thing" 151 *a*.

*Setting* (Hof). V. "Marginal Zone."

*Shape*,—S. as transcendent Essence 61 *c*; S. of a Thing and sensory data 85 *c*.

perience 39 *b*; T. of the world and of the pure Ego 46 *bc*; T. of the world and marginal consciousness 47 *c*; T. in phenom. reduction as components of the noema 90 *c*; potentiality of the T. and neutrality-modification (Vide) 113 *a*, 114; creative engendering of the T. as spontaneity (actuality) and its modifications 122 *a;* T. of expressing and expressed strata essentially one 124 *c*, 127.

*Thesis and Protodoxa* (Vide): doxic primary T. and further concept of T. 113 *c*, 117; every thetic act a modality of Being in the widest sense, extension of the concept of T. to all act-spheres 114 *b*; every thetic act-character generally conceals in itself a doxic primary T., special advantage of primary T. over modalities 115 *c*; generic community, in essence, of all thetic characters (positional characters) 117 *a*; doxic modalities present in all thetic characters 117 *c*.

*Secondary* (*grounded*) *Theses:* plain thetic consciousness and polythetic (many rayed and single rayed) consciousness 119 *a*; Archontic T. of secondary acts 117 *a*, 120, 131 *c*; plain T. as foundation for secondary T. 120.

*Thesis and Reason:* Rationality of the positional character on the ground of a primordial filled-out dator meaning 136 *b*; rational consciousness as the highest genus of the thetic modalities 137 *bc*; weight of T. 138 *b*; right (justification) of every rational T. 139 *a*; transferability of all theses into actual rational positings 140 *ab*.

[The term *"Urthese"* translated as "primary theses" might be conveniently rendered as *"protothesis,"* just as "Urdoxa" has been translated "protodoxa."]

*Thing* (v. also "Reality"). T.-Appearance (v. "Appearance"), real (*wirkliches*) T. (v. "Reality").

(A): *General:* T. itself as original objectivity 10 *a*; the T. that appears and the "true" (physical) T. 40 *b*; unity of the T. and variety of the experiences relating to it as an example of the constituting function 41 *a*, *b*; 135 *a*, *b*; the Being of the T. and the Being of experiences 42; existence of T. contingent 46 *b*; the region "T." as exemplifying a clue [to phenomenological inquiry] 149, 150; T. as *res temporalis* and *res materialis* 149 *c*. T.-schema and spatiality 150 *b*; strata in the constitution of a T., the schema of a T., substantivo-causal and intersubjective T. 151.

(B): *The Perception and Givenness of a T.* (v. also "Experience (i)" and "Perception, transcendent"): intrinsic inadequacy of T.-perception 3 *a*, 44, 138; description of a T.-perception 41 *a*, *b*; 97 *a*; perceptivity of the T. and perceptivity of experiences 45 *b*, *c*; concept of T.-transcendence; essential structure of the experience of a T. 47 *b*; T.-perception as generic essence 75 *b*; T.-perception as primordial experience 78 *b*; T.-significance of perception 133 *b*; adequate presentation of a T. as Idea 143; "T." as Idea and limitlessness in the development of intuitions 149 *b*, *c*.

*This-There* (Dies-da, τοδε τι),—T. and the formless ultimate essence as substrative categories 114; subsumption of T. under an essence 2 *c*, 13 *c*.

*Thought:* (i) = *Denken:*—(v. also "Predication," "Judgment"),—T.-synthesis, T.-functions. V. "Synthesis," "Function"; "I think" = cogito 34 (v. "Cogito"); ambiguity of T.; vague and clear T. 125; *Supposal* (Sichdenken) and abstention from judgment 31 *c*, Supposal and neutrality-modification 110 *a*, 114 *a*; supposal and assumption 110 *b*.

   (ii) = *Gedanke*—, "mere" T. as neutrality-consciousness 109 and 114 *a*, and cf. 31, vague T. 123 *a*; "unthinking" as not primordial 136 *a*; T. represents the Idea in consciousness 149 *a*.

*Time,*—temporal horizon of the world 27 *c*; phenomenologist T. as the necessary unitary form of all experience of the Pure Ego, and objective (cosmic) T. 81; the constituting of experiences as members of *one* phenom. T. unaffected by their essential foreignness to one another 118 *a*; T. as the form of thinghood 149 *c*.

*Time-Consciousness,*—the stream of experience constituted in T.C. 81 *c*, 85 *a*, 114 *c*; original T.C. and its fancy-modification 113 *b*; T.C. as primary or as protosynthesis 118 *a*.

τοδε τι = This-there (Vide).

*Total Act,*—(v. also "Act," polythetic, and "Synthesis") 131 *b*.

*Transcendence,*—T. of the Thing (v. "Thing"); T. of the Thing and immanence of consciousness 42 *a*; intrinsically impossible for transcendental Being to be given except through appearances 44 *ab;* T. as intrinsically experienceable 45 *c*, 47 *b*, *c*; T. as mere intentional Being, constituted in pure consciousness 49 *c*, 76 *a*, 135 *b*, *c*; 143; T. of God and T. of the world 51 *c*. Note, 58 *b*, *c*; T. of the physical Thing 52 *b*, *c*; T. of empirical consciousness 53 *b*, 54 (v. also "Consciousness"); T. in the immanence of the Pure Ego 57; T. of the eidetic 59; everything transcendent an object of phenom. Inquiry 76 *ab*; T. as infinitude of the noematic correlate, 144 *a*; T. as limitlessness in the development of intuitions 149 *bc*.

*Transcendental,* t. and transcendental Being 76 *a*; t. problems as problems of the constituting function 86 *c*, 97 *c*.

*Truth* (Wahrheit),—pure T. concerning meaning and pure T. concerning the object 10 *c*, essential T. formal and synthetic 16; concept of T. in a definite manifold as a derivation from axioms along the lines of formal logic 72 *c*; to be true and to be demonstrable, logical correlates 136 Pref.; T. as correlate of the character of primary rationality (of the protodoxa), theoretical, axiological, and practical T. 139 *b*, 147 *b*; Eidos "True-Being" correlate of the Eidos "Being that can be posited as self-evident" (that can be adequately given) 142 *a*, 144 *a*; the forms of predicative synthesis as *a priori* conditions of possible T. 147 *b*.

*Turning to, or towards* (Zuwendung, Richtung auf), directedness towards,— T.t. as simple act of the Ego 28 *a*; T.t. (orientation) as focal (wakeful) actuality 35, 84 *b*; T.t. and grasping (apprehending) in complex (consolidated: fundierten) acts are not one and the same 37; T.t. in neutral consciousness cannot actualize real theses 113 *a*.

*Type* (Typus),—treatment of types (Typik); treatment of types of positions (Sätze 133 *c*. T. of essence 47 *c*; *a priori* prefiguring of T. 144 *b*. "Type" is also used as an equivalent of kind, class or species,—as a translation, for instance, of "Art."

## U

*ύλη*,—hyletic data,—(v. "Sensory data," "Sensation," and "Material"); sensile *ύλη* 85; *ύλη* not intentional 85 *a*; *ύλη* as a real (reelles) phase of experiences 97 *b*; *ύλη* not apprehended objectively prior to reflection 98 *a*; hyletics as a self-contained discipline of phenomenology 86 *c*.

*Unity*,—collective U., v. "Collective Function,"—synthetic U., v. "synthesis";— U. of the stream of experience and transcendent U. 38 *b*, *c*; all U. of consciousness a U. through synthesis (v. also "Experience, Stream of," and "Time-consciousness").—U. presupposes community of essence 70 *a*, *b*; psychophysical U. as consolidated U. 53 *b*; empirical (real) U. as *indicators* of absolute systems of experience (unities of meaning) 54 *b*; noematic U. and noetic variety 97 *b*, 98 *c* (v. also "Noesis" and "Noema"); objective U. and noematic variety 98 *c* (v. also "Object"); objective U. constituted in consciousness 86; objective U. not unambiguously indicated in the material contents themselves 98 *b*; U. and multiplicity 119.

*Universality*.—V. "Generality."

*Unreason* (Unvernunft), phenomenology of U. 145 *a*.

## V

*Vagueness*, confusion (Verworrenheit),—V. and distinctness as modes in the fulfilling of synthetic acts 123; V. of the lower layers and logical distinctness 125 *b*; V. and incompleteness of expression 126; V. and rational character incompatible 136 *c*.

*Validity* (Gültigkeit, Geltung)—v. also "Right" and "Proof"—absolute V. of logical axioms for Phenomenology also 59 *c*; "Being" equivalent to "being validly posited" 108 *c*; synthetic forms as *a priori* conditions of possible V. 147 *a*.

*Value, valuing* (Wert, werten),—cf. "Worth, worthfulness" as a synonym. Vide "Feeling."—World of values and world of facts and affairs; characters of V. inhere in objects before us as belonging inwardly to them 27 c; Inclining to and apprehending in the process of valuing 37 b; mere matter of fact, worthfulness and objectified V.—Substantive meaning and meaning in terms of V., objectified V. *simpliciter* and objectified V. as noema 95 b; V. as secondary (grounded) noema, the valued as such as nucleus of meaning 116 bc; V.-consciousness as positional, and its modalized forms 116 c; logic and theory of value analogous (v. also "Axiology") 117 a, 147 a; the valuing consciousness as objectifying (object-constituting) 117 c, 152 b; formal Ontology of V. 148 b.

*Verification* (Bewährung),—v. "Confirmation."

*Visual Thing* as a stratum in the constituting of a Thing 42 a, 151 a; Cf. "visual phantom" 15 c.

# W

*Warranty* (Berechtigung). V. "Right." W. apart from self-evidence 140.

*Weight,*—W. as a modality of Belief 103 b; W. as motivating power of experience 138 b; degree of W. and motivating power 138 b; only motivated possibilities have W. 140 b. Note.

*What, Somewhat* (Was),—W. as import or meaning-content, v. "Matter (Materie) B"—W. as essence of an individual 2 b, c; 3 a; W. as judged content, the noematic correlate of the judging process 94 a; W. as noematic meaning 95 b, 130 c; W. as noematic nucleus (v. "Nucleus") 129 b.

*Willing* (Wollen),—W. generally as generic essence 75 b; W. as secondary (grounded) act 95, 116 b; noesis and noema in the domain of Will, deciding and decision 95 c; W. as an act of positing, acts of Will as objectifying acts, sources of new regions of Being 117 c, 148 c (cf. also "Practical Science"); the W. that refers beyond itself as an example of a synthetic act of a higher level 118 c, 147 a; collective W. 121 a; W. and spontaneity 122 a; reason in the sphere of W., practical Truth 139 b.

*Wishing* (Wünschen),—W. as a positing act 117 a; every sentence conveying a wish can be transformed into a doxic statement 117 b; generality and incompleteness of the form of W. 126; direct and indirect expressions of W. 127 b.

*Word,*—the layer of verbal sound and the layer of conceptual expressing 124 b, 124 c; understanding of the meaning of a W. and the vagueness of an underlying stratum 125 b.

*World, Natural World:* Concept of the W. 1 a; W. of the natural standpoint 27; W. as the W. about me 28; relation of the natural W. to ideal Worlds 28 c; the natural world about me related to intersubjectivity 29; intersubjective world as correlate of intersubjective experience 151 ab; the natural W. continually present 30 b; source of the general thesis of the

# Index to Proper Names

ARISTOTLE 67.

BERKELEY 116, 153, 265.

BOLZANO, *Wissenschaftslehre* 254, ftn.

BRENTANO, FRANZ, *Psychologie* 229, 334; *Vom Ursprung der sittlichen Erkenntnis* 359.

CANTOR, G. 254, ftn.

COHN, JONAS 212, ftn.

DESCARTES (CARTESIUS) 93, 97, 98, 99, 104, 107, 132, 133, 166, 369.

ELSENHANS, *Lehrbuch d. Psychologie* 79, ftn.

FRISCHEISEN-KÖHLER, *Jahrbücher d. Philosophie* 212, ftn.

HILBERT, D. 188, ftn.

HUME, D. 39, 166.

HUSSERL, E. *Philosophie der Arithmetik* 188, ftn., 226, ftn., 308, ftn., 319, ftn.; "Bericht ueber deutsche Schriften zur Logik" i.d. Jahren 1895-99 i *Archiv. f. system. Philosophie*, Bd. X., 38 ftn.; *Logische Untersuchungen (Logical Studies)* 36, 36 ftn., 42, 49, ftn., 56, ftn., 61, ftn., 63, ftn. #8, 63, ftn. #9, 68, ftn., 76, ftn., 77, ftn., 79, ftn., 80, ftn., 124, ftn., 132, ftn., 134, ftn., 157, ftn., 164, 188, ftn., 204, ftn., 211, ftn., 224, 226, 226, ftn., 238, ftn., 250, ftn., 252, ftn., 281, ftn., 288, ftn., 311, ftn., 321, ftn., 324, ftn., 328, ftn., 332, ftn., 340, 340, ftn., 369, ftn., 370, ftn., 374; "Philosophie als strenge Wissenschaft," i Logos, Bd. I, Introd. 38, ftn., 50, ftn., 80, ftn., 212, ftn.; *Lectures* 63, 124, ftn., 188, ftn., 217, ftn.; Paper read before the "Mathematical Society" of Göttingen 168, ftn.

KANT—156, 166, 383; *Kritik of the Pure Reason* 70, 166, 382, ftn.; *Metaphysic of Morals* 379, ftn.; "Idea" in the Kantian sense of the term—42, 191, 221, 366, 382, 383.

KÜLPE, O. *Die Realisierung* I 49, ftn.

LIPPS, TH. 204, ftn., 205, 250, ftn.